BY WILLIAM NICKERSON

How I Turned $1,000 into a Million in Real Estate—In My Spare Time

My Odyssey Around Three Worlds

How I Turned $1,000 into Three Million in Real Estate—
In My Spare Time

NICKERSON'S NEW
REAL ESTATE GUIDE

# How to Make
# a Fortune Today-
# Starting from Scratch

**REVISED AND UPDATED EDITION**

SIMON AND SCHUSTER *New York*

SBN 671-22064-0
Library of Congress Catalog Card Number: 75-4037
Designed by Irving Perkins
Manufactured in the United States of America

2   3   4   5   6   7   8   9   10

*To my son and daughter, Robert and Nancy*

# *Preface to Second Edition*

This revised book is the feature text for the renowned Lowry-Nickerson Real Estate Investors Seminar, a series of advanced lectures, based on William Nickerson's proven teachings. Each session is followed by a no-holds-barred question-and-answer period. More than ten thousand part-time investors and realty professionals have speeded their way to a fortune by attending this Seminar in its initial four years.

Given periodically in major cities across the country, the Seminar is constantly updated to fit current economic conditions. Albert J. Lowry designed its unusual procedures to allow adults to absorb and retain a large volume of practical knowledge in a relatively short time. Students are given a unique "workbook," which structures their note taking and reinforces their retention of complex lecture material. As national demand for seminars grows, highly qualified lecturers are chosen from successful real-estate professionals, who must be both knowledgeable and inspirational. All instructors must complete intensive teacher-training programs under Mr. Lowry's direction in order to win certification by Lowry and Nickerson. The instructors use chalk talks, diagrams and other visual aids to illustrate their lectures, and are always available for individual questions during recesses and after classes. They stay in the classroom until the last avid student leaves.

Lowry is himself an example of the usefulness of the Nickerson methods taught in the course. In 1963, while employed as a butcher, he began to study real estate and bought small duplexes and triplexes with minimum down payments. In 1970 he devoted his efforts toward a millionaire portfolio specializing in residential property. By 1973, ten years after starting from scratch, his net worth topped the million mark. He is now a full-time lecturer, author and teacher.

For information about the Lowry-Nickerson Real Estate Investors Seminar and when it will be scheduled in your area, write the Education Advancement Institute, 3505 Broadway, Oakland, California 94611.

*January 10, 1975*

# Contents

# Foreword

My first book, *How I Turned $1,000 into a Million in Real Estate,* and its second edition, *How I Turned $1,000 into Three Million,* have inspired thousands of fan letters from all over the world. Postmarks from every major country and every section of the United States—from Alaska to Florida and from Hawaii to Maine—show that people everywhere are vitally interested in learning how to make money in real estate. There are letters, too, from such faraway places as Bangkok and Calcutta, Cape Town and Stockholm.

Most writers ask about investment matters. Some letters are personal. Some are comical. A dozen or so cranks have called me a sinner; about half of them say it is a sin to believe in free enterprise, and the others say it is sinful to believe in God!

Most of the letter writers thank me for giving away my secrets of success. They frequently give examples of how they have used my proven formula to make even more than a million in real estate in less than twenty years. These current examples of success prove over and over how real-estate investment can turn small nest eggs into large fortunes.

People who have asked me questions by letter and during lecture, radio, television and other personal appearances have couched their questions in terms of how much money they have to start with —all the way from none to millions. Examples:

"How can I save a nest egg to start investing, when all I have now is a goose egg?" (See Chapter V.)

"With only $2,500 saved, how can I pyramid to a million dollars today?" (See Chapter II.)

"How will your pyramid progress if I throw in a million in cash?" (See Chapter II.)

Although my replies have often been delayed several months by lecture and writing commitments, I have tried to answer every pertinent question. This new book is an up-to-date compilation of my answers to questions about real-estate investment, along with a smattering of the personal and comic.

References to pages "in my first book" are tied to numbers in its revised edition, *$1,000 into Three Million.*

WILLIAM NICKERSON

*Alamo, California*

# 1

# Can I Make a Million Dollars Today?

# I

# *Are the Days of Opportunity Over?*

I've often wondered why people of accomplishment spend so much time worrying whether their success will last. Ambitious neophytes tend to ask similar questions. Does success depend on a lucky fluke that may not be repeated, like breaking the bank at Monte Carlo? At any given time the average person feels that success, like peace, was easier to win yesterday, but is elusive today and doubtful tomorrow.

## Are the Days of Opportunity Over?

This question, a typical one, was asked by Jack Eigen on his WMAQ radio show, broadcast from the Kennedy family's $75-million Merchandise Mart in Chicago.

Appearing with me on the midnight show were Geneviève, the pixy Parisian night club entertainer, and Gloria Lind, Chicago's talented opera star. Geneviève likes to make startling statements at the slightest opportunity, as she does on many TV interviews. She said, "A man should not marry or buy property, *chéri,* until he is thirty-five or forty years old. It takes a man that long to grow up. Especially if he is an artist, his job is to make people happy, not to save money. He should get the most pleasure from spending it to make a woman happy. So why should he tie himself down with a wife and property before forty?"

Gloria Lind challenged this, saying, "My earnings are successfully invested in Chicago real estate, under the guidance of my father. I know of many TV and movie stars who plan for the future and invest their money in real estate. I think people should start at an early age."

We discussed various performing artists who were successful investors in income property: Dana Andrews, Bing Crosby, Bob Hope, Lucille Ball, Desi Arnaz, Lloyd Bridges and Don DeFore. Also Red Skelton, Hugh O'Brian, Lloyd Nolan, Dennis Weaver, Loretta Young, Carolyn Jones, Fred MacMurray, John Wayne, Burt Lancaster and Lawrence Welk.

### Can Anyone Make a Fortune?

Anyone who really wants to can make a fortune in real estate. To succeed, one requires only the initiative to start and the determination to keep applying the three R's of Renovating, Refinancing and Reinvesting.

There are always a number of pessimists who go out of their way to discourage you. During the depression days of 1931, when my wife, Lucille, and I were newlyweds, our Fresno State College economics professor said, "The days of opportunity are over. There's no longer any use trying to save for investment. The best you can hope for is to keep a steady job and stay off relief."

My wife and I were obsessed with the idea of additional security, probably because we both came from poor families. We determined to save a nest egg, even though at the time we had no idea where to invest.

During World War II, when I withdrew my savings to buy a duplex (two-family) house, my banker said, "You're crazy to buy income property under rent controls. Your income will be held down so you won't even be able to pay your mortgage, and we'll have to foreclose."

Although rent controls curtailed maximum investment potentials, it turned out that most owners made a fair net income, sometimes greater than normal. Because of the housing shortage, dwellings were 100 per cent rented, and there were many legitimate ways to increase rents. Operating costs were reduced. Customary upkeep, such as painting, was omitted. Supplies and equipment that were usually provided just were not available, because of wartime shortages. Afterward, when boom times came along, my economics professor at Fresno State and many others said, "It's too late for opportunity. Success depends on having started back there during the depression."

### Is It Possible to Succeed Today?

That was the question asked by the five leading publishers who turned down my first book. In every case the editors I dealt with directly were enthusiastic. But the more their senior editors thought about it the more it seemed just too good to be true for current markets. So they submitted my first chapters to outside experts.

One editor wrote, "Our outside expert tells us you were just lucky and rode the market up from the depression, and nobody else could duplicate your success today."

Another editor told me, "It's a funny thing. We checked your financial statement with Dun and Bradstreet and know you have proved your case. But our expert who says it can't be done is a stock analyst and knows nothing about real estate. Furthermore, he doesn't even have a thousand dollars saved up!"

I'm a pretty patient man, but finally I got mad and decided to prove that these skeptics were wrong. At the time I started writing my first book I had only a half-million dollars. I went out on the current real-estate market, shopping exclusively from ads that realtors put in metropolitan papers. I had no intention of increasing my estate; I only wanted to prove there were still good buys available. My wife and I were perfectly satisfied to sit back and enjoy the fruits of a half-million dollars' net worth in investments.

But we found so many good buys we couldn't resist them all. We borrowed on our apartments and used the money to buy and fix up more properties to increase their revenues. In two years we doubled our net estate to over a million dollars, then we coasted along, past a net of $3½ million.

Of course it made a more rounded title to write *How I Turned $1,000 into a Million* (then 3 million)—instead of a half million. I can certainly thank those pessimistic editors for pushing me into becoming a multimillionaire.

## Are Opportunities Always Present?

Although opportunities are greater during boom times, I have come to the conclusion that opportunities are always present, in good times or bad. Opportunity in America knocks not only for the favored few, but for everyone who aspires to better himself; it knocks not just once, but many times. All you have to do is open the door.

## Who Have Opened the Door?

I have previously mentioned popular entertainers who have taken advantage of real-estate opportunities. Since the publication of my books, the door of opportunity has been opened to many thousands of lesser-known people in different localities. Among them is Roy Dygert of Portland, Oregon, a retired carpenter, who bought a three-apartment, or triplex, building for $8,000, paying only $800 down. In seven months he spent $600 for materials and used his own labor to make improvements. After a total cash outlay of $1,400 he sold the property for $14,500 and made a profit of $5,900.

According to Shirley Camper, whose article "Can Reading a Book Make You Rich?" appeared in the April 1961 *Cosmopolitan,* "Gerard Pinault of Pawtucket, Rhode Island, didn't graduate from grammar school, never earned more than five thousand dollars a year in the furniture business. Enter Nickerson's real-estate book. Now, less than two years làter, Pinault has seven buildings, a total of fifty units, and about eighteen thousand dollars a year income from rentals—all accomplished in his spare time and on credit."

Victor J. Zaro started his first realty investments in Philadelphia after my book came out and in three years pyramided from scratch to a net worth of a third of a million dollars in apartment equities. He writes, "And some brokers told me your program wouldn't work in Philadelphia! For the first time in my life I feel I have achieved complete economic security. I know I wouldn't even have started investing except for the inspiration and know-how of your book, and for this I shall be forever grateful.

"I honestly feel that on the basis of the last three years—counting my current holdings and deals I am working on—I should hit the one-million-dollar mark in about six years. If I quit right now (and I would have to be a fool to give up this new, exhilarating way of life) my present investments will be worth a million dollars in twenty years."

To cite one of many examples outside the United States, John Connor of Brisbane, Australia, also improved run-down properties. In four years he increased his estate a hundredfold, from $2,500 to $250,000.

### Is Real Estate Headed for Another Major Depression?

A widowed teacher in Pittsburgh writes, "I bought a $10,500 triplex a year ago with $1,200 down. I spent $960 painting and fixing it up, and increased the income so it's worth $6,000 more than I paid. I want to keep going, but have to be careful because I'm all alone in the world. In view of the troubled world situation, and acute unemployment in some areas, is real estate headed for another major depression?"

No. There are many indications that we are heading in the opposite direction, a leveling period followed by a boom. I go along with the optimistic long-range forecasts of tough-minded business corporations. The huge Bell Telephone System, for example, made plans to spend $9 billion for expansion in 1973 and many billions more in the next ten years on the basis of these carefully considered and generally agreed-on assumptions:

There will be no major war.
Defense spending will be above current levels.

There will be no major depression.
There will probably be increased welfare expenditures.
The political and social structure will not change materially.
National growth will continue to rise, in some areas very fast.
Real income will continue to rise.

In 1963 A.T. & T. board chairman Frederick Kappel stated the ongoing Bell System policy: "Of course there will be ups and downs in the business cycle, but we aren't going to let temporary things scare us. We're backing our faith in the near months and the far years with the biggest construction outlay in our history. We are moving full steam ahead with this big construction program. We are doing it because of our faith and confidence in the future of business and the nation. Surely, the course of America is upward."

## What Are the Built-In Safety Measures?

There are many built-in safety measures to help prevent a major depression—Federal Deposit Insurance, Social Security, unemployment insurance. Significant safeguards against a depression affect both the stock market and real estate. In the 1929 crash, stocks could be bought for only 10 per cent down, and many fortunes were wiped out when stock dropped more than the margin that was put up. Now stocks are bought with considerably more cash.

Real-estate mortgages at that time were short-term; most of them ran for only three years. Five years was considered a long-term mortgage. When the loan fell due during a tight money market, it was often impossible to renew and the lender had to foreclose, with little possibility of redemption.

My father, Alonzo Nickerson, made such a short-term mortgage loan to pay for imported fruit trees which he planted over most of the acreage of our farm in Wilderville, Oregon. The loan fell due before the fruit produced an income. The bank refused to renew and foreclosed. When I was eight years old my family moved to California, where my discouraged father worked as a farm hand for the rest of his life.

Today foreclosure laws are considerably more lenient, allowing a reasonable time to raise the money for redemption. The main stabilizing factor of present property loans is that they are generally on an amortizing basis. You pay so much a month until the loan is paid off, and you do not have the problem of renewal.

In our dynamic economy, minor recessions are bound to alternate with boom times, but existing real-estate investments are not significantly affected by minor recessions.

## How Big Is the Business of Real Estate?

This question was asked by realtor Bill Tillman following my lecture at an educational conference of the California Real Estate Association in Pasadena.

The transfer of real estate in the United States amounts to approximately $72 billion a year. Total value of real estate in 1974 reached approximately $3 trillion making this by far the nation's largest investment.

## Am I Too Young or Too Old?

John Semrad of Milwaukee, Wisconsin, writes, "I am retired on an annuity at sixty-five and would like to know whether at my age it is too late to start."

Milton Wahlberg, a seminary student in Houston, Texas, writes, "I am a twenty-two-year-old student, supporting myself and wife and baby by part-time preaching. What I want to know is, am I too young to start following your plan?"

It is never too late or to early for those who can visualize the possibilities. Age has little to do with one's ability to succeed. Sixty-five-year-old John Semrad is a youngster compared with some of the people who have written to me.

Sam Stark of Leander, Wyoming, who writes of his plans "for the next ten years," gives his age as eighty-four. He built seven apartments in Rock Springs, Wyoming, in 1920 and allowed them to deteriorate until they were giving him a poor income. Stark writes, "Your book inspired me to dress that building up a bit. Now it pays off so good I'm looking for another good buy in apartments that some other fool has let run down, so I can rejuvenate them."

Then there was my grandfather, John Robinson, of Grant's Pass, Oregon, who at ninety-seven was still looking for ways to improve farm properties.

On the other hand, I know of some teen-agers who have already started investing. One of them is nineteen-year-old Sherman Furlong of St. Paul, Minnesota, who paid $1,400 down for a $13,900 triplex. He writes, "In a few months' time I made minor improvements which made it possible to raise the rents to a total of $190 monthly. My present value, according to comparable buildings in the neighborhood, is $17,000."

## Why Give Secrets Away?

One question I am asked frequently is, "Why are you giving your hard-won secrets away?" Realty board secretary Isabelle Veech asked this question in Hawaii; it was repeated soon after by television interviewer James Kerr of station WBAP in Dallas.

First, I sincerely believe that all investors today, and the whole world, will be better off if as many people as possible know how to reap the fruits of free enterprise. It is healthier for our economy if widespread property ownership is encouraged. This has been the case in the United States, where the percentage of resident-owned dwelling units has about doubled in the last fifty years—from a one-third minority to almost a two-thirds majority.

I started writing about investment opportunities when friends and relatives asked how they could copy my success. It gives me a feeling of satisfaction to be able to tell them just what to do and to see them successfully follow my advice.

Additionally, I have wanted to be a writer since my school days, when I never dreamed of becoming a millionaire. I just stumbled into success, first investing on a hit-or-miss basis, then analyzing the underlying principles of real-estate pyramiding. In common with many writers, I have an urge to share my secrets. Some writers tell of their experiences with alcohol and drugs and sex. I have written about how to make money, while others have written about how to make merry.

## What Is the American Dream?

This is a question that seems to preoccupy many people. New Yorker Lillian Friedman of Brentano's asked me what I thought it was when I appeared on her WEVD radio show, *Let's Look at Books*. It was also one of the questions most frequently asked by the Russians of a robot at an American exhibit in Moscow.

Our official government answer was, "That every person shall be free to seek a better life for himself and for his children."

Of course, a better life includes more than financial success, although it is usually dependent upon it. For a time in New Deal days the subject of making money seemed out of fashion, both politically and socially. In some circles, making profits was called sinful, and people shunned talking about investment, even though it might be uppermost in their minds.

Now, as in the days of Benjamin Franklin, profitable investments are an acceptable and sometimes exciting topic of conversation at tea and cocktail parties. Five of our last seven Presidents have been millionaires: Hoover, Roosevelt, Eisenhower, Kennedy and Johnson. America's wealthiest multimillionaire President took office in 1961, with a major portion of his Kennedy family's one-third-billion-range fortune invested in real estate. The Vice President at this writing, Nelson Rockefeller, is even wealthier.

In 1961 also, the seven original space-bound Astronauts pooled their half-million dollars earned from books and magazine articles and invested it in real estate. One of their purchases was a Washington, D.C., apartment house.

In 1960, 1961 and 1962 over a million earthbound Americans became new "capitalists" by buying their first stock or real estate.

## Isn't It Harder to Start Today?

Teacher Tom Chun asked this question after my lecture to the Lowry-Nickerson Real Estate Investors Seminar in Waikiki, Hawaii, emceed by Al Lowry. Chun continued, "With the tight money market and high prices we are having now, isn't it much harder to make a million than when you started during the depression?"

No, it is much easier. Every day a great many say it is harder to succeed in their particular day than at another time. But success today is much easier for the average person than ever before in history. The proof is in the growing number who actually succeed. There were over 10,000 new millionaires created in the United States in 1973, more than the total number of 8,500 when I started during the depression. The ranks of new millionaires keep expanding, making a total of over 100,000 in 1974.

# II

# *How Can I Pyramid to a Million Today?*

When I appeared on the *Today* show, Dave Garroway piled one million dollars in currency around me and asked, "Can you tell me how to start with an average nest egg and pyramid to a million dollars today?"

Henry Morgan on his New York TV show paraphrased this by saying, "I challenge you to show me in three minutes how I can start out today with only twenty-five hundred dollars and pyramid to a million."

Such questions call for boiling down the step-by-step formula of the real-estate pyramid set forth in my first book. After I've given a capsule report of three minutes or so, interviewers invariably request more details; so do audiences following my lectures.

At my Ambassador Club lecture appearance in Sacramento, California, for example, Judge Murle Shreck asked, "Where do you get the financing mentioned in the first step?"

Following my Cleveland, Ohio, Apartment and Home Owners' Association lecture, executive secretary Karl Duldner asked, "Where did you ever get the inspiration for such a clear-cut pyramid in the first place?"

These are typical of the many questions involving my million-dollar pyramid. After divulging some behind-the-scenes information about the *Today* show, I'll give a consolidated answer, starting with how the idea first came to me.

## Was That Million in Real Money?

The million dollars in currency pyramided around me by Dave Garroway, with Frank Blair assisting, provoked a number of unexpected questions from the television audience. J. F. Hanak of Salem, Wisconsin, wrote, "Was that real or phony money?"

Newspaper publisher Semmes Gordon of Danville, California, asked, "How did the government let you photograph real money for TV shows?"

Others have asked how my wife and I transported the money from California to New York. Our children, Nancy and Robert, wanted to know, "Where did the money and all those armed guards come from?"

The money wasn't in gold, but it really was a million in good U.S. currency.

My $3 million-plus net worth is tied up in real-estate equities, not in cash. The money displayed on the show was borrowed from the Bankers Trust Company. Simon and Schuster obtained clearance from the F.B.I. to photograph the money. The government agents stipulated that no individual notes could be photographed and all the currency must be left in bundles. Mike Clancey, NBC chief of protection, arranged for the presence of three NBC guards, three Bankers Trust men in uniform, three U.S. Trucking armored-car guards, and three New York City policemen. Each man was armed with a Tommy gun or a sawed-off shotgun.

## Don't You Worship Money?

The show was broadcast live in the East, starting at 7 A.M. The million dollars arrived by armored car at the same time my wife and I appeared at the studio for rehearsal, at 5:30 A.M. Several members of the press were on hand. A reporter from *Life* magazine said they wanted to run a two-page spread with pictures of the million dollars and me, surrounded by the *Today* cast and the armed guards.

*Life*'s photographer took many candid shots and asked me to pose for various seated and standing pictures, then requested, "Will you please kneel down and face the money so I can get a shot from that angle?"

I replied, "No, it would look like I worshiped money, and that's not right."

"Don't you worship money? How else could you be a millionaire?"

"I appreciate having enough money to do the things I really want to. I would never think of worshiping money, or posing as though I did."

The photographer got quite angry at my refusal. *Life*'s reporter said, "Well, maybe we'll run the story anyhow." But they didn't.

Shortly thereafter, however, *Time-Life* photographer Jim Truitt made a special trip to my Alamo home. His photo of me in a Hawaiian shirt beside my swimming pool was run with *Time*'s gratifying review of my book.

Another who asked, "Don't you have to worship money to be a millionaire?" was deaconess Bella Campbell of the La Selva Beach Community Church on Monterey Bay. She asked the question just prior to my Layman's Sunday sermon, "Heaven Is All About You."

I said, "Please ask me after my sermon." After the service she said, "Sorry I asked. Your inspiring sermon showed so many worthwhile interests that have nothing to do with money."

### How Can We Copy Your Success?

In March 1951 I retired from the telephone company at the age of forty-two to live off my property income. Friends and relatives asked how they could duplicate my investment success. How could they retire early with an independent income?

I was able to answer specific questions about how to shop for good buys, what kind of property to look for and how to operate it.

But then I was asked if there was an underlying secret that would help them tell whether or not they were on the right road. My advice was to borrow heavily to invest in real estate and improve it, then keep reinvesting. But there was such a forest of details that I could not chart a clear path. I pondered over this for several months and studied the conclusions of others.

A typical answer was given by Henry Kaiser at a symposium of corporation chiefs. The subject was, "What Should You Do to Achieve Success?" Kaiser stated, "The one who works the hardest at his present job is bound to rise to the top."

Kaiser's answer was sincere, I'm sure, but if it were true the hardest-working laborer should always be the one chosen for company president. Even so, I couldn't think of a better answer as I continued studying in my office in the mornings and gardening in my sunny San Ramon Valley acre in the afternoons.

Then I awoke at three o'clock one morning with a clear-cut step-by-step formula in mind, as simple as the ABC's. I'm no mathematical wizard, but something told me it would work out to a million dollars. I got up and went to the office in my home and ran the figures up on my adding machine. Sure enough, they topped a million.

Before explaining the formula I should mention that you can start investing with $1,000 today, as my wife and I did. Many people have written to me telling how they started with that little or less. A San Francisco widow tells of buying a desirable triplex for only $500 down. I know of many recent buys with nothing down. But today, in order to have a sound start on the current market, and to be in a position comparable to mine when I started with $1,000, I figure the average investor should have somewhere in the neighborhood of $2,500. Older wage earners tend to have greater savings, but this $2,500 sum happens to be the average savings for a family in the United States where the breadwinner is between the ages of twenty-five and thirty-four. This amount can be accumulated in four years by saving $50 monthly and adding the interest.

You take your $2,500 in savings and borrow three times as much, $7,500, for a total of $10,000. With this you buy a run-down house that is basically sound but needs fixing up. The $7,500 financing could be in the form of a first mortgage that the owner might take back, or it could be a loan from a savings bank or insurance company. What if the first mortgage is insufficient to cover needed financing? The growing practice all over the country is for the seller to take back a second mortgage to make up the difference.

You take an average of two years for renovation, including such items as painting, modernizing electrical and plumbing fixtures, and sprucing up the yard. This increases the rental value. You raise the rents an average of 25 per cent, either in steps or all at once, depending on how the improvement work is handled. This increases the sale value 25 per cent, as the market value of rental real estate is based on income. The national yardstick for apartment values is ten times the net scheduled annual income.

### Is Saving Absolutely Necessary?

Many are like minister-teacher Benjamin Seruya of Brooklyn, New York, who asks, "For sustained investment, is saving $50 a month absolutely necessary or just advisable?"

A savings program is not absolutely necessary, but helps a great deal to speed your progress when you start out with a small nest egg. Some think that as soon as they buy their first small rental property they can immediately start living like millionaires. Then they wonder what keeps them from further advancement.

In this example you keep plowing back the net rents, plus your continued $50 monthly savings. At the end of two years you sell or trade your property for a gross turnover profit of 25 per cent. This average of 12½ per cent a year is rather nominal for anyone who follows my suggested program. Out of the 25 per cent gross profit you pay sales costs, which will average about 5 per cent, covering realty board fees. They usually start at 6 per cent with small properties and drop lower with larger sales. This leaves you with a net worth after two years of $5,800.

Then you take your accumulated nest egg of $5,800 and use it as the down payment on a larger income property, perhaps four flats. Or you might buy at this stage a six- to eight-unit apartment house. Again you seek 75 per cent financing. At each step you try to borrow three times as much as your own down payment.

## What Is the Most Important Single Factor in Making a Fortune?

This question was asked by Seattle *Times* classified-advertising manager Lester Jenkins at a press conference when I spoke to the Chamber of Commerce and the Real Estate Board in Seattle.

The most important consideration is the power of O.P.M. After my Waikiki, Hawaii, lecture, Dr. Lucy Ma asked, "Do you mean opium?"

I replied, "No, I mean Other People's Money!"

It is impossible to make a fortune today without heavy borrowing. That is what banks and insurance companies actually do when they take your deposits and premiums. In effect, they borrow from you. They perform a real service at a nominal charge by acting as money wholesalers. Money would earn no return for those who save if it were not for borrowers. You become a money retailer when you borrow for investment purposes.

## How Can Borrowing Be Sound?

This question was asked by a saleswoman when I lectured at Lit Brothers department store in Philadelphia. She was hesitant to speak until urged on by Lit's Good Neighbor director, Elma McCarraher. Then she said, "I know my neighbors and relatives have more than I do because they borrow. I have about ten thousand dollars to invest in apartments and am anxious to get started. But I've always been so indoctrinated against going into debt that I'm afraid to owe a cent."

Borrowing for investment is sound as long as you can take care of loan payments plus expenses from income. Many people are afraid to borrow, usually because they confuse money consumption with investment. It is a wise precaution not to borrow too heavily for personal pleasure, for then you are only a money consumer.

Don't forget that Henry Ford had to borrow 100 per cent to found his billionaire fortune. Henry Kaiser and many others achieved major success through heavy borrowing.

Christopher Columbus had no money, but he too was obsessed by a dream. It's a good thing he wasn't afraid to borrow, for it was entirely with borrowed funds, advanced chiefly by Queen Isabella of Spain in exchange for 90 per cent of all proceeds, that he discovered America.

### Must I Follow Your Formula Exactly to Achieve Success?

This question is frequently asked by those who want to be sure they are not going astray. A typical questioner was a salesman of twenty-five who worked in William Chleboun's book department at the Emporium in San Francisco. He was determined to invest in real estate, following the suggestions in my book, in order to provide comfort and security for his wife and two children.

He was perturbed by the "deviations" of two little old ladies dressed in black. They were looking through my book while I was autographing.

One said, "I have ten thousand dollars to invest. But I'd be satisfied just to make a hundred thousand."

The other said, "I already own a duplex. And I'd be satisfied just to learn how to collect the rents!"

My formula is intended as a guide to show the potential inherent in real estate for anyone who has the courage to start and the determination to keep at it. Some investors will move slower at given steps, some faster. Profits may be less at certain steps and greater on others. There are no hard-and-fast rules regarding the time to be allotted and the profit that may be made.

Some may start off like the white-haired painter who jumped up after my lecture at Capwell's store in Hayward, across the bay from San Francisco. He said, "When I read your book I had only four hundred dollars in the bank. But I couldn't wait to save that twenty-five hundred you recommended. I bought a ratty-looking house that mainly needed paint. Then I bought paint on credit and painted it inside and out myself. In one month I sold it for a four-thousand-dollar profit."

Or, to put it another way, the painter's investment earned 1,000 per cent in one month.

If this seems fantastic, there is a modified example in the Bible. Jesus tells the parable of the talents to show His endorsement of investing. While their master was gone on a journey, two servants invested talents (we call them nest eggs today) and increased their value twofold. Here we have an example of a short-term profit of 100 per cent.

But let's get back to my fairly conservative formula, with a gross turnover profit in the range of only one per cent per month. We will continue to plan an average gross capital profit of 12½ per cent a year on an average turnover time of every two years.

At the end of two more years, or four years after you start with $2,500, you would have a net worth of $11,575. At the end of six years you would have $21,681, at the end of eight years $39,363, and at the end of ten years $70,548.

### Is This a Get-Rich-Quick Scheme?

This question was asked by San Francisco Town Hall impresario Dr. Albert Rappaport when he was arranging for my lecture.

This is in no sense a get-rich-quick scheme, but is a planned program, based on sound principles, that requires a reasonable amount of time. You will notice that your progress, although gratifying, is not spectacular in the early stages. That's the way all sound pyramids work. When I was in Egypt gathering material for my second book, *My Odyssey Around Three Worlds,* I learned that it took twenty years to build the Great Pyramid of Cheops at Gizeh. To hold up the two million stone blocks, weighing 2½ tons each, it took ten years just to prepare the foundation and lay the first step.

Succeeding steps rise much faster as you approach the apex. If this is kept in mind it helps to prevent discouragement and promotes confidence. After ten years, or when you have passed your fifth step, you find that your progress is much more rapid.

At the end of twelve years you would have $124,884, at the end of fourteen years $219,972, sixteen years $386,376, eighteen years $677,583. And at the end of twenty years you would top a million, with $1,187,195.

A number of readers have written that they felt compelled to check this computation on their own adding machines. All found that it actually works out.

### How Would You Pyramid Past a Million?

A retired Detroit industrialist of sixty-two writes, "I'm worth over two million and am anxious to convert most of my stock into real-estate investment. How will your pyramid work if I throw in a million or so in cash and keep reinvesting for ten years?"

A trial lawyer of fifty asked a question along similar lines after my lecture to the National Association of Claimants' Counsel of America in Denver. "I have seventy-five thousand dollars to invest. How far would it go if I started at the ten-year step on your pyramid and kept at it for twenty years?"

Suppose the attorney takes $70,548 and invests it for ten years. He follows the average pattern in my pyramid of 75 per cent financing, 25 per cent gross turnover profits each two years, and 5 per cent sales costs. At that point he will be on the same past-the-million-mark level at which the Detroit industrialist wants to start investing.

Assume that the industrialist now and the attorney ten years from now start out at the twenty-year level on my pyramid, with $1,187,195. Where will this same average experience take them in ten more years?

At the end of two more years each will have a net estate from this investment of $2,079,016.

At the end of four years this will have grown to $3,639,703.
At the end of six years, to $6,370,905.
Eight years, $11,145,769.
Ten years, $19,506,521.

In actuality, after you make a million, additional millions are easier to accumulate if you want to keep at it, just as the second thousand is much easier than the first. Some, like myself with writing and lecturing, to encourage others, are more interested in other challenges. Some, like Henry Kaiser, want to see how far they can expand, setting their sights on $10-million, then $100-million, then billion-dollar levels. Many people have overshadowed by far my comparatively modest success.

According to the *J. K. Lasser Tax Report*, "Starting from scratch slightly more than ten years ago, real-estate developer Kanavos at thirty-six now has a net worth of more than five million dollars."

*Time* magazine reported that Dave Murdock made his first million in Phoenix, Arizona, real estate in two years by the time he was thirty-one.

Another Southwestern realty investor pyramided $200,000 to $10 million in three years. It is well known that Texans Clint Murchison and Sid Richardson topped the $300-million and $700-million marks. In both cases they developed their estates by heavy borrowing on their real-estate investments all over the country. Some investors, like Howard Hughes and Paul Getty, have passed the billion mark.

### Is Yours a System That Depends on Inflation?

This frequently repeated question was asked by Pat McCarty, Minneapolis *Tribune* reporter, when I lectured to a Minnesota Realtors Association educational conference.

No. Inflation helps, of course. But if you had no inflation at all you could still succeed.

Continuing inflation is expected for the foreseeable future. Property tends to benefit from two built-in bonuses normally tied in with population increase. Real-estate values go up when there is general inflation and a period of active community development. These increases can be offset, or more than offset, by depreciation of buildings and equipment. Normal upkeep is expected if you want to stay abreast of depreciation, neither gaining nor losing except for gradual obsolescence.

The improvement and modernization program that I advocate overcomes both depreciation and obsolescence and accelerates increases in value. My recommendations are not based on inflation or other outside influences, but on putting something into the property, and improving it to enhance the value. Thus your success is determined by your own decisions.

"As you sow, so shall you reap," the Bible truly says; it is my conviction that if you put worthwhile improvements into property, then you can earn a worthwhile return.

This process of improvement gives you an added safety factor. After fixing up property you can often borrow as much as you have invested in it, or more, including the purchase price plus improvement costs. I know of many who have done this. It makes your investment as sound as the bank's when it lends you the money.

### Will You Invest for Me?

Some facetious questions I've received help expose fallacious thinking and thereby point to reality. An example I have in mind came from one of the deans at a Southern university.

He wrote, "I have not read your book, but saw the publicity about your million-dollar pyramid in *Forbes* magazine. I should like to make you a proposition. I will send you $600 in cash and $50 a month for five years which you invest in your pyramiding scheme for financial accumulation. At the end of five years you send me $10,000, and you keep whatever additional balance has accrued to the fund as payment for your services. According to your table this should yield you about $5,000. How about it?"

My reply was as follows:

Since the publication of my book, I have received requests from readers all over the world, asking me to invest cash funds on a fee basis or in partnership. The amounts offered for investment thus far have ranged from $1,000 to $1,000,000. Thank you for your proposition (tongue-in-cheekish, I suspect) to broaden this base. Your offer of your initial nest egg of $600 is the first that has come from one who has not yet read my book.

Previous correspondence has arrived from several universities and from many states and foreign countries. It is impossible to accommodate all requests for my participation in investment; therefore I am refusing all. I am not interested in any further expansion, preferring to devote most of my efforts to lecturing and writing and answering thousands of serious inquiries.

Your proposition might focus itself better if I made a counter-proposition: I'll send you the tuition and fees necessary for you to earn a doctorate in philosophy. You take the necessary courses and write the required thesis. When you get your degree, please arrange for the university to send one to me also. You can keep yours "as payment for your services."

Would the university send me a degree unless I earned it myself? The same considerations apply to free enterprise. If you sincerely aspire to reap the maximum benefits of free enterprise, you have to earn them yourself. You have to develop the courage to jump in and get your own feet wet.

If you decide to sit back and have someone else do your investing for you, then you should be satisfied with more nominal returns. They will range, perhaps, from 10 per cent in a real-estate syndicate to 4½ per cent from regular bank savings.

## What Are My Chances for Success?

Some get so enthused about real-estate possibilities they are apt to stray into other fields, thinking the opportunities may be the same. An unexpected example involved the owner of a Chinese res-

taurant who phoned from San Francisco. He said, "I got excited
after reading the *Chronicle* ads about your book. I took a thousand
dollars out of the bank and invested it. And I lost it all in one
night."

"How in the world did that happen?"

"I invested it in the dollar slot machine in Las Vegas!"

He added, "I'm a gambler at heart. But I like to figure the odds
against me before I pay my money. I'd like to read your book and
copy your ideas. But first I have a question: What are the odds
against me if I buy apartments?"

Fortunately we have both government and insurance-company
studies on mortgage experience, as cited in my first book. They
show that if you take out a mortgage to buy property the chances
are four hundred to one in your favor that it will be paid off.

By comparison, if you take out a life insurance policy, the
chances are one in twenty that it will be canceled for failure to pay
out. Thus the chances of paying off a real-estate mortgage are
twenty times greater than the chances on a life insurance policy.
Compare these odds with those of going into business, where the
chances are four to one that you will go broke. This makes the
chances for success in property investment 1,600-to-one better than
the chances on going into business.

### Why Doesn't Everyone Make a Million When It Looks So Simple?

This logical question was asked at a press interview in St. Louis,
Missouri, by *Globe-Democrat* reporter Carl Major.

Most of those who read about successful investment only dream
of the results. They are interested in how it can be done, but they
don't expect to exert the necessary effort themselves. Others make
plans and start shopping for possible buys, but many never make
the decision to go ahead. All who do take action find there is con-
tinuously expanding room for investment opportunity.

## With a Devaluing Dollar, Isn't This a Bad Time to Buy Real Estate?

This question was asked after my lecture in St. Louis at a Lowry-Nickerson Seminar, where my co-lecturer was realtor Don Straub of Long Beach, California.

No, devaluation of the dollar increases the value of real estate. In addition, the value of land will continue to rise as it keeps getting scarcer. And the value of existing buildings will continue rising with the increased cost of construction.

## Shouldn't I Hold Off Buying at Today's High Prices Until Costs Drop?

This oft-repeated question, companion to the previous one, reflects wishful but erroneous thinking.

It's better to buy now, as land and construction costs will continue to rise. Even with improved factory methods of construction, over-all building costs will continue to increase along with leaping escalation in labor and raw material costs.

Land values will continue rising because of four basic factors, besides inflation, affecting the dwindling supply of usable land:

1. Increasing U.S. population, requiring more dwelling use to handle an absolute minimum for the foreseeable future of one million new housing units per year.

2. Increasing world population, requiring maximum additional agricultural use of marginal land to help overcome worldwide food scarcities.

3. Increasing commercial and industrial facilities, requiring more land to serve greater U.S. and world populations.

4. Increasing reservation of land by federal, state, county and local governments for recreational use, to meet the demands of

greater leisure time by a growing population. The U.S. Department of the Interior alone proposed in 1974 to ask Congress to double the land under the National Park System from 30,285,139.68 acres to over 60 million acres.

# III

## Can I Succeed with Average Ability in a Dwindling City?

A Detroit auto worker writes, "Since reading your book I put $2,000 into a brick duplex, fixed it up and sold it in six months, pocketing $3,500 net cash. I started looking for a larger piece of property and found a five-unit apartment house that fits your improvement recommendations to a *T*. I almost bought it, then held off after I saw the new census figures. They scared me plenty.

"Our city population has dropped 156,543 in the last ten years, from 1,670,144 in 1960 to 1,513,601 in 1970. Does this mean there is little chance of continuing to succeed by following your formula in Detroit?"

I have received letters with similar questions and comparable experiences from every major city where the 1960 and 1970 censuses showed a population drop. Reactions have no doubt been distorted in some cases by alarming newspaper stories quoting anguished politicians who demanded census recounts.

As I have verified from firsthand appraisals, I would say Detroit offers tremendous real-estate investment opportunities today, despite a falling city population. This answer also applies to other leading cities throughout the country which have lost population in the last decade. Included are San Francisco and Oakland in northern California, where my investments are located.

In these and in all cities above 300,000 (except Pittsburgh) where the population has dropped, the greater metropolitan areas have increased; they have followed the area pattern of the mush-rooming pace setters where city population has increased. Among the latter, Jacksonville, Nashville and San Jose have all jumped over 100 per cent. Every major metropolitan area in the United States shows a potential growth factor that offers investment opportunities in city investments.

## Do Many Prefer City Living?

Although many people like myself prefer country living, a high percentage of the movement to the suburbs is not dictated primarily from choice, as is commonly supposed, but more from necessity. Many who prefer city living leave for the suburbs because urban living quarters have become run-down, or the land has been converted to higher-valued usage for commercial, industrial and governmental purposes. A striking example of this pattern is in New York City, where older apartment houses on Park Avenue are being torn down. The kind of new construction that is displacing apartments and homes includes:

Offices of corporations, including utilities, banks, insurance companies, etc.

Office buildings primarily for rental purposes

Government buildings for municipal, county, state and federal offices, post offices, museums, libraries, etc.

Schools and churches

Hotels and motels

Medical and hospital buildings

Terminals for air and surface transportation

Throughways and expanded streets

Parking lots and garages

Recreational facilities such as theaters, cabarets, auditoriums, bowling alleys, skating rinks, stadiums and parks.

The Detroit-area population increased from 3,762,360 in 1960 to 4,435,051 in 1970. This is a jump of 672,691 in contrast to the 156,543 decrease in city population.

The table on p. 44, compiled from figures sent to me by Vincent P. Barabba, director of the Bureau of the Census, shows the fifty cities above 100,000 that shared Detroit's experience of a population drop within city limits and an increase in the metropolitan area; the area increases are net figures, arrived at after offsetting the city decreases. It should be noted that a metropolitan area is defined by the Census Bureau as a central city of at least 50,000, with adjoining counties and communities predominantly urban and closely integrated. Only cities that had populations of more than 100,000 in 1970 are shown here. The six cities that lost both corporate and area population are shown at the bottom of the table along with four that have no metropolitan area outside their boundaries.

(A table in Chapter VIII lists the ninety-six cities with population above 100,000 which gained population. Of the thirty growing metropolitan areas exceeding one million, sixteen of these million-plus areas lost population in their central cities and fourteen gained.)

It is interesting to note some wide variations between city and area rankings. While they match for cities like Philadelphia and Detroit, others are considerably different. Showing much larger area populations than the city rankings would indicate, for example, Boston city ranks 16 while its area ranks 6, Albany city 126 and area 45. Three Connecticut cities of Hartford, Bridgeport and New Haven rank 85, 86 and 102, while their areas rank twice as high at 42, 44 and 49.

Some cities show a reverse ratio, with areas ranking much lower than cities. Interesting examples are Baltimore with a city ranking of 7 and area ranking of 13; New Orleans city 19 and area 33; and Spokane, site of Expo 74, with a city ranking of 79 and area ranking of 117.

## Can You Give More Current Examples of Success?

The proof of the pudding is in the eating, and the best proofs of opportunities are examples of those who are actually experiencing success. I've received many fan letters from readers in the cities listed in the population chart, citing examples of real-estate investments they have made since publication of my first book. All are doing well. Most of them, like my Detroit correspondent, the Pittsburgh widow and others previously mentioned, are ahead of my million-dollar schedule. And hundreds all over the country have advised me of passing the million mark in five to ten years, some starting from scratch.

A San Diego attorney asked for my autograph when I lectured before the local realty board. He mentioned that he was following the suggestions in my book and had far exceeded my million-dollar formula. On a net cash outlay of $30,000 his net worth had jumped to over $300,000 in the previous fourteen months.

When I lectured at a realtors' seminar in Mankato, southern Minnesota, a small-town investor told of making $50,000 by improving one local ranch, bringing his net worth to a quarter million at the age of thirty-one. Another realtor in Mankato told how he made over $100,000 with 100 per cent financing by fixing up small run-down single-family homes.

According to *Parade* magazine, singer Johnny Mathis pyramided record royalties and night club fees into a million-dollar real-estate fortune, making him one of thirty-five American black millionaires.

In my files are many thousands of successful case histories from more than a million readers. Only a representative cross section can be cited here. While speculators may lose money by straying from my proven methods, not one investor has advised me of failure as a result of following my suggestions.

## Is There a Booming Rush to City Apartments?

As fan letters with case histories and queries piled up in my office, Sam Meyerson of Simon and Schuster suggested that I compile this question-and-answer sequel to my first book. But before starting this project I wanted to verify actual cases and the over-all picture in every section of the country. I visited every one of the aforementioned cities with populations above 200,000, plus many others, that had experienced population gains. In every case, my

## 50 Cities Above 100,000 That Lost Population While Their Areas Gained
### (From 1960 and 1970 Census Bureau Figures, with Corrections Issued May, 1974)

| Rank | | CITY POPULATION | | AREA POPULATION | | |
|---|---|---|---|---|---|---|
| | | 1970 Census | Decrease | 1970 Census | Increase | Rank |
| 52 | Akron, Ohio | 275,425 | −14,926 | 679,239 | 165,670 | 55 |
| 126 | Albany, N.Y. | 115,781 | −13,945 | 777,977 | 120,474 | 45 |
| 7 | Baltimore, Md. | 905,757 | −33,267 | 2,071,016 | 343,993 | 13 |
| 123 | Beaumont, Texas | 117,548 | −1,627 | 347,568 | 41,552 | 97 |
| 48 | Birmingham, Ala. | 300,910 | −39,977 | 767,230 | 132,366 | 47 |
| 16 | Boston, Mass. | 697,197 | −56,126 | 3,376,328 | 787,027 | 6 |
| 86 | Bridgeport, Conn. | 156,542 | −206 | 792,814 | 458,238 | 44 |
| 28 | Buffalo, N.Y. | 462,768 | −69,991 | 1,349,211 | 42,254 | 25 |
| 135 | Canton, Ohio | 110,053 | −3,578 | 393,789 | 53,444 | 86 |
| 121 | Chattanooga, Tenn. | 119,082 | −10,927 | 370,857 | 87,688 | 91 |
| 2 | Chicago, Ill. | 3,369,357 | −181,047 | 6,977,611 | 756,698 | 3 |
| 29 | Cincinnati, Ohio | 451,455 | −51,095 | 1,385,103 | 313,479 | 22 |
| 10 | Cleveland, Ohio | 750,619 | −125,431 | 2,063,729 | 267,134 | 14 |
| 59 | Dayton, Ohio | 242,917 | −19,415 | 852,531 | 157,908 | 40 |
| 64 | Des Moines, Iowa | 201,404 | −7,578 | 313,562 | 47,247 | 111 |
| 5 | Detroit, Mich. | 1,513,601 | −156,543 | 4,435,051 | 672,691 | 5 |
| 110 | Erie, Pa. | 129,231 | −9,209 | 263,654 | 12,972 | 130 |
| 99 | Evansville, Ind. | 138,764 | −2,779 | 284,959 | 85,646 | 119 |
| 67 | Flint, Mich. | 193,317 | −3,623 | 508,664 | 135,351 | 73 |
| 75 | Gary and | 175,415 | −2,905 | 633,367 | 59,819 | 58 |
| 141 | Hammond, Ind. | 107,885 | −3,813 | | | |
| 85 | Hartford, Conn. | 158,017 | −4,161 | 816,737 | 291,530 | 42 |

| | City | | | | | |
|---|---|---|---|---|---|---|
| 39 | Louisville, Ky. | 361,704 | −28,935 | 867,330 | 142,191 | 39 |
| 12 | Milwaukee, Wis. | 717,372 | −23,952 | 1,403,884 | 209,594 | 21 |
| 32 | Minneapolis and | 434,400 | −48,472 | 1,965,391 | 483,366 | 17 |
| 46 | St. Paul, Minn. | 309,714 | −3,697 | | | |
| 68 | Mobile, Ala. | 190,026 | −4,830 | 376,690 | 62,389 | 89 |
| 106 | Montgomery, Ala. | 133,386 | −1,007 | 225,911 | 56,701 | 149 |
| 36 | Newark, N.J. | 381,930 | −23,290 | 2,057,468 | 368,048 | 15 |
| 149 | New Bedford, Mass. | 101,777 | −700 | 152,642 | 9,466 | 184 |
| 102 | New Haven, Conn. | 137,707 | −14,341 | 744,948 | 433,267 | 49 |
| 19 | New Orleans, La. | 593,471 | −34,054 | 1,046,470 | 177,990 | 33 |
| 1 | New York, N.Y. | 7,895,563 | −113,579 | 11,571,899 | 877,266 | 1 |
| 4 | Philadelphia, Pa. | 2,002,512 | −52,516 | 4,824,110 | 481,213 | 4 |
| 131 | Portsmouth, Va. | 110,963 | −3,810 | 732,600 | 154,093 | 50 |
| | (Part of Norfolk, Va., Statistical Area, listed in Chapter VIII) | | | | | |
| 49 | Rochester, N.Y. | 296,233 | −22,378 | 961,516 | 375,129 | 37 |
| 18 | St. Louis, Mo. | 622,236 | −127,790 | 2,410,492 | 350,389 | 10 |
| 74 | Salt Lake City, Utah | 175,885 | −13,569 | 705,458 | 322,423 | 52 |
| 13 | San Francisco and | 715,674 | −25,642 | 3,108,782 | 325,423 | 7 |
| 38 | Oakland, Cal. | 361,561 | −5,987 | | | |
| 122 | Savannah, Ga. | 118,349 | −30,896 | 207,987 | 19,688 | 156 |
| 22 | Seattle, Wash. | 530,831 | −26,256 | 1,424,605 | 317,392 | 19 |
| 114 | South Bend, Ind. | 125,580 | −6,865 | 280,031 | 41,417 | 122 |
| 79 | Spokane, Wash. | 170,516 | −11,092 | 287,487 | 9,154 | 117 |
| 84 | Springfield, Mass. | 163,905 | −10,558 | 583,031 | 104,439 | 66 |
| 66 | Syracuse, New York | 197,297 | −18,741 | 636,596 | 72,815 | 57 |
| 144 | Trenton, N.J. | 104,786 | −9,381 | 304,116 | 37,724 | 112 |
| 9 | Washington, D.C. | 756,510 | −7,446 | 2,909,355 | 907,458 | 8 |
| 73 | Worcester, Mass. | 176,572 | −10,015 | 637,037 | 313,731 | 56 |
| 96 | Youngstown, Ohio | 140,909 | −25,780 | 537,124 | 28,118 | 72 |

SIX CITIES ABOVE 100,000 THAT LOST
BOTH CITY AND AREA POPULATION

| Rank | | CITY POPULATION | | AREA POPULATION | | |
|---|---|---|---|---|---|---|
| | | 1970 Census | Decrease | 1970 Census | Decrease | Rank |
| 111 | Amarillo, Texas | 127,010 | —10,959 | 144,396 | —5,097 | 191 |
| 151 | Duluth, Minn. | 100,578 | —6,306 | 265,350 | —11,246 | 128 |
| 54 | Jersey City, N.J. | 260,350 | —15,751 | 607,839 | —2,895 | 63 |
| 24 | Pittsburgh, Pa. | 520,117 | —84,215 | 2,401,362 | —4,073 | 11 |
| 71 | Providence, R.I. | 179,116 | —28,382 | 769,789 | —46,359 | 46 |
| 146 | Scranton, Pa. | 103,564 | —7,879 | 234,107 | —424 | 146 |

FOUR CITIES ABOVE 100,000 THAT LOST POPULATION AND HAD NO CENSUS
BUREAU METROPOLITAN STATISTICAL AREAS OUTSIDE THEIR BOUNDARIES

| Rank | | 1970 Census | Decrease |
|---|---|---|---|
| 152 | Cambridge, Mass. | 100,361 | —7,355 |
| 147 | Camden, N.J. | 102,551 | —14,608 |
| 145 | Dearborn, Mich. | 104,199 | —7,808 |
| 128 | Pasadena, Cal. | 112,951 | —3,456 |

personal inspection showed encouraging signs that metropolitan-area growth is accompanied by renewed interest in the central city area.

The more an area grows, the more in demand the central-city land becomes for all uses, including commercial, industrial and governmental, plus residential. Area population constitutes a truer measure of growth than city figures. Some cities, like Phoenix and Jacksonville, increase population more through annexation than from growth within the city limits. For others, like Boston and San Francisco, annexations are prohibited by natural geographic boundaries or by bitter opposition from adjoining communities.

With intensified demand, conveniently located city land becomes too valuable for economical residence use except for multistoried apartment houses. Thus, single-family residences will continue to decrease within city limits, but well-maintained older apartments plus competitive new high-rise apartments will always be in demand. These dwelling units will experience an over-all increase in order to meet the country-wide trend toward moving back to the city.

### Why So Many Cliff Dwellers?

Most newly married couples prefer to start housekeeping in close-in city apartments. Besides them and the confirmed cliff dwellers who have stayed in the city all along, retired couples, widows and widowers constitute a rapidly growing segment of the population. After raising their families the average pensioners become tired of caring for their houses and yards and paying rising taxes and costly labor. Their first choice becomes a carefree apartment close to city attractions and conveniences.

A growing number of country dwellers want to move nearer the heart of the city to avoid congested and costly commuting. They also want to avoid rising suburban taxes that pay for new local governing bureaucracies and the voracious dollar devourers of spreading communities—$chools, $ewers, and $treets.

Department of Commerce figures measure these trends dramatically. They show that the percentage of apartment construction has boomed almost five and a half times in twenty years, from 7.3 per cent of total dwelling units in 1954 to 40.1 per cent in 1974.

This national average was pulled down by rural home building, naturally, and was considerably exceeded in larger cities. Apartments constituted about 60 per cent of privately owned dwelling units constructed in 1973 in Philadelphia, 78 per cent in New York, 80 per cent in Houston and San Francisco, 82 per cent in Chicago, 83 per cent in Los Angeles, and 92 per cent in Washington, D.C.

Every major city offers tremendous opportunities to meet this growing demand for apartments. Requirements can be filled partially by new construction, but by far the greatest answer in any given year will be the rehabilitation and modernization of existing apartments.

### Is Apartment Living a Worldwide Trend?

What is happening in Sweden demonstrates a worldwide trend toward apartment living. Sweden's National Housing Board estimates that about 75 per cent of all postwar housing construction has been in urban apartments. As elsewhere, the Swedish government considers apartments the fastest and most economic method of relieving housing shortages.

### How Can I Best Understand Technical Terms?

Ann Willis of San Francisco remarks, "My husband, Mosby, and I have found your book absorbing, and most of it is easy reading. But some of the high financing slows us down. What is the best way to understand technical terms?"

Robert Sanders of Kansas City writes with similar purpose, "Now, I'm a fellow with a college education, supposedly above average intelligence, and have been making a good living at broadcasting for over twelve years. I'm convinced that you are right in your contention that real estate is the best place to accumulate wealth. Your book is fascinating, but I'll be darned if I can keep from becoming bogged down in the technical terms involved in a real-estate transaction. With this in mind I am suggesting that you look into the possibility of setting up a 'William Nickerson Course for Prospective Real Estate Investors.' I would be your first enrollee in Kansas City, and I'm sure many others would welcome the opportunity."

In answer to the tremendous demand, my Lowry-Nickerson Real Estate Investors Seminars are spreading all over the United States, under the direction of Al Lowry. Many neophyte readers find they can understand technical points better by not trying to grasp them fully at first reading. They finish my book rapidly, as if they were reading a novel, to get the general picture. A surprising number have written of staying up all night to discover how my million-dollar formula works out with Joseph Enterprise, hero of my first book, and other examples. After this cover-to-cover reading they then reread carefully to absorb the factors which apply to their particular stage of investment.

### Is There Any Chance for Success in Overbuilt Areas?

A Los Angeles-area utility worker cites a 30 per cent vacancy factor in his recently bought Anaheim apartments, near Disneyland. "They are two years old, and were bought before I discovered your book," he writes. "Now that I know better, should I sell out at a sacrifice? Or is there any chance of following your formula for success in such an overbuilt area?"

I have considered questions concerning dwindling city populations and have found increases in the populations of nearly all areas. Here we are on the other side of the fence, where even the city populations have increased. In fast-growing areas, like Los Angeles and San Diego, many builders have become overoptimistic to the extent of supplying new apartments faster than they are needed. Questions along this line, usually pertaining to suburban districts, have come from other areas where rapid new construction has moved ahead of demand. Sometimes slightly and sometimes considerably overbuilt in specific districts, these new construction projects have about 20 per cent vacancies.

Many rental owners are doing well, however, in the general areas where there are overbuilt districts, and even in the overbuilt neighborhoods. Close-in apartments that are kept up and rented at competitive levels still stay comparatively full. Population influx will eventually catch up with most of the new construction. In the meantime, owners can usually increase their net income by taking a look at what the other fellow is doing and seeking ways of improvement, either of the property itself or in operations.

Recently I appraised a number of apartment houses in the Anaheim district, when I lectured to the Orange County Apartment House Association. Their magazine publisher, Ed Mee, discussed local conditions, and I made individual inspections over a wide area. Block after block of new buildings, mostly with one- and two-bedroom apartments, have been erected. They appear quite similar for the most part except for some contrasts in exterior paint. In the same neighborhoods some owners had quite a few vacancies and others had full or nearly full houses. What were the differences in their operations?

Most of the apartments in the buildings with vacancies were unfurnished and catered to adults only. Many had no air conditioning to counteract the sultry, smoggy atmosphere. Some of the successful owners had departed from the going custom merely by installing air conditioning or by providing furniture. Other owners, with two-bedroom apartments, catered to families with children, in most cases leaving their units unfurnished. Playground equipment, and in some cases baby-sitting arrangements for working mothers, helped to draw family tenants. Renting to families with children as a house practice, so that all apartments in the same building have children, can work out well in unfurnished apartments. Most of these owners required damages deposits as a way of encouraging care and discouraging breakage. The deposits were as high as a month's rent on brand-new apartments and as low as a quarter of a month's rent on older apartments.

Competently managed and economically purchased apartment houses, new and old, can pay off so handsomely that new builders may be tempted to follow personal inclinations and stray from economical construction. If they do not follow competitive construction practices, their resulting costs may require higher rent schedules than the going market, thus inviting high vacancies. My first book repeatedly warns of pitfalls to avoid, especially in unproven new construction. *Time* magazine referred to my book as an encyclopedia of investment knowledge and said that half of the information was in telling what not to do. But anyone who carefully reviews the yardsticks set forth should be able to avoid mistakes and achieve success.

## Can a Simple Person Like Myself Achieve Success?

Mrs. Frances Michael of La Mirada, California, writes a diverting letter which reveals chiefly a desire for reassurance that success is possible not only for the lucky stranger in distant, greener pastures, but also for the average reader:

"There is nothing hypocritical about me, and although I don't smoke a certain brand of cigarettes, I'm a woman who thinks for myself. Today is a typical lovely Sunday afternoon, and I'm relaxing with the Los Angeles *Sunday Times* in my charming, modest abode. There's nothing extraordinary about this scene, as I'm sure it's being repeated in millions of homes throughout the country.

"However, today is different from all other days because you opened an avenue of doubt in my simple little mind as to what perfect contentment should be! Why did you, a perfect stranger, have to come into my life?

"The full page in the *Times* about your financial success fascinates me. I read the page from top to bottom, oblivious of the fact that my delicious dinner was burning to a crisp. Honestly, I didn't really care, because I would make it up to my family as soon as I made a million. It read so easily, I just knew I would amass a fortune in short time.

"I started to survey my modest holdings and became discontented. I was tempted to follow your suggestions immediately, and then I made some mental reservations about my emotional and mental capabilities as compared with the rest of the human race.

"I could have put you out of mind at this point, and just remain a has-been the rest of my life, but the temptation to satisfy my curiosity got the better of me. I have to have your answer to my questions that would otherwise plague me forever. Without your answer I'll end up being a powerless female without even a spark left of my radiating personality!

"These questions aren't meant to be facetious. It is important to me that you answer me in all sincerity. If an average person can win a fortune, what distinguishes those who actually do from those who don't? Could a simple person, like myself, actually succeed in making a million if I strive toward making a fortune in real estate?"

### Can an Average "C" Student Achieve Success?

Questions similar to Mrs. Michael's have come from widely scattered sources. A student at my University of Toledo lecture remarked, "You state that anyone with average ability, average savings and average luck can make a million in real estate if he really wants to. I am an average C student and would like to believe I can succeed. I wonder if I can with average ability? It's obvious not everyone who wants to can do it. There must be some special qualifications needed. What are they?"

The same question was phrased almost identically by a Stanford University economics professor who participated with me in a KQED Educational TV seminar in San Francisco.

By the "average" ability needed for investment success I mean average mental ability. On the other hand, above-average intelligence is needed even to achieve C grades in a recognized university; you have to exceed an average I.Q. just to stay in school.

Some special qualifications certainly are needed, however. But they are qualifications that I believe almost anyone with average intelligence can acquire by trying hard enough, if he does not already possess them. Five helpful attributes are:

*Ambition:* Many dream of greater success, but really care little about changing their modes of existence. For investment success you need a fairly strong ambition to be financially independent.

*Imagination:* Anyone who says "It can't be done" limits himself by his own shortsightedness. But those who have the imagination to visualize the potentialities inherent in sustained realty investment stand a very good chance of achieving the goal they earnestly aspire to.

*Courage:* Those who wait for success to drop into their laps will seldom embrace it. You need the courage to mount the high ladder, sometimes to climb out on a limb, in order to reach for the fruits of success.

*Determination:* Many get off to a small start, like buying a home or duplex, but they may fail to pursue the course of property investment which they have modestly begun. Maximum success demands the determination to keep at it.

*Judgment:* Fortune is surer for those who have the judgment to stick to my proven investment methods, where the odds are 400 to one in their favor. Some get so enthused about real-estate potentials that they digress on speculative tangents where the odds are against them.

James Tyson of Savannah, Georgia, had no previous experience when he read my book. He then mushroomed $1,000 into $30,000 in six months, buying eighteen apartments in three different buildings.

Two San Francisco-area professional men also had no previous real-estate experience when they read my book. One is now successfully launched on an eighteen-apartment investment with a $2,000 down payment. The other has mushroomed a $70,000 investment to over a quarter-million net in fourteen months.

Clyde Foster of Evanston, Illinois, has built his real-estate investments to produce an annual income of $40,000. He writes, "One project pays me more annually than my original investment."

## When Is the Best Time to Start?

This question is asked at almost every Real Estate Seminar, often accompanied by dire statements regarding the local, regional, national or international situation. Timid procrastinators are prone to seek any weak excuse for postponement.

The answer is always, "Now."

# 2

# How to Turn
# a Goose Egg
# into a Nest Egg

# IV

## *Who Married Money, You or Your Wife?*

A teacher earning $9,500 a year writes from Philadelphia, "My family tries to live as economically as possible, but living costs and obligations eat up every small raise in pay, and we can't save a dime. Our bank balance the day before payday usually winds up a goose egg."

### How Can I Save a Nest Egg to Get Started?

Of the thousands of people who have written to me, only a few have asked this question, but, oddly, it comes up frequently at personal appearances, lectures, autograph parties and radio, television and press interviews.

Sometimes the questioner is facetious. When I was interviewed by Bill Gordon and Dorothy Fuldheim on the WEWS-TV *One O'Clock Show* in Cleveland, Bill Gordon asked, "How can I start making a million when I've got only ten dollars to my name?"

Dorothy Fuldheim whispered that he was probably worth closer to a million. But a question like Gordon's demands an answer in kind, so I retorted, "Buy my book. It will give you the incentive to save more."

Most questioners, however, are as serious as the Philadelphia teacher, for the inability to save is a basic and widespread problem.

If you are one of the seven out of ten who have saved a nest egg, you have already overcome the toughest obstacle and, if you are interested in investing in real estate, you have won at least half the battle toward making a million. More determination is needed to save a nest egg than will be needed thereafter to make a fortune in income property investment.

Chances are your present savings may approach the American family average of $13,900, and you are ready to start investing. Or you may be near the $8,000 level of the Denis Gilmers of Palo Alto, California, when they started investing. Gilmer writes, "I'm a forty-two-year-old grocery clerk with a wife and three children. We saved $8,000 by eating a lot of hamburgers. Then, in three years of investing, our assets climbed over the $100,000 mark. We owe less than $45,000, which gives us a net worth of better than $55,000."

But let's assume that you are one of the numerous company who haven't yet established a definite aim in life, and that your net assets are closer to the $300 typical for ages eighteen to twenty-four. You want to get the most out of life, but you have been drifting, perhaps, because you didn't know how to get started. You realize that the achievement of other ambitions may depend on financial freedom, so you are eager to make financial independence your definite goal.

Many are like nineteen-year-old Alan Heywood and his wife, Gerri, of Seattle, Washington. He has written that they have started to save, but that they are finding it difficult to keep on. This section, then, is intended for people who want to save more, in addition to those who have been unable to save at all. I will try to answer their over-all question, "How can I save a nest egg to start investment?"

## How Can I Get an Incentive?

The chief incentive is the potential goal ahead; try to visualize how a carrot dangled in front of a balky mule inspires it to move. After you start investing, you have something tangible, like apartment houses, to spur you on.

Althea Bliss of Orlando, Florida, writes that lack of incentive kept Bliss and his wife from saving. Once they realized the potentials of real-estate investment they decided to save a $2,500 nest egg in two years, half the average time mentioned in my first book. They're off to a good start, with leeway for slacking off. Mrs. Bliss states, "In three months' time we have saved $365 by cutting and scrimping. We keep constant check on the ads in order to have a better idea of values before we start shopping." Many single persons prosper, of course, but success is much easier when you have a mate to plan and work with, like the Blisses and my wife and me.

## Which One Married Money?

Why is it that some new business friends are like the San Francisco banker who remarked, "I suppose you married money. Is that what got you off to a good start?"

Curiously enough, my wife's new friends are often like Women's Club member Erika Polson of Alamo, who asked the same question.

To set the record straight on how Lucille and I got our start, we were both stone broke when we married, with high hopes, at sunrise on July 11, 1931. We were working our way through Fresno State College in the depths of the depression. Instead of waiting for graduation, we figured we might as well work our way together. Lucille, who had been working for room and board, became a housewife, while I sold Realsilk hosiery on commission to support us.

I was still selling Realsilk when we left Fresno State in the spring of '33. Although we had not married for money, we shared a willingness to plan and save together to achieve financial independence for our mellower years. We determined to save a nest egg for future investment, but we couldn't afford to set aside a dime out of my uncertain Realsilk earnings. My commissions averaged about $12 a week. Salesmen who earn substantial sums often find it difficult to save a worthwhile nest egg. It is more of a problem to hold to a savings budget when income is subject to marked fluctuation, where high pay may be followed by periods when it is difficult to pay the rent. That is one reason why so many real-estate salesmen are unable to take advantage of bargains dropped into their laps.

## Does It Help to Set a High Goal?

One experienced realtor in Southern California cited his experience following my lecture to his association in Santa Barbara. He had sold millions of dollars' worth of property as a broker, but, because he couldn't save a nest egg, he had never invested. It seemed that debts always piled up beyond his income. After reading my book he decided to try to become a millionaire in ten years. In one year, starting from scratch, his savings and realty investments gave him a net worth of $14,000. This put him well past my four-year mark of $11,575 on a twenty-year pyramid, starting with $2,500.

I guess Lucille and I didn't have a high enough incentive to save on my commission income. Although we wanted to save a nest egg, we had no idea how we would use the money for investment. I quit selling hosiery and got a steady job with the Bell Telephone Company in Oakland, California. I said, "I'll take any job but selling. I'm sick and tired of pushing doorbells selling Realsilk."

So, naturally, they hired me as a salesman, selling telephones to people who didn't have them. The company started me at the lowest wage allowed under the provisions of the National Recovery Act. Jim Raycraft, the employment officer who hired me, said, "Your pay will be fifteen dollars a week. Of course the first week, while you're learning, it will be only twelve."

That turned into a lucky break. Lucille and I figured out a budget that would allow us to continue living on $12, which had been my average weekly Realsilk commission. When the $15 pay checks started we made it a regular practice to save the extra $3 every week. Besides the $3 weekly, we skimped a little here and there so that we could put a minimum of $15 a month in the savings bank. We lived on what was left over.

One who followed the same budget was Al Athearn, who started the same day with me, and is still a good friend and fishing buddy. Now retired, he lives with his wife, Lola, in Santa Cruz, California, where he served as telephone company manager for twenty-one years.

## Can I Save by Economical Living?

An auto salesman we'll call Bill Spencer said, "I make two hundred and fifty dollars a week. It would take a wizard to show me how to bank a penny. My wife and I live as economically as possible so's we can save what's left over, but there's never any money left. In fact, we have to keep jumping to stay ahead of the bill collectors. Why can't we save, when we try so hard to economize?"

One fundamental of saving is to adhere to a rigid savings budget, setting aside a definite amount, even if it's small to start with, and live on what's left. Many people with good intentions wind up like the auto salesman; at year's end they find they have arrived nowhere, like aimless squirrels in a revolving cage. Many say they will live as economically as possible and save what's left over, but they rarely have any money left.

More than one third of those who reach sixty-five find themselves poverty-stricken. How many could at least live in comfort if they had followed a savings and investment plan from their early years? It takes only a few adjustments now to make you independent of the sacrifices often expected in later years.

As Dickens' Mr. Micawber says in *David Copperfield,* "Annual income twenty pounds, annual expenditure nineteen nineteen six, result happiness. Annual income twenty pounds, annual expenditure twenty pounds ought and six, result misery." Dickens wrote not only from observation but from experience based on the unhappy sojourn of his father, John, in the Marshalsea Prison for being unable to pay his debts.

## How Could You Budget a $15 Pay Check?

Many of our friends were unable to save even though their salaries at the time seemed munificent to my wife and me. Several asked, "How were you and Lucille able to save your nest egg to get started?"

My wife and I have analyzed the factors which enabled us to save, and we have studied the successes and failures of others. The details of how we and others saved may help those who have difficulty take a closer look at their budgets and find ways to start putting away the nest egg which can be used to build to a fortune.

Our son, Bob, and daughter, Nancy, are among those who have remarked, "Everything must have been awfully cheap." It's true that costs were low to go with our small income in 1933. But it can readily be seen that there was a lot less leeway then than there is with the sample budget in Chapter VI, which shows current expenses on today's average income.

### OUR FIRST MONTHLY BUDGET
*For Earnings of $65 ($15 a Week)*

| | |
|---|---:|
| Savings | $15.00 |
| Furnished apartment | 15.00 |
| Food and entertainment | 20.00 |
| Utilities | 5.00 |
| Clothing, including upkeep | 5.00 |
| Miscellaneous (Contributions, carfare, paper, shows, etc.) | 5.00 |
| | $65.00 |

We answered ads till we found a furnished apartment for $15 a month. The generous sunshine-filled windows exposed faded wallpaper, blackened varnish, dingy ceilings and smudge-stained kitchen and bath. The landlady, Mrs. Ceil Smith, a middle-aged widow, apologized for the run-down condition. She said the low rent she charged to get tenants didn't pay her enough to fix her places up. We said we'd try to clean it up ourselves.

We kept well within our food budget by weekly shopping at the Housewives' Market in the lower end of town, toward the estuary. The best bargains were on Saturdays, in fully ripe fruit and vegetables that wouldn't keep much longer. A nickel usually bought three heads of lettuce, two pounds of tomatoes or half a dozen grapefruit. Such flavorful and nutritious fruit and vegetables were cheap the year round in California.

We bought meat twice a week. On Wednesdays we often bought two pounds of stew meat for fifteen cents. This formed the base of a savory stew, good for three substantial meals when combined with four bunches of carrots and turnips along with potatoes and onions. On weekends, instead of spending a dollar for a tender roast, we bought a cheap but nutritious shank or chuck roast for thirty cents and steamed it tender in our pressure cooker. We bought margarine for one-third the price of butter, canned milk for half as much as fresh milk, and bacon trimmings for half the cost of packaged bacon.

Buying with conservative taste at the end of each season, we found that our clothing allowance of $5 a month was sufficient to keep us presentable. Having practiced on her sister and brothers for several years, my wife was able to cut my hair almost as expertly as a professional barber. She also shingled and feathered her own hair and gave herself permanent waves. Our first month of home barbering paid for our initial investment in a good pair of barber scissors and clippers. After that we eliminated the cost of haircutting from our budget.

## How Much Insurance Did You Carry?

This question was asked by my insurance broker, Kenneth Bone, with whom I have since placed several million dollars in apartment-house fire-and-extended-coverage insurance.

The Bell System Employee Benefit Plan provided sickness pay and free life insurance up to a maximum of one year's salary. That was all the insurance we had. Although Ken Bone was shocked at this information, we believed that our own funds would soon grow large enough to provide us with adequate additional insurance against the eventualities of accident or death. We expected to pay for medical care out of accumulated savings, if necessary, but we were fortunate in never being ill.

It should be mentioned that we considered Lucille's B.A. degree and teaching-credentials certificate, earned at Fresno State, as a better protection for her than any amount of life insurance we could have paid for. She could have secured a teaching job if I were unemployed or out of the picture. But, with the spread-the-work rules of those depression days, she was told by several school boards that she could never be hired as long as her husband was working.

## How Can You Have Fun Today If You Save for Tomorrow?

My wife and I believe in finding some enjoyment in each day, even as we plan for the future. When we saved on $65 a month our frugality filled our lives with more joy rather than less, enriching us with the satisfaction that we were able to plan together to build for the future.

There was usually something left over from our food allowance to finance an occasional party or bridge get-together. A lot of conviviality came out of a forty-nine-cent gallon of California port or sherry spigoted from a wooden barrel into your own jug. Although our savings kept growing, we always did as much entertaining as our friends who spent every cent they earned. Besides giving and attending parties, we enjoyed swimming and tennis. We often hiked a mile to a public beach where we could swim and acquire a suntan without cost. We borrowed books from the public library. We enjoyed most of the movies rated highest by the critics, even though we waited until they were playing the third- or fourth-run theaters.

In two years we found that our $15 a month in savings, with average interest of 2½ per cent, had grown to $402. Although my basic wage remained at the N.R.A. minimum all this time, I earned additional sums in sales commissions and bonuses. We felt that our rigid savings budget need not be added to at this point until my base salary increased, and we put the additional income into family betterment. In 1934, for example, we bought a 1928 Model A Ford for $165. My first paid vacation came in September, one year after starting the job. We took our first car on a flying 2,000-mile one-week vacation trip from San Francisco to Vancouver, British Columbia. We drove up the scenic Pacific Coast Highway and returned along the slopes of the Cascades by way of Crater Lake. We slept under the stars every night on a strip of canvas (fortunately, it did not rain), for we didn't own an umbrella tent until a few years later. Although we bought a gasoline stove later on, all our cooking on this trip was done over coals from a wood fire in an open pit.

After two years with the telephone company, in 1935, my boss, Gordon Wheeler, called me in for a meeting with his superior, Emil Maloney, who said my incentive commissions and bonuses were getting too high. One big week, which included bonuses for a month, I received a paycheck for $101.92. This exceeded Maloney's weekly pay and resulted in the whole incentive plan's being questioned by the company. A lowest-echelon employee like myself could not be allowed to receive as much as a third-level supervisor, even though I was the only salesman to approach this sum. The solution was to give me a promotion and a fixed salary. My pay arrangement would have to be changed from a $15 weekly base plus bonuses to a flat $27 a week.

With this dependable income, Lucille and I were able to save $50 monthly for the next twelve months. In the meantime interest rates at the savings bank dropped to 2 per cent. Nevertheless, my total savings and accumulated interest after three years with the telephone company grew to $1,060.

### Did You Belong to a Union and Pay Dues?

While I was autographing books at Horne's Department Store in Pittsburgh, Pennsylvania, a member of the Teamsters' Union asked, "Did you belong to a union and pay dues while you were saving your nest egg?"

Yes. I not only belonged but took an active part in union affairs until I became a sales supervisor. For two years I served as president of my local.

## Where Did You Learn to Fix Up Apartments?

This question was asked by Oakland banker-author Kendric Morrish.

During the last year of accumulating our $1,000 nest egg we finally fixed up our small apartment. Our landlady, Mrs. Smith, said she loved the dark varnish that covered the woodwork running halfway up the living-room walls, but eventually gave us permission to remove the varnish and paint with light, cheerful colors instead.

She said, "I have my doubts that it will look much better when you get through. I don't charge much, but you can't cover up the fact that these are little, dingy apartments. Your amateur work won't help things any. I wouldn't give permission if you weren't getting expert advice from your cousin. You understand, it's your own expense. I'm not putting out a penny. Go ahead and stop pestering me."

After painting the woodwork, we covered the upper portion of the walls with attractive wallpaper. Then we put in new dime-store curtains and drapes and a new electrical fixture. The materials cost about $12. There were no labor costs. Lucille and I enjoyed the time we spent working together.

When she saw the final results our landlady said, "I would never have believed it. Why, this is just beautiful. The light paint makes these little rooms look bigger, too. I'll fix up all my other apartments the same way. Maybe it will help me get the place filled with more tenants who pay their rent, and get rid of my vacancies and deadbeats."

My wife's cousin, Robert Mosby, had advised us on the varnish removal, painting and papering. Mrs. Smith hired him to paint and paper and make minor modernizations in her other seven apartments at a cost of about $50 apiece.

Then Mrs. Smith said, "Of course, these nice places are worth lots more now. I'll give you kids credit for your work, but I'll have to raise all the rents—including yours."

She raised the rent of the other tenants $5 a month. When two couples moved out she readily rented the vacancies at the higher rent. Last of all, our apartment was raised $3 a month. "Your apartment will go up five dollars like the rest if you move," Mrs. Smith said.

### What Decided You to Buy Your First Property?

Oakland banker Fred Miles said, "I suppose you studied economics and the real-estate market for a long time before you bought your first property. What was it that decided you?"

We didn't study real-estate investment at all. What really decided us was the series of circumstances just related. We figured that Mrs. Smith earned a $60 annual income increase for each $50 in renovation expense, giving her a yearly return of 120 per cent. We told ourselves, "If fixing up run-down housing improves values to this extent, we ought to do it for our own benefit."

Lucille answered ads in the Oakland *Tribune* and shopped for houses during the week. She looked for homes that were intrinsically better than we could afford, but that had been allowed to deteriorate to the point where they fell within our price range. I looked over her selections on weekends. We finally chose a run-down house that was basically sound, and paid $650 as a down payment. We soon spent an additional $300 for renovation materials. We painted inside and out and put in some new plumbing and electrical fixtures and landscaping.

It took us two years to finish our improvements, doing most of the work ourselves. Our renovation and modernization naturally increased the value. We traded our increased equity for a basically sound but run-down pair of flats which we could fix up.

Here was an example of "casting your bread upon the waters." What we had learned by fixing up Mrs. Smith's apartment pointed the way to a foolproof formula of buying deteriorated properties and increasing their value by judicious improvement. We had no spectacular goals in mind when we bought our first income property. Our most imaginative dreams never touched on the idea that we might someday be millionaires. In fact, I remember telling a fellow employee, Ed Harding, "We're shooting for a side income of a hundred dollars a month by the time I'm sixty-five and retire from the telephone company with a modest pension."

Primarily on a hit-or-miss basis Lucille and I traded into larger properties. Within seventeen years of our start with $1,000, we had pyramided to over a million.

In the next two chapters we will explore ways to help you save with an average income and average costs today. Then, in the rest of the book, we'll proceed with questions and answers concerned with how to get the most out of your savings through buying, selling and trading properties, and financing and improving them.

### Would You Change Anything If You Could Start All Over?

This question is frequently asked in letters and seminars. After an Oakland, California, Lowry-Nickerson Seminar a concerned State of California counselor, Margaret Noah, asked, "Would you have stayed as long with the telephone company if you knew what you know now?"

With my present knowledge I would have quit the phone company much sooner and devoted more time to real estate while I was younger. During most of my seventeen years with the phone company I stumbled along with spare-time realty investments, and with no guidance to follow like my books and seminars. I never dreamed of the tremendous pyramiding potential until a financial statement showed that my net estate had mushroomed to over a half million.

# V

## How Can We Start Saving?

A New York suburban correspondent sent a detailed and impressive two-page history of his education and employment. He wrote, "This is my first fan letter to anybody and I'm forty-three. The ideas proposed in your inspiring book have hit me at a time in my life when you were already 'half a millionaire.' "

### How Can I Keep from Losing Everything That Counts?

"In my search for financial security," he continued, "I've been a sales manager, general manager, contracts manager, vice president and general manager, staff engineer, and various other things. When it's all studied and assembled into a résumé prepared by an expert, it sounds just wonderful, but, truthfully, twenty years have been spent only to find myself right now about to lose everything that counts, for lack of money. How can I keep from losing my wonderful family, my lovely wife and three daughters, prestige, reputation, etc.?

"People have always said I'm a top salesman because I establish confidence. Maybe so, but something is lacking. And that's why I'm impressed with the stimulating ideas you advocate, and that's why, even at forty-three, I want to follow the guidance of a man who has done it himself.

"I'm enclosing a factual résumé, and after you read it, if you will, may I have the benefit of your criticism? I shall be grateful for any additional guidance you might give me."

My answer was as follows:

You no doubt have drawn my book's conclusion that financial independence can be achieved only through investment. Your present problem appears to be not so much financial independence as financial stability, which you indicate is not now in the picture. The reasons can probably best be answered by self-analysis, just as you are the only one who can take corrective measures involving yourself. Not knowing details, I can only make assumptions. Perhaps you might find the answer by honestly asking yourself, "What is the true reason for so many changes of employment?"

Anyone who really applies himself consistently can achieve the goals set forth in my book. Many who start will not stick to it and will settle for a lower step on the pyramid. This same lack of consistent effort also applies to many in industry, particularly in sales, where peak achievements can be followed by valleys of lethargy.

Such dips can best be overcome by building up faith in your ability to progress consistently, once you set your mind to it, in order to achieve a worthwhile goal. Your morale can be sustained by the respect and love of a wonderful family, and nurtured by the knowledge that there is a power greater than yourself upon which you can draw for renewed strength.

It appears that your "top salesmanship" makes it too easy for you to get a new job when the spirit moves you to leave an old one. Even though it means compromises in your choice of employment, you might try harder to settle down longer in one place with an assured income. This kind of stability will help you prove your capability of setting aside the nest egg necessary for future investment that can lead you to financial independence.

## Should I Lend My Fiancé the Money to Start?

In a long-distance call from San Jose, California, a telephone operator told me, "My fiancé works in a Standard Oil station and does odd mechanical repairs in his spare time. He wants me to lend him my three-thousand-dollar savings to open his own garage. He wants to delay our marriage till after his new business gets going. He lives with his folks now and I rent an apartment. I say wait until we get married before we use my money for investment. After reading your book I want to buy a duplex. We would live in one unit and rent the other. I don't want to lose my fiancé or my money. Which is the best course, his or mine?"

Yours. If you lend the money for business or investment, love is apt to fly with it out the window. Lending before marriage would probably be a mistake. It might work out in exceptional circumstances, but the odds are four to one your fiancé would go broke. If that happens, isn't it likely that your engagement would be broken, too? Save your money for investment and you are more apt to save your engagement.

San Jose offers good duplex buys. As you suggest, you might do well to buy a duplex to give you both income and a place to live when you are married. Afterward you might offer to pool your remaining resources while your husband gains more experience along with further savings with which to start in business.

A Christmas card and an accompanying message mailed almost a year later informed me that the couple were happily married and living in their nice two-bedroom duplex unit. They were expecting a baby around Easter, when they would need the extra bedroom. The husband had been promoted to manager of the gas station. He had decided to keep working for a steady income and was going to concentrate his spare-time efforts on buying and fixing up apartments.

### Have You Ever Belonged to a Credit Union?

This question was asked by Dr. Leslie Carlin of Michigan State Teachers' College at Mt. Pleasant. He pointed out with pride that his state has the world's biggest teachers' credit union, in Detroit.

Yes, as a telephone company employee I served on various boards and committees for many years. This was entirely a labor of love. However, like many a contribution of time and effort, it was another case of casting bread upon the waters. The experience gave me my first insight into some of the fundamentals of financing, my first realization that money wholesalers, such as banks, are as anxious to make loans as borrowers. My first writing in the field of finance was done as editor of our local monthly *Credit Union News,* which was widely quoted by similar publications all over the United States.

In every issue I included at least one background article on the history and philosophy of financing, one article on how to save money, and one on how to borrow it. The borrowing information covered the value of shopping for loans and how to compare costs, emphasizing that most installment loans are on a discount basis, where you pay almost double the usual interest. For example, a 6 per cent discount equals almost 12 per cent of regular interest. The discount is charged on the full amount for the entire period of the loan, even though installment payments keep reducing the amount owed.

Most people join the credit union initially in order to borrow from the savings of older employees. After their loans are paid off, often through payroll deduction, they are encouraged to set the same monthly payment aside and start saving. The authorization to the company to make a payroll deduction of a fixed amount continues without change.

Credit unions have experienced a phenomenal growth nationally, with two million new members joining in 1974. Total membership at the end of 1974 came to 29 million with assets in all 23,000 credit unions of $32 billion.

## Is There an Easy Way to Get a Nest Egg?

Among those who haven't yet started saving, some waste a great deal of time trying to find easy ways to get a nest egg.

An interesting letterhead comes from Cebu City, Philippine Islands. It reads "Star Radionics General Merchandise, Aquilino Ca-

linawan, Chief Technician, Prop. & Mgr." Mr. Calinawan writes a
five-page letter in fine script about his business operations, family,
religion and personal affairs. He states, "I am a deacon in our
church, twenty-nine years old—no children yet from a three years'
marriage . . . I was always business minded since my childhood
. . . I took a radio course and became a licensed ship's operator.
After two years of savings I quit employment and opened my own
establishment, which is prospering. I am making a good living from
the business, but no more savings.

"I just finished reading your book, and now I see many opportunities here in Cebu City to follow your example which I had
not realized before. I am so greatly inspired with your revealing
thoughts . . .

"Now to come to why the main reason is I am writing you. How
about extending a helping hand to me? How about if I ask a personal loan of $1,000 from your personal savings? Grant me this
loan and I can pay you $35 a month including interest, so it will be
paid in three years.

"You can trust me because I consider it a cardinal sin if I do not
fulfill my promise. According to Ecclesiastes in the Bible it says,
'Better act now if thou canst fulfill.' I do not hesitate to ask you this
personal loan because I know I can pay, and I am definitely capable
of paying. One miraculous thing for the good of your soul is that
you will forever be carved in my memory. May I hear from you
soon?"

These closing words "May I hear from you soon?" are identical
with those in a letter I received from a truck driver's wife in Tampa,
Florida. She asks for a loan of $2,500. The phrase appears again in
a letter from a lumber dealer's widow in Southern California. She
asks for a "substantial check" and says nothing about any repayment plans. The Tampa housewife assures me that she can repay
at the rate of $50 a month from her husband's good wages. They
already own the home they live in and have paid $500 down on a
second house which they are renting and fixing up. But they want
to move faster by personal borrowing.

The Tampa and Cebu City correspondents are to be congratulated on already making a good start. All they have to do is turn their goals of repaying personal loans at $35 and $50 per month into regular savings in those amounts. Then they should try to keep saving until their investment programs are well launched.

Or, if business or credit is well established, perhaps the down payment for further investment can be borrowed from a regular lending source, such as a local bank. With such borrowing you must prove your ability to repay from your income, expenses and experience.

The Ecclesiastes quotation is double-edged, for I can use it to point out that it is better to act at once to start saving than to use the same amounts for loan repayment. Among the Bible's many marvels are rejoinders for almost any quotation you can find. A logical answer for Mr. Calinawan is, "The Lord helps him who helps himself."

There are few easy short cuts to success. You have to follow the necessary steps and keep at it. What is apt to happen if any steps (such as getting a nest egg or down-payment funds for further investment) are accomplished too easily? You will probably be handicapped rather than helped, because then it will be harder to discipline yourself to the extent necessary for sustained progress.

## When Should I Start Saving?

A realtor at a Miami, Florida, autographing party said, "I make about twenty-five thousand a year, but I don't see how I can save anything right now. I bought a yacht this spring and am still making high payments on my Cadillac. I'm really going to start saving, though, beginning the first of next year."

When I was autographing books in Rochester, New York, an Eastman Kodak executive said, "I'm going to start saving a nest egg right after the next promotion."

A neighbor who works at the Livermore Radiation Laboratory as a nuclear physicist said, "My son gets his B.A. from Stanford next year. I'm going to start a heavy savings budget right after that."

After telling of the sizable sums they plan to budget for savings with their expected changes in circumstances, each of these procrastinators asked, "Don't you think that's a good idea?"

What is most likely to happen when the stated impediments to saving drop away? When the Cadillac payments are completed? When the Eastman promotion brings a higher salary? When the physicist's son graduates and the school expenses cease?

For those who are prone to procrastinate, some new obstacle nearly always arises after the present one is overcome. The Miami realtor may buy a new Cadillac. The Eastman executive or his wife will probably decide that a promotion requires greater expenses, such as buying a bigger house. And the scientist's son will probably emulate his father and continue with graduate studies. The prospects of accumulating a nest egg are slim unless the would-be saver starts in right now. The road to poverty is paved with the good intentions of those who want to save but never get around to it.

Another neighbor asked me, "How can Mom and I save, when we can't spare a dime? Have a tough time getting by as it is. We have to scrimp before every payday because the money runs out."

"Sounds rough," I replied. "But suppose you had a salary cut of ten dollars a week? Would you have to make a major change in your present way of living?"

"Of course. And would the missus scream!"

"Would you have to move to a smaller house or sell your car? Or do you think you could get by with a few minor adjustments, like maybe dining out a little less often?"

"Let's see. If we went out for dinner one less time a month? That always kills at least twenty bucks, and usually more, after you pay for drinks, transportation and baby sitting."

"What else can you think of that you and your wife could each cut?"

"I should cut down on my heavy lunches. Getting too paunchy

anyway. Mom could cut out some of her weekly trips to the beauty parlor. Talks about doing her own hair every time she sees those do-it-yourself jobs on TV. If you put it together we could save at least five dollars apiece each week, besides the twenty a month on dinners."

"That would come to sixty-five dollars a month. You could shade it to fifty dollars and still save twenty-five hundred in four years, with your interest. You get paid twice a month, don't you? If you really want to save, why don't you have your boss put twenty-five dollars in your savings account every payday? You can spend all that's left in your check the same as if you had a salary cut, and by the end of the first year you'd have six hundred saved."

"O.K., I'll do it. I always turn my check over to Mom, so I'll give it to her with the twenty-five dollars already deducted. I'll tell the boss to start deducting with my next pay."

Though my friend loved procrastination, in this case he actually kept his resolution. He had expected his wife to complain, but she was as eager as he to share in a planned spending and savings program.

## How Should I Adjust for a Larger or Smaller Income?

A larger income should permit larger savings, holding to a 10 per cent minimum, to speed the growth of a nest egg in order to make investments. If both husband and wife work they might try living on the husband's earnings and saving the wife's entire income. This is a laudable plan followed by many couples to obtain the down payment on a home.

A smaller income normally forces smaller savings, but the saver should attempt to maintain the same percentage. Small incomes leave less leeway for savings, but even the smallest can allow for setting something aside, if only one or two dollars a week. Forming the habit now makes it easier to add to savings as income increases. Your investment future depends on starting to save now.

If it is impossible to save under present living circumstances, the only alternative for the earnest is to change the mode of living. If food expenses are too high, try more effective menu planning and shopping and less eating out. If housing payments are excessive, consider moving to less expensive quarters, a smaller house or apartment or one having fewer conveniences. In each expense category, out-of-line savings can be effected if there is sufficient desire —as may be seen in the next chapter, where we will cover expense items in more detail.

Before leaving the subject of savings, let's look at an outstanding example set by Los Angeles banker Gordon Baskin and his wife, Delia. In 1946, when he was twenty-two and she twenty, they arrived in California from Albany, New York, with $3.60 in their pockets. Both worked at odd jobs while Baskin studied at U.C.L.A. He started as a dishwasher and his wife as a waitress.

Within two years the couple saved $1,200. They too regard this as by far the hardest step on the road to a fortune. The Baskins started building up their fortune by heavy borrowing to buy old, run-down apartments, which they modernized. They did the papering and painting themselves in the beginning, just as my wife and I had done, and found they were able to double the rents with nominal outlays of money.

The Baskins kept pyramiding from their initial investment. In sixteen years, their apartment investments pyramided to several millions in property and the major (11 per cent) holding of stock in the Continental Bank, which they founded. Included in their holdings is the $1.5-million Sans-Sunset Motor Hotel on Sunset Boulevard, near Beverly Hills. Delia Baskin manages the motel, and her husband is president of the $24-million bank.

## Isn't It Useless to Save When the Value of Money Keeps Falling?

This question has been repeated often, along with continuing inflation and the resulting drop in the purchasing power of money.

It always pays to save a nest egg so you can start investing. Pessimists like my economics professor during the depression always find reasons not to save or invest now. Those who fail to save today will regret tomorrow. But if you do save today you are bound to look back with fulfilled satisfaction when your enhanced tomorrow comes.

# VI

## Can You Suggest a Budget for a Family of Four?

Sometimes this request arises: "Will you tell us exactly how to budget our earnings so that we can save a nest egg?"

My wife and I tried budgeting with fixed percentages that did not allow for deviations. But such exact spending plans seldom work out in practice. You can set aside a fixed minimum amount for savings, and then you can establish recommended percentages for spending. Every family is better off if it recognizes from the start that there will probably be some fluctuation in spending.

Some families wish to spend more proportionately on recreation, on interests such as stereo or the theater, or on some hobby. Others may want to step up their contributions by tithing to their churches. Larger families naturally spend more on food. Budgets can only be cited as guides into which each family fits its own interests.

### Can You Suggest an Average Budget?

As a guide, I have worked out after careful study a reasonable savings budget for a family of four. It is a composite of several budgets recommended by the following authorities: the U.S. Department of Agriculture, the U.S. Bureau of Labor Statistics, the American Bankers' Association, the Institute of Life Insurance, the Household Finance Corporation, and the National Association of

Secondary School Principals, Consumer Education Study. This budget is based on the 1974 median income of $12,000 estimated by the Department of Commerce for families in the United States.

Expenses like real-estate taxes, vacations and insurance should be budgeted on an annual basis and divided by twelve to calculate the monthly allotment. Out of the total income of $12,000, taxes may approximate about $1,920. This comes to 16 per cent for Social Security, unemployment and disability, and income taxes, leaving a net after-tax income of $10,080. We thus have $840 monthly from which to make our savings and spending allotments.

SAMPLE BUDGET BASED ON $840 NET MONTHLY
SPENDABLE INCOME

|  | Percentage of $840 | Amount |
|---|---|---|
| Savings account | 6% | $ 50.40 |
| Food | 27% | 226.80 |
| Housing, including utilities | 25% | 210.00 |
| Clothing | 9% | 75.60 |
| Transportation, including auto | 9% | 75.60 |
| Medical care, including health insurance | 7% | 58.80 |
| Life insurance | 4% | 33.60 |
| Personal care (barber, beauty, cosmetics) | 3% | 25.20 |
| Personal allowances, miscellaneous (tobacco, stationery, school) | 3% | 25.20 |
| Contributions, gifts | 3% | 25.20 |
| Reading, recreation | 4% | 33.60 |
| TOTALS | 100% | $840.00 |

## SAVINGS

Many sample budgets place savings last. Since fluctuations are bound to occur among expenditures, I advise putting savings first, for then you can meet your savings goal by managing on what is left. Our budget is based on what a determined saver can reasonably expect to allot from an average income.

The $50.40 monthly savings allotment should be deposited in a savings account where it can accumulate compound interest until the total is sufficient for your first long-term investment. Even starting from scratch, the savings account would exceed $2,500 in four years, enough to start a million-dollar pyramid on a sound basis. With adequate financing you could buy your first productive income property in the $10,000 range.

## How Can I Save a Definite Amount Every Payday?

The saver should resolve to set aside a definite amount each month, no matter how small, and live on the balance. A windfall may be added to savings, but it is usually fatal to set up a budget on the premise that there will be windfalls. On the other hand, an inviolable rule should be that savings are to be used solely for investment, except in the case of extreme emergencies. Turn away from temptations to dip into savings "just this once." Failure to hold faithfully to the savings portion of the budget will detour and possibly wreck your progress on the road to a fortune.

To help save a definite amount every payday, take advantage of every possible habit-forming aid. Because savings contribute to the welfare of their employees, most companies gladly handle savings by payroll deduction, so you don't see the money at all. The company deposits a designated amount in your savings bank, your credit union or another institution of your choice. Then you can automatically regulate your expenses to live on the balance of your pay. Payroll deduction multiplies your chances to build the highest potential savings, since it is a form of contract. The Federal Reserve System estimates that 70 per cent of the "dis-savers," who spend more than they earn, manage to save something by "contractual savings," mostly in the form of life insurance.

If payroll deduction is not feasible, consider the next-best substitute to help form the saving habit: Cash your check, if possible, at your savings institution. Have the cashier deposit in your savings account a fixed amount or percentage each payday.

## How Can We Control Our Spending?

The wife of a Cincinnati, Ohio, brewery worker writes, "My husband and I spend every cent we earn. His take-home pay averages about $800 a month. How can we control our spending so we can save the nest egg to start on the road to wealth?"

If all earnings are spent, obviously there can be no savings. The ability to save the suggested 6 per cent depends upon the ability to spend the remaining 94 per cent wisely. Now that we have covered savings, we can review the allocation of the remaining income to keep it within the over-all spending budget of 94 per cent.

# FOOD

By judicious menu planning and shopping, the householder can enjoy well-balanced, savory meals and still stay within a 27 per cent food budget. Make a weekly shopping list that includes lower-priced foods with high nutritional value, and avoid expensive spur-of-the-moment buying.

## How Can I Eat Hearty on a Slimmer Budget?

Food normally sells for less in high-volume cash markets. The best time to buy is when weekly specials are offered at lower prices. Buy fruits and vegetables in season, when abundance creates more reasonable prices. Potatoes are about the cheapest nutritious food and can be prepared in scores of ways. Margarine can be bought for one-half the cost of butter, and tasty bacon trimmings and bacon ends for one-third the price of regular bacon. Canned and powdered milk average one-half the cost of fresh milk; their distinct flavors do not detract when used in cooking. Both may have the same nutritional value as fresh milk. Powdered milk may be ordered dried whole or as dried skim milk with the butterfat removed.

Meat can be the most expensive part of the food budget, but cost can be considerably reduced while taste and quantity stay high. Try tenderizing with cheap red wine less expensive cuts like bottom-round steaks and chuck roasts instead of buying higher priced T-bone steaks and rib roasts. Try mutton instead of lamb. Try inexpensive frozen fish, like perch, smelt, turbot, whitefish and whiting. Try more pork and poultry, and organs like heart and liver. Through advantageous cooking methods and utensils, generous portions of steaks and other meats can be enjoyed at low cost.

Experiment also with more varieties of delicious stews and chowders, like bouillabaisse, jambalaya and cacciatores.

Helpful investments for thrifty cooks include:

A time-saving, tenderizing pressure cooker
A good hand chopper for steak tenderizing
A fairly heavy chopping board
Seasoning, spices, bulk wine and other chemical tenderizers
A refrigerator with sufficient freezer space to handle bulk buying
   and leftovers

Many cookbooks contain valuable recipes for tasty low-cost meals. Pressure cookers usually include excellent booklets. A free list of helpful booklets, prepared by the Agricultural Research Service, may be obtained from the Office of Information, U.S. Department of Agriculture, Washington, D.C. 20425. One of their informative publications, *Family Fare, a Guide to Good Nutrition,* is obtainable for 95 cents from the Superintendent of Documents, Washington, D.C. 20402.

### How Can I Drink Hearty Without Squandering?

The food allowance should cover all meals, as well as snacks at coffee breaks and teatime, all beverages, and home entertainment such as cocktail parties and beer- or bridge-fests. Each item should be scrutinized as a possibility for economizing. People who work, for example, can save on lunches by eating in the company cafeteria, if one is available, or by carrying lunch from home. Many a busy executive budgets his time and money by carrying lunch and business reading to his office in a brief case.

The earnest budgeter should take a quizzical look at expense items that often develop into serious budget drains, such as habitual dining and drinking in night clubs and bars. Food and beverages served at home cost a great deal less.

In the office where I formerly worked, one of the employees observed a five-o'clock ritual of stopping with various cohorts at a nearby bar. His daily quota was four highballs. Of course, if a crony dropped in when he was about to leave for home, additional rounds were automatically ordered. His after-work drinking averaged 100 drinks a month and cost him $100 for what amounted to 100 ounces of bourbon. An equal amount, about three quarts of package whiskey, could have been bought for around $18. These spending habits thwarted my co-worker from saving a nickel out of his $1,000 monthly salary.

Liquors and wines can be bought at considerable savings by the gallon or half-gallon and by the case. For example, very palatable California wines are sold for substantially less by the gallon, about half the cost of bottled wine, with a 10 per cent further discount by the case of four gallons.

### How Can I Keep Bulk Wine from Souring?

"After I pour a serving of wine from a gallon jug it starts deteriorating and finally turns sour," states a Pomona, California, housewife. "How can this be avoided?"

Once a gallon of wine is opened, decanter it into convenient-sized bottles, such as quarts, fifths or pints. If well sealed with a tight cap or cork, it should keep like originally bottled wine. Wine left in a partially emptied jug tends to sour from absorbing the excessive air that has displaced the poured wine.

## HOUSING

The housing allotment covers payments for shelter, furniture, household cleansers, and such utilities as fuel, electricity, water and telephone service. For the majority of city people the most economical way to spend the housing dollar is to rent a furnished apartment with utilities included. Then additional household expenses can be confined to a telephone and sundry supplies like soap, kitchen cleansers, dishcloths, scouring pads and light bulbs.

Homeowners should include under housing their loan payments, taxes, fire insurance, amortized improvements and maintenance costs, covering repairs, painting and decorating.

### How Can I Live in a Nice Home for Less?

A few people on budgets allot as little as 15 per cent for housing. Most agree on 27 per cent as the absolute maximum. If housing expenses exceed 25 per cent, consider seeking less expensive living quarters. Suitable accommodations can usually be found through the classified-advertising section of leading newspapers. Those listings that fail to show rent rates are apt to prove too high-priced. Be alert for such phrases as "needs painting," which should lead to the best buys in housing. More space, better location and better all-round livability for less money are often found by the renter who deliberately seeks what almost everyone else shuns—a dwelling unit with smudged paint and faded wallpaper.

Though ads seldom mention such shortcomings, an otherwise desirable dwelling crying for paint can often be found. Tremendous savings may be made by doing things yourself. If this appeals to you, you might suggest that you will provide the labor for redecoration if the owner will furnish the material. Most owners will welcome such an opportunity, since material may cost as low as one-fifth of a contractor's charge for labor. An owner may refuse to buy material if the rent is considerably lower than the market. It might still be advantageous to secure a desirable accommodation at low cost by painting one room at a time, perhaps monthly, in order not to strain the budget.

If an apartment cannot be found by answering ads, the next step is to place an ad under "Apartments Wanted." A surprising response may be received from a minimum ten-word or two-line ad such as "Responsible couple desires $95 furnished apt. Will decorate. 237-4314."

If you have children they should be mentioned so that only owners who accept children will respond. In advertising, more is accomplished in the long run by revealing rather than concealing pertinent factors.

### How Can I Learn at a Rental Owner's Expense?

Frank and Mary Self of Sacramento, California, said they had little decorating experience and no apartment-managing experience. They have two children, Linda and Terry. Mrs. Self would like to stay home and still be a breadwinner. They asked, "Would it be possible for us to learn maintenance and management at our landlord's expense?"

If you don't mind doing things yourself and are anxious to save, don't be hindered by lack of experience. Painting and papering are fairly simple to learn. Paint and wallpaper dealers gladly give all the advice needed, and so will co-operative owners. Varnish remover, paint and wallpaper can transform a dreary apartment into an attractive and cheerful home and give a great deal of satisfaction in the bargain. As my wife and I found out, such experience proves most helpful when you are ready to start improving your own property. So welcome the possibility of training at the owner's expense instead of waiting to get it entirely on your own.

The greatest experience can be gained—and savings increased— by working as an apartment house manager or assistant. This is an especially advantageous position for a couple with children, because the wife can be a breadwinner and still remain at home. Look under "Help Wanted" in the classified ads. If a job does not materialize, advertise under "Positions Wanted." A sample ad: "Trustworthy couple will manage apartments. Inexperienced, ambitious, willing. 932-4132."

### How Can You Advance from Debt to Duplex Owners?

On Frank's instructor's salary, the Selfs were in debt when Mary took an apartment manager's job. Together they handled painting and decorating and other maintenance, besides routine manager duties like showing and leasing apartments and collecting rents. In two years, the resulting savings and experience enabled them to make good buys on two new duplexes, each of which consisted of two bedrooms per unit. Mary Self writes, "We were able to buy the places for no money down by arranging to do the painting, installing linoleum-tile floors, and most of the inside and outside finish work ourselves."

A Denver, Colorado, couple are going in the same direction as the Selfs. Robert Larson writes that he and his wife, Mickey Ann, were going into debt instead of saving after three years of marriage. "After reading your book we decided that it would be good experience for us to manage an apartment house while saving money toward our own future income property. By managing an apartment house, rent free, spending much less and saving money instead of wasting it, we are now able to save $400 a month. In the spring we plan to purchase our first duplex or other income property."

## CLOTHING

The clothing allotment includes initial cost plus upkeep expenses like cleaning, pressing, laundry and mending. Some people look strikingly well dressed at little cost, while others look awkwardly dressed at great expense.

### How Can I Dress Well for Less?

Choose durable material in conservative taste. Avoid the flashy, which may soon prove shoddy and out of style. Wear colors that complement your skin, eyes, and hair. In the comprehensive book on clothing, *Singer Sewing Book,* published by the Singer Sewing Machine Company, Mary Brooks Picken includes color charts for light blondes, medium blondes, medium brunettes, dark brunettes, grayheads and redheads. Within each general type there is a good range of desirable colors, and, of course, your own preferences prevail among the suitable colors. To help maintain a well-dressed appearance at reasonable cost, both husband and wife should choose all their suits and other major clothing items within their individual color ranges. Then the same accessories, like shirt, tie, hat and shoes, can match regardless of the outer clothing worn.

Plan your clothing purchases well in advance. Avoid spur-of-the-moment and height-of-the-season shopping. Real bargains can be bought at end-of-season sales. Rock-bottom clearance sales of winter clothing are usually held after Christmas, through January; summer clothing sales are generally in August. Better-looking, longer-lasting quality for less money can often be found in reputable department stores rather than in a hole in the wall or a so-called manufacturer's outlet. Some such establishments offer good buys, but many of their bargains turn into shoddy material sold for as much as the traffic will stand. On the other hand, discount houses that feature good buys are springing up all over the country. It pays to make a careful inspection of material and workmanship when comparing prices between stores in order to tell the difference between a good and a bad buy.

National retail organizations, like Sears, Montgomery Ward, Penney, Macy's and other large department stores feature true bargains. They sell good-quality material and workmanship at reduced costs. When legitimate department stores buy merchandise at below-normal cost as the result of bankruptcy or because of style changes, they usually add their normal markup and pass their bargains on to the consumer.

Obviously, it saves money if you can keep clothing maintenance and mending costs to a minimum. Business suits last longer and require less pressing if worn on alternate days and placed on hangers when the wearer returns home from work. Inexpensive, comfortable sports clothes are universally acceptable for home and recreational wear. Do as much clothing maintenance as possible at your own home. A secondhand sewing machine can be bought inexpensively and is an invaluable aid in making and mending clothes. Many housewives press and spot-clean suits, thereby reducing the wear and cost of complete cleaning. Self-service coin-operated cleaning machines also reduce costs. If you do not own a washing machine, you can cut your laundry bills by doing the wash at a neighborhood launderette.

## TRANSPORTATION

Probably more budgets break down on auto, taxi, bus and carfare expenses than on any other item. All transportation costs, the monthly auto payments, gasoline, oil, tires, service, repairs, taxes, licenses and insurance should be accounted for. It is often difficult to keep these expenses in line except with a low-priced car.

### How Can I Ride Farther in a Lower-Priced Car?

To hold to the budget while getting started, stay away from high-priced cars. Drive standard models of proven popular makes. Low-priced cars not only sell for less initially, but save on operating, repair and insurance costs. Trade-in values are comparatively higher and are not subject to drastic slashes.

One of my acquaintances, a salaried corporation attorney, continually gripes about his low income and his inability to save because he is always in debt. He makes $17,500 a year, is married, but has no children. Almost half of his take-home salary is spent on payments and maintenance for a new Cadillac. His high car payments never cease, for each year he trades in the one he has for the latest model. After his last cream-and-maroon purchase I asked him if his wife was still complaining; her secondhand washing machine had broken down and she needed a new one, which he kept telling her they couldn't afford.

He protested, "My friends would all think I'd gone broke if I drove anything but a new Cad hardtop. Some people can put up with cheap cars. I can't afford to be seen in anything but a Cad."

"Don't you think you would enjoy life more in the long run if you drove a less expensive car now, so you could save and be in a better position to afford a Cad when you have an independent income?"

"For my position I think I'm being conservative now. You ought to see a friend of mine who's a sports-car fiend. He makes fifteen G's a year and just spent a whole year's salary—went into hock for the next three years—to buy an Allard with a special Cad motor."

He fools only himself who has a Ford income and says he buys a Cadillac for greater safety or performance. Present designs of popular cars eliminate much of the former marked differences between high- and low-priced cars in comfort, road performance and safety. High-priced cars of course possess many refinements. Like mink coats, their chief sales value is a visible sign of opulence, which can be better afforded after financial independence is attained.

## MEDICAL CARE

Medical and dental expenses include hospital and professional services, medicines, first-aid materials and health insurance. Ill-health can throw any budget topsy-turvy. Financial safeguards formerly were few, except for trying to stay healthy.

### How Can I Save on Doctor and Hospital Bills?

Now, fortunately, comprehensive hospital and medical insurance can be bought for the entire family at moderate continuing cost. Special rates and greater coverage are often available on a group basis, with company, union or other organization health insurance plans. Prepaid medical care can keep emergency costs low. Not only does it pay for sickness and accident expenses, but many coverages help keep you healthier by preventive care.

## LIFE INSURANCE

Four out of five U.S. families are protected by some form of life insurance, according to the Institute of Life Insurance. Insurance plans and costs vary considerably. Annuities pay the highest yield, but generally provide no protection to survivors except the return of the amount paid in. Term insurance provides the highest protection per premium dollar, but has no investment return.

### Should I Buy Life Insurance for Protection or Investment?

Protection is the chief purpose of life insurance, with investment secondary. Over-all investment returns cannot exceed the earnings of life insurance companies on their total investments. Their returns consistently average in the 6 per cent range after taxes, according to the Institute of Life Insurance.

Normally the best insurance buy is ordinary life, which combines protection with a nominal investment return and comprises 52 per cent of all life insurance in force. Business and professional men, whose chief asset is their personal production, may load heavily with life insurance because they fail to make higher-paying investments. But if you want to follow a consistent investment plan that leads to wealth, you should consider buying ordinary life insurance as a protective necessity to tide survivors over emergencies.

Insurance provides the maximum stand-by estate for your survivors in case you die young. But the preponderant odds today are that you will live to a ripe old age. The average American at age twenty-five, according to the Federal Office of Vital Statistics, can expect to live past seventy. Increasing age adds to your total life expectancy, so why not chart your main course to get the most out of your prospective years? It is wise to plan for probable eventualities, but isn't it tragic to toil and save chiefly for death when all the time you're really seeking an abundant life?

Mortgage insurance provides an additional safeguard, paying off loans in case of death of the breadwinner. This type of nominal-cost life insurance can be combined with home loans. It merits consideration for beginning investors with heavy mortgages. Insurance for investment pays only for the one out of five who is unable to save by any other method except by contracting for life insurance.

## PERSONAL CARE

Included here are barber costs, beauty care and cosmetics. Lotions, creams, powders, and so on *ad infinitum* can be bought for prices ranging from a few cents to astronomic sums. Studies by Consumer's Research show that you pay plenty for fancy containers and exotic names, and that cosmetics bought in discount stores serve as well and are often made of the same ingredients as those sold under far more expensive labels.

### Does Do-It-Yourself Beauty Care Really Pay?

With rising labor costs, sizable amounts can be saved by doing for yourself the work that is performed in barber and beauty shops. Inclinations and capabilities vary considerably on this score. Many wives take care of their own permanents, hair tinting and other beauty care. With the clever ones it's true, you can't tell the difference. Others go in for hair trimming now and then. Some go all out, as my wife and I did when we started saving, and buy a pair of clippers. Especially with a large family, it pays for itself in one month of haircutting.

## PERSONAL ALLOWANCES

Tobacco, in most cases, proves the costliest personal expense. Other items include education, stationery and postage. Education covers school expenses, lessons in music, dancing or art, special studies, lectures and generally any methods for gaining knowledge. This excludes reading costs, which are grouped later with recreation. Adding new knowledge makes up for the inevitable sloughing off of previous learning and need not necessarily be costly. Public night schools, for example, provide many desired courses.

### Can Investment Income Pay for College?

Many families plan ahead for the college education of their children by maintaining a special savings account or paying off an endowment policy. If early savings are channeled into rental property, by the time the children are ready for college any necessary expenses can normally be handled from income.

Travel is properly included under education in many budgets and is especially appropriate in fields like teaching. Domestic travel, where costs can be kept relatively low, should be budgeted under vacations. Some people have the good fortune that I had in being able to vagabond afar on my own, as described in *My Odyssey Around Three Worlds,* before settling down with a regular job and family. Others, like my son, Robert, with his Navy hitch, see the world when they serve in the armed forces. Otherwise, extensive overseas travel should probably be deferred until independence is gained.

## CONTRIBUTIONS, GIFTS

For differing spiritual requirements a church can almost always be found which will fortify inner resources and provide strength in times of disappointment or sorrow. Churches add to the moral soundness of a community. Many members tithe, others contribute between one and five per cent of their earnings.

### How Can I Contribute My Share?

The beginning budget keeper cannot afford overgenerosity in church and with other philanthropies, but should plan some minimum contribution, such as one or two per cent of his income, to carry at least part of his share. Higher gross incomes permit stepped-up contributions. In addition to a share of income, time should be contributed to help operate churches and philanthropic organizations, such as Boy and Girl Scouts and Community Chest. People starting out with slim budgets can help offset their low money contribution by offering a greater share of time.

The personal-gift budget is apt to be hit hardest at Christmas. Birthdays and other anniversaries need to be accounted for. Gifts to family and friends should be selected well in advance, with taste and care and a close eye on the pocketbook. Instead of smothering generous impulses, take time to review personal tastes and take care in making pleasing selections. In gift buying it isn't high expenditure that counts most, it's thoughtfulness.

## READING, RECREATION

As mentioned previously, my wife and I have always believed in enjoying each day while saving and planning for the future. There are many ways of having fun at low cost.

### How Can I Have Fun While Saving?

One of the most practical sources of home enjoyment for the entire family is, of course, an inexpensive table-model television set. Other recreation that adds to the family's health and enjoyment with minimum expense includes hiking, tennis, and swimming at public pools and beaches. Many neighborhood organizations, including enlightened schools and churches, sponsor social and folk dancing and other activities where a lot of fun can be shared with convivial companionship at little cost.

It is difficult to keep up with the world without a newspaper and one or two periodicals. Being surrounded with clothbound books in the home adds to convenience and pride of ownership. Having books readily available encourages family reading and improvement, a most worthwhile objective. But most books, except those on specialized technical subjects, can be obtained in inexpensive paperback editions or at the public or lending library. Libraries are important sources which should be heavily utilized while you are getting started.

## How Can I Enjoy a Good Vacation for Less Money?

Vacations have been left until the end of this chapter as an important part of living to look forward to. The most dedicated worker and saver should plan some time out on a weekly and annual basis for pure relaxation. Taking periodic time out renews inner resources and enables you to go further in the long run than if you kept your nose continually applied to the grindstone. Vacations provide the greatest renewal if they combine play and relaxation differing from the usual surroundings of home and work.

The most fun at the least cost can be enjoyed by going on camping trips to green hills, cool lakes, rushing streams or sandy ocean beaches. Near most of the populous centers of the United States are public camp areas maintained by the U.S. Park and Forest Services, and by state and municipal agencies, where you can vacation in the open for a small fee or without charge. According to the U.S. Forest Service, the 155 national forests and 19 national grasslands hold over 187 million acres of land, almost one acre for each person in the United States. In addition there are over 30 million acres in the 157 parks and monuments in the National Park System's 298 areas, and millions of acres in the hundreds of state, regional and municipal parks. Of the 759 million acres of forest in the United States, federal and state governments own 212½ million, about 28 per cent.

At least one national park or forest, and often several, can be reached from practically any locality in the nation within a few hours' or at most a day's driving time. Many states, like California, publish a list of forest and beach campsites. For an interesting booklet covering the locations, special features, recreation facilities and accommodations of all national forests, send 90 cents to the Superintendent of Documents, Washington, D.C. 20402, and ask for *National Forest Vacations,* prepared by the U.S. Department of

Agriculture, Forest Service. Also ask for the free *Price List 35,* in which the National Park Service lists 288 publications covering national parks, monuments and historic sites. Included is *Camping in the National Park System,* price 55 cents.

## Can Camping Equipment Be Inexpensive?

The camper can start with no special equipment, although he may eventually splurge on an umbrella tent, a gasoline stove, sleeping bags, air mattresses, compact cooking utensils and other gear. Lack of a tent would be the chief shortcoming. In many areas summer showers may result in uncomfortable car-cooped hours when no shelter is available. It is often advisable to rent equipment at nominal cost until experience tells what fits family needs and inclinations best.

Many campers manage with a square of canvas or a small used tent bought from an army surplus store. Sheets can be tied between trees for privacy. Blankets from home can be spread over a one-dollar plastic sheet or a soft bed of leaves. For cooking, a coffee pot, a heavy skillet and two or three pans from the home kitchen will suffice. Often deadfall wood can be burned for fuel in stoves, boulder pits or fireplaces provided in many camping areas. Food usually costs less than at home. An outdoor-whetted appetite makes the mouth water over the simplest fare like beans, spaghetti, chowders and stews.

Some innovators wire a well-wrapped pot roast to the manifold of their car when they start a trip, add potatoes, carrots and onions after three hours or so of driving, and have a delicious dinner cooked in about four hours.

Campers can anticipate exhilarating recreational experiences, especially with children, whose eyes open in wonder at each new aspect of nature. The health-stimulating relaxation of a camping trip makes waking to each new day's fun a pleasure to be remembered. There is a likelihood of meeting many sincere fellow campers, some of whom may grow into lasting friends. Hiking, fishing, swimming, basking in the sun or relaxing and reading in the shade, along with refreshing sleep out of doors, return the vacationer homeward soothed and refreshed.

## What If I Spend More Than I Earn?

"Is my case hopeless?" writes telephone operator Elsie Middleton. "I want to save so I can invest, but I wind up each month a little more in debt. For the past year I spent about 5 per cent more than I earned, mostly on credit-card charges. What chance have I got to get ahead?"

Your chances are good if you conscientiously review all your expenses and make obvious corrections of overspending on budgeted items. Credit counselors agree that budgets can readily be adjusted to balance and include savings if not off more than 10 per cent.

Your modest 5 per cent deficiency can easily be corrected if you arrange for the telephone company to deposit your savings allotment in your local credit union, and you adjust your spending to live on the balance of your paycheck.

# 3

# Getting Started

# in

# Income Property

# VII

## How Can I Get Started
## in Real Estate?

Many of the serious questions I've been asked carry overtones of humor. A Hollywood housewife accuses me of almost wrecking her home, while a Miami couple thank me for saving their marriage. Both correspondents doubtless exaggerate somewhat, but each brings out interesting points.

### What to Do When the Husband Wants to Invest and the Wife Doesn't?

The Hollywood accusation:

"My husband has read your book through twice and filled it with underlining, but I've just started it. He's so anxious to follow your suggestions that he wants to borrow on our home and start right out investing. We're both getting along with a fine income now, and I'm perfectly happy to stay the way we are.

"I say don't borrow on our home. It will be harder to sell with a larger loan. Wait till we have saved the cash in the bank before we think of investments. My husband says since the home is in his name only, he is going ahead with the new loan, come what may. I say if he does I will divorce him. Do you know you are about to break up our marriage? Please give us your advice. We are both forty-three."

The husband writes separately, "I'm hot as a pistol to get started, and don't want to wait any more to get ahead. Sure, we have a good income, but we've saved less than $1,000, except for our home equity. I can borrow $4,500 net cash from a new loan on our home. It will cost us about $600 in various fees. I say it would be worthwhile in view of all we could make by following the advice in your book. Please give us the benefit of your experience and advise us what is the best thing to do. The way things are now, our marriage is really going on the rocks."

To begin with, husband and wife should come to an agreement before either makes too irrevocable a decision on investments. In California and many other states it is legally necessary for both husband and wife to agree before any loan or sale can be arranged on community property bought since they were married. Thus it is up to the eager spouse to convince the reluctant partner. Each should respect the other's wishes and strive for a harmonious compromise in order to preserve a marriage. Couples achieve much greater success by continuing to plan and do things together, as they did when they started on their honeymoon.

Many find that a home equity is the only substantial savings available. It could well be worth $600 to borrow a net of $4,500, which would make a fair-sized nest egg to use as a starting investment. When you're ready to sell later, it will help more than hinder to have as large a loan on the house as possible. Basically, although home loans are tied to the market value of the property, your "fine income" might help you get a larger loan than could a buyer with a lower income.

However, before arranging a new loan on the home, I would wait until a good income-property buy is found. A good deal may be consummated soon, or there might be considerable delay. A purchase offer can be made "subject to buyers obtaining loan to net $4,500 on their present home." Then the home loan can be arranged after this offer is accepted by the seller.

Other good alternatives are:

A possible trade of the home equity as the down payment on income property

A purchase offer with the proviso "subject to buyers selling their present home for [for example] $25,000."

Happily, the couple phoned a few weeks later to thank me for helping them find harmony. They had been enjoying themselves shopping for income property. They found a desirable fourplex that fitted my suggestions, and their offer to trade their home for it had been accepted. They were already making plans for improving their newly acquired property and expected to be ready in about six months for their next pyramiding step.

## What About Specializing in Single-Family Homes?

The Florida husband mentioned previously writes, "My wife and I are in our fifties, and have been drifting apart the last few years, mostly, I guess, from boredom. We used to plan things together and talk over my C.P.A. work a lot. I've built up a fair income and have done a little investing on the side, but my wife has completely lost interest in my work. To tell the truth, I've become bored stiff when she tells about her little social and club doings. We got to bickering a lot, and last year even talked of divorce.

"Then your book came along. I first read it through and felt I learned more from it than any other book. I then gave it to my wife to read. She has never taken any interest whatever in investments, but she became so enthusiastic about the possibilities you have so clearly shown, she wanted to go right out with me shopping for property.

"We have already bought and fixed up a run-down house, and in six months put through a sale that nets us $8,500. My wife and I talk over deals all the time now, both those we are working together on and also my own work. For the first time, she seems to understand what I am trying to do, and this has given me a new interest in her separate affairs.

"Our marriage has been transformed from the brink of divorce to the happiness in planning and doing things together that we knew in our honeymoon days. All this is due to your inspiration, and we want to thank you for saving our marriage.

"In view of our outstanding success on our first deal, should we continue to invest in single-family homes?"

You might make good profits by continuing to buy and improve single-family homes and duplexes. These might represent the only property-improvement opportunities in smaller communities, the same as fixing up run-down farms in farm areas. Outstanding large-city results have been achieved by a Boston investor, now a multimillionaire, who has specialized in improving single-family dwellings and has modernized, remodeled and rehabilitated over six hundred so far.

Moving from the Atlantic to the Pacific Coast, a Portland investor advises that he has made $40,000 in four years working spare time on improving run-down single-family dwellings.

There are hundreds of small towns across the country from which investors have written of successful real-estate ventures achieved by improving single-family homes and two-, three- or four-unit apartment buildings. In some cases they have merely fixed up run-down homes. In others they have converted larger homes to duplexes. Some of the communities I have heard about include Port Angeles, Washington; Hancock and Holly, New York; Santa Rosa, California; Mabel, Minnesota; Wausau, Wisconsin; and Bluffton, Indiana.

One example comes from Salem, Massachusetts, where a correspondent bought a fourplex for $15,000, paying $3,000 down. Nominal improvements were made, and within one month the net income went up at the rate of over $400 a year, increasing the sale value $4,000. Other rent-raising improvements are still under way.

### Can You Have Too Many Peanuts?

In cities where larger properties are available, the average investor can progress faster and easier by pyramiding into bigger apartment houses. A good example is the twenty-four-unit Cynthia Court mentioned in my first book. Larger properties, in this or the thirty- or forty-apartment range, are far easier to operate than several smaller ones. The income on larger apartment buildings is sufficient to hire a resident manager who can handle all the day-to-day operations. As compensation you can give a manager a free apartment plus cash spending money, an offer that usually creates a wide field of desirable applicants to choose from.

Smaller properties, such as a two-unit or a single-family rental house, are fine to start out with when you have a small nest egg. But it pays where possible to turn these into large properties as you go along. Many small properties may represent too many peanuts, as described in my first book. They require more personal supervision or higher management costs by comparison. You would usually spend more time looking after a couple of two-unit flats, showing vacancies, collecting rents, and so forth, than you would dealing with a manager who handles these things in a thirty-unit apartment building. Thus, the more larger properties you own, the less time you need to spend on operating details, and the more attention you can give to over-all supervision and planning.

## Would Starting in Real Estate Be Sensible for a Penniless Preacher?

Jerry Davis of Oklahoma City writes, "Everything in your book sounds very logical and sensible and I feel it will be of considerable help to me. I am a minister and have a very low income. This means, of course, that my wife and I are not able to save nearly so much as $50 a month. I plan to finish my college education in Oklahoma City, and will be earning only a part-time income.

"We have given a great deal of thought to starting a pyramid on the same order as yours. We have much apprehension, however, due to our lack of cash on hand. We are not in debt, but all that we have is enough only for tuition.

"We would like to buy a duplex, feeling we would have better living quarters than we could afford by paying rent. But we would have to obtain 100 per cent financing. I believe I could borrow the down payment plus a little more from a private individual who would take back a second mortgage. I know several people both in banking and in insurance companies who would finance the necessary first mortgage.

"There are questions peculiar to my situation that I would deeply appreciate your giving studious consideration and the benefit of your advice: First, would it be wise to try financing 100 per cent on my first venture? Second, if so, how much over the down payment should I borrow from the private individual to cover the improvements necessary for pyramiding? Third, would even trying to start in real estate be sensible for one in my comparatively penniless situation? Last, would Oklahoma City be a good place to start a pyramid? (I ask this because you said that Oklahoma is expected to lose population in the next 10 years.)"

Financing 100 per cent on your first venture can be sound if you have a backlog of employment income. It will be somewhat risky if there is no income except from the investment. The chief objection is that payments might be higher than what you might get from income. This could be offset by having secondary financing stretched out with low payments, say by paying only interest for a year or so until you have taken care of improvements and increased your income. You should have a clear idea of the improvements that need to be made and their approximate cost before you can decide how much to borrow for this purpose.

Starting in real estate, or in any investment program, would definitely not be sensible where you have no income and would have to borrow over 100 per cent. However, it might be possible if you and your wife have a strong enough determination. Normally it would be advisable to wait until you complete your training and are called by a church that will pay a fair income.

When you work out compensation arrangements as a minister, try to plan a situation where you will receive a rental allowance rather than the use of a church-owned parsonage. Many ministers, including two I know in nearby churches, are getting started in real estate by using their rental allowances to buy property. A rental allowance, designated as such by the church, is nontaxable as income whether it is used to pay rent or to purchase dwelling quarters.

Oklahoma, like other farm states, is expected to lose population from farm areas, not metropolitan areas. Oklahoma City is expanding rapidly and should be a good place for realty investment.

## What Is the Difference Between Co-operative and Condominium Apartments?

Zeanette Roberts of Orinda, California, is considering investment in a condominium. She asks how this "new idea" differs from a co-operative, and also what are the chances of profit from reselling her interest.

Condominium housing, blessed by F.H.A. financing, is rapidly spreading in different parts of the country, especially in California, Hawaii and Florida. However, it is far from new; it started in Rome at the time of Caesar. It has been popular in Europe and Latin America for many years.

With co-operative housing, you buy stock in the corporation that owns and manages the apartment house. The corporation pays operating expenses and charges you for your share. However, you can deduct your proportion of taxes and interest for income tax purposes. Even though you keep up your payments to the corporation, you may be subject to loss because of the default of other tenants.

In a condominium you purchase an apartment or cottage unit usually intact, including its proportion of the land. You are directly responsible for paying separate real-estate taxes and mortgage installments. Default by another owner affects only his condominium unit. You can deduct interest and realty taxes just as an individual homeowner does. Realty laws concerning condominiums are hazy in some states. Texas courts have ruled them illegal on the grounds that they are not a true form of real-estate ownership.

Co-operatives and condominiums with their varying applications offer an opportunity to own or share in ownership of a single apartment in a multi-unit project. You can decorate and improve your individual unit, but you have as little control over your close neighbors as you do when you own a single-family home. You stand a chance of selling at the price you paid, at a discount, or at a modest profit. I know of unit buyers in Hawaii who have sold at a good profit under the impact of skyrocketing realty prices in choice areas. But in most new investments of this type your chances for profit as an individual unit owner are no better than those of a buyer of a new single-family home.

However, the original builders or developers can do quite well. An example of success by a beginner is described by columnist Bill Fiset in the Oakland *Tribune:*

Jim Knuppe, 32, has just about sold out all the units in Oakland's first condominium apartment. . . . Knuppe's project is a success although he's new at the game. He's a railroad engineer by occupation and two years ago read William Nickerson's book, *How I Turned $1,000 into a Million in Real Estate—in My Spare Time.*

Knuppe started with $2,000, now owns two apartment buildings and is starting a third. He invested $91,000 in borrowed money in the condominium and is clearing $43,000 profit.

Although Jim Knuppe and his wife Bobbie had no previous experience when they read my book, they mushroomed $2,000 into a net worth of a quarter of a million in apartment equities in three years.

### Should I Start Out Only with a Small Buy?

Among those who wonder if they should follow my guidance to the letter are many people with larger-than-average nest eggs. They ask if their first buy to start a million-dollar pyramid should always be a single-family home or a duplex. Such questions have come from a fifty-year-old college professor who had $10,000 to start, an about-to-retire farmer of sixty-five with over $100,000, and the previously mentioned retired industrialist who had over a million dollars. All are eager for their initial real-estate investment.

Typical is a Chicago salesman, who writes, "I have cash assets of $13,000. Do you think it wise for me to follow my inclination to

shop around for a $40,000 apartment as a first venture, using all
your tips? Or would you think it more prudent to seek a $10,000 to
$12,000 house to get my first experience? I tend toward the larger
project because I believe that with your book as a foundation and
belonging to a rental association, etc., I have confidence that I can
do it. Most important—what do you think?"

As indicated in my first book, I favor starting as far up the ladder as your resources allow and you feel you can handle. The modest start of the Joseph Enterprises mentioned in the book is based
on their having only the average young couple's nest egg of $2,500.
If their funds had been sufficient, it would have been advisable to
make an initial investment in the B Boulevard or Cynthia Court
range.

## Will You Be My Partner?

In Chapter II, in my reply to the Southern university dean, I
mentioned that a number of readers have made sincere requests for
me to invest for them or go into partnership. Some tell of heart-
rending personal problems. Others are strictly businesslike. Some
offer fees, some ask that I share alike in investing funds, and some
offer to put up all the money if I will put up my management experience. It might be of interest to mention a few specific requests,
along with a composite answer.

Marian Christenson of Colorado offers me a "goodly commission" for acting as agent in the investment of $15,000.

A New York City spinster writes, "In the terrible depression of
1929–34 my father lost in Wall Street a nice nest egg my mother
struggled to save. The private school where I taught went bankrupt, so I started teaching in public schools. You must have read of
the trying situation in Harlem and the Bedford-Stuyvesant area
where Principal George Goldfarb threw himself from the roof
and another principal suffered a heart attack. These and many
other terrifying incidents have hastened retirement of many teachers, including myself. I am fifty-six years old, the sole support of my

aged mother and myself. My disability pension is $1,308 per annum, and I earn $3,000 per annum in a private school. Your wonderful book has inspired me to seek investment income, and has won my confidence in you. Would you, therefore, be willing to begin investing for me? I'll send you $1,000 as soon as I receive your gracious answer, and then I'll keep sending you $60 monthly."

Thomas Sweeney, a retired insurance company executive and a former state senator of West Virginia, offers "to match $25,000 cash with your know-how and tenacity of purpose."

Lucy Pierce of Wisconsin asks, "Please, Mr. Nickerson, would you be so good and kind to invest for me if I send you the money I have saved?"

Allen Wooldridge of South Orange, New Jersey, writes, "I am considering a $750,000 purchase of a fairly large apartment house that is in need of repair. I have experience in engineering, construction and renovating, and my objective in real estate is essentially the same as yours, to improve property in order to increase values. I would like to know, would you care to go in on this proposition on a fifty-fifty basis?"

An Australian publisher wants to send me $50,000 to invest, with an offer to share the profits.

A Toronto, Canada, corporation executive, C. H. Strub, asks me to go into partnership in Canadian realty investments.

A Singapore physician, a South African teacher, a Hong Kong businessman and a Hungarian refugee, among others whose letters are in my files, all want to send me money to invest.

Some of the requests are appealing, some tempting, some intriguing. As much as I would like to in some cases, I cannot possibly comply with all requests to invest for others and feel it fairest to give the same answer to all. Although I continue to develop my properties, I am not interested in extending investment, either on my own or on a partnership basis. I am glad to share my knowledge by answering questions that arise, both directly and in my books and seminars. I have seen many good opportunities in metropolitan areas throughout the United States, but am glad to leave them for the benefit of other investors. I know of a number of people, like the writers of the foregoing letters, who are doing well on their own in each city or area from which these requests have come. Their example should give courage to those who hesitate to start without experienced personal assistance.

## Could You Recommend a Real-Estate Corporation?

Anthony Polack of New York City writes, "I am disposing of my holdings in nonproductive vacant lots, vacant acreage, oil and gas leases and speculative stocks. As you say, I know now it doesn't make any kind of sense to throw good money after bad. I will invest in income-producing properties, just like you write about in your fine and concise book. I would like to know, are you starting an investment corporation? If so please let me know and I will send you my savings and money from sales. If not, could you recommend and explain the operation of a good and stable corporation in the same investment and pyramiding real-estate operation as you are?"

My wife and I prefer to operate on our own and are not contemplating an investment corporation. However, for those who would like to share risks and profits, rather than start on their own, there are many such corporations and syndicates in operation. Some are restricted as to ownership, being composed, for example, of a group of doctors or lawyers. In New York, as in Hawaii and many foreign countries, syndicates fairly open to the public offer a common form of investment. A number of investors with comparatively small nest eggs can thus band together in order to buy larger, more desirable properties.

A growing form of multi-owner operations is through investment trusts, where there must be a minimum of one hundred participants. Real-estate trusts must be somewhat passive in their activities, because they look chiefly for investment return. Syndicates can go more into real-estate management, pyramiding and speculation.

The chief determinant of success in a trust or a syndicate is the caliber of management. In many cities absentee managers have not proven out so well in the long run as experienced and alert local managers who are more familiar with tenants and local conditions.

For suggestions on where to locate sound syndicates, you might get in touch with your local real-estate board. Its representatives should be able to give you some good advice on competent operators or direct you to leading realtors who specialize in this field. Also, your local banker might be of help.

## What Do You Think of This Syndicate?

Arthur Rein writes from Nassau County, New York, "I know you warn people to approach new construction only after some experience, but here is a likely proposition I have had presented to me. I would certainly appreciate it if you would tell me what you think of this syndicate.

"A group well known to a broker friend of mine is going to build a thirty-five-unit apartment house here in Nassau County, one of the top growth counties in the country. This group is made up of the principals of a consulting-engineering firm in New York. They are consultants to several leading N.Y.C. banks and have an outstanding list of completed projects. They seem to know their business and will hire a general contractor.

"Land is costing $50,000 and building about $440,000. They have offered me a 5 per cent interest for $5,000. Naturally, I am going to consult an attorney on the risks involved, protection of my interest, etc. But I would like to have your opinion from a real-estate investor's standpoint as to what my risks are. They project a 20 to 25 per cent net return per year on our investment. This seems high on the surface, but other apartment projects in town are returning the same. Of course this includes the profit on total funds, including all the money borrowed."

The syndicate deal you mention looks very attractive. Such a syndication enables a smaller investor like yourself to participate in a large, desirable, well-located holding such as the one you describe. Check out as thoroughly as you can the dependability of projected building costs, income, and operating expenses. The ability and experience of management usually decide the success of this kind of project, and it appears that you are in good hands.

### Does a Two-Time Business Failure Have a Chance?

A Southern California correspondent writes, "I was adjudged bankrupt March 19, 1959. Was in the lumber business. This is the second time. Sure have learned a lot, but feel a little down now. I'm forty-eight years old, still ambitious, and just can't think of myself as a failure. I have three boys I want to send to college. I still have hopes. I want to start afresh and save enough for a start in real estate. Would you please answer these questions: What chances have I after two business failures? What would you advise?"

It is never too late to start. This applies also to making a fresh start, regardless of previous disappointing experiences. If you have failed twice in business, you can still fail in the same field a couple of more times before you strike the average. As I noted in my book, the ratio of failures to business starts is four to one. If your judgment and experience keep you from having any more failures, you can still consider yourself above average in your capabilities!

This emphasizes the difference between going into business and making real-estate investments, where the odds are four hundred to one in your favor that you will succeed. In view of your previous discouragement you might prefer trying another field. Or you might want to re-enter as an employee the field in which you have experience, in order to develop a nest egg for investment. Your specific choice on what to do depends, of course, on your talents and your present inclinations.

If I were to start from scratch today, I would begin as a real-estate salesman with an established realtor. Your experience in the lumber business would probably be especially valuable in sales involving new construction, such as subdivisions, and remodeling. The potential income is good if you are willing to apply yourself.

The real-estate education would help lay a foundation for making investments.

## What Is the Basic Difference Between Real-Estate Speculation and Investment?

A general contractor in Cleveland asked this question. He has recently started investing on his own. He states, "I have built for other owners many new homes and apartments, and have remodeled plenty more. Even though I've been in the building game for over thirty years, I never had an inkling of the possible profits as an owner until I bought your book from Anne Udin at Higbee's department store. I'm still contracting for others, but am making more from remodeling older apartments on my own, in my spare time. In fact, I didn't have anything saved up when I started investing a year and a half ago. Being a contractor, I was able to buy entirely with borrowed money, on the promise of extensive improvements. I've built up a net worth of over $20,000 already and feel like I've only scratched the surface.

"I hear so much talk about the dangers of speculation, I want to ask this question: What is the basic difference between real-estate speculation and investment?"

With pure speculation, such as buying vacant land, there is no income to offset continuing costs such as taxes and interest. Some say you can't miss if you buy land by the acre in sight of City Hall and hold it until it can be sold as city lots. This can be highly profitable if you happen to guess right and don't have to wait too long for turnover profits. But you are apt to guess wrong on both direction of expansion and timing. The city may build away from you, and delayed profits may be eaten away by continuing costs.

When you buy nonproductive lands for speculation you have to sit back and wait for the action of outside forces over which you have no control. And you do not build large investment pyramids by waiting a long time for a big profit on a single transaction. Such a practice makes you a slave to the slower process of arithmetical progression.

Continuing turnover and expansion, even with modest profits at each step, harness the phenomenal pyramiding power of geometric progression and can be kept on a sound investment basis. With investment, the property pays for itself as you go along. This might apply to rental homes or apartments, or to commercial, industrial or farm property. But you pay all expenses plus loan payments from the income, earning a return on your costs from the start.

An investment-minded owner improves his property, as you have, so that it will earn a higher income. Instead of waiting for outside forces, as the speculator must, you can make immediate changes that increase values. You are not only on a safer footing, with little chance of losing your property, but you are also much surer, in the long run, of making a fortune.

### Have You Ever Lost on a Real-Estate Deal?

This question arises from time to time, especially at seminars, as could be expected, when I always invite questions "with no holds barred." One who asked it somewhat hesitantly was travel bureau agent Renée Berg of San Jose, after a Lowry-Nickerson Seminar.

Sometimes I have made spectacular profits, sometimes moderate, but I have never lost money on a real-estate investment.

The only venture where I lost money was the White Sulphur Springs Resort, St. Helena, in the Napa Valley, California. Like hotels and motels, resorts are a purely business operation, much more prone to failure than real-estate investment.

At least this experience, described further in Chapter XII, added to my education, helping me to perceive clearly for the first time the basic contrast between business and real estate ownership. Business ventures inherently carry a heavy risk of failure, with odds against you. Property investment contains minimum risks, with odds for success overwhelmingly in your favor.

# VIII

## *Where Can I Find Good Buys?*

My mail and personal contacts have brought inquiries regarding various investment possibilities in every major city in the United States. My personal inspections and many case histories that people have sent me prove that all these cities offer opportunities. Still, it may be of interest to include a few typical queries I have received, as they pertain to different parts of the country and different neighborhoods.

### How About San Jose, Sacramento, San Francisco, Oakland, Los Angeles and San Diego?

Bryce Baker of Minidoka, Idaho, writes, "In two years in my 'spare time' I have increased my capital valuation from $4,000 to approximately $32,000 by developing a 160-acre farm from sagebrush to sugar-beet production. I have tentatively considered relocating in San Jose or Sacramento. Could you offer your opinion as to their possibilities for rental-real-estate investment? Also, how about San Francisco, Oakland, Los Angeles and San Diego?"

San Jose and Sacramento are both good cities for realty investment. So are all the others. I have lectured several times in each of the cities mentioned, know of many people who have succeeded there and have inspected many excellent opportunities in each. Some of my own properties are in Oakland and Sacramento. If I wanted to expand, I would not hesitate to buy in the other cities.

## What Do You Think of New York?

Gerhart Irving of Brooklyn writes, "Do you think that in Brooklyn and elsewhere in New York City, where rent controls and building requirements are so rigid, one can still apply your methods and achieve success?"

Yes. Rent controls present some obstacles which discourage many owners from keeping their buildings on a par with competing rentals, but this situation helps create better bargains for the alert operator. Perhaps you would benefit by rereading the chapter entitled "How to Operate under Government Regulations" in my first book. New York's constantly changing skyline is tangible evidence of the terrific real-estate potential in that city. There are thousands of examples of smaller operations involving the improvement of older structures from Manhattan's Bowery to Harlem, and in the other boroughs as well.

## What Do You Advise About Washington, D.C.?

Colonel James Bishop writes from Arlington, Virginia, "Another Air Force colonel and I have pooled our assets, about $62,000 equity in our homes, and set about finding an apartment house in Washington, D.C., that meets your criteria. Properties that might come close to the buy standards of your book as to price are in run-down neighborhoods where the whites have moved out and blacks have taken over. What do you advise about Washington?"

There should be a wide choice of possibilities if you keep looking and spread your sights. I was in Washington recently to lecture to the National Apartment Association convention and saw major possibilities in both urban and suburban areas. White tenants who move to outlying areas—when there is virtually no older housing available—create a tremendous demand for new apartments. In suburban areas the best opportunities lie in erecting new structures on nonproductive or low-income-producing lands. You may prefer the latter course after checking, although it is usually best to gain experience with older apartments.

The Arlington Apartment House Association has many members who are doing well. Why not check with that organization? One active member is Jerry Reinch, former president of the National Apartment Association, whose multimillion-dollar apartment projects return good profits. I inspected his apartments with Oscar Brinkman, former national executive secretary of the association. We found that Reinch kept his buildings full at middle-bracket rents.

Urban renewal, redevelopment, economic growth, and integration are working together to accomplish two major conversions of properties close to the center of large cities. One is a changeover from residential to higher-paying commercial usage, the other is a fast-moving change from white to black residential occupancy. Both these changes offer opportunities for property improvements and resulting increases in rents and resale values. Apartment owners can do very well by providing better housing for minority-race tenants who pay their rents.

Elmer Klavans, a contractor who specializes in renovations, reports many profitable examples of Washington property improvements in both the aforementioned fields. His experience exceeds that of anyone else in the area, as he has completed over $3 million worth of remodeling jobs in each of the last three years. In one spectacular conversion of a thirty-unit apartment building to a commercial office building, the owner's annual rentals zoomed from $35,000 to $240,000. A more typical remodeling job changed some archaic flats that Washington might have slept in to desirable modern apartments. This improvement increased the annual income from $2,500 to $12,500.

## Would Seattle Be a Good Choice?

Julian Wachsmuth writes from Wisconsin, "I would appreciate your opinion as to whether or not Seattle would be a good choice—

not necessarily the best, but good to follow your investment program."

Seattle offers very good opportunities for real-estate investment. I made a number of personal inspections during an extensive tour of the city when I went there to lecture to a joint meeting of the Chamber of Commerce and the Realty Board. Among the people who welcomed my wife and me were two representatives from the Seattle *Times,* both of whom knew several examples of real-estate success. The *Times* people were classified-advertising manager Lester Jenkins and real-estate editor Alice Staples.

### Should I Leave Dayton and Go to Florida?

William Kilgore writes from Dayton, "I will be sixty years old come October, and have been employed at Frigidaire thirty-three years. I would love to take what I have and get a good start by the time I retire. I have my $12,000 home paid for, which I could trade or sell, plus $4,000 in the bank. I would like a little of your advice: Should I invest here in Dayton, or do you think I should go to Florida?"

It's chiefly a matter of where you prefer to live. In either locality there are many good buys in older, close-in property that can be modernized. You should be able to trade or sell your home in order to buy apartments either in Florida cities or in Dayton. Some areas of Florida are considerably overbuilt in hotels, motels and other rental units that depend on seasonal income. However, you might want to explore the opportunities offered by regular apartment rentals in one of the larger cities where you could have stable tenants.

Why not gain experience by taking a look at the market where you live, where you are more familiar with local conditions? If you find what you want in an apartment house, you might be able to trade your home as the down payment and live in one of the rental units. That way most of your cash could be kept as a reserve for emergencies and improvements.

### Should I Move from My Small Home Town to a Nearby City or to a Distant Metropolis?

A. N. Hartnagel writes, "I live in Port Angeles, Washington, a small town of 16,000 population, and I prefer to invest in a larger community. I have around $20,000 to invest, plus a $35,000 home which might be used for a trade. Would you advise moving to a large city like nearby Seattle, or to some mushrooming area like Santa Clara Valley or Los Angeles County?"

The San Jose and Los Angeles areas both offer excellent opportunities. If you prefer to stay in the Seattle area because of your associations and familiarity with local conditions, you no doubt could do as well there as anywhere. If it suits you, you could invest in Seattle and continue to live in Port Angeles. Your chances for success would be enhanced, of course, if you moved and operated your first apartment house yourself, assuming that you wish to make property investment your chief interest.

### What Do You Think of a Four-Hour Drive?

Irvin Scheel writes, "I own and publish the Mabel *Record,* a weekly Minnesota newspaper in a small town of 900 near the Iowa line. I have considered trying your formula in Rochester, a booming city of 54,000 only little more than an hour's drive from my house. I like the possibilities better in Minneapolis, about a four-hour drive from here. I am eager to try, but would like to know what you think of my starting in Minneapolis and living that long a drive from the city."

Many property owners, like Roger Stevens of Detroit and the Murchisons of Texas, successfully operate their investment holdings all over the country. They delegate on-the-spot supervision to local management, either a building manager or an over-all manager for a geographical area. If you decide on an area manager, you might consider a realtor who specializes in property management.

Jet air travel makes it possible for an individual to oversee wide-flung real-estate holdings. New York builder Alvin Dworman personally looks after his multimillion-dollar properties in New York, Florida and California; he has made appointments to cover all three in one day, checking New York City before he leaves in the morning, stopping off at Miami at midday and flying on to Los Angeles in the afternoon.

I favor the idea of owning property within one day's round-trip drive of your home, so that traveling and necessary supervision can be handled in one day. I usually make supervisory visits twice a month on a routine basis, and at least once a week when I have remodeling, redecorating, financing, sale, trade or purchase projects under way. In the latter cases it might be in order to stay overnight once in a while.

For you to follow a similar pattern of being able to personally supervise your properties without taking up too much travel time and expense, Minneapolis could well be handled within your sphere of operations—but that is just about the distance limit if you plan to drive.

On the basis of all I hear about Rochester, it is indeed a booming city that is drawing new industries. You should find it worthwhile to shop there for possible good buys. When my Rochester friend Leo Shapiro was president of Minnesota Realtors he told me of profitable deals there, and so have others. You might find a limited number of apartment houses in Rochester or the town where you live, but there could be good potentialities in single-family homes, duplexes and fourplexes. It generally pays to keep your investing in properties as close to home as possible.

I prefer pyramiding into larger buildings, because then more efficient managers can usually be afforded and the supervision becomes easier. However, many investors in smaller towns and rural communities do very well by concentrating on single-family homes and farms. Such properties can often be sold more readily than a large apartment house, and the capital profits can be used faster for further investment. Higher profits are earned by heavy financing of sales, usually where the seller takes back a second mortgage. The total amount of such subsidiary loans constitutes profit in most cases. They can then be turned in as down payments to buy additional properties.

### Does One Ugly Duckling Kill a Neighborhood?

Mrs. Tilden Helvenston of Columbus, Ohio, writes, "My husband and I are enthusiastic about following your suggestions in real estate. We have found a double in the $12,500 range in run-down condition and perfect for renovating. It is the second-worst-looking property in the block. The general neighborhood is good, but the house next door is very shabby-looking and unfortunately not for sale, or we could buy it also to be repaired and resold at a profit. My question is, Would this one shabby neighbor kill our chances of making a profitable resale?"

Don't worry too much about one shabby house next door, as long as the general neighborhood is good. When I was in Columbus for a Realty Board lecture arranged by executive secretary Larry Chambers, I noted many handsome new apartments being erected right next door to eyesores. In Columbus, as in other cities, both new and improved buildings make money in spite of shabby neighbors.

Neighbors are prone to keep up with the Joneses, and improvements are contagious. A number of correspondents have told me how their improvements have stimulated their neighbors to copy them. Often one eye-catching start spreads down the block and transforms an entire neighborhood. After your duplex is fixed up, it is likely that your neighbor will spruce up his property. Perhaps you can help with suggestions on painting and renovating at low cost, and how to finance improvements. If your neighbor doesn't improve his property, consider screening him off as much as possible with shrubbery or a wooden fence along your side line.

### Does New Construction Hurt Older Properties?

Following my lecture at Foley's in Houston, Texas, Mario Galindo asked, "Does a new building next door pull down an older building? I bought a fourplex for fourteen thousand dollars. Paid three thousand down. Fixed it up in a year and got my rents raised so it's worth twenty-two thousand, besides having a commercial potential. Some new commercial buildings have gone up in the neighborhood. Now they're building a big new apartment house right next door to me, and I'm worried. Will this pull my rents and my value down?"

On the contrary, it will raise your rents and your values, as long as you keep up your property. True, new construction accentuates the undesirability of run-down property, but new construction costs more than judiciously improved older rentals, and new builders have to charge more. These factors tend to raise rent levels in the area.

One of many examples with which I am familiar involved a thirty-unit apartment house in Oakland, California, similar to the Cynthia Court described in my first book. It was well kept up, and the owner charged $95 monthly for one-bedroom apartments. A sixty-four-unit new building was put up next door, with rents at $150 monthly for slightly smaller units. The only significant drawback in the older property was that it had a breakdown-prone community refrigeration system; the box in each apartment was approximately four cubic feet. The new apartments had ten-cubic-foot individual refrigerators. They cost the owner approximately $150 apiece, and each contained a sizable freezer compartment across the top.

Tenants in the older building who compared the accommodations complained about the archaic refrigeration. Many said they would gladly pay more and stay in the older building if they could have a decent-sized refrigerator with a compartment to take care of frozen foods. Through the local apartment house association, the

owner contacted Kelvinator apartment sales manager Gordon Layman, from whom he bought twelve-cubic-foot refrigerators for
about $135 apiece. Kelvinator financed the purchase so that the
monthly payments were less than the owner's increased income. He
raised all thirty rentals $10 monthly as soon as the new refrigera-
tors were installed. Then he obtained additional $5 raises every
three months until, by the end of one year, the rentals reached
$125.

### Does a Run-Down Area Preclude Profitable Improvements?

Mary Cole of Los Angeles writes, "My husband, Joseph, and I
began with great enthusiasm to look for our first piece of property
even when we were only halfway through reading your book. For
various reasons we limited our field to Hollywood and certain adja-
cent sections of Los Angeles. We are ready to start, if need be, with
step number two on your pyramid, as we have around $6,000 to in-
vest. After marking ads, telephoning, talking with brokers and in-
specting properties, we have found two projects. One is a triplex,
the other a four-flat. They meet all the requirements except for the
fact that in each case they are located in old, run-down slum areas.
Would this preclude attracting qualified tenants who would pay the
increased rent schedule after improvements? Also, would the street
and general locale prevent us from trading up?"

The triplex and fourplex you mention might merit further consideration. Neighborhood is, of course, number one in importance
to tenants. But many tenants prefer an area closer in, even though
it is somewhat run-down, to a better-looking outlying area that requires long-distance commuting. If these properties are close in,
the areas are bound to improve in time. A question to take a look
at is, How much time? You may be in on the ground floor if neighborhood improvement has already started or is just about to start.

My wife and I have visited the Los Angeles area every year since
my first book was published in 1959. We have observed a number
of very good buys that would fit into my recommended program.

Some were fairly close in and in areas that are presently on the run-down side. Also, I have received scores of letters from Los Angeles–area readers who have recently purchased moneymakers. It seems to me you may be restricting yourselves too much as to area and other factors. Why not consider being more open-minded in your shopping?

### Where Is the Best Place to Invest?

This frequent question was asked by telephone company secretary Ann Raumaker following my Portland Apartment Owners' Association lecture. It was repeated by a brewmaster in Milwaukee, who wrote, "I'm about ready to retire and want to start investing in apartments. I like it here in Milwaukee, but wonder if I should sell my home and move to Southern California, which shows the greatest growth in the country. Are investment opportunities better in Los Angeles, or perhaps San Diego? Or would you recommend some other part of the country? How do other areas compare with Milwaukee and Los Angeles as to opportunities and to growth?"

Although larger areas may have greater over-all opportunities, they also have more opportunists. Each area in the United States offers a high degree of individual opportunity. In most cases the average investor can do best in the area with which he is most familiar. This is especially true if he likes its economic, social and geographical climate and is not influenced toward moving for health or other personal reasons.

Your neighbor's grass may look greener to you at the same time that yours looks greener to him. A case in point involves two Texas oilmen who heard me lecture in Dallas. They said they wanted to follow my real-estate experience as closely as possible and therefore had decided to start operations in California. I said, "You can do just as well in Dallas." Nevertheless, they insisted on investing in California; I have been advised that they are doing exceedingly well in buying, improving and financing apartments.

On the other hand, many people have written of equal success in

## 96 Cities Above 100,000 That Gained Population Along with Their Areas
*(From 1960 and 1970 Census Bureau Figures, with Corrections Issued May, 1974)*

| Rank | | CITY POPULATION | | AREA POPULATION | | Rank |
|---|---|---|---|---|---|---|
| | | 1970 Census | Increase | 1970 Census | Increase | |
| 58 | Albuquerque, N.M. | 243,751 | 42,562 | 333,266 | 71,067 | 103 |
| 132 | Alexandria, Va. | 110,927 | 19,904 | No Census Bureau Area | | — |
| 136 | Allentown, Pa. | 109,871 | 1,524 | 594,382 | 102,214 | 64 |
| 81 | Anaheim and | 166,408 | 62,224 | 1,421,233 | New Area | 20 |
| 87 | Santa Ana and | 155,762 | 55,412 | | | |
| 118 | Garden Grove, Cal. | 121,357 | 37,119 | | | |
| 27 | Atlanta, Ga. | 497,421 | 9,966 | 1,595,517 | 578,329 | 18 |
| 56 | Austin, Texas | 251,808 | 65,263 | 323,158 | 111,022 | 108 |
| 83 | Baton Rouge, La. | 165,963 | 13,544 | 375,628 | 145,570 | 90 |
| — | Bayamon, P.R. | 147,552 | 132,443 | No Census Bureau Area | | — |
| 125 | Berkeley, Cal. | 116,716 | 5,448 | 163,213 | 26,314 | 179 |
| 133 | Cedar Rapids, Iowa | 110,642 | 18,607 | 557,785 | 285,674 | 67 |
| 60 | Charlotte, N.C. | 241,178 | 39,614 | 239,288 | 95,546 | 140 |
| 103 | Colorado Springs, Col. | 135,060 | 64,866 | 322,880 | New Area | 109 |
| 127 | Columbia, S.C. | 113,542 | 16,109 | 238,584 | 20,599 | 141 |
| 88 | Columbus, Ga. | 155,028 | 38,249 | | | |
| 21 | Columbus, Ohio | 540,025 | 68,709 | 1,017,847 | 334,885 | 34 |
| 62 | Corpus Christi, Texas | 204,525 | 36,835 | 284,832 | 63,259 | 120 |
| 8 | Dallas and | 844,401 | 164,717 | 2,378,353 | 721,537 | 12 |
| 33 | Fort Worth, Texas | 393,476 | 37,208 | | | |
| 25 | Denver, Col. | 514,678 | 20,791 | 1,239,477 | 310,094 | 28 |
| 129 | Elizabeth, N.J. | 112,654 | 4,956 | No Census Bureau Area | | — |

| | City | | | | | |
|---|---|---|---|---|---|---|
| 45 | El Paso, Texas | 322,261 | 45,574 | 359,291 | 45,221 | 94 |
| 98 | Fort Lauderdale and | 139,590 | 55,942 | 620,100 | 286,154 | 62 |
| 142 | Hollywood, Fla. | 106,873 | 71,636 | | | |
| 72 | Fort Wayne, Ind. | 176,021 | 14,245 | 361,984 | 129,788 | 93 |
| 150 | Fremont, Cal. | 100,869 | 57,079 | No Census Bureau Area | No Census Bureau Area | — |
| 82 | Fresno, Cal. | 165,972 | 32,043 | 413,329 | 47,384 | 82 |
| 107 | Glendale, Cal. | 132,664 | 13,222 | No Census Bureau Area | No Census Bureau Area | — |
| 65 | Grand Rapids, Mich. | 197,649 | 20,336 | 539,225 | 176,038 | 71 |
| 95 | Greensboro and | 144,076 | 24,502 | 724,129 | 477,609 | 51 |
| 105 | Winston-Salem, N.C. | 133,683 | 22,548 | | | |
| 148 | Hialeah, Fla. | 102,452 | 35,480 | No Census Bureau Area | No Census Bureau Area | — |
| 44 | Honolulu, Hawaii | 324,871 | 30,677 | 630,528 | 130,119 | 59 |
| 6 | Houston, Texas | 1,232,802 | 294,583 | 1,999,316 | 756,158 | 16 |
| 124 | Huntington Beach, Cal. | 115,960 | 104,468 | No Census Bureau Area | No Census Bureau Area | — |
| 101 | Huntsville, Ala. | 137,802 | 65,437 | 282,450 | 165,102 | 121 |
| 130 | Independence, Mo. | 111,630 | 49,302 | No Census Bureau Area | No Census Bureau Area | — |
| 11 | Indianapolis, Ind. | 746,303 | 270,044 | 1,111,352 | 413,785 | 30 |
| 90 | Jackson, Miss. | 153,968 | 9,546 | 258,905 | 71,860 | 132 |
| 23 | Jacksonville, Fla. | 528,865 | 327,835 | 621,827 | 166,416 | 61 |
| 26 | Kansas City, Mo., and | 507,330 | 31,791 | 1,273,926 | 234,433 | 26 |
| 80 | Kansas City, Kan. | 168,213 | 46,312 | | | |
| 76 | Knoxville, Tenn. | 174,587 | 62,761 | 409,409 | 41,329 | 85 |
| 109 | Lansing, Mich. | 131,403 | 23,596 | 424,271 | 125,322 | 80 |
| 113 | Las Vegas, Nev. | 125,787 | 61,382 | 273,288 | 146,272 | 125 |
| 138 | Lexington, Ky. | 108,137 | 45,327 | 266,701 | 134,795 | 127 |
| 91 | Lincoln, Neb. | 149,518 | 20,997 | 167,972 | 12,700 | 176 |
| 108 | Little Rock, Ark. | 132,483 | 24,670 | 323,296 | 80,316 | 107 |
| 134 | Livonia, Mich. | 110,109 | 43,407 | No Census Bureau Area | No Census Bureau Area | — |
| 3 | Los Angeles and | 2,809,813 | 330,798 | 7,041,980 | 256,904 | 2 |

## 96 Cities Above 100,000 That Gained Population Along with Their Areas (continued)
### (From 1960 and 1970 Census Bureau Figures, with Corrections Issued May, 1974)

| Rank | | CITY POPULATION | | AREA POPULATION | | |
|---|---|---|---|---|---|---|
| | | 1970 Census | Increase | 1970 Census | Increase | Rank |
| 40 | Long Beach, Cal. | 358,879 | 14,711 | 179,295 | 23,024 | 167 |
| 92 | Lubbock, Texas | 149,101 | 20,410 | 226,782 | 46,379 | 147 |
| 117 | Macon, Ga. | 122,423 | 52,669 | 290,272 | 68,177 | 116 |
| 77 | Madison, Wis. | 171,767 | 45,061 | 834,103 | 207,084 | 41 |
| 17 | Memphis, Tenn. | 623,530 | 126,006 | 1,267,792 | 332,745 | 27 |
| 42 | Miami, Fla. | 334,859 | 43,171 | 699,271 | 299,528 | 43 |
| 30 | Nashville, Tenn. | 448,003 | 277,129 | | | |
| 100 | Newport News and | 138,177 | 24,515 | 333,140 | 108,637 | 104 |
| 119 | Hampton, Va. | 120,779 | 31,521 | | | |
| 47 | Norfolk and | 307,951 | 3,082 | 732,600 | 154,093 | 50 |
| 78 | Virginia Beach and | 172,106 | 164,105 | | | |
| 131 | Portsmouth, Va. | 110,963 | (−3,810 loss) | | | |
| 37 | Oklahoma City, Okla. | 368,377 | 44,124 | 699,092 | 187,259 | 54 |
| 41 | Omaha, Neb. | 346,929 | 45,331 | 542,646 | 84,773 | 69 |
| 153 | Parma, Ohio | 100,216 | 17,371 | No Census Bureau Area | | — |
| 94 | Paterson, N.J. | 144,824 | 1,161 | 1,358,794 | 171,921 | 23 |
| 112 | Peoria, Ill. | 126,963 | 23,801 | 341,979 | 53,146 | 98 |
| 20 | Phoenix, Ariz. | 581,562 | 142,392 | 969,425 | 305,915 | 36 |
| — | Ponce, P.R. | 128,233 | 13,947 | No Census Bureau Area | | — |
| 35 | Portland, Ore. | 379,964 | 7,288 | 1,007,130 | 185,233 | 35 |
| 116 | Raleigh, N.C. | 123,793 | 29,862 | 419,394 | 250,312 | 81 |
| 57 | Richmond, Va. | 249,431 | 29,473 | 542,242 | 133,748 | 70 |

| | | | | | | |
|---|---|---|---|---|---|---|
| 97 | Riverside and | 140,089 | 55,757 | 1,141,307 | 331,525 | 29 |
| 143 | San Bernardino, Cal. | 106,867 | 14,945 | | | |
| 93 | Rockford, Ill. | 147,370 | 20,664 | 272,063 | 62,298 | 126 |
| 55 | Sacramento, Cal. | 257,105 | 65,438 | 803,793 | 301,015 | 43 |
| 15 | San Antonio, Texas | 654,153 | 66,435 | 888,179 | 201,028 | 38 |
| 14 | San Diego, Cal. | 697,027 | 123,803 | 1,357,854 | 324,843 | 24 |
| 31 | San Jose, Cal. | 445,779 | 241,583 | 1,065,313 | 422,998 | 32 |
| — | San Juan, P.R. | 452,749 | 20,372 | No Census Bureau Area | No Census Bureau Area | — |
| 69 | Shreveport, La. | 182,064 | 17,692 | 333,826 | 52,345 | 101 |
| 120 | Springfield, Mo. | 120,096 | 24,231 | 168,053 | 41,777 | 175 |
| 137 | Stamford, Conn. | 108,798 | 16,085 | No Census Bureau Area | No Census Bureau Area | — |
| 140 | Stockton, Cal. | 109,963 | 23,642 | 291,073 | 41,084 | 115 |
| 89 | Tacoma, Wash. | 154,581 | 6,602 | 412,344 | 90,754 | 83 |
| 50 | Tampa and | 277,753 | 2,783 | 1,088,549 | 316,096 | 31 |
| 61 | St. Petersburg, Fla. | 216,159 | 34,861 | | | |
| 34 | Toledo, Ohio | 383,105 | 65,102 | 762,658 | 305,727 | 48 |
| 115 | Topeka, Kan. | 125,011 | 5,527 | 180,619 | 39,333 | 165 |
| 104 | Torrance, Cal. | 134,968 | 33,977 | No Census Bureau Area | No Census Bureau Area | — |
| 53 | Tucson, Ariz. | 262,933 | 50,041 | 351,667 | 86,007 | 95 |
| 43 | Tulsa, Okla. | 330,350 | 68,665 | 549,154 | 130,180 | 68 |
| 70 | Warren, Mich. | 179,260 | 90,014 | No Census Bureau Area | No Census Bureau Area | — |
| 139 | Waterbury, Conn. | 108,033 | 703 | No Census Bureau Area | No Census Bureau Area | — |
| 51 | Wichita, Kan. | 276,554 | 21,856 | 389,352 | 46,121 | 87 |
| 63 | Yonkers, N.Y. | 204,297 | 13,663 | No Census Bureau Area | No Census Bureau Area | — |

both the Dallas and Houston areas. A couple who moved to Dallas from Southern California appear to be doing better than the Texas oilmen in California!

I know of several new investors who are doing as well in Milwaukee as others who are succeeding in San Diego and Los Angeles. Such cities offer high opportunity in real-estate investment because of comparatively fast population growth. There are compensating factors in any city. Boston, Chicago, New York and Philadelphia, for example, have a much higher proportion of older close-in buildings, which offer the greatest opportunity for capital gain from moneymaking improvements.

The sixty cities above 100,000 that have dropped in population were listed in Chapter III, along with metropolitan-area figures. For comparison, see the chart on p. 126 showing the ninety-six cities exceeding 100,000 in population that have experienced increases.

## What Are the Sources of Good Buys?

Following my lecture at the Hilton Hotel in Pittsburgh's fabulous Golden Triangle, Dave Bollinger, book and real-estate editor of the *Press,* asked, "Why would anyone sell you a good buy instead of holding on to it? What are the sources of good buys?"

Some that I know personally are mentioned in my first book. They include properties that were allowed to deteriorate by shortsighted owners, and liquidations by heirs, spendthrifts, older owners who preferred to sell and take back a mortgage as a source of income, transferred employees, or those who decided to put their equities into other fields.

In addition, there are some tax sales and foreclosures, especially on properties financed with no down payment by F.H.A. or other agencies with loans at or exceeding building costs. In some areas such recovered properties are available for improvement and resale with virtually no down payment.

A great deal of property is coming on the market because of business mergers, which release choice downtown land for industrial and apartment development. Government consolidations such as those which eliminate scattered armed-forces posts release tracts of land for private investment. Immense acreage is often bought by right of eminent domain for use as throughway and other governmental purposes; then substantial portions of this land are sold off as excess property.

Often, properties are sold with a valuation based on their present use, which may be far short of the potential. When you buy with the intention of improving the usage, through rehabilitation, modernization, remodeling or new construction, your maximum assured profits are based on your improvements.

## What Are the Future Population Prospects for My State?

This is a common question from every state. One who asked it is stockbroker Melvyn Yap of Honolulu, after my lecture to the Lowry-Nickerson Seminar. He continued, "My wife, May, and I aren't sure whether to buy apartments in California or Hawaii or both. It would help make up our minds if we had a better idea of the future population growth in both states."

The Census Bureau has compiled population estimates for 1980 and 1990 for every state, showing a continuing general upsurge in the Southeast, Southwest, Central States, and the Eastern Seaboard except for Maine. Population is expected to dwindle in Maine and also in Idaho, Montana, North Dakota and Wyoming.

## U.S. Census Bureau Estimates of State Population Changes

| Rank | | 1973 Actual | 1980 Estimate | 1990 Estimate | Rank | POPULATION Change 1973–90 | |
|---|---|---|---|---|---|---|---|
| 21 | Alabama | 3,539,000 | 3,747,000 | 4,090,000 | 20 | Gain | 15.6% |
| 51 | Alaska | 330,000 | 333,000 | 391,000 | 50 | " | 18.5% |
| 32 | Arizona | 2,058,000 | 2,226,000 | 2,701,000 | 29 | " | 31.2% |
| 33 | Arkansas | 2,037,000 | 2,087,000 | 2,271,000 | 33 | " | 11.5% |
| 1 | California | 20,601,000 | 22,403,000 | 24,982,000 | 1 | " | 21.3% |
| 28 | Colorado | 2,437,000 | 2,586,000 | 2,890,000 | 28 | " | 18.6% |
| 24 | Connecticut | 3,076,000 | 3,358,000 | 3,710,000 | 24 | " | 20.6% |
| 47 | Delaware | 576,000 | 627,000 | 707,000 | 45 | " | 22.7% |
| 43 | District of Columbia | 746,000 | 750,000 | 750,000 | 43 | " | .5% |
| 8 | Florida | 7,678,000 | 8,926,000 | 10,978,000 | 7 | " | 43.0% |
| 14 | Georgia | 4,786,000 | 5,147,000 | 5,907,000 | 14 | " | 23.4% |
| 40 | Hawaii | 832,000 | 848,000 | 979,000 | 40 | " | 17.7% |
| 42 | Idaho | 770,000 | 708,000 | 738,000 | 44 | Loss | —4.2% |
| 5 | Illinois | 11,236,000 | 12,091,000 | 13,056,000 | 5 | Gain | 16.2% |
| 11 | Indiana | 5,316,000 | 5,784,000 | 6,384,000 | 12 | " | 19.7% |
| 25 | Iowa | 2,904,000 | 2,913,000 | 2,993,000 | 26 (tie) | " | 3.1% |
| 30 | Kansas | 2,279,000 | 2,228,000 | 2,281,000 | 32 | " | .1% |
| 23 | Kentucky | 3,342,000 | 3,609,000 | 3,982,000 | 21 | " | 19.2% |
| 20 | Louisiana | 3,764,000 | 3,744,000 | 3,937,000 | 22 | " | 4.6% |
| 38 | Maine | 1,028,000 | 972,000 | 992,000 | 39 | Loss | —3.5% |
| 18 | Maryland | 4,070,000 | 4,473,000 | 5,275,000 | 16 | Gain | 29.6% |
| 10 | Massachusetts | 5,818,000 | 6,267,000 | 6,876,000 | 10 | " | 18.2% |
| 7 | Michigan | 9,044,000 | 9,743,000 | 10,645,000 | 8 | " | 17.7% |
| 19 | Minnesota | 3,897,000 | 4,119,000 | 4,553,000 | 19 | " | 16.8% |

| | | | | | | | |
|---|---|---|---|---|---|---|---|
| 29 | Mississippi | 2,281,000 | 2,328,000 | 2,450,000 | 31 | " | 7.4% |
| 15 | Missouri | 4,757,000 | 5,071,000 | 5,439,000 | 15 | " | 14.3% |
| 44 | Montana | 721,000 | 670,000 | 665,000 | 46 | Loss | —7.8% |
| 35 | Nebraska | 1,542,000 | 1,499,000 | 1,557,000 | 35 | Gain | 1.0% |
| 48 | Nevada | 548,000 | 616,000 | 761,000 | 42 | " | 38.9% |
| 41 | New Hampshire | 791,000 | 843,000 | 919,000 | 41 | " | 16.2% |
| 9 | New Jersey | 7,361,000 | 8,080,000 | 8,923,000 | 9 | " | 21.2% |
| 37 | New Mexico | 1,106,000 | 1,055,000 | 1,131,000 | 37 | " | 2.3% |
| 2 | New York | 18,265,000 | 19,352,000 | 20,946,000 | 2 | " | 14.7% |
| 12 | North Carolina | 5,273,000 | 5,736,000 | 6,465,000 | 11 | " | 22.6% |
| 46 | North Dakota | 640,000 | 579,000 | 563,000 | 48 | Loss | —12.0% |
| 6 | Ohio | 10,731,000 | 11,651,000 | 12,609,000 | 6 | Gain | 17.5% |
| 27 | Oklahoma | 2,663,000 | 2,762,000 | 2,993,000 | 26 (tie) | " | 12.4% |
| 31 | Oregon | 2,225,000 | 2,335,000 | 2,537,000 | 30 | " | 14.0% |
| 3 | Pennsylvania | 11,902,000 | 12,649,000 | 13,416,000 | 4 | " | 12.7% |
| 39 | Rhode Island | 973,000 | 1,032,000 | 1,115,000 | 38 | " | 14.6% |
| 26 | South Carolina | 2,726,000 | 2,819,000 | 3,122,000 | 25 | " | 14.5% |
| 45 | South Dakota | 685,000 | 655,000 | 648,000 | 47 | Loss | —5.4% |
| 17 | Tennessee | 4,126,000 | 4,557,000 | 5,191,000 | 17 | Gain | 25.8% |
| 4 | Texas | 11,794,000 | 12,167,000 | 13,580,000 | 3 | " | 15.1% |
| 36 | Utah | 1,157,000 | 1,160,000 | 1,310,000 | 36 | " | 13.2% |
| 49 | Vermont | 464,000 | 482,000 | 519,000 | 49 | " | 11.9% |
| 13 | Virginia | 4,811,000 | 5,295,000 | 6,135,000 | 13 | " | 27.5% |
| 22 | Washington | 3,429,000 | 3,550,000 | 3,836,000 | 23 | " | 11.0% |
| 34 | West Virginia | 1,794,000 | 1,832,000 | 1,845,000 | 34 | " | 2.8% |
| 16 | Wisconsin | 4,569,000 | 4,737,000 | 5,013,000 | 18 | " | 9.7% |
| 50 | Wyoming | 353,000 | 331,000 | 334,000 | 51 | Loss | —5.4% |
| | UNITED STATES | 209,851,000 | 223,532,000 | 246,039,000 | | GAIN | 17.2% |

# 4

# Realtors

# versus

# Lawyers

# IX

## Does It Pay to Deal with a Realtor?

Many investors after getting a little experience try to bypass brokers and handle all their own deals in order to save the commission. I am often asked my opinion and experience concerning this aspect of investing in real estate.

### Are You a Broker and What Is Your Fee?

Georgia Deems of White Plains, New York, asks, "Would you let me know the fee for your consultation service?"

Some, like Joan Polsdorfer of Ross, California, send along a check to pay for my answers to their questions.

Others, like Noel Roseman of Auckland, New Zealand, who wants to send me $50,000 cash to invest, ask my broker's fee for finding suitable apartment buys.

All such checks are invariably returned. I have gladly answered specific questions as soon as I could get to them after my lecture tours and other commitments.

I am purely an investor myself, not a broker. I have taken a course in California brokerage practices to add to my education, and could, if I wished, make my own deals. But every piece of income property I have ever bought or traded has been handled through a realtor. Requests from friends, relatives or anyone else that I act as a broker, associate or adviser in a sales or management capacity are, therefore, all referred to realtors who specialize in these activities.

## Could You Advise Me on Gas Station Leases?

Typical of such requests is a letter from Raymond Poole of San Francisco. He writes, "Could you recommend a formula or advise me concerning gas stations with respect to the following:

1. Valuation of property where one owns both land and improvements
2. Valuation of the land—consideration given only to ground leases
3. Basis for rentals in both of the above cases
4. Kinds of leases—with regard to protection against inflationary trends
5. Gallonage clauses—how determined
6. Tax clauses—kinds

"I have three stations—two with ground leases and one under lease, in which I own both land and improvements. Past negotiations with the oil companies have led me to feel that I have always been at a disadvantage in dealing with their real-estate representatives—who seem to have all the answers to any kind of argument. Any information or recommendation would be greatly appreciated."

Regarding gas station or other business leases, I would suggest your asking the San Francisco Real Estate Board to recommend a qualified realtor who specializes in your field. There are a number of leading realtors who handle many kinds of business leases and are quite familiar with the ramifications peculiar to your area.

You would no doubt come out ahead in the long run by handling your negotiations through competent realtors. Their knowledge will help you obtain the most advantageous terms, which should save you more than enough to pay their commissions.

## Why Pay Commissions to a Broker?

This question was asked by a Hawaiian housewife when, during an interview on a Honolulu radio program, I answered telephone calls for two hours. She said she had been trying to sell her home—unsuccessfully—without benefit of broker in order to save the commission. The same query was made by a multimillionaire apartment owner after my lecture to the Cleveland Apartment and Home Owners' Association.

A similar question comes from David Dudenhoeffer of Hartford, Connecticut, who writes, "What are the advantages of buying property through a real-estate agent versus buying directly from the owner? I realize that the seller pays the realtor's commission, but it seems that he could sell for less if there is no commission involved. Yet I notice that you mention buying through an agent most of the time. What has been your experience in this matter?"

I believe the average investor is better off dealing with realtors. I am often asked why I am so emphatic about this. My reasoning is clear, I think, if I compare real estate with pheasant hunting. With no dogs to help you, you will probably return with an empty bag. Take a couple of bird dogs along, and you are more apt to bag the limit; they will find more game than you would ever come close to finding on your own. Then they will flush it out and help you retrieve it.

In this respect (and I don't mean any disrespect), realtors are just like a pack of hunting dogs! They turn up more buyers and sellers than an investor could possibly find by himself. Additionally, they will usually work out the financing and other negotiations to bag more and better deals than an investor could work out on his own.

Familiarity with the essential problems of a particular community, with current market conditions and with the preparation of bona-fide contracts is the stock in trade of a realtor. Buyers who try to handle purchases on their own run the danger of duplicating the original "swindle" of Peter Minuit when he bought Manhattan Island from the visiting Long Island Canarsie Indians—who didn't own it. Today's hoodwinked buyers are not so likely to be able to correct their mistakes by getting the actual owners to sell cheap, as Minuit did. When the Manhattan Weckquasgeeks returned from a hunting trip, the Dutch leader rebought the island for $24 worth of beads, muskets, knives and cloth.

Often a buyer and a seller who confront each other directly will be so far apart in their thinking and bargaining that it will be impossible for them to get together. A buyer, for example, may say, "I won't pay a penny over twenty thousand." The seller may say, "I won't sell for a cent less than twenty-five thousand." The result of such a conversation is likely to be an unconsummated deal. In contrast, a realtor in the middle can negotiate back and forth until he concludes an agreement on a compromise, say, of $22,500.

## What Do You Think of "For Sale by Owner" Signs?

This question was asked by reporter Ben Thompson of the Honolulu *Star-Bulletin*.

Such signs usually cheapen property. Buyers and sellers do, of course, work out successful deals on their own. On the other hand, I know of many sellers who tried to dispose of their properties, sometimes at unrealistically high prices, by putting up a "For Sale by Owner" sign. They thought this would make prospective buyers feel they had stumbled on a bargain. Almost invariably, though, the seller winds up getting less for his property than he would have netted by dealing originally through a realtor. Even if he changes his mind later and puts it into a realtor's hands, the property by then may have a reputation for being "distress merchandise." Inept advertising and sales attempts by an owner have a tendency to pull his price down.

## What Is Your Opinion of Women Realtors?

This question was asked by Houston realtors Lucille Beckner and Pauline Moore after my noon lecture to the women's council at a convention of the National Association of Realtors in Dallas. There were close to a thousand women in the audience and only a smattering of men. I gave the same answer I have given at lectures with an audience composed wholly or mainly of men.

Many women do an outstanding job as realtors. They are especially adept at handling home sales and apartment sales and management. After all, most homes, and apartment houses too, are managed by women.

## Where Can I Find a Reliable Real-Estate Broker?

This question was asked by Gene Brendler when I appeared on his *Better Half* KPTV show in Portland, Oregon.

Any broker who belongs to the local real-estate board, which entitles him to the use of the registered designation of realtor, promises reliability. Brokers who do not belong may be well qualified, but you may occasionally find one who is not. You are safer, generally, to deal with a member of your local real-estate board. Every salesman is out to make sales, naturally, but most realtors do a conscientious job of observing the fine code of ethics and educational practices of the National Association of Realtors.

When I gave a morning talk to the Dallas Real Estate Board, Ebby Halliday, as program chairman, introduced me and concluded by saying, "I know you'll all be happy to learn what Bill Nickerson had just told me—every income property deal he has ever made has been through a broker."

I challenged this, saying, "I have a correction to make. Ebby has misquoted me. What I actually said was that every deal has been made through a *realtor*. I make it a point to deal with realtors and can therefore thank your associates in California for finding and consummating the deals that made me a millionaire."

I have lectured to realtor conferences, conventions and educational seminars throughout the United States and have always found the realtors eager to improve their knowledge and ability. The educational programs they sponsor are not usually available to brokers who do not belong to realty boards. What this means in a man's qualifications is exemplified by the experience of Minnesota realtor Herman Heldt. He told me that he attended every educational meeting he could. He had started working in the realty field as a salesman for a broker who never attended such meetings. "Last year my additional knowledge enabled me to buy him out," Heldt told me. "This year he's working for me as a salesman."

### How Can I Avoid an Unreliable Broker?

An unfortunate example involving a nonrealtor broker is described in a letter from Wally Valiquette of Boston:

"Before I bought your book I paid $450 down to a Massachusetts broker for a two-and-a-half-acre piece of country land, total price $4,500, that I still think is a good buy. The broker ran a small grocery store and sold insurance and real estate on the side. He has a state license, but I don't think he belongs to the Real Estate Board. How can you tell?

"He has gone bankrupt and I have lost my deposit. I realize it's a little late to ask for advice, but I wanted to have some reassurance before giving another broker a deposit. How can I avoid an unreliable broker in the future?"

Editor Donald Hansen of *Buildings* magazine has sent me the *Official Roster of Realtors,* listing the name of every bona-fide realtor in the United States. Your broker's name is not included among those in Massachusetts. You are right, therefore, in thinking he does not belong to the Real Estate Board. If he had been a realtor you probably would have been spared your discouraging experience. Most states are tightening their realty licensing laws; in California they are fairly strict. Unfortunately Massachusetts and some other states have blanketed in an ungainly crew of untrained practitioners as real-estate brokers.

When my wife and I visited the Massachusetts Real Estate Association office in Boston, we were advised by executive vice president Ray Hofford and research director Frank Mann that many nonrealtor licensed brokers are sadly uneducated. Not long ago, Massachusetts allowed any crossroads filling-station operator, grocer, fisher, farmer or tinkerer to sell real estate without any study or special qualifications. Today, examinations are conducted before licenses are granted to new realty salesmen or brokers, but even the tightened laws permit any of the former unqualified licensees to keep puttering around with real-estate sales. Many of them are afraid to write up a contract involving a simple sale without consulting a lawyer.

The foregoing criticism made by Boston realtors paints a somewhat biased picture in favor of members. However, my personal investigations showed that the realtors' statements were not exaggerated. For the greater protection of clients a board member includes the word "realtor" in his advertising, on his stationery and in his place of business.

In most states it is general practice and law that earnest-money deposits to buy property must be placed in a special trust account that the broker cannot draw from for personal expenditures. If you have qualms about future transactions, you can make your deposit check payable to the title company or attorney who will be handling your real-estate escrow.

### Where Can I Find Rehabilitation-Minded Brokers?

Steve Blauner writes from New York City, "Are there any real-estate brokers in the metropolitan New York area or in New Jersey or Connecticut who lean toward, or concentrate in, realty subject to rehabilitation? Where could I look for them to latch onto, particularly for starters?"

Dr. Cecil Bowlby asks, "How can I find a rehabilitation-minded broker in Des Moines, Iowa?"

Newspaper ads covering the communities which interest you list the brokers who advertise apartments, including property needing rehabilitation. An ad which appeals to you usually leads to a broker who has a number of unadvertised properties of a similar nature.

On recent trips to New York, my wife and I noticed that newspapers in outlying areas carried a fair number of for-sale ads. The New York *Times,* on the other hand, had a limited number of ads in proportion to the properties for sale. Brokers in New York City tend to keep listings in their offices and do not advertise them as heavily as do brokers in other parts of the country. Some brokers told me that advertising was unnecessary, because they were approached by plenty of buyers. Others said that owners asked them not to advertise—their prices might raise a red flag at the rent control office and stir up agitation among tenants.

You might find it advisable to ask realtors in the neighborhoods that interest you about listings in your shopping range. Other sources that may be helpful are:

Local borough, city, county or area real-estate boards
Apartment or other property owners' associations
Contractors' associations
Home builders' associations
Telephone and city directories.

### Are There Similar Sources in Iowa and Elsewhere?

Property manager Wilma Hefti of Des Moines served as a panelist on a round-table discussion of "Modernization and Rehabilitation" at the National Realtors' convention in Dallas when I lectured there. She stated, "Older buildings must be modernized in order to compete with new construction for tenants at profitable rents."

Many hundreds of realtors representing all parts of the country attended the Dallas seminar. All of them advocate modernization and rehabilitation of properties. They and like-minded realtors can be found in Des Moines and other cities by checking the sources mentioned for New York.

### Are Realty Commissions Sacrosanct?

After my lecture before the Fresno, California, Medical Auxiliary, Helen Matlock asked, "Are real-estate commissions subject to change, or are they sacrosanct? My husband, Wilson, figures certain medical charges for office calls, operations and so forth. There are certain standard fees recommended by the Medical Association.

But charges vary some according to circumstances. Is this true with real-estate fees?"

No. Real-estate boards establish recommended commission rates; they have gone from 5 per cent to 6 per cent for lower-priced sales in a good part of the country. These rates are usually based on a sliding scale; they tend to get lower on costlier sales. Realty boards have been rigid about asking members to hold to their rates. However, the legality of enforcing these rates has been challenged. There is some deviation, as there is with medical fees.

When a realtor sells at a price approximating the market value, he expects the full commission, which he has earned. However, if he brings a reduced offer to a seller, especially if the reduction is severe, he may share in the price cutting by discounting his commission. This often happens at one end or another of a trade where values have been inflated. Usually the broker's discount is not apparent on paper. He may take a piece of property or a note, or both, at somewhat ballooned values for all or part of his commission.

I traded a Santa Cruz County resort cabin as down payment on a twenty-eight-unit apartment house in Sacramento. Jim Bequette of Coldwell, Banker and Company's Sacramento office represented me, and Jim Claitor of the same firm's San Francisco office represented the apartment sellers. The two salesmen and their superiors agreed to take the cabin as their commission on the deal, splitting the ownership three ways, with their company as third owner. They subsequently sold the cabin, taking back a mortgage. The ownership of this too was shared by the company and the two salesmen, who later opened their own brokers' offices.

Brokers may discount notes taken as commission for cash, or they may hold them until they are paid out. After Bequette opened his own realty office, with his wife, Marguerite, and his brother Al, he accepted $1,000 cash and a $3,000 note as full commission on another deal I made. The note could have been discounted to obtain cash, but the broker held it until it was paid in full at the end of two years.

Realtor John Grimes of Southfield, Michigan, tells of working out an exchange of a $16,500 property, involving an $8,500 home and nine lots, for two land contracts. One was for $10,500 on the home and lots, and the other was for $6,000 on a different piece of property. The broker took a 6 per cent mortgage as his entire fee. Although the face value represented the full recommended Board commission, Grimes indicates that the cash value was 20 to 25 per cent less.

Sometimes commission arrangements get complicated by combinations of cash, notes and property. This happens especially on trades, where more than one property is subject to a commission, and where more than one broker may be participating. According to their report in the *California Real Estate Magazine,* realtors Richard Smith and Leo Bonetti of San Jose's Stevens Creek Realty accepted their full $12,000 commission on an exchange deal as follows: $4,300 in cash from one trader; $300 cash from the other trader; a $5,700 note and second deed of trust on a ranch, with one-half undivided interest to each broker; and a $2,000 note and second deed of trust on an apartment house.

### Should I Change Brokers When I Resell?

After my lecture to the Honolulu Realty Board, a charming but irate realtor with fire in her eyes, Dorothy Tyrrell, charged, "I just lost a good client because of your book. I found him a good apartment buy. After he fixed it up and was ready to sell for a good profit I asked for the listing. He quoted your book and said everything in it had worked out so far and he was going to follow it to the letter and change brokers in order to sell. Why did you write that the realtor you buy from is not the one to sell your property?"

This advice is based on my own experience and that of others I know of. Some salesmen have the imagination to appreciate the resale value of improved property they originally sold in run-down condition at a low price, but a different salesman is more likely to give a true appraisal of increased values. Some brokers keep reminding you of the price you paid, in an attempt to pull your resale price down. Some give no consideration to the money and time you've spent on improving the property and operations.

Some unimaginative brokers have a mania for keeping track of original costs. I know one who spends 90 per cent of his time checking courthouse records daily and writing meticulously in his huge file of every property selling price in his metropolis. If he spent half as much energy on selling as he does on record-keeping he might be a millionaire.

With income property, the chief measure of value is the present income, regardless of whether original costs were greater or less. Original costs have little to do with present market values. As an example, do you suppose that a prospector for gold, diamonds, uranium or oil should be paid on the basis of his original investment for his gear?

On one side of the scale, I know of resort properties with real castles that originally cost millions of dollars to build. They are virtually worthless today except for nominal junk and land values, because they pay no income.

On the other side, the classic example is Manhattan Island. Should it be valued at $24 today because that was Peter Minuit's original purchase price in baubles and sundries? To establish property value you have to account for three general factors:

Improvement of the individual property toward its highest-paying use

Area or city growth and development

General economic growth and inflation.

I tell investors that the original broker should be given first consideration for his services, but should not be considered indispensable. If the selling broker is open-minded enough to appreciate present values, regardless of cost, he should be given a chance to prove himself. Also, the selling broker might be given a resale listing and another salesman in his office may take as fresh a look at values as a new broker. The broker who sold you the property originally could do as well as anyone else at listing on a multiple basis. This practice of giving the pertinent sales information to all participating realtors in the area is growing more common.

### Should I Give an Exclusive Listing?

This is a question often asked by sellers and traders. A utility company secretary writes from Baltimore, "A year and a half ago I gave a six months' exclusive listing to sell my home. The broker didn't do a thing until a couple of weeks before the listing ran out. Then he put a small ad in the paper. By then I got desperate and accepted a sacrifice offer. I took the cash and bought a duplex, which I fixed up. Can sell at a $3,500 profit, but I want to trade for a larger apartment building. Another broker insists I give an exclusive listing before he will work on the property. What do you advise?"

It's all right to give an exclusive when you want to sell. Otherwise most brokers won't advertise your property. But don't make it too long. Some brokers ask for as much as a year. The longer the term, the greater their tendency to let properties sit unattended, like yours, till the expiration date approaches. Sixty to ninety days is usually time enough for an alert realtor who really wants to work at selling. Get as much of a commitment as possible in writing as to advertising and promotion. If your broker advertises and otherwise actively tries to sell your property, you should expect to renew the listing if it expires before a sale is made. In some cities a certain specified minimum period, such as 120 days, may be required as a condition of listing your property on the multiple mart, a usually desirable practice.

A trade usually works out best if you shop for the property you want and then offer your duplex as down payment. Your broker may need a listing in order to work out a three-way trade, or to consummate an exchange in other ways. Such a consideration should be incorporated in the listing instructions, including, for example,

"To be sold only in order to consummate trade for 10410 B Boulevard apartments."

Where you list your property for trade purposes it usually works out best to keep it on an open rather than exclusive basis. That way you will be free to shop for advertised properties. With each ad you answer that leads to a suitable realtor, you can give the realtor an open listing on the basis of trading for a property that meets with your approval.

## Why Don't Brokers Snap Up All the Good Buys?

This question was asked by Dr. Lucy Ma soon after she and her secretary had decorated my wife and me with leis at the Honolulu airport. They greeted us on our flight back from a lecture to Hilo realtors. Dr. Ma's question covers a common misconception; I have heard it repeatedly at many lectures, including one I made to the Santa Monica Apartment Owners' Association. Honolulu's leading obstetrician was about to conclude negotiations on an advantageous commercial property. She said, "Before I sign the papers I feel I must ask you a question. Don't you think there must be something wrong with this property? Realty Board President Philip Won knows about it. If it's as good as it looks, why doesn't he or the realtor handling it buy the property?"

I told Dr. Ma, "There are many reasons for selling good properties. Each purchase has to be desirable to the buyer, or he wouldn't take it. Your specialty is delivering babies. For various reasons some very desirable infants are put out for adoption. What if you were asked, 'Why don't you keep all these adorable babies yourself when the mother puts them in your care, instead of placing them for adoption?' It's just as unreasonable and as physically impossible to expect the approximately one hundred thousand realtors in the United States to personally take over the more than seventy billion dollars in annual realty transactions. That would amount to an investment of seven hundred thousand apiece per year."

### Why Don't More Real-Estate Men Buy and Invest?

This question was asked by Bob Merrick of Houston's KPRC-TV when I appeared on his *Midnight with Marietta* show.

Most real-estate salesmen are trained to sell property as brokers, not to buy it. The average salesman hasn't the means or the inclination to invest. The average realtor, unless he specializes in apartment sales, is not familiar with apartment operations and investment potentialities. He passes the seller's information on to prospective buyers and leaves the good buys for the investor.

Many realtors are discouraged from investment because of the possibility of greatly increased taxes compared with nonbroker investors. Brokers are under a heavy burden of proof to show that investment is not a part of their business, in which case turnover profits are subject to ordinary income taxes rather than the reduced capital-gains taxes.

Some realtors, such as the firm of Coldwell, Banker, which operates throughout California, forbid their salesmen to buy their own listed properties. Other realtors and their salesmen make apartment investments, however, and this can turn them into better-qualified brokers. Still, such brokers can purchase only a small percentage of total investments. There are plenty of good buys for everyone in a continually expanding market.

### Can I Find an Apartment Buy in San Francisco?

This question was asked by Mel Venter when I was interviewed on his KTVU-TV show, *I Want to Know*. A leading San Francisco attorney commented, "I suppose you can find good buys across the bay, but none in San Francisco." Similarly, in other cities I've heard people suggest that no good buys are available in their area, although they may be found elsewhere.

You can find good buys if you study ads placed by realtors and follow up their listings. A roster sent me by Albert Wray, managing editor of the *California Real Estate Magazine,* indicates that San Francisco has 2,468 realtors and associates. As in any other city, realtors have to make sales in addition to managing property and handling leases in order to stay in business. Recorded title changes show a continuing turnover in San Francisco apartments.

A San Francisco realtor, David Goodwin of the statewide William Goodwin Company, told me in a recent letter that his organization had made the following sales and trades in the San Francisco Bay area in one year:

San Francisco:
　　Geary near 45th Avenue, 4 units—$41,000
　　Bush near Powell, 42 units—$350,000
　　Francisco near Bay (trade), 12 units—$155,000
　　Post near Leavenworth, 113 units—$712,000
Oakland:
　　College near Lawton, 9 units—$112,000
　　27th near Foothill (trade), 36 units—$300,000
Berkeley:
　　Hilgard near Scenic, 15 units—$110,000.

Goodwin writes, "Some sellers have depreciated older buildings to the vanishing point and can get more depreciation to offset income only by trading for more modern and valuable buildings. Others have built up their estates to where they no longer need the additional income from operating apartments. They can enjoy all the steady income they want by selling and earning the interest on loans carried back. Capital gains are spread out and higher prices obtained by selling for 29 per cent down or less.

"The Geary Street property was resold in one year for $49,000, after the exterior was painted at a cost of $1,000.

"The 42 units on Bush Street were resold in one year for $600,-000, almost double the previous year's purchase price. The first buyers increased the annual net income from approximately $30,-000 to $60,000. This was achieved by making the kind of improvements recommended in your book: painting the exterior and interior, modernizing kitchens and bathrooms, putting in new furniture and changing the management.

"The College near Lawton property was resold by our firm in one year for $130,000.

"In addition to the above, here are examples of San Francisco buys that we recently negotiated:

Bush near Hyde (trade), 13 units—$112,000
25th near Lake, 12 units—$275,000
Vallejo near Steiner, 11 units—$105,000."

Similar examples are mentioned by representative realtors in every major city. The Julius Kislak organization in Jersey City, a leading New Jersey realtor, reports that in a twelve-month period the firm sold 165 apartment houses with a total value of $45 million.

### Can an Alien Get a Broker's License?

Several aliens have asked this question, including Dimitri Papadopolous from Greece, Kiku Mitsubashi from Japan and Jesus Hernandez from Mexico. All three have advised that when they applied for real-estate broker's licenses they were turned down because they are aliens.

A 1974 U.S. Supreme Court ruling holds that such state laws discriminating against aliens are unconstitutional. The door is now open for qualified aliens to obtain a real-estate broker's license in any state, provided they meet other legitimate, nondiscriminatory requirements.

# X

## Do I Always Need a Lawyer to Deal in Real Estate?

I have been asked many questions about the need for an attorney in connection with rental operations and turnover transactions. A somewhat ticklish query, in view of the audience, came up following my lecture to the national convention of trial lawyers in Denver. A Philadelphia attorney asked, "Do you think a lawyer is always needed to prepare a trade or sales contract?"

No. A qualified realtor is perfectly capable of filling out standard approved exchange or purchase contract forms. He is licensed to do so by his state government.

According to Camden, New Jersey, realtor, C. Armel Nutter, the National Association of Realtors, of which he was president, has participated for years in the National Conference of Realtors and Lawyers; and both his group and the American Bar Association have approved the Conference agreement which states that realtors are qualified to prepare approved contracts and other standard legal forms used by a broker in transacting his business.

### Can a Qualified Realtor Handle Most Realty Contracts?

Yes, providing he is a "qualified realtor," a bona-fide member of his local realty board. Many salesmen and brokers, such as the inept old-timers who were given blanket licenses under Massachusetts license laws, lack the training to prepare even a simple sales contract. They need a lawyer to complete the most routine transaction. Most of the questions raised by buyers or sellers concerning the preparation of documents can be straightened out by a title company if one is used. This highly recommended practice is almost universal in the West and is rapidly spreading eastward. If there is ever any doubt, however, as to the ability of a broker or the legality of a contract, then it is wise to check with an attorney versed in real-estate law.

When any question of a legal nature arises that varies from the straightforward buying, selling or trading of property, it makes good sense to consult a lawyer. An example of unusual matters that an attorney should handle is a transaction involving property tied up in an estate or in the process of being liquidated as part of a divorce settlement.

An estranged Philadelphia couple owned an apartment house valued at $155,000; it carried a $62,000 mortgage. They listed their building with a realtor, agreeing to take other income property in trade. The main stipulation was that all acquired properties must be subject to equal division, with neither spouse gaining an advantage. The imaginative realtor worked out a trade with a happily married couple who desired to consolidate their scattered investments—five different parcels, including two duplexes, one fourplex and two pieces of commercial property.

There was considerable give-and-take in computing the respective net equities in the various properties—that is, the values over and above the outstanding mortgages. It was finally agreed that the estranged couple had an equity of $7,750 more than the happy couple. This difference was equalized when the apartment sellers took back a $7,750 second mortgage, which they turned over to the realtor as their part of his commission. The husband took the fourplex and one commercial property. The wife took the remaining commercial property and the two duplexes, one of which she planned to live in.

None of the parties had to put up any cash to pay commissions. The realtor agreed to take an increase of $8,600 in the second mortgage on the apartment house to cover the commission owed him by the happily married couple.

The realtor was perfectly capable of filling out the necessary exchange papers. It was necessary for an attorney to draw up legal-settlement papers between the husband and wife and file these with the court as part of the divorce proceedings.

## What Real-Estate Course Did You Take?

Dr. L. Schecter of Dallas, Texas, writes, "Was the real-estate law course you took and recommend in your book a business-law course or a law-school course? Do you have sample forms of the necessary bookkeeping data—ledgers, leases, etc.—that you could mail me (postpaid) and that I could turn over to my printer?"

The course I studied was conducted by Assistant District Attorney (now judge) William Brailsford in an Oakland, California, public business-school evening class. Your local real-estate board can undoubtedly tell you about the availability of similar courses that you can take in your local schools or neighborhood. The course I took was designed for real-estate salesmen and brokers. The final exams were California state tests for a broker's license. Many of the students became brokers. I completed the tests satisfactorily, but did not apply for a license and have always retained the status of an investor.

Also, courses in real-estate law may be given by a school that specializes in real estate, a business college, or a law school. Any such courses should cover the information you will want for investment purposes; they are not designed to make a lawyer out of you. However, they are useful in that they inform you of legal points involving real estate that may protect your interests and help you avoid lawsuits. A rudimentary legal knowledge helps in making contracts and dealing with tenants on a sound basis. In my first book I covered the legal information I consider essential for average operations.

Sometimes I have been asked about the sample forms included

in my book. They were developed for my personal use, and although they have not been printed for distribution as yet, some consideration has been given to arranging for such service for those who request it. Meanwhile, Simon and Schuster and I are glad to give you permission to copy any forms in the book as long as they are for your own use and not for resale.

### What Do Lawyers Say?

I have lectured to lawyers and have received a number of interesting letters and queries from them. There have been gratifying compliments too. Attorney Olan Lowrey of Houston, Texas, writes, "I have found your book to be extraordinarily reliable." Another attorney said, after a lecture, "Your book makes so many unequivocal statements of fact and opinion that I was challenged to go through it with a fine-tooth comb, looking for flaws. I must say I couldn't find a single statement that didn't stand up under inspection."

Attorney-accountant Hubert Howes of North Canton, Ohio, writes, "Your book ties everything together and shows how to apply your past-gained knowledge today. Every accountant and attorney who has a client with rental properties should read your book. Not only that, but your book shows every attorney and accountant with investment capital where to put it to work.

"I should be in the position to start on the road to realty riches in about a year, and believe me, when I am, I'll be off with a bang. I have clients who are in the position to go and should have been going years ago. The information I got from your book is starting these clients to move."

A lawyer from northern California writes, "I paid $25,000 for some duplex units, cleaned and repainted inside and outside and eighteen months later sold at a profit of $22,000.

"The information you give in your book on the handling of tax matters on income property is very valuable. One question I would like to ask is whether you have had any experience in the matter of trading vacant lots for an apartment house. Do you know whether the Internal Revenue Service will accept such a trade without my paying a capital-gains tax? I own fifty-seven lots in northern California. Have you any suggestions regarding the tax angles on selling or trading them? I plan to trade for a thirty-unit apartment house."

It is my observation that the Internal Revenue Service accepts nontaxable exchanges of almost any kind of real estate, subject, of course, to many ramifications. Exchanging vacant lots for an apartment house may be tax-free as long as the lots have been held for investment purposes. I have made such tax-free trades, and they have been approved on audit.

You should have no tax problem if you can exchange the entire property in one transaction for an apartment house, or can trade substantial portions. You should guard against disposing of more than five parcels in separate transactions within a five-year period, as six sales in the same tract normally mark you as a dealer rather than an investor. A dealer is deprived of favorable capital-gains treatment and must pay full income tax rates on turnover profits.

### Should I Get a Lawyer or a Realtor to Settle Condemnation Separation?

A Midwestern farmer phoned long distance to ask, "Shouldn't I get a bonus from the government for cutting my farm in half? They're taking half of my twelve-hundred-acre farm for a missile site. They're paying me the going land price, but no bonus. My son at Iowa State College says I'm entitled to a bonus because my farm with all the equipment and everything is set up for twelve-hundred-acre operation. Should I get me a lawyer or a real-estate appraiser to protect my rights?"

You probably could use both a realtor-appraiser and a lawyer. You are not necessarily entitled to a bonus just because your land is reduced by half. It has to be established that there is a relative loss of value in the remaining acreage because of reduced efficiency.

Your nearest real-estate board can recommend a qualified M.A.I. (Member, Appraisal Institute) realtor, who will charge a reasonable fee to appraise your claim. He will determine your value before the condemnation and the value of the remaining acreage afterward, based on the highest and best use and efficiency before and after.

An M.A.I. should be qualified to testify in court for you as an expert witness. If he concludes that you have a bonus coming, and the government disagrees, you will need a trial lawyer to handle your claim in court. Many trial lawyers will agree to charge a fee on such a claim for damages only if you win, on a so-called "contingency basis." If your case is lost, you pay no fee. If you win you pay a percentage of the awarded damages. Percentages vary, depending to some extent on local customs and the amounts involved. They generally run from a range of 33⅓ per cent on cases settled out of court to 50 per cent on cases that go to court.

### Is the Owner Responsible for Equipment Ordered by a Tenant?

A number of apartment owners have raised questions regarding an owner's responsibility for unauthorized equipment ordered by a tenant. Bee Mueller of Sacramento, California, for example, tells of one of her tenants who, without authorization from her, ordered a room air conditioner installed. Later he moved out, leaving the equipment unpaid for. The appliance store sent a bill to her, the owner, threatening to place a lien on the property if she didn't pay. Is the owner responsible in such a case?

No, not when it involves a removable appliance, such as a room air conditioner, that is installed for convenience and is not a matter of a needed repair. On the other hand, unless there is a lease provision to the contrary, the owner would normally be responsible for repairing necessary equipment, such as a water heater. If such equipment breaks down or stops operating, the tenant would be obliged to notify the owner and give him a chance to repair or replace it. What if the owner does not remedy the breakdown within a reasonable time? Then the tenant would be justified in ordering a repair or replacement, and in such a case the owner would be liable for payment.

Even though no emergency repair or replacement is involved, some appliance dealers might try to bluff the owner as the one mentioned above did. They may be under the false impression that the owner has authorized such a purchase, and may turn such a claim over to an attorney. The attorney is apt to inform the owner by letter of the information given by his client. If a contest appears inevitable an apartment owner should have an attorney defend him. However, an owner who feels his case is clear-cut should first contact the claimant attorney and state his position. I know of many cases where conscientious attorneys have advised their clients to drop dubious claims.

My own experience bears this out. One of my tenants once ordered a forty-gallon water heater without my authorization, then moved away without paying for it. It appeared that the tenant had told the appliance dealer that I would pay. My first knowledge of the matter came when I received a registered letter from a law firm containing a bill for $139.82 and the following message:

I would like to take this opportunity to inform you that on behalf of our client, ——— Plumbing Company, we have placed and recorded a mechanic's lien on your property located at ———. This lien was placed as the result of labor and materials furnished in the installation of a forty-gallon hot-water heater at the request of one ———. This lien is in the amount of $139.82. Unless we hear from you within the next seven days in regard to this matter, we shall be forced to commence foreclosure proceedings under this lien.

Following is my reply, which disposed of the only nuisance claim of this nature I've ever received:

It appears your client has possibly labored under a misapprehension regarding his bill, which you mention. At no time have I ever authorized this company to perform work reported by them at my ———

property. It would seem that they should be aware of this, as at no time prior to this have I received a bill from them for such work.

As I understand it, a tenant in the single-family cottage at this address, ———, who has since vacated the premises, placed an order with your client to disconnect my operating twenty-gallon hot-water heater and connect a forty-gallon heater for his convenience to facilitate use of his privately owned automatic washer and dryer. At no time was any emergency involved, as the twenty-gallon heater operated perfectly and is still operating in good condition.

When the tenant moved he arranged to reconnect my twenty-gallon heater that had been left on the premises, and disconnect the forty-gallon heater belonging to your client. He left the forty-gallon heater temporarily stored, disconnected, at the premises. If your client wishes, he may take possession of same upon giving a receipt for it to my resident manager in the adjoining apartment house, at ———.

Any further claims by your client against my former tenant, ———, should be addressed to him at his new address, since he is no longer a resident of my property.

The plumbing company picked up the water heater and gave the manager a receipt for it. That's the last I heard of the matter.

### Is the Tenant Liable for Attorney's Fees?

Insurance agency owner Robert Briggs writes from Eugene, Oregon, "In your rental contract, as shown in the book, you include the provision whereby the tenant pays for attorney's fees in enforcing any provision within the contract. From a legal standpoint, have you been able to enforce this provision in the state of California?"

Yes. I've enforced it the few times it was necessary, and so have other rental owners using similar lease clauses. Courts have not questioned the legality of such a provision as long as it is included in a written lease. If it is not, tenants may be liable for court costs, but not for attorney's fees. This added expense in case of court action helps persuade obstreperous tenants to pay fair claims before going to court. The more expense they may be liable for, the more likely are they to settle before incurring the added costs.

## What If I Agree to Buy, Then Find a Better Bargain?

Once about midnight an agitated newspaperwoman phoned long distance from Pasadena. She said she had signed a sales agreement to buy a duplex. It looked like a fair buy and she had put down a $1,000 deposit. Then another broker, whom she had contacted previously, called to her attention a fourplex he had just listed. It cost almost the same as the duplex, and she considered it a much better buy. She asked, "How can I cancel the duplex contract and buy the fourplex?"

My questioning revealed that the sellers of the duplex were out of town and were returning the next day. They had not yet accepted the offer. My caller had told the duplex salesman to cancel because she had changed her mind. She had not mentioned the fourplex. He had told her she could not cancel until after the thirty-day period stipulated in the contract for acceptance by the sellers. After some second thoughts and rereading portions of my book, the newspaperwoman had decided to phone me, hoping I would give some helpful advice. I told her the following:

The California Real Estate Law, with which all licensed brokers should be familiar, provides that you can cancel your offer at any time prior to its acceptance by the sellers. Once they accept, you are bound by the terms of the offer. The salesman was probably trying to reassure you. A lot of buyers, especially novices, get cold feet after making an offer, even on a real bargain.

If this is your wish, feel free to wake the salesman up immediately. Tell him you're withdrawing your offer because you have found a better bargain. If you have any further problems, you should consult an attorney.

## Is the Buyer Released by a Counteroffer?

A question of similar nature came from a San Francisco school-teacher, who wanted to back out of purchasing a single-family home. She had made a $500 deposit which would constitute her full down payment. Since making the offer on the house she had read my book, had decided to buy a duplex instead and had found a desirable one near her school. She planned to live in one half and rent the other, which would carry all expenses, giving her, rent-free, a more desirable dwelling than she could otherwise afford. Questioning brought out that the home sellers had accepted the price the teacher offered. However, they had stipulated that their acceptance was "subject to payment of additional $500, making total of $1,000 down."

Any change in your offered terms constitutes a counteroffer. This frees you to reject the whole deal if you desire. Tell the salesman you have decided to cancel and are going to buy a duplex instead.

## What If I Agree to Sell, Then Get a Better Offer?

This question came up following my lecture to the Portland Apartment Owners' Association: "My wife and I agreed to sell our apartment house for $86,500. The next week another buyer offered $90,000, including more cash down and assured financing. The first buyer had asked for sixty days to obtain his financing, and is having difficulties. He says he still wants the property, but his financing looks doubtful. Does this free us to take the better offer?"

Questions like this should be referred to a real-estate attorney. The legal answer would depend on the exact statements made and the specific wording of the sales agreement. However, I'm glad to offer general observations based on my experience and study.

Once you sign a contract agreeing to sell, you are bound to wait out its terms, even though it may appear that the deal won't go through. What if the buyer states positively that he cannot go through with the deal because required financing is unobtainable? At that point the buyer should be asked to sign a written statement confirming the facts, whereupon the deal can be considered as canceled. The buyer has the property tied up for as long a period as the contract stipulates, even though he may express pessimism about getting the financing he needs.

It often happens that once an agreement of sale has been signed another legitimate buyer shows up. The property somebody else wants always looks more attractive than a property nobody else wants. The second buyer, unwilling to wait sixty days for the agreement of sale to expire, may look for another property. To hold on to the second customer, try to take a deposit from him and tie him up on a sales contract that reads, "Subject to seller being able to obtain release within sixty days of existing sales agreement, selling to John Doe." Then, if the first buyer fails to consummate the deal in sixty days, the seller can proceed automatically with completion of the sale to the second buyer. A comparatively small bonus, such as $1,000, may influence a questionable buyer to release a deal—a good investment for the seller if he can make, for example, $10,000 more from a second buyer.

## Am I Liable to Prospective Buyer for Refusing to Sell?

Jane Robertson phoned from San Francisco with this story: "I manage a twenty-unit apartment house on Russian Hill. Two sons, aged twenty-one and twenty-six, inherited the property from their father. They figured on selling and reinvesting in other property and signed an exclusive listing to sell for two hundred thousand dollars. Now that the broker has come up with a buyer in short order, the boys have looked around a bit. They haven't found other property they like as well and have decided not to sell. The broker says if they don't sign the sales agreement they're liable to the buyer for damages for not fulfilling the listing agreement. Are they liable to the prospective buyer for refusing to sell?"

No. There is no obligation to the buyer until a sales agreement is signed. After that the buyer has a claim for damages if the deed and other necessary papers are not signed.

But the boys are liable to the broker for his commission. I would recommend that they consider fully whether it may be more advisable to sell after all. The fact that the broker came up with a buyer so soon doesn't mean it isn't a fair deal. They could wait a long time and not do as well. If the boys don't plan to improve the property and the new buyer does, this could be a good deal for both parties. The boys may not be able to improve on it for their particular interests and circumstances. If they definitely determine not to sell and the broker presents a bona-fide offer under the terms of the listing, the law in California and other states provides that they are liable to the broker for the sales commission he would have made if the property sold.

One point to bear in mind is that the owner is not liable to the broker except in the case of a complete, bona-fide offer for the full amount and with all terms as cited in the listing, and with a sufficient deposit to constitute earnest money, not just a token payment. An offer for less than the full amount and terms does not obligate the seller if he decides to reject it.

### Would It Be Advisable to Insert Loophole Clauses?

Donald Wahle of Cincinnati, Ohio, writes, "In your chapter entitled 'How to Make a Three-Way Trade' you give five steps which, if followed, will almost always make possible a three-way trade. I find one disturbing question, which is this: Would it not possibly be catastrophic if you were caught in a situation where the second party refused to follow your plans and you were forced to either lose your deposit or pay the tax on your accumulated gains if you went ahead and closed the deal?

"Would it be advisable to close up this loophole by inserting a clause in your purchase agreement which reads, 'Subject to seller accepting a three-way trade or paper trade whereby the deed of seller's property be exchanged for the deed of the buyer's property and then the seller takes the proceeds from the sale of his newly acquired deed to the third party'?

"If an offer was accepted with this clause inserted, there would be no chance of losing the possibility of a trade."

A clause such as you suggest might well be inserted. Every broker is apt to use different wording in the preparation of a contract. The objective is to be as simple as possible in order to avoid misunderstandings. Concerning the purpose you have in mind, the seller is already committed to deed his property to the buyer. Therefore you might simplify the wording to read, "Subject to seller's taking title to buyer's property, the Belvedere Apartments, and being able to sell said property."

I would avoid any reference in the contract to "paper trades," for income tax reasons. Such wording makes the transaction more subject to questions as being a nontaxable exchange. An exchange agreement would normally be used to make an offer involving a three-way trade, and the standard wording should provide for an exchange of deeds.

The Giacolinis mentioned in my first book were allergic to trades, having turned down previous exchange offers for the Cynthia Court Apartments. The story about them followed the intricacies of turning a trade-resistant seller into a trader, to the point where an exchange agreement could be prepared. Such a seller would have good reason not to sign papers when the property was not ultimately sold as contracted for. However, it would be unusual to refuse to co-operate in the preliminary paperwork which brought the contracted results. The original exchange of deeds would be held in escrow by the title company until after the buyer's B Boulevard property had been sold to a third party. Thus the seller of the Cynthia Court would have no valid reason to refuse to sign.

## When Can You Insert Stipulations in a Contract?

W. L. Montgomery of Forth Worth, Texas, writes, "On page 81 of your book and in the paragraph entitled 'You May Stipulate as

Many Inspections as You Wish,' you stated that after the previous provisions had been made one could feel safe to go ahead and make an offer. The question I would like to ask is this: When would a person have an opportunity to insert the other stipulations he might wish to place in the offer contract?"

The stipulations you want inserted would normally be included with your original offer. However, if you find reasons for further stipulations, they may be added later, at any time before the offer is accepted by the seller. Once the purchase contract is accepted by the seller, you would be bound by the written arrangements. The contract could then be changed only by mutual agreement between buyer and seller.

### Should I Sue for Lost Potential Profit When Seller Can't Convey Good Title?

Sue Balfiori phoned excitedly from Sacramento with the following story: "I'm a divorcee who has to watch my money. I found a honey of a two-story fourplex near the Sutter Hospital in a commercial zone. All it needs is paint to make it worth a lot more. I planned to live in one of the downstairs flats and set up a beauty parlor in the front living room. I figured I could make a real good profit. The owner signed an agreement to sell at my price. Now, the fly in the ointment is, the fourplex is tied up in such a way that the owner can't give me a clear title. I'm a redhead and believe in fighting for my rights. What I want to know is, should I sue for the profit I would have made if the deal had gone through?"

The usual sales agreement calls for returning the deposit and canceling the contract if a title cannot be cleared within a specified time. Evidently the seller acted in good faith and ran into hard luck. In any event, it is doubtful that a court would award damages for profits you cannot prove, even though you have every expectation of making them.

I'd forget the deal and take my deposit back. Lawsuits can waste a lot of time; I'd spend it looking for another property. In less time than it takes to sue, you are almost sure to find another deal you will like just as well or perhaps even better.

This story has an epilogue that proved my point in a different way than visualized. A few months later the divorcee phoned me again. "I'm at the San Francisco International Airport. I want you to know how happy I am for your advice not to sue, and to spend my time looking for a better deal. The fourplex owner thought I was so nice about losing his place that he started courting me. We just got married. My husband and I both want to thank you for your part in our happiness. We're waiting for our plane to take us on our honeymoon to Hawaii."

## Why Won't Lawyers Give You a Straight "Yes" or "No"?

"Whenever I ask my lawyer for a straight 'yes' or 'no' he beats around the bush," writes Ronald Stratemaier of Montreal, Canada. "Why won't he give me a clear-cut answer like you do in your books?"

Even competent attorneys hate to answer a straight "yes" or "no" on a legal question, because they are well trained in all the imponderable "ifs" and "supposes" that might influence a specific situation. And then, even though the law may clearly favor one side, a sympathetic judge may make a contrary ruling because of his personal inclinations or prejudices.

He may favor a litigant who strikes his fancy even though that position is unquestionably opposed to the clear-cut law. And most of these anti-legal decisions are seldom appealed because of the cost in time and money.

You will find my straightforward answers to legal questions affecting my lifetime field of real-estate investment to be as unequivocably "yes" or "no" as possible because every cited example is based not on theory but on my actual experience or the meticulously verified experiences of others.

# 5

# How
# to Appraise
# Property Values

# XI

## How Can I Tell a Good Deal?

Wherever I've gone I've been asked a number of questions about significant factors to look for, and their meaning, in appraising and buying property.

### Which Gives Truer Value, Gross or Net Income?

Robert Dench writes from Hollywood, "I saw a 'For Sale' ad in the Los Angeles *Times* on a sixteen-unit apartment house. The annual gross income was given at $14,484 and the net at $4,800. Square feet at 11,600.

"The broker said the property was priced at seven times the gross income, which comes to $101,388. I told him your book said you should not pay more than ten times the net, which makes only $48,000. The property is only three years old, and the broker says depreciated cost of building should be about $8 per square foot. This makes approximately $92,800. The lot is worth about $16,-000. Adding this to the depreciated building cost gives you a total reproduction value of $108,800.

"Would you kindly answer one question: Which income figure gives the fair market value, the gross of $101,388 or the net of $48,000?"

Neither the net nor the gross figure given is reliable without more detailed information. The national yardstick, ten times the annual net, with stipulations covering what should be included for income and expense, is recognized by leading realtors from Los Angeles to Boston.

However, there are all kinds of "nets." Some commercial leases provide that the tenant will pay all expenses, including taxes and insurance. By this calculation, the net income is the same as the gross—a graphic demonstration that you have to establish what kind of net you are talking about. The different kinds of rentals— office buildings, industrial properties, hotels, motels, apartments —yield different ratios of income to value. There are varying costs of operations and vacancy factors, as well as widely ranging arrangements on the share of expenses borne by owner or tenant.

The owner of apartments may or may not provide furniture, furnishings, utilities, janitor or maid service; each of these items may make a major difference in the operating costs. The cost of each service included in the rent naturally lowers the net income and also the gross ratio figure.

Some appraisers rightly apply gross ratios as a check, thus arriving at the seven times the gross cited by your broker. This is fairly common practice for certain types of rental property under usual operating conditions in certain areas. The gross-ratio figure of $101,388 seems in line with the estimated reproduction cost of $108,800. Because operating can vary so greatly, gross-income ratios are usually far less accurate than net ratios in establishing fair market values.

In your example, a look at the gross income shows there is something out of line in the net figures. One common rule for checking purposes is to make sure that the net should never (or hardly ever) fall below 50 per cent of the gross. Only actual operating figures showing an excessive number of vacancies could normally produce such a low net in relation to gross. I would guess that the $4,800 quoted is not the net usually figured in arriving at ten times the net to establish a market value. Loan and other payments, such as those for capital expenditures, may be included in the operating expenses. Such payments are usually left out when computing valuations, and are taken into account only when you want to arrive at a "spendable" or "in-pocket" net.

## What Income and Expenses Are Usually Applied to Get 10 Per Cent Net?

This question was asked by realtor Joanne Soviak, following my lecture at Waikiki, Hawaii.

On commercial valuations, the common practice is to figure actual rentals for the previous year or years and deduct the actual total expenses.

The gross income on an apartment valuation is usually based on the rent roll—the market rental value of all apartments on a full-house basis. Actual rent schedules in a building are always used except on completely vacant new construction, where estimates must be based on proposed rents. To determine whether an owner's statement of rental values is high, low or at market levels, check existing rentals in the building and in the neighborhood.

Appraisers for lending institutions usually deduct a certain percentage, ranging from 5 to 10 per cent depending on the area, for estimated vacancies. This deduction is usually added to expense items and should be taken into account when you are figuring in-pocket income. It is not usually applied in figuring ten times the net income. The expenses usually deducted for this purpose include:

Management (including the value of the manager's quarters if they are listed under income)
Property taxes and licenses
Insurance
Utilities included in rents (water, fuel, light, power, sanitation, telephone).

An accepted standard income-and-expense statement is listed on pages 306 and 307 of my first book, covering the Cynthia Court Apartments.

## What Other Expenses Can Be Expected?

This question was asked by James Goodrich of Lazarus Store, Columbus, Ohio, following an autograph party in the store's book department.

Operating costs, such as supplies, repairs, maintenance, and replacement reserves for new equipment and other capital expenditures, are not included in computing the 10 per cent fixed net. When they are included, a different ratio applies; twelve times the net is a figure used by some apartment appraisers. These are all expenditures deducted in order to arrive at net in-pocket income before computing interest and depreciation. The last two items often come close to balancing with net in-pocket income, thus freeing spendable income from income taxes.

## What Is Scavenger Service?

In a letter from Parkchester, New York, Robert McFadden writes, "I find that the majority of people, including young persons, enjoy sitting back and discussing your suggestions. But most of them will never take the chance and do anything about it. My wife and I firmly believe the principles in your book, so we shortly expect to look for our first property.

"You mention scavenger service. This term is unfamiliar to me. Could you please explain it?"

Sanitation service in some cities is called scavenger service in Metropole. These terms for garbage pickup are, possibly, attempts to dignify the occupation, attract prouder workers and justify higher rates. Garbage by any other name does smell sweeter. A wife who would balk at saying, "My husband picks up garbage," might be glad to say, "My husband is in the Sanitation Department. He handles scavenger service."

### How Can You Expect to Earn 20 Per Cent and Sell on the Basis of 10 Per Cent?

Mr. McFadden had a second question: "You also mention that in buying apartment property you should pay about ten times the yearly net income. You state that these earnings are conservative and that most real-estate purchasers expect to earn 15 to 20 per cent. How can you sell or trade on the basis of 10 per cent if most real-estate buyers expect more?"

The figures apply to two different breeds of cats. The 10 per cent net-earnings figure applies to total investment. This is the total market price, including down payment and loans, at which you would buy or sell.

The 20 per cent expected-earnings figure refers to the personal investment, the down payment. In the survey I mentioned in my first book, developers stated they would not go into a real-estate venture unless they expected to earn at least 20 per cent on their personal investment.

### Have You a Special Checklist?

"God bless you for sharing with others the experience and secrets of your rise to a fortune," writes Eugene Henry of Long Beach, California. "I am forty-eight years old and work as a route man, delivering fresh eggs to private homes. I have felt for some time a need for a more realistic financial future, and your book has inspired me to embark on the challenging adventure of pyramiding my savings into a modest retirement sum. In your early practice, did you use any type of checklist for insuring positive analysis and procedure? If you did and such is for sale, I most appreciatively will welcome it."

Quite a number of other correspondents have also asked for a checklist. Interestingly, a heavy percentage of such requests have come from Air Force and civilian pilots. Nearly all the pilots tell of the exhaustive checklists they make before take-offs.

I have used no checklists other than those mentioned in the book. As you shop the market for actual buys you may, perhaps laboriously at first, check off the items that pertain to your particular project. After you have gained experience these items will come to mind almost automatically, so you will be able to readily recognize the earmarks of a good or bad buy. Here is a résumé of major checkpoints:

## PRIMARY APPRAISAL CHECKLIST

PRESENT INCOME

*What is the present gross income?* Are the present rentals on a level with or below the going market for condition and neighborhood?

*What are the present expenses?* Are the usual expenses included and in line? If they are questionable, have expenses been verified?

*What is the present net income?* (Deduct expenses from gross income.)

PRICE

*Is the price good, or at least fair?* Is the price based on present income? (The price should not exceed ten times the present net income.)

FINANCING

*Can the required loans be obtained?* Is the amount of the loans available sufficient to complete purchase with your planned down payment? Are the monthly installments low enough to be paid out of rental income? (The longest possible loan period and the lowest possible interest will be points to check.)

POTENTIAL INCOME

*Can the present net income be increased?* Are market levels already above the present rentals? Can rents be increased by improving operations through better management and advertising? Can the present expenses be decreased by more efficient and streamlined management? Can the physical property be improved to increase the market value a minimum of $2 for each $1 of renovation costs? What will physical improvements cost? What will the fair rental and market values be afterward?

These are the key questions a buyer should have in mind. Even one uneconomical answer, such as an excessive price for the present net income, often eliminates a property without further consideration. For this reason, before looking at a property, insist on seeing an operating statement that shows income and expenses. A glance can often tell whether it will pay to spend further time making a physical inspection.

There are a number of supplemental points to consider before arriving at a final decision. For example, a buy that looks good on paper may turn out to be in the wrong neighborhood for rental housing. Obviously, you'll want to avoid a property near a vinegar works, a tannery or a garbage dump. The same income-and-expense statement on a property in a close-in neighborhood that is on the upgrade, or that is likely to be upgraded soon, would point to a very good buy.

## SUPPLEMENTAL CHECKLIST

NEIGHBORHOOD

*Are the immediate and general neighborhoods good for drawing prospective tenants?* (A good neighborhood is number one in a tenant's desires. This means a neighborhood that looks good in the tenant's eyes. A close-in neighborhood draws tenants, even though some of the other details may be less desirable than those in outlying areas.)

ZONING

*Is the property zoned for the intended use?* If you intend to build or remodel, will there be any zoning problems? (Plans to add apartments, for example, might not be permissible under existing zoning.)

INSPECTIONS AND BUILDING CODES

*Will the property satisfy city, county, state or district inspection codes without prohibitive expense?* (Many cities have passed *post facto* ordinances, some applying only when there is a transfer of ownership.)

CONVENIENCE OF LOCATION

*Are transportation and shopping convenient? Are schools convenient for rentals catering to families with children?*

PHYSICAL ASPECTS OF PROPERTY

*Spaciousness: Are the rooms, plus closets and storage cabinets, large enough to satisfy tenants?* (These details are the strongest desires of tenants after they approve a neighborhood.)

*Are the laundry arrangements satisfactory?*

*Is the room layout convenient?*

*Is there adequate working or eating space in the kitchen?*

*Is the building and lot layout pleasing?* Are there open spaces, desirable landscaping?

*Are the garbage or parking facilities satisfactory?*

*How old are the buildings?* What is their general condition?

REPLACEMENT VALUE

*Is the price lower or no greater than the cost of erecting a similar building in a comparable neighborhood, figuring depreciation?* (Obviously, it pays to find out if you can reproduce for less by buying a lot and erecting a new building.)

MARKET VALUE

*Is the price favorable compared with listings or recent sales of similar properties in the area?*

ITEMIZED CHECK OF IMPROVABILITY

*What is the probable cost of repair, modernization or rehabilitation of:*

*Foundation?*

*Roof, gutters and downspouts?*

*Exterior painting and sealing?*

*Interior painting and papering of walls and ceilings?*

*Floors?*

*Heating and air conditioning?*

*Other plumbing, as in kitchen and bath?*
*Electric fixtures?*

## Do You Expect Every Appraisal Point to Check Out on Each Purchase?

After my San Diego Real Estate Board lecture, Woods Caperton, Jr., of the Percy Goodwin Company said, "I was surprised to see all the items in your appraisal lists. Surely you don't expect every one of them to check out on each purchase, do you?"

No, you're right. Appraisal points would never be 100 per cent affirmative. The sample purchase in the book accepts some items that are marginal or can be corrected. You expect a good percentage. Some things weigh more than others to certain tenants. A close-in neighborhood that has convenient shopping and transportation, for example, might outweigh extensive landscaping and convenient schools in an outlying area if you cater to tenants without children. If your prospective tenants are large families, the reverse would apply.

## How Do You Measure Cubic Feet?

George Robinson writes from Chicago, "I'm thirty-one years old, with a wife and daughter. We heard you on Jack Eigen's radio show the other night. I am going to follow your book like a Bible, and have already begun with the purchase of a two-flat brick building. I would appreciate your answering one question: How do you measure the cubic feet of rooms? I became confused on the problem when I tried to figure it out."

My mother's maiden name was Robinson, so maybe we're third or fourth cousins!

Apartment appraisers usually measure only the square feet, which you find by multiplying the width of the room by the length. If you want the cubic feet, you then multiply the square feet by the height. This last figure is seldom used by appraisers except when there are unusual space conditions, such as in a church. You might want to know the cubic feet for other than appraisal purposes. For example, you might want to determine how much heating capacity, air conditioning or paint is needed.

### Should I Use My Wife's Eyes and Legs?

Carl Karrfalt of Erie, Pennsylvania, writes, "While I'm not in a youthful position, as you were when you started, my wife and I believe we can use your formula to build our future. A couple of deviations from your experience will be necessary because of a personal situation. I have multiple sclerosis and will need to implement the personal inspection of properties you speak of with my wife's eyes and legs. Do you think this will be satisfactory?

"Further, the regular income from a job you mention will have to be implemented by an income from the sale of a number of subdivision lots. It is my opinion that this subdivision places me in a considerably advanced position from the one you described yours to be. Please comment."

You certainly should be able to make sound decisions using your "wife's eyes and legs." My wife did all of our preliminary shopping for property while I was working for the telephone company, leaving final choices for our joint inspection over weekends. Many widows and single women buy and operate income property on their own. Your wife's shopping, in conjunction with discussion and planning with you, should work out fine.

### Can Lot Sales Take the Place of Job Income?

I agree that the potential funds that would be available from selling the lots you mention give you an investment nest egg considerably larger than average. A regular income from a job, plus continued savings, helps to assure progress when one starts out with a small nest egg. However, this is cited only as an example. Your plan to obtain supplemental income from selling lots should put you in an advantageous position.

## Is $12,500 per Unit Too High?

A Santa Cruz County, California, resident writes, "My wife and I had the pleasure of hearing you speak yesterday on San Francisco Town Hall in the Alcazar Theater. I wanted to ask two questions, but there were too many others for me to have the opportunity.

"We have a large equity in a home and eighteen-acre property, and want to trade for an apartment building in a metropolitan area, say San Francisco. In the examples in your book, the average purchase price of the properties was roughly $8,000 per unit. Is it possible to find sound properties at this price now? Would it be unwise to buy property at a higher price, say $12,500 per unit, assuming a total price of ten times the annual net?"

There are many sound properties on the market that can be bought for $8,000 per unit. Newspaper ads and leading realtors carry many listings in this range in the San Francisco area and around the country. A higher price, such as the $12,500 per unit you mention, would not rule out making a good deal. The unit price could be much higher, as long as present income in the range of 10 per cent net and other possibilities are there.

## Is Property Too Young, or Too Old?

Some prospective investors wonder if an apparently good buy is too young, and others whether a property is too old. Jack Steinberg writes about age from Los Angeles: "From my own personal experience with real estate, everything you have written is extremely logical and practical. I've bought and sold a house and a four-rental apartment at a profit. I've just modernized and painted a duplex. It is in tiptop condition now. The rentals and sale value are considerably increased, and I'm working on a trade for an eight-unit building.

"Please answer one question for me about the age of a building: Is a thirty-year-old building too ancient to modernize, and will the repairs and maintenance eat up all the profits?"

There are a lot of choice bargains far older than the one you have been looking at. Rental owners in the East often succeed with buildings that have passed the century mark. For example, Manhattanite William Clifford showed my wife and me his attractive Greenwich Village fourplex apartment building that had been modernized from a 120-year-old house. His wife, Joan, said they loved the convenience of living close in.

When my wife and I were in England, G. C. Dinnis of Eltham, London, showed us some successfully modernized buildings that were several hundred years old. A Manchester, England, correspondent tells of the spectacular profits he earned after following my suggestions for improving flats that were three or four hundred years old. Some looked terribly run-down, with broken windows and rickety front steps. Vandals had wreaked havoc while the dilapidated buildings lay vacant. But the flats were structurally sound, and they were rehabilitated and modernized at nominal cost. Then they were easy to rent.

Age is not so much the criterion as sound basic construction and location. The best rental locations are usually close in, and, unless they are older, can seldom be found in most cities.

### Is Youth a Problem?

A typical question concerning the problems of youth in buildings arose after my Waikiki lecture to the Honolulu Realty Board. Bookseller Harlo Dillingham said, "Here in the youngest state, Hawaii, there is a great deal of expansion and new construction. Are there any opportunities to follow your suggestions by putting up brand-new buildings?"

Yes, you can make good profits by building new, as long as you erect what the public wants in a competitive rental range. My basic thesis is that sound investment profits in real estate are made by improving property. Building from the ground up is one form of property improvement.

However, I recommend an older building with proven rentals for the soundest first buy. The average investor will have a better knowledge of what to build, what to include and what to be on guard against, if he gains experience with an existing structure. Assuming you have the kind of adequate knowledge that a realtor, contractor or astute student of real estate has, you might safely make new construction your first venture.

While you can profit from building anew, keep in mind the fact that a great deal of new construction on the market is overpriced. If you are thinking of buying a newly built structure, you should compare it with the cost of reproduction—or how much it would cost to build for yourself on a comparable lot.

In 1974 I appraised a number of new construction projects. Some of the builders had established fair prices for resale purposes, taking only nominal construction profits. Their sales prices averaged about $20 per square foot, which is approximately what it would cost an investor if he set out to build for himself.

### Do Crumbling Chimneys Make a Fifty-Year-Old House Too Old?

From the state of Washington, Mark Buchanan writes, "Found a bargain, a cheap-priced house fifty years old. The foundation and roof are good. Needs paint and the brick chimneys are crumbling. Looks easy to fix up and double my money. But I'm sending a few questions: What about that condition? Is the house too old? How can I protect myself?"

No, the house isn't too old for profitable improvements. Often a dilapidated eye-catcher, like your crumbling chimney, may not be too costly to repair. Like askew front steps and porches, its unsightliness may lower the sale price and enable you to get a bargain, yet the repairs may be fairly inexpensive. You could easily protect yourself if you're in doubt as to the costs of repair after making further inspections. Include in your offer the proviso "Subject to buyer's obtaining satisfactory bid to repair chimneys."

## Can a Property Be Worth More Than the Listed Price?

A number of buyers find on appraisal that a property seems priced quite a bit under a fair market value. Then they wonder if there is something wrong with their prospective purchase, something that has been hidden. Can it be possible that an owner would put a selling price on a property below its fair market value?

Don Coombs of Palo Alto, California, telephoned to say, "I'm one of the telephone employees that you used to work with. Been with Ma Bell for fourteen years. I'm thinking of buying a house that looks like a steal. What worries me is that when I applied for a loan the bank appraised it at forty-five hundred more than the owner is asking. Do you think there is something wrong about a house that's so underpriced?"

Retiring Army officer Jack Carter phoned from San Rafael, California. "I've a chance to buy a piece of property with only three thousand dollars down," he said. "The owner is asking thirty thousand. This looked like such a bargain, I thought there must be something wrong. I paid a licensed appraiser, an M.A.I., seventy-five dollars to go over the property. He came up with an appraisal of forty-nine thousand. That's what he thinks the property is really worth. Can this appraisal be trusted?"

Yes. You can depend on an honest appraisal from any one of the two thousand-odd M.A.I.s in the country. Membership in the Appraisal Institute is awarded only to realtors whose education, experience and integrity enable them to pass very strict examinations.

All appraisals are subject to some human factors, inasmuch as they are judgments of individuals based on study and evaluation. If an appraisal is near your own valuation, be satisfied. If it is different from your own, and you are still in doubt, you can double-check by getting a separate appraisal from another M.A.I.

Actual fair market values may be higher than listed prices, just as they may be lower. An owner may overprice a property because of exaggerated personal appreciation, sentimentality or some other such motive.

Carl Wente, chairman of the Bank of America, mentioned an example of overpricing at a national Appraisal Institute convention that I attended in San Francisco. A farmer wanted an extra $10,000 for his Sierra foothill acreage because his home overlooked a beautiful view of the San Joaquin Valley. Wente told the farmer, "The view may be worth that much to you, but to another buyer it may be worthless. The market value of your farm is based on dirt alone and what it will produce, nothing more."

A different owner may underprice his property because of low costs; another, because he is anxious to sell in a hurry for personal reasons—in order to move to another neighborhood, to take advantage of a once-in-a-lifetime business opportunity, to stave off a business bankruptcy, to settle a divorce. As mentioned earlier, cost may have little to do with the present market value of a property. By the same token, neither has price, although the latter is usually more realistic than original cost.

A seller usually sets a price that he feels is fair to him. For a buyer to be interested, he usually has to decide that for his particular plans the price is favorable. It is surprising how many real-estate transactions are completed where both the buyer and the seller feel that they have worked out a good deal.

## What Is the Safest Moneymaking Property Investment?

This question was asked by Dorothy Fuldheim on her TV program in Cleveland.

Dwelling units, either apartments or one-family houses, are the safest property investment for the owner interested in capital gains. They meet a prime necessity of life and are needed regardless of shifts in the economy. Any average housewife knows what makes a livable apartment and can figure how to fix it up to a tenant's satisfaction.

The safest of all property investment is usually commercial, on long-term lease to tenants with top credit ratings. Such properties normally offer less net income than dwelling units. The very stability of long-term commercial leases against loss of income holds down the chances for capital gain, because, in most cases, these leases lessen the opportunities for increasing income.

The best apartment or one-family-house buy for rental purposes will be an older building as close to the center of town as possible, in a neighborhood which attracts tenants. It will be a building that has been allowed to run down and can readily be fixed up. When it is judiciously improved its rental value and sale value automatically increase. Older property is safest because the rents can be scaled to compete favorably with new construction.

In 1973 the national vacancy factor for all rental housing units, including new and run-down older ones, was 5.8 per cent. In many areas higher-priced new apartments were 20 per cent vacant on the average. Modernized older apartments, with more reasonable rents, are the most competitive of all and tend to have an average of only 2 per cent vacancies, or 98 per cent full.

### Have You Ever Lost Money on Apartments?

This question comes up from time to time. One who asked it was Norman Cousins, editor of the *Saturday Review,* at a press interview in New York City.

No. I've lost money when I've strayed into less familiar fields than property investment, such as business ventures. Sometimes real-estate profits have been only fair, sometimes exceptional. But I've never failed to make money on apartments.

### What Is the Meaning of "Cap Rate"?

This question was asked at a Lowry-Nickerson Seminar in Rochester, New York, where my co-lecturer was realtor Jim Howard of

Los Angeles. The term has been used for many years, but has come into vogue among appraisers in the '70s.

"Cap rate" means *capitalization rate*. I heard an appraiser spend two hours explaining its meaning in a condemnation suit. Technical tables and jargon can be quoted ad infinitum to mystify the meaning of "cap rates," but I'll try to simplify as much as possible. A capitalization rate is a predetermined figure, representing the ratio of income to value, used in appraising property values. It is similar to our oft-repeated figure of "10 times the annual net" to establish apartment house values.

For example, 10 times an annual net of $10,000 would give a value of $100,000. If you multiply the annual net by 10 in order to set a value, then, obviously, your capitalization rate or rate of return is 10 per cent. To establish value, using the cap rate, you divide the net of $10,000 by .10, arriving at the same result of $100,000.

With any other figure but 10, the multiplier and divisor would be different. For example, if you establish 8 per cent as the desired cap rate on a sound commercial property, you divide .08 into the $10,000 annual net, or multiply by 12.5, and arrive at a value of $125,000. On a less desirable, more risky, hotel you might figure a cap rate of 12 per cent. Dividing $10,000 net by .12, or multiplying by 8.3, would give a valuation of $83,333.

# XII

## *How Can I Judge Risky Deals?*

After a sampling of questions regarding good deals and safe investments, it is appropriate to examine questions about risky deals.

### What Is the Riskiest Property?

This question was asked by Dr. Don Ball of Cincinnati at a dental-convention lecture in Columbus, Ohio.

The riskiest property is probably a resort. Like hotels and motels, resorts are not basically investments, but are business operations. They require a lot of know-how and personal attention on the part of the operator. I have examined the financial statements of many resorts; most of them show that the places fail to meet expenses. Rare exceptions are resorts owned by large families, all of whose members work their shirttails off.

Resorts suffer from two fatal diseases, seasonitis and weekenditis. They are empty off season, and often during the week at midseason. Fifty years ago, according to Cleveland Amory in *The Last Resorts,* people stayed at resorts all summer. Now, thanks to fast highways and fast cars, many come only for weekends. The average resort is only about 10 per cent full on a year-round basis, but high operating costs keep eating away at income the year round. This situation is in sharp contrast to apartment houses, which tend to stay comparatively full. Even hotels and motels with their seasonal fluctuations average 65 per cent full on a year-round basis.

### Have You Had Any Personal Experience with Resorts?

Yes, in 1951 my wife and I bought the White Sulphur Springs resort at St. Helena, California. It was the worst mistake we ever made. Expenses far exceeded income right from the start. We ran the resort for six months trying to recoup our losses. The whole family took on various responsibilities. My wife, Lucille, was in charge of the restaurant and the kitchen; our daughter, Nancy, ran the swimming pool and the hamburger stand; our son, Robert, was the overseer for the picnic grounds, the bathhouse and the sulphur-water concession; our shepherd dog, Teddy, guarded against human and woods varmints who tried to steal liquor and food; and my main jobs were renting rooms, tending bar, and hiring and firing help.

We had a good crew at season's end and were starting to make an operating profit. Even so, we were glad to exercise the option in our purchase agreement which enabled us to return the resort to the seller. Despite all our efforts and attention, our losses were so high that we would have gone broke if it hadn't been for the substantial income we got from our apartment house holdings.

It was a disappointing experience, but it helped me to appreciate better the marked difference between such business operations and sound income-property investment. And I have been better able to point out the advantage of the latter to other investors.

### Should I Buy Housing in a Resort Area Like Kennebunk, Maine, or St. Petersburg, Florida?

A Rhode Island insurance man writes, "I am sixty years old. Have worked for the Metropolitan Life Insurance Company for thirty-one years, and been a manager for them for the past seventeen years. I have a son and two daughters, all married, and we have ten grandchildren. I plan to retire soon, but still want something to do to take up my time and keep me from growing old physically.

"We have a 211-acre farm in Kennebunk, Maine, with a twelve-room house, our present summer home, where we hope to retire. I would like to buy some rental property there from the proceeds of selling our Rhode Island home, which is worth about $30,000. Our farm is close to Kennebunk and Kennebunkport. Both are small towns of about five or six thousand each, but a very good summer resort area with beautiful beaches and summer playhouses where many big stars come in summer. Some, like Jane Morgan, own farms or other property, and others rent for the season.

"Do you think this would be a good place to invest in housing for rental and resale?"

A question along similar lines comes from an Ohio farmer. He writes, "I'm getting ready to retire from farming. Will have about $100,000 to invest after selling my land. What do you advise about buying apartments in St. Petersburg, Florida?"

Generally the safest area for investment in rental housing is where there is a relatively stable year-round backlog of potential tenants, rather than seasonal renters. If you invest in conventional apartment housing in resort areas, of course you won't be getting into as risky a business as running a resort. However, you will have to face the possibility of heavy off-season vacancies. Your tenants will stay longer than overnight and weekend motel tenants, but your over-all annual vacancies may turn out as bad as those of a motel—almost empty off season. Therefore you have to take an especially close look at the potential income on a seasonal basis. A resort-area-property investment will be highly speculative if you live in a distant location and are unable to supervise it personally.

Some resort areas, such as the two mentioned here, are overbuilt in motels and hotels but have a shortage of apartments for more permanent tenants. You should consider the opportunities for building new apartments or improving older ones, or converting money-losing motels into apartments by installing kitchens and catering to longer-staying tenants. Your expectations of making a good income may still look appealing after you review seasonal fluctuations. Further consideration may be merited if you intend to live in a resort area and can personally supervise your investments.

## Is High-Valued Land a Risky Investment?

This question regarding the advisability of paying high land costs comes from Ward Meeks, the owner-operator of a truck rental business in Seattle, Washington. He writes, "Seattle's Century 21 World's Fair of 1962 used some eighty acres of semi-business and apartment-house space as the site. Existing buildings were demolished and the area was entirely rebuilt. Land values have inflated to double in the past ten years in this lower Queen Ann area. Empty lots of 90 to 120 feet are bringing $40,000 to $50,000.

"Would a six-unit apartment house needing a face-lifting be worthwhile buying, repairing and selling or trading if the land and building can be bought for $50,000? Present income of $385 per month can be raised to approximately $450, and possibly $500 per month. What is your opinion of this as an investment with a land overvaluation from an income standpoint? Is it too risky?"

The six-unit apartment house certainly appears to be overpriced for the income. You should carefully recheck the figures to see if you can arrive at a basic value of ten times the annual net. Gross income is, of course, meaningless as a yardstick unless you know what the expenses are. However, an operation of this size often returns a net similar to that of a duplex, where tenants normally pay utilities. Two months' rent usually offsets other expenses, such as taxes. This type of operation gives you 100 times the present monthly gross as a possible measure of value, making $38,500. This shortcut gives the same answer as multiplying the monthly rent by twelve to get the annual gross income, then deducting estimated expenses to get the annual net, and multiplying the remainder by ten.

The soundest way to buy is on investment-income value, which must be based on present income. You should guard against prices that exceed income value. However, many listings present appraisals that are neither all black nor all white. Nor do they merit absolute rejection or unqualified acceptance. Based on comparable sales, the land value in a promising area may be too high for the income on the existing land usage. The purchase in this case might still pay off well, but it should be considered as partial speculation rather than pure investment.

Do not undertake purchase where the income is insufficient to cover expenses and loan payments, unless you have sufficient additional income to carry the property. It may take some time to convert the property from, say, residential to business usage, or to wait for prices to go up. In general, overpriced land should never be bought until after you have verified the prices on a number of recent sales in the area.

### Have You Ever Speculated in Raw Land?

After my lecture to the Contra Costa County Realty Board in Richmond, California, executive secretary William Leonard asked, "Have you ever branched out into speculative fields, such as raw land? And if so, did you make a profit or lose money?"

Yes, and I've made fair profits on selective buys. All of them represented a small percentage of my total holdings. I strongly advise against putting all your savings into ventures that produce no income, such as raw land or vacant lots. Speculation may be safe if your total investment income from other sources is sufficient to pay all expenses.

My caution against investing all resources in raw land also applies to single-tenant commercial and industrial buildings. You should always be able to meet your expenses and mortgage payments in case of a vacancy. When an owner loses the only tenant on a property, he faces a total loss of income that may take considerable time to replace. On the other hand, the loss of a tenant in an apartment house constitutes a loss of only a portion of the entire building income, and it is much easier to find a new tenant.

### Is a Dream Desert Lot a Gyp or a Bargain?

A St. Louis furniture store owner writes, "I'm planning to sell out and buy property. I have an offer of $20,000 cash for my business and I want to put it all into a real bargain I have stumbled onto in Utah desert land. Everybody knows how property like that has made fortunes for the smart early buyers in Palm Springs, California, and Las Vegas, Nevada. Well, I'm one who wants to get in on the ground floor in Utah. It's only $49.50 per acre lot, supposed to be restricted to one lot per buyer at that price. But I have got an O.K. to buy all the lots my money will handle.

"They will give me a chance to pay only $10 down per lot, and finance the rest in easy payments of $10 per lot a year. The salesman says I can make enough money selling some of the lots at a profit to take care of the payments on the others. Then I'll wind up with some of the most valuable land free and clear. I'll have my choice of land right in the center of the development, where there is a casino planned. I was all set to sell out and buy this property when my wife bought your book and gave it to me for my birthday. According to what you say, I should invest in property that pays an income, and buying raw land like this is dangerous.

"Please advise at once by airmail, or phone me collect. What is your opinion of this desert land deal? It seems like a dream to me although I haven't yet seen it. Want to save all I can so I can buy the most property possible. Do you think I should snap up this bargain?"

Don't do it. At least spend enough money to look the property over before you invest a cent. Some speculators make fortunes subdividing worthless raw land, while many of the lot buyers take a loss. The Federal Trade Commission, alarmed by increased mail-order advertising of vacant lots and unproductive land, warns, "Never buy land sight unseen, no matter how low the price."

You would be far better off to keep your going business a while longer and invest in income property in your home town of St. Louis, starting on a spare-time basis, as I did.

California Real Estate Commissioner W. A. Savage says that most such land has been bought by gypo swindlers for less than $5 an acre. Prospective buyers like yourself who purchase such property without first seeing it are being bilked out of about $500 million a year. Typical undeveloped-land swindles range from Florida swamps under twenty feet of water to Hawaii mountains covered with lava. Most of the current big promotions in gyp deals are in the Southwestern desert, in Arizona, Colorado, Nevada, New Mexico and Utah.

Gerald McBride, executive secretary of the Nevada Real Estate Commission and chairman of the Rackets Committee of the National Association of Law Officials, has a further warning about raw-land speculation:

Raw-land rackets have mushroomed in the past few years, with an increasing number of investors (with more money) interested in easy money from property speculation.

Swindlers advertise by newspaper, radio, television and mail, aiming often at those ready for retirement. They prepare brochures showing boating, trees, water and green meadowland where there is actually nothing in sight but cactus and desert sand. They talk of such land being "minutes away from Las Vegas," or some other well-known recreational center. These minutes must be measured by rocket spacecraft, as the actual distances may be hundreds of miles. Buyers are urged to send money without seeing the property, usually to a post office box where the swindlers are harder to trace.

Outside the U.S., "choice retirement-home property" is now being sold in Central and South America, where the "grass is greener." At least the land is green rather than a barren desert, but it is virtually inaccessible virgin jungle.

## Do You Want to Buy Cemetery Plots?

A Southern California promoter phoned long distance and raved, "This Hillside Rest development is the highest-concentrated use of land that you could get into without putting up a building. You can't beat the number of lots you can subdivide there out of one little old acre. Don't you want to buy a block of these cemetery plots?"

No.

### Do You Want a Run-Down Hotel in Tonapah, Nevada?

A Reno broker phoned about a hot bargain in a run-down hotel in Tonapah, in an abandoned mining area that came to life from time to time whenever there was a Nevada nuclear test. "The hotel is kind of empty now," he said, "but that's because it doesn't have gambling or girls yet. You can easily get licenses for both with a little of my pull at the State Capitol. And I've got a real 'in' with the local officials. You'll need parking and swimming to help draw crowds. There's no extra land, but you could put a garage in the basement and a pool on the roof. Slot machines could go in the lobby and show girls in some of the rooms. How about it? Do you want to get in on this gold mine?"

No.

### Do You Want to Buy Uranium and Oil Land or Stock?

A San Francisco widow phoned to ask me about a proposition she had received from Canada. She was on the verge of selling her apartments and blue-chip stock when she read my book and decided to call me first. "A nice man phoned me long distance from Montreal," she told me. "He offered me the choice of a lifetime, either to buy land outright or to invest in stock in a company that's right in on the ground floor. It's the hottest land buy in history. It's got both oil and uranium, something almost unheard of. Everybody knows that this choice Canadian property has oil. It's lying a couple miles down, waiting for the smart investors to pump it out. The thing they're keeping quiet, except for the insiders, is the fact that some of the best uranium-producing ore in the whole world has been found right under the surface.

"I know this man who phones me is nice, because he has such a sweet voice. He says they have all the Canadian money they need, but they want to get a few select American investors who will build up the prestige of the company. Of course you know I've served many years as Women's Club president. I guess all my hard work that nobody ever thanked me for is finally paying off.

"Would you advise liquidating my other assets and buying either a share of the land or stock in the explorative company? Would you like to take advantage of the same deal yourself, if I ask them to let you in?"

No. No.

## Do You Want to Invest in a New Steam Engine?

An Illinois machinist writes, "For the past few years another inventor and I have been developing a new kind of steam power plant for autos. This is a big improvement over the old Stanley Steamer. Our new steam engine is perfected now, and all we need is money to promote it. It will make big money with trucks, buses and taxicabs. Do you want to get in on the ground floor by buying a piece of our new invention?"

No.

## Do You Want to Beat the Speed of Light?

A surprise New York visitor said, "I'm in on a new ray invention that puts laser behind the times. By using its principles you can travel in space faster than the speed of light. The scientists said it couldn't be done, but we've done it. Inside a year after this is perfected, every partner in the deal will be worth at least a hundred million. The thing is, my life savings are all spent, and everybody else's money is all used up. We'll cut you in for thirty or forty thousand to keep us going. Wouldn't you like to be in on a scientific breakthrough that will beat the speed of light?"

This proposition sounded so fantastic, I thought it would be interesting to have the visitor repeat it to my neighbor Professor Clyde Polson, supervisor of science teaching at the University of California.

We both said no.

### Do You Want to Buy a Lighthouse?

A Portland salesman writes about an opportunity to buy an abandoned lighthouse on a rocky island off the Oregon coast. "It has complete privacy for writing and other pursuits that require seclusion," he told me. "The only access is by derrick when the tide is just right. Don't you think this would be just the place for you to take your secretary and do your writing?"

No.

### Will You Be My Partner in a Housekeeping Venture?

An Omaha rooming-house operator writes of a huge development "with access to 20,000 tenants." Small sleeping rooms will be provided, with community baths, recreation areas, cooking and other housekeeping facilities, at low cost to single men and women. "I'm a divorcee in my thirties. I have a way with people, so I can easy rent out as many rooms as we can build. This is cheap construction, with the smallest square footage the law allows. I haven't read your book, but saw about it in the paper. I intend to read it as soon as I get the time. I've got the experience to run this deal, but need your credit to finance it. The profits would be tremendous for both of us. As a financial partner, would you be interested in backing me?"

No.

## Can Hotel Experience Pay Off?

Milos Hamza writes from Birmingham, Alabama, that he and a fellow Czechoslovakian have saved $50,000 to invest in a hotel. "Our decision is hard to make after so many years of experience in the hotel line, operating our own company. Now we don't know whether we should buy a hotel or apartments. What do you think we should do? Will our experience pay off?"

For most people, investment in income property such as apartment houses offers the greatest opportunity to make a fortune. But you and your partner should certainly consider carefully the possibilities in a field where you have already proven yourselves. Hotel operation, as I have mentioned, is more a business than an investment. Normally your chances of failure are hundreds of times greater. However, your years of successful experience in this field give you a better chance for success.

As you well know, success in the hotel business usually demands that you put in many hours of personal labor, as you must in most businesses. As long as you are prepared to contribute the extra time and effort, there is good reason to assume that you will continue to succeed. Two bulwarks against business failure are ample experience and capital. With the cash you have, you should be able to make a substantially worthwhile deal and still hold a healthy reserve to tide you over the first rough spots on a new operation.

## What Do You Think of Trailer Parks?

Albert Beinert of Indianapolis writes, "I am determined to follow your step-by-step blueprint toward financial success, which will also emulate my two uncles. They have both made over $150,000 in apartments, even though they came over from Denmark with no money and little education to speak of. Both are over sixty and they got their start in the butcher business.

"I have saved up $9,000 from selling kitchenware and knitting machines, and making a profit from fixing up four flats and selling them. Two of my friends are making good money with trailer courts. One has a sixteen-space park in Detroit and the other a forty-eight-unit park in Bay City, Michigan. This puts me in a quandary on my next move. What I want to ask you is, what is your opinion of trailer parks?"

Trailer parks, like well-located motels, often pay off exceedingly well when you consider the cost of the land plus improvements. However, many trailer parks on the market are far overpriced in relation to actual income. They are subject to heavy seasonal fluctuations in many areas. Caravans of trailer owners follow the birds south in the fall and north in the spring.

With businesses like trailer parks, accepted values are based on actual income and expenses, including management and operating costs. Vacancies average considerably higher than apartments. On the whole, owners of trailer parks have benefited by a favorable property-tax loophole. House trailers have usually been subject to nominal vehicle taxes but no real-estate taxes comparable to a similarly valued house, even where the trailers have been permanently located for years. On a country-wide basis this application appears to be undergoing a change adverse to trailer ownership. The possibility of heavily increased taxes should not be overlooked if you are considering a trailer park. Another anticipated cause of greater expense in many areas is the enactment of stricter ordinances, requiring more space per trailer and more shower, toilet and washroom facilities. If you can take all this into account in going over actual operations with a fine-tooth comb, you may do very well.

### Should I Buy Property That Will Profit Only My Children?

Eloy Chavez of Albuquerque, New Mexico, sends a financial statement showing assets of $42,390 in his home, other properties and cash. Debts are listed at $23,165, giving him a net worth of $19,225. He writes, "this was earned by my wife and I giving up many luxuries and good times that the average couple enjoys. I am a postal clerk earning $5,200 per year. We bought a house three years ago for $450 down. We spent $300 for paint and plaster improvements, and increased the value $1,500. We bought another house a year ago for $1,000 down, put in $200 worth of paint and landscaping, and increased the value $2,750. Of course to make these profits my wife and I had to do a lot of the work ourselves, like you and your wife did to get started.

"In 1949 I bought a business lot for $1,000 cash and in ten years sold it for $3,200 cash. Had to wait much longer for this easy profit, but it appeals to me more than the work on rental property. My wife and I have a lot of faith in real estate, but now I am thinking of putting our equities and cash into vacant land.

"Two of my brothers, Alex and Frank, have made good money fixing up apartments. Alex put $2,000 into a run-down duplex and increased the value by $5,200. Frank paid $2,600 for a beat-up triplex that he fixed up and sold for a gross profit of $7,400. My brothers advise me to invest, not so much in vacant land, but in income property, as your book recommends. I am beginning to believe they are right, but hope you will advise me what is the safest thing for me to do. Is it sound to buy property on the basis that even though I may be unable to do any good with it in my time, it should pay a good profit to my children?"

The answer to your last question is no.

Your brothers are certainly right. Success is much more assured in income property that pays for itself as you go along. You may make a killing by buying undeveloped land, but you may have to wait so long that your profits will be eaten away by taxes and interests. Also, you may waste a lot of investment time that could better be spent on a surer success. The one- and three-year profits on your single-family homes are good examples to compare with the ten years you had to wait before you could profit on your lot.

Let's figure 6 per cent interest for ten years on your initial $1,000 lot investment, plus estimated over-all taxes of only $100. This would pull your $2,200 gross profit down $700, leaving $1,500. Without taking sales costs into account, you would have a net profit of 150 per cent over a ten-year period. Let's say you take the whole

$3,200 from your lot sale and reinvest it the same way, doing as well over another ten years. A net profit of 150 per cent would come to $4,800. Your total net worth after twenty years would be $8,000 after an initial investment of $1,000.

On one of your houses the profits were $2,750 in one year, on the other $1,500 in three years. An accounting average would be less than half the four years' time for the two investments, because of the higher profit in the one-year deal. But let's take a more conservative average turnover time of two years. Your initial investment of $1,450 in the two houses has increased by the $1,372 you show as your reduction on the mortgages. Normally, all costs would have been paid from rental income. This includes your total of $500 in improvement costs and your loan payments.

Let's assume, to be conservative, that all but $100 of this $1,372 loan reduction could be charged to sale and other costs. The $100 added to your increased value would make a profit of $4,350, or 300 per cent. This considerably exceeds the average profit for a million-dollar pyramid cited in my first book. Suppose you continue to earn a 300 per cent profit, with an average two-year turnover time? At the end of another ten years you would have $1,484,800.

Therefore it seems to me that the safest thing you can do is consolidate as much as possible in dwelling rentals. You have progressed to the point where you should consider hiring more labor for improvement and devoting a greater portion of your spare time to supervision. Single-family homes are better than lots, of course, for sound income-producing investment. Larger apartment buildings will take up less of your time than scattered homes, enabling you to hire resident managers to handle operating details.

As to buying property on the basis that it may not be worth much now but should pay a good profit to your children, my answer is the same as the one I give a San Francisco Bay–area realtor who phones me periodically. This realtor always starts out with a similar saw: "This is it! I've got something for you to pick up. It will be good for your children and your grandchildren."

"How does it pay now?" I ask. "What are the income and expenses?"

"Well, it doesn't pay very good right now, you know. But it's got a great potential. Think of your grandchildren—what a sweet piece of property they'll have."

"My children and my grandchildren will be much better off if I buy only sound property that pays for itself and has a good income right now."

## Can We Use Your Name?

A Chicago promoter phones about a realty syndicate he is forming. Around three hundred professional people are expected to invest an average of $10,000 each to establish a kitty of $3 million. It is expected that they will earn about 12 per cent, virtually tax-free because of depreciation and interest deductions.

"There'll still be plenty left for high expenses and salaries to the promoters," the promoter tells me. "We'd like to give you a free investment share, plus a liberal travel allowance for you and your family any time you want to come to Chicago, plus a divvy of management profits. All we ask you to do is let us include your name on our promotional literature, as a management consultant and sponsor. It won't cost you a cent. Can we use your name?"

No.

## Should I Spend More Than One Weekend Shopping?

Some eager buyers, especially younger ones, may get impatient and expect to accomplish a worthwhile investment program overnight. They are in too big a hurry, like my Chinese friend who "invested $1,000 in the slot machines in Las Vegas and lost it all in one night."

Bertram Heddlon, twenty-five, a San Francisco appliance salesman, writes, "I got to Chapter 4 of your truly stimulating book last Saturday night. I went right out and spent all day Sunday looking at houses and duplexes in the $10,000 to $15,000 range. The ones that suited me required too much down. The ones that would take my $2,500 down, the same amount you show as a recommended down payment to get started, didn't suit me. Now, before I go any further, would you answer four questions?

1. Would you suggest continuing to look in that price range?
2. Would $2,500 still be a sufficient down payment to work with?
3. Would you say that San Francisco is a good place to make my start?
4. Considering all this, have you any other suggestions?"

1. Keep looking.
2. Yes, $2,500 is sufficient for a sound start today.
3. San Francisco offers top opportunities.
4. Finish reading the book!

### What If the Sky Should Fall?

A clerk at one of the motels along the Strip phoned from Las Vegas and said, "I bought an old duplex for thirteen thousand dollars. It looks like a sweet deal. I could get my money back anytime and a thousand or two profit without doing a thing. I can make five or six thousand more by fixing it up, putting in air conditioning and new furniture. It would cost me another couple thou' for all the improvements I've planned. But then a friend from Florida came for a visit, and he stopped me. He says, 'What if they stop gambling in Nevada? Where would you be then? Better dump and not spend any more money.' I know he's wrong, but I need a little reassurance. What do you think I should do?"

You're right, he's wrong. He's like Chicken Little asking, "What if the sky should fall?" I'd go ahead and fix the place up. Nobody knows what will happen in the future. The odds are in your favor that you will at least have your profit made before Nevada outlaws gambling. And the Census Bureau predicts that Nevada will keep growing faster than any state in the union except Florida.

## What If Russia Drops an Atom Bomb?

Surprisingly enough, a query along similar lines came up at a board of directors meeting I attended. The organization was the Northern California Congregational Retirement Homes. F.H.A. and other financing, to the extent of about $3 million, was being used to build nonprofit Carmel Valley Manor, about a hundred miles south of San Francisco. Our construction site and other costs had all been checked and double-checked. We were discussing my motion to go ahead and approve the construction contract. It had been arranged by our administrator, Dr. William David Pratt, and our board chairman, Hugh Davy, with the guidance of top architects Skidmore, Owings and Merrill.

An accountant who was present commented, "I'd advise going slow on approving this. What if you contract to spend all this money, and then Russia drops an atom bomb on San Francisco? Where would you be then?"

What was the response of the Congregational directors? Besides insurance executive Davy and myself, there were Pan American executive Charles Gregg, retired Scripps College president Dr. Ernest Jacqua, who seconded my motion, United Church of Christ conference minister Dr. Richard Norberg, and lawyer Harley Spitler.

Perhaps it is needless to report that we all possessed enough faith to rise above the fears of Chicken Little and the Russian shadow. Our unanimous approval established enchanting retirement years for close to two hundred alert senior citizens.

## Should You Allow Tenants to Sublease Without Your Approval?

This question was asked by Eleanor Warren, talented executive director of the Mt. Baldy Area Apartment Association, after my lecture to her group in Claremont, California. She said that her printed leases provided that tenants may not sublease. But she had many tenants in her apartments who were teachers from nearby Pomona University. They often asked for the privilege of subleasing so they could keep their apartments on a year-round basis and not have to move. They planned to sublease to others, like summer school students and teachers, when they took their three-month vacations elsewhere. Eleanor's practice was to rule out and initial the cancellation of the clause prohibiting subleasing. She asked, "Do you think I am doing wrong, and if so, what would you recommend?"

It is risky to remove your control against subtenants. You should retain the privilege of approving or rejecting them. If you want to retain year-round teachers by allowing them to sublet, tell the prime tenant that subleasing would be acceptable, provided you approve the subtenants.

A kindly widow told me that she allowed unrestricted subletting in Berkeley, California, and one two-bedroom apartment was filled with about twenty hippie drug addicts. Their wild parties and obnoxious behavior caused most of her desirable tenants to move out.

Another unwary manager, who operated a luxury building for a syndicate of musicians, allowed a comely matron, a Mrs. Ava Folsom, to sublet a $1,000 three-bedroom apartment without restriction. Mrs. Folsom said she wanted to lease her apartment for a year, but would keep renewing, as she wanted to stay permanently. She was taking a six-month tour around the world and wanted to sublet, including her nice furniture. She bought expensive furniture on 100 per cent credit through a local store, following the recommendations of their exclusive interior decorator. Then she advertised her newly furnished apartment:

$1,000 monthly unfurnished, apt. for $500 monthly bargain furnished to responsible family who will be good caretakers while owner is gone on six months vacation. Swimming pool and all luxury conveniences. On lakeshore. Phone 452-8291

A flood of prospects answered, all anxious to sublet the luxury apartment with its expensive furniture. Many took the precaution of asking at the building office if it was O.K. for them to sublet. As agreed with Mrs. Folsom, the answer was "yes."

In one month Mrs. Folsom signed six-month leases with 156 tenants, collecting $1,000 from each for the first and last month's rent. The subleases were to start one month after signing. After a month the master tenant decamped with $156,000, forfeiting only her last month's rent of $1,000. She left the furniture store the responsibility of repossessing all her unpaid-for furniture. And she left the apartment management the onerous task of explaining to the 156 irate "subtenants" why they could not move in to the vacated, furniture-stripped apartment.

# 6

# How

# to Exchange

# Properties

# XIII

## Where Can I Make Advantageous Trades?

From New York City, Jesse Dean writes, "The concept of trading is completely alien to all the New York brokers I have met. They conceded that it was possible but assured me it was a very rare occurrence. Are tax-free trades such as you recommend actually being made?"

According to the American Research Council, over $100 million in tax-free exchanges take place in the United States annually. In 1950 such exchanges came to only $2 million. The volume of tax-free exchanges keeps growing. Recently, a high-rise deluxe apartment house in Oakland was traded for three older apartment buildings in nearby Berkeley; the value of the various buildings exchanged came to over $1 million.

Early Yankees boasted of being avid swappers. Eastern owners and brokers as a group have failed to keep up with their Western associates in exploring the advantages of tax-free real-estate exchanges. They're catching up, though, as the practice spreads rapidly over the entire country, spearheaded by alert realtors who usually relish trading after they consummate their first exchange. Many have told me how they made such deals by following examples in my books.

Exchanges in the same cities have been fairly common for some time in the West and the Southwest, and the volume of such activity between cities has accelerated. A recent example mentioned by Georgetown, Texas, realtor Owen Sherrill involved the trading of property in Austin for the Port Arthur Telephone Building.

Brokers who have never handled trades tend to shun them. As more brokers around the country affiliate with realty boards and their Exchange or Traders Clubs, a bigger percentage will welcome the opportunity to study and make trades. Many realty salesmen have told me they were afraid to try working out a trade until they attended realtor conferences and seminars, such as those in which I have participated.

There is nothing especially intricate about the mechanics of a property exchange. Basically, it is merely a combined sale and purchase. One trader is the seller and one the purchaser on each property changing hands. Often, participation in one such transaction turns a reluctant realtor or investor into a confirmed trader.

### Have You Made Any Tax-Free Exchanges?

Betty Holst-Jensen of Santa Barbara tells of increasing the value of two dwelling units from $18,000 to $22,500. Then she traded at the latter price for a desirable seven-unit property valued at $78,000. She asks, "Have you made any tax-free exchanges yourself?"

Yes, I've made a number of up trades for larger properties—in lots, stores, duplexes and apartment houses. Most of my present real-estate holdings, exceeding $5 million in value, have been obtained through trades.

In addition to simple exchanges, several have been of the multiple variety. In one series of exchanges I traded a lot for a duplex equity, then traded the latter for a fourplex equity in a different city. In another chain I traded a rental house for a Safeway-leased grocery-store building, then traded it for a forty-unit apartment building. In another multiple exchange I turned in a resort-area lot for two commercial buildings, then traded them as part payment for a forty-eight-unit apartment house. More recently I traded a deluxe duplex as the full down payment on another forty-eight-unit apartment house.

Besides my personal exchanges, I am familiar with hundreds of similar transactions. A relatively new but rapidly growing practice is the trading of homes. A New Jersey realtor, for example, tells of arranging an exchange of a $15,000 for a $22,500 home. From the Atlantic seaboard to the Pacific and from St. Paul to Miami I have been advised of various home exchanges. Homes are traded for larger or smaller homes, for apartments and for other properties. Apartments, business property and farms are freely swapped across the country. (Various kinds of trades will be cited in this chapter; further tax implications will be covered in Part 10, under income taxes.)

## Could You Refer Me to a Broker Who Specializes in Trades?

This question is asked by Liberace's neighbor Dr. Stuart Clarke of Sherman Oaks, California. He states that he can't find a broker who will handle trades in Palm Springs or in Van Nuys, in the San Fernando Valley. Similar questions have come from cities across the country.

Good brokers who specialize in handling trades or exchanges often indicate their readiness to arrange such transactions in newspaper ads and in the classified section of the telephone directory. Your local real-estate board can direct you to realtors who belong to the Traders Club, Exchange Counselors, Exchange Committee, or similar affiliate.

Suppose you find a property you wish to trade for, and the broker admits to an unfamiliarity with the mechanics of handling trades? Suggest that he obtain information from the local Traders Club or by studying the examples in my books. Here again you find a mark in favor of realtors as opposed to brokers who are not members of their local realty board. Only realtors can belong to affiliates like the Traders Club, where members exchange properties and experiences.

## Can I Trade City for Farm Property?

This question has been asked by many people, including business editor Charles Vaughan of the Indianapolis *News*. Farm owners want to move to the city and vice versa. Both want to make better deals and save taxes by exchanges.

It's being done all the time. Roswell, New Mexico, realtor Wayne Adams confirmed this when he described such exchanges to a national convention of the Institute of Farm and Land Brokers and stated, "Exchange of city and farm property is rapidly increasing among realtors."

Realtor Richard Smith of San Jose, California, tells of working out a trade of a twenty-acre walnut orchard for a twelve-unit Santa Clara apartment house. Both properties are near San Jose. Each was valued at $100,000, making an even exchange.

Following my lecture to the Mankato Realty Board, realtor Frank Baumann of New Ulm, Minnesota, told me of a southern Minnesota deal. Two city houses with a valuation of $23,000 were traded for a 200-acre farm valued at $64,000. The ranch seller took back a mortgage for the difference, payable in ten years.

A San Francisco realtor tells of arranging a trade of an eighteen-acre vineyard for a twenty-four-unit apartment house.

Salem, Oregon, realtor Cliff Bowder tells of working out a trade of a farm valued at $90,000 for garden-type apartments valued at $150,000.

A Connecticut realtor recently consummated a fine trade for a bedridden farmer of a 220-acre farm valued at $65,000 for Hartford rental dwellings of comparable value. The farmer wanted income property that required little care, since he could no longer work. If he had sold outright, a capital-gains tax would have applied to his profit over the original purchase price of $15,000, paid thirty years previously. The city businessman who traded his rental property for the farm was more interested in the potential profit from future development.

## Can I Trade Commercial Property for Apartments?

A Cincinnati correspondent writes, "My husband is sixty and I'm fifty-three years old. We own a restaurant and bar business worth about $15,000, free and clear. Also, we paid $19,000 for a two-apartment building ten years ago, worth about $25,000 market value today. Bought a five-room bungalow two years ago for $17,000 with a $15,000 mortgage to pay out. Have about five thousand insurance and a couple of thousand cash for a rainy day.

"We want to trade our commercial property for larger apartments. Can this be done? Now, accounting for our age and all our investments, what would you recommend we do to have better days for the future?"

It is fairly common to trade commercial property for apartments, as I have. There are many choices you and your husband could make. Your chances for further progress would be good if you could trade all or part of your holdings for the largest apartment house you can safely handle. For example, you could trade the restaurant and bar for a desirable apartment house, reserving your other property for a separate pyramid. You might trade the two-apartment building plus the bungalow as the down payment on an apartment house.

You might consider the possibility of borrowing on the business property. That way you could retain its income as a backlog while starting your investment expansion. Then you could use the cash proceeds from the loan to sweeten a trade of the two-apartment building for a larger one.

Here are some case histories of exchanges of commercial property for residential homes and apartments:

Realtor Sheldon Good of Chicago tells of arranging an exchange of a Chicago Loop property for a suburban apartment building, with total values of about $210,000. Another Chicago deal he co-operated in was a multiple trade involving four apartment buildings at a valuation of approximately $1,300,000.

From Hawaii, realtor John Phillips tells of a swap in Oahu involving a $150,000 apartment house and commercial property valued at $250,000. As in all income-property trades, it was a matter not only of gaining a tax advantage but also of keeping the income continuous while disposing of one property and acquiring another. When you make an outright sale and then have to spend time shopping for a different kind of property, there can be a long waiting period when your funds are tied up without giving you any appreciable income.

A California realtor worked out a trade of a San Francisco commercial building valued at $200,000 for a deluxe eighteen-unit Hollywood apartment house valued at $275,000. Another San Francisco commercial property was traded for an Oakland apartment house. And the William Goodwin Company, realtors in San Francisco, arranged a trade of a triplex for a forty-eight-room hotel. The hotel was converted into twenty-four studio apartments at a cost of $17,000, and the value of the building increased from $135,000 to $195,000.

Realtor Dale Dean of Coldwater, Michigan, tells of an exchange worked out by his salesman John Dean: a $25,000 home against a $110,000 motel. The motel seller wanted to liquidate and figured the home would be easier to dispose of. In addition to the possibility of postponing capital gains, easier liquidation is often the motive that will prompt a large-property owner to trade down.

Sure enough, the salesman next traded the $25,000 home for a $10,000 home, which was still easier to sell. The original motel owner finally liquidated his property ownership completely when the salesman sold the $10,000 home. The seller took back a sizable land contract to expedite the sale. As often works out in exchanges, both of the original parties were completely satisfied. The home-owner who wanted an income-producing motel was happy, and so was the motel owner who wanted to liquidate. Suppose they had sat back, as some owners do, demanding that their properties be sold for cash? It is likely they would have had to compromise on their original prices, or else they might still be waiting.

## Is It Possible to Trade Between Cities?

A Boston insurance salesman writes, "I possess a piece of property which should be a good springboard for trading up into income property. For three weeks I've systematically scanned the Boston Sunday papers. Much income property is advertised, one edition having 203 such ads. But I've yet to discover one that suggests trading.

"Further, I've interviewed about ten brokers. All of them considered my suggestion of trading as slightly 'odd.' Hence my questions. Is it possible that trading is a process used in some parts of the country and not in others, like staid old New England? I live in the suburbs of Melrose and wonder, is it possible to trade between communities? What means of accomplishing the same would you suggest? Do you have personal knowledge of such trading?"

Intercity trades within the same area are fairly common. Several of my exchanges have been between different cities, and I know of many others. It is more unusual to trade between distant cities, but this too is a growing practice.

Trading in "staid old New England," the home of the "Yankee trader," has been prevalent from early times. However, as previously pointed out, most brokers are reluctant to attempt the ramifications of a property exchange unless they happen to specialize in this field. After handling a deal or two, they realize the advantages of accepting such a challenge. For performing a real service that many owners desire, they earn a double or multiple commission, one from each party to an exchange.

Realtors who belong to the rapidly expanding ranks of exchange specialists relish trades. With other brokers you may seldom accomplish a trade merely by telling what kind of property you have and what you want. You stand a better chance if you shop for the property you desire, then offer yours as all or part of the down payment. It is easier to work out an up trade for larger property if you can throw in some cash to enhance the deal. Most for-sale ads of income property do not indicate a willingness to trade, but the seller will often entertain such an offer.

All of my investments are in northern California, within the range of a one-day round-trip drive from my home. In some of my intercity trades I disposed of scattered properties in the Santa Cruz County resort areas, about fifty miles south of San Francisco. I traded one Santa Cruz mountain cabin as the down payment for twenty-eight Sacramento apartments, another Santa Cruz cabin as down payment on twenty-four Oakland apartments. A Santa Cruz lot was exchanged for a Santa Cruz duplex, the duplex was exchanged for a Stockton fourplex, then the fourplex was traded for Oakland apartments. I traded a Santa Cruz lot for a commercial building in Tracy, and five other Santa Cruz lots as part of the down payment for a Sacramento apartment house.

More examples of inter-city trades:

Coldwell Banker and Company's San Francisco office recently arranged a $1-million property exchange of a garage and store building in San Francisco for a thirty-two-unit deluxe apartment house in San Jose.

Prudential Realty and Finance Company of Oakland, California, put together a $1¾-million exchange of a 208-unit senior citizens project in San Jose for an apartment property in San Francisco.

### How Can I Value an Ohio Duplex and Exchange It for Maryland Property?

Retired Army Captain Willard Dressler of Coraopolis, Pennsylvania, writes, "My wife and I paid $12,750 for a Canton, Ohio, duplex, occupied it for two years, and have rented it constantly since, through a local agent. The downstairs tenant pays $85 and the upstairs tenant $75. Each unit has four rooms. It is in a middle-class neighborhood, on a bus line, across the street from stores, near school and churches. It is in good condition except it needs exterior paint. The interior was redecorated last spring.

"We paid $350 for the first-floor furniture when we bought the place, and also furnished the second. Both units are rented furnished. Expenses total $762 a year, including taxes, gas heat, water, maintenance and insurance, thus leaving an average net income of $1,155. Now we want to dispose of the duplex and acquire a similar property in Maryland, between Baltimore and Washington, D.C.

"In summary here are my questions: What is the fair sale price for the duplex? I feel that $14,950 should be agreeable. What is the best method of trading or otherwise disposing of it and acquiring Maryland property?"

The usual ratio for establishing market value on apartments is to calculate ten times the annual net, which would give you a price of only $11,550. However, under normal operations the expenses on single-family homes and duplexes should be held close to two months' income. Thus 100 times the monthly gross would give a result similar to the figure reached by computing ten times the annual net. A common practice for a duplex owner, therefore, is to multiply the monthly rents by 100. This would give you a sale value of $17,000. Such an application is predicated on the assumption that the property is in fair condition. It should pay you to paint the exterior.

The foregoing comparisons indicate that your ratio of expenses to income is high. It would appear that you should either receive more income or be able to reduce expenses. Perhaps your expense figures have been distorted by the inclusion of maintenance costs, which are usually omitted when applying the yardsticks of value. If you are paying for yard maintenance, for example, consider that most duplex tenants are willing to handle such chores if this is stipulated in the rental agreement.

In the usual single-family home or duplex operation, tenants pay their own utilities. Bills are sent directly to them if separate meters are installed. If the building has community meters, arrangements can be made for the tenants to split the charges. Perhaps you can arrange to have the tenants pay for the utilities, or else raise rents to compensate.

As for your second question, although trading within a city or between nearby cities can readily be worked out, it is more difficult to trade between distant cities. Even so, you might negotiate a trade by shopping for the kind of property you want, then offering your property as all or part of the down payment. You might also try advertising in papers covering the desired Maryland area.

An alternative might be more readily worked out if you sell the Canton duplex, obtaining a better price by taking back a second mortgage. If you succeed, you can then use the second mortgage as all or part of the down payment on the property you buy. If you find a good buy, and the seller won't trade, you might contract to buy the property "subject to sale of buyer's Canton duplex." Or you could give a newly created mortgage on the Canton duplex as the down payment for Maryland property, then sell the duplex subject to the mortgage. Many sellers are willing to take mortgages as down payments when they are reluctant to acquire distant property.

### Do You Know Any Examples of Inter-Area Trades?

This question, a frequent one, was also asked by reporter Jim Connally of the Baltimore *News-Post*.

I know of many trades between more distant cities. Dallas realtor Winston Nowlin tells of completing a trade of 3,000 acres of undeveloped Arkansas pastureland, valued at about $150,000, for a more developed 2,800 acres of Texas land, valued at approximately $250,000. The $100,000 difference was covered by a fifteen-year first mortgage.

In a fourteen-property inter-area trade, realtor Warren Blosil of Oakland, California, won the Snyder Trophy for arranging the most outstanding exchange in the United States in 1972. Two apartment buildings totaling 116 units in San Leandro and Walnut Creek in northern California were traded for a $1,321,000 shopping center in Southern California. To complete the exchange Blosil had to work out a fourteen-property deal, where the two apartment buildings were, in turn, traded for eleven houses. Then these were sold to different buyers before closing the escrow, and the original shopping center developer wound up by cashing out.

Another inter-area exchange was made by the John Burt Terhunes when they moved from the Rockies to the Pacific Coast. They traded equities in three parcels in the Grand Junction, Colorado, area, consisting of a small motel, a ranch, and a city home, for a modern forty-eight-unit garden-type apartment project in Rancho Cordova, California, near Sacramento.

A Southwestern deal of which I was told after lecturing to the national realtors' convention in Dallas involved a trade of Texas cotton acreage for Los Angeles apartments.

A San Francisco realtor tells of arranging a trade of apartments in his city for apartments in Los Angeles, with combined valuations in the $600,000 range.

A Montana rancher traded his property plus $62,500 in cash for a Kansas farm.

A Miami, Florida, realtor tells of arranging an exchange for a $97,000 apartment house in his city. The down payment was a North Carolina duplex.

Realtor W. S. Lighthall of Scottsdale, Arizona, tells of arranging a trade of Midwestern commercial property for an Arizona business property.

In Hawaii I was advised by a general contractor that he had acquired his desirable Waikiki apartments by trading his apartments in Hollywood. He had been able to make the swap when he told a Los Angeles realtor of his desire to settle in Hawaii. The Oahu apartments had been listed by an owner wanting to move back to his former community on the mainland. Again, all parties to the exchange were extremely happy. The realtor was gratified to earn a double commission, one from each seller. And each exchanger was able to acquire apartments where he really wanted to live and own income property.

Honolulu-based Dillingham Corporation acquired their first mainland residential realty outside of California by trading for a luxury twenty-one-story 102-unit apartment house, 3525 Turtle Creek, Dallas, Texas.

# XIV

## *How Can I Dispose of Home and Other Equities?*

Many would-be investors in real estate are puzzled regarding the best way to utilize their homes or other equities to start pyramids. Some are willing to dispose of their homes in order to speed their progress. Others want to keep their homes but still make use of their accumulated net worth for investment. Many people are like a former colleague of mine, a telephone company executive, who didn't appreciate what a high investment nest egg he owned in his home.

He was complaining because he had no funds with which to take advantage of the investment opportunities I told him about. Further discussion revealed that he owned a home worth about $35,000 and that all but $3,000 of his mortgage was paid off. If he sold or traded his home, he could net in the neighborhood of $30,000 after paying sales costs and the balance of his present mortgage. But, like the Hollywood couple mentioned in Chapter VII, he wanted to keep his home. To raise money for investment, he was able to get a new mortgage that netted him about $20,000.

### How Can I Tell If I'm Building Up Equity?

My telephone company friend was in the same boat as many others who don't realize how big their equities have grown until they prepare a financial statement. John Curry of Atlanta, Georgia, writes, "Besides other property (list enclosed) my wife and I own a $25,000 home. It has an $8,000 mortgage. Sometimes I feel that I have done all right. At other times my wife comes up with the statement that we don't have any more money than we did when we started investing. We just owe more! She is not griping, but is sorta like me. Can't see that it is doing too much good to own property, although my head tells me we are building up equity. How can we know where we stand?"

Prepare a financial statement, using the sample in my first book. Add up the fair market value of all your personal and realty properties, then deduct what you owe. The amount left represents your total equities, or net worth. You and your wife may be surprised to find what the figures in your list reveal—that your equities have already pyramided to the $100,000 range.

## Does Reduced Mortgage Plus Improvement Costs Equal Equity?

Since a considerable number of inquiries have involved the figuring of equities, it may be helpful to give another example. William Lizer of Seattle, Washington, writes, "I have a problem in figuring my home equity and what I should do with it. Bought a house for $500 down seven years ago for a purchase price of $8,550. The balance owing is $6,690. The mortgage reduction of $1,360 plus my down payment makes $1,860 I have paid against the purchase price. I have also paid out $2,200 on improvements. Included are new permanent transite siding, a new automatic oil furnace, insulation overhead, knotty-pine and mahogany paneling in living room. I am handy at making improvements.

"Should I combine my mortgage reduction and improvement costs to figure equity, giving me an estimate of $4,060?

"Would you advise trading this place? Have three children and need a larger home. Would also like to get started in apartment investment if it can be worked out. This house has two bedrooms and nursery upstairs, with part basement and a nice lot with fruit and berries."

Your present sale value minus the balance on your mortgage is your equity, regardless of what you have paid to buy and improve the house. Some improvements made to satisfy personal tastes may not pay off. They may not increase the value to the extent of their cost. The same holds true for purchase costs. The property may not be worth as much today as you paid for it, especially if it has been allowed to run down.

However, property values have gone up generally nationwide. The improvements you describe should increase the value at least by double your cost, especially since you did some of the work yourself. As long as the property is well maintained and has been judiciously improved, your present value should be considerably more than you have paid out.

You certainly have sufficient equity for a down payment on such income property as a duplex or a fourplex. You could trade for income property or a larger home. Taking over larger mortgage loans would make up the difference in value.

If your desire is strong enough and your income sufficient to handle the financing, you could have your cake and eat it, too. You might consider trading your home equity for income property. At the same time you could buy a larger home with a small down payment, such as the $500 you paid down on your present home. Or you could sell your home, taking part cash—as the down payment—and a second mortgage. The second mortgage could be used as all or part of the down payment on income property, with some of the cash as a down payment on a larger home.

### Can I Trade My Trailer for a House?

This question was asked by a real-estate salesman after my lecture to the Orange County Apartment House Association in Anaheim, home of Disneyland. The questioner then apologized: "This is what my wife and I want, but I guess it's too outlandish a dream to accomplish."

I had noticed ads mentioning such trades in Anaheim-area papers, and I asked the audience if they knew of any examples. Several volunteered the information that they had participated in such trades or knew of others who had experienced them. The association's executive director, Ed Mee, said that a number of Anaheim-area realtors specialized in this type of trade.

## Can I Trade a Fishing Boat for Apartments?

Following my San Diego Realty Board lecture, another questioner asked if there was any possibility of trading his forty-one-foot commercial fishing vessel for an apartment house.

Any exchange you can conceive of has a possibility of being consummated. I know of a commercial fishing boat that was traded as the down payment for an apartment house in San Francisco. Sacramento realtor Jim Bequette worked out a trade of a showboat restaurant plus a swimming pool for a desirable city restaurant property. He accepted the pool as his commission. It was built of redwood planking and had a blue plastic inner lining. Bequette had to dig up the pool and install it in his own back yard before he could enjoy his commission.

## Should I Trade Home Equity for an Empty Duplex?

James Deitt of Pittsburgh, Pennsylvania, writes, "I work for the telephone company, as you once did. I'm thirty-three years old and have a family of six children. I know that what you say about the possibilities of financing and trading is true, because I've tried both. I bought my first house by borrowing $1,000 on my life insurance. Then I traded my Plymouth for the owner's older Ford to make up a $500 difference in the down payment. After four years I was able to borrow again and buy a larger house for my family. I rented out the first place, making a nice profit.

"I'm now at the point where I want to invest in more rental property, but am a little confused because of conflicting information. When I mentioned investing and improving property to a real-estate agent here he said, 'It's O.K. elsewhere, but it doesn't apply to the

Pittsburgh area!' He says, for one thing, you can't buy a good home here for $10,000, let alone a duplex.

"Since all this fellow tried to do was discourage me, I found another agent. He picked me out a piece of property just like you mention in the book. It is a five-room brick double with a double garage. 'Basically sound, but needs improvements.' Can do at small expense. The problem is that one side is rented for $73 a month, and the tenants are moving in one month; the owner lives in the other side. This means the place will be empty when I buy. Do you consider this a poor risk? Do you think your method of investing and improving can continue to work in Pittsburgh?"

Empty rental units point to an element of risk, particularly with new, untried properties, because the rents quoted may exceed actual market levels. On the other hand, and especially with older properties, market values may be much greater than the rents quoted. Empty units may also pull the price down and help you drive a good bargain. Thus, empty units, like the advice of pessimistic agents, call for extra caution, but the potentialities may turn out good instead of bad.

The duplex mentioned might very well present a good opportunity if all the other yardsticks for value are met. You would want to verify other rentals in the area to see if you can work out a worthwhile return on your purchase price plus your improvement costs. What are the actual rentals for comparable space and location, as is and when you've made the improvements you contemplate? Does $73 compete favorably with rents for properties in similar condition? If the answer is yes, then vacancies can readily be rerented. Very likely the upcoming vacancy may be rented for more before you take possession. A purchase price based on the present rent level would therefore represent a bargain market value.

What are the rent levels for a similar five-room flat that has been fixed up? You may find, for example, that $95 per month represents the going rate unfurnished, and $110 furnished. Each dollar of increased monthly rental that is not offset by increased expenses is multiplied by twelve to give you the annual net, increasing the market value by $120.

If the rents can be raised from $74 to $95 per unit, you would have an over-all monthly increase for both of $44, or $528 annually. This would enhance the market value by $5,280. If the improvements can be made for $2,500 or less, you have a good buy, following my yardstick of $2 in increased value for each $1 spent in improvement costs.

## Will Investing and Improving Work in Pittsburgh?

Pittsburgh offers very good opportunities for success in real-estate investment. If this duplex pans out as it promises, the second agent who bird-dogged the property has already proved wrong the Gloomy Gus who said there was nothing like it available. There are many letters from Pittsburgh in my files describing actual cases of people who have successfully followed my suggestions. I spotted several good deals there during my various visits.

John Schultz is improving four run-down flats in the Pittsburgh area that he bought for a total of $9,100. Most of the other correspondents are also doing better than the average mentioned as a guide in my first book. None has had results lower than the average I suggest. Some who seek success in their own back yards are making spectacular profits. This pattern fits every major city in the United States.

## Will "Settlement Costs" Eat Profits Away?

Mary Roysdon of Baltimore, Maryland, writes, "Regarding the first Enterprise venture, the A Avenue house discussed in your book, I can't find any mention of the loan cost. It is called 'Settlement Costs' here, and usually amounts to $500 to $800. Please advise me, should these costs be figured in real-estate pyramiding?"

Settlement or transfer charges are a cost factor in real-estate turnover and should be taken into account in figuring profits. The charges on page 93 of my first book that apply to the A Avenue house are typical for such a transaction in California.

My pyramiding is based on average sales costs of 5 per cent. In most parts of the country commissions usually start at 6 per cent on smaller transactions and diminish on larger deals. In my statements on the B Boulevard and Cynthia Court properties, the major transfer cost is in the commissions. Both commissions are covered by financing, to be repaid from future income, and therefore do not show up in the cash reconciliations, or settlement. When you own larger, more desirable apartments, like the Cynthia Court, it usually pays to save turnover charges by holding the property and refinancing it in order to secure funds for further pyramiding.

The settlement costs you speak of would not apply in most parts of the country where the seller takes back a mortgage, as happened on the A Avenue purchase. In this example the seller paid for title insurance. Community practices vary, however. In some areas the buyer pays these costs, in others they are shared. The total for the A Avenue purchase was only $79.50.

The additional costs you mention are common only in some areas where an F.H.A.- or V.A.-type loan is involved, as on a home purchase, and the interest rates are below market levels. The bank or other lender then charges a bonus, called "points," to make up for the low government-regulated interest rates. Such points are not regularly charged with conventional financing when you are buying a duplex or other income property.

### Should Turnover Costs Include Operating Expenses?

Rita Rosen of Philadelphia writes, "My husband and I plan to invest $3,000 as the down payment on a duplex. Then, if we become courageous enough, we'll continue to reinvest in the manner you suggest. However, there is one matter that is troubling us. When we purchased our $11,000 home a year ago we paid approximately $700 in settlement costs. Now if we were to continue to buy and sell or trade every few years, wouldn't the settlement costs keep growing so they would eat greatly into any profit we make?"

Mrs. Rosen appends a list of her "settlement charges." They are shown here in full in order to help explain possible misconceptions.

CHARGES ON PHILADELPHIA HOME PURCHASES

| | | |
|---|---|---|
| 1. | Real-estate taxes | $136.00 |
| 2. | Acknowledgment of deed | 1.00 |
| 3. | Title company charges | 105.00 |
| 4. | Recording deed and mortgage | 12.25 |
| 5. | Notary fees | 5.00 |
| 6. | 1 per cent transfer fee | 110.00 |
| 7. | Triangle Home Sales, Inc., conveyancing | 50.00 |
| 8. | Homeower's insurance | 93.60 |
| 9. | Eastern Mortgage Service Co. service fee | 102.00 |
| 10. | Prorate 3 months' taxes | 57.09 |
| 11. | Prorate 1 month F.H.A. mortgage insurance | 4.22 |
| 12. | Prorate 1 month fire insurance | 3.00 |
| 13. | Mortgage-inspection fee | 5.00 |
| 14. | Photos and credit report | 5.00 |
| 15. | Prorate 1 month water and sewer | 2.25 |
| | Total Settlement Charges Paid by Us | $691.41 |

Many items in your statement, such as taxes, insurance and utilities, should be included as prorated and full-term billing when calculating operating expenses. They are not part of your costs for transferring property; the only transfer costs that customarily apply on income-property purchases are title company, recording and notary charges—items 2 through 5 in your statement. Your prorated operating expenses include one month's insurance and three months' taxes of $57.09. Also, in the first item, you apparently have an additional half year's tax payment in advance of $136. The $93.60 insurance charge evidently covers you for the next three years.

The transfer tax of one per cent applies only in certain communities; for investment purposes it must be added to capital costs. The $152 in service and conveyancing fees would not normally apply on a purchase or trade of income property. However, such charges may crop up when financing is handled through a mortgage service company, such as the one you list. You are more apt to get such charges when buying a new home.

You might also have to pay for "point discounts" in the loan itself, if you get a low-interest F.H.A. or V.A. loan. The points are not charged for in cash (if they were, they should be included in settlement costs). They are added to the loan and should be allocated to capital costs. For example, assume you need a $10,000 F.H.A. mortgage, and the banker charges three points. This 3 per cent, amounting to $300, is added to the mortgage. You then have to repay a mortgage of $10,300, although you or the seller receive loan proceeds of only $10,000.

### Should I Incorporate to Keep Pyramiding?

Realtor Phil Clark asked this question after my lecture to his Rockford, Illinois, Realty Board. Several successful investment case histories were mentioned by Clark and by realtors Marian Schwab, Paul Gambino and Wilbur Bankord. Clark said, "In one deal I handled that follows your formula, the investor put in about $1,000 to buy a triplex that cost $13,500. After fixing the property up he sold inside one year for $18,500."

Richard Kratsch writes from Waupun, Wisconsin, "I have read your book several times and consider it a bible on property investment. I started on a program of real-estate investment with only $1,000 three years ago. So far I have acquired four properties of twenty-four apartments. With your book as a guide, plus a background in mechanical engineering, I plan to keep pyramiding. I would like to ask what your opinion is of incorporation before I grow much further.

"P.S. Are you incorporated?"

No, I'm not incorporated. One of the advantages of incorporation is that of limiting liability to the assets of the corporation, but this may also limit credit. Another advantage, of course, is limiting the maximum income tax. While these two factors can be of prime importance in other fields, such as a business, I see no special advantage for the average individual investor.

If you are thinking of incorporating in order to handle investments for a large group of people on a syndicate or other basis, that is an entirely different matter. Group investments are becoming more common in various parts of the United States from New York to Hawaii. If you are contemplating this step, it would be advisable to consult with a local attorney who specializes in this field.

### Should I Have Traded My Home When I Traded Husbands?

A Hollywood divorcee writes, "Your book is terrific and has inspired me to take a new look at my life after suffering the depths of disillusionment from perfidious males. I am reading your book again, the second copy I have bought. The first one was stolen by my last divorced husband.

"I have been running my own business as a health-studio operator since I was nineteen and first came to Hollywood to be a starlet. Now I'm forty-nine and still considered attractive by the opposite sex. When I was twenty I married a no-good, lazy sponger. He was a wrestler, but after marrying a meal ticket he stopped wrestling—except with me. I kicked him out. He got a job as a ship's recreation director and I've never seen him since.

"Then I met another man who was an exercise-equipment salesman. He wooed me until I got my final divorce papers and married him. Then he sold me down the river. He cheated, lied and humiliated me in every way he could, stopping at nothing short of murder. Then he finally left me, to my utter shock. It took a full year to get over this second disappointing husband. But thank God I am left with my health studio and the ownership of one good house in which to heal my wounds.

"When I first read your book just before I traded husbands, I sold my house that I owned by myself for $13,000 cash. Then I bought two houses and fixed them both up. Each one after my improvements was worth as much as my former home. Rented one out for enough to pay for both. I thought I was doing very well. I felt I was walking on a gold mine, and planned to keep pyramiding, borrowing, buying, improving and moving upward just like your book says.

"Well, my no-good second husband talked me into selling one of the houses for $12,500 cash, 'so I could buy more property.' But he skipped out to Mexico with the money and your book, and I haven't seen him since. After a year of moping, my natural affectionate inclination has repossessed me, and I am again taking an interest in the opposite sex. Now I am considering a third husband, who is the sole proprietor of his own health studio. He is a nice widower and I feel secure with him.

"But I don't want to put temptation in his way. I don't want to take chances again on losing cash from selling property. Yet I want to keep pyramiding with the other house that I still have for my new start. I feel your reassurance would be a great help to renew my confidence. What would you advise that would have protected me from losing money in the first place? Should I have traded instead of selling? I haven't talked to any brokers yet who handle trades. Are there any such in Hollywood?"

You have already figured out a good safeguard for removing the temptation of available cash. Trade up for larger property instead of selling. There are plenty of live-wire realtors in Hollywood and the general Los Angeles area who handle trades. The names of those who belong to the Traders or Exchange Club can be obtained through your local real-estate board. Let's hope that from now on you enjoy the best of success and happiness in all your enterprises.

### Should We Live Where We Invest?

The James Hislers of Philadelphia write, "We have only $600 in cash savings, and in selling our house we would net about $2,300. Reason why we should live where we invest, we think. Do you agree? Husband is chemist assistant at Du Pont's, and we have six children. Could you tell us if there is any chance of taking the little we could get hold of and doing something with it to provide a better today and future for us?"

You have arrived at a wise decision. You can get off to a sounder investment start by disposing of your home equity and living in your income property. Find a run-down but basically sound pair of flats that you can fix up with the aid of your family. Some older properties have plenty of extra space to accommodate all your family.

In my files are a number of examples of recent good buys in the Philadelphia area in the price range you are considering. Sometimes it takes a lot of looking, at other times very little. Keep at it till you find what suits you. The husband's steady job provides a good credit reserve that will help pay for emergency expenses or improvements.

## Should I Pay an Advance Fee to Trade or Sell Property?

An upstate New York correspondent writes, "I am seventy-two years old and going blind, so I can't operate my farm any longer. I want to trade it for apartments in Florida or Southern California. I answered an ad in a farm journal advertising such trades. The city slicker who came to see me said he could work out a trade of my farm for a nice apartment house in Tampa, Florida. He showed me the picture in a pretty colored catalogue. He gave me a financial statement on the Tampa place and said he could easy arrange the trade. But I had to pay him a fee in advance to cover expenses and to show that I meant business.

"My farm that I don't owe a cent on was to be traded at a value of $80,000. The commission, when the deal was completed, would be 10 per cent, or $8,000. He wanted half of this in advance. Well, we dickered over how much I would pay and I finally gave him $1,000 in cash. He said he would go to Florida and wind up the deal. I would be hearing from him shortly about transferring titles and so forth, so I could take over the Tampa property.

"That was four months ago and I've never heard a peep from him since. I still want to make a trade. Who should I contact to get the trade I want without being gypped? Should a person pay an advance fee to get the right kind of deal?"

No advance fee should be paid. Commissions should be paid only when a transaction is consummated. Some realtors take care of all advertising in order to make a sale. Others may ask that you pay a nominal advertising cost. In no case should you pay any kind of fee in advance, either for a prospective sale or for financing your property.

Ask for a list of members of the Traders Club at your nearest real-estate board and tell them what you have in mind. If there is no metropolitan realty board conveniently near, you can write to the New York State Association of Real Estate Boards, 274 State Street, Albany, New York 12210.

### Can I Trade a Note for Apartments?

In a long-distance call from Phoenix, Arizona, a widow said, "I want to trade my home for apartments in San Diego, where my sister lives. I'd like to move there as soon as possible. My husband died and left our home without debts. He had mortgage insurance on it, which paid off our fifteen-thousand-dollar loan. I have an offer to buy from an Army officer who will pay twenty-five thousand, about the right price. He wants to pay five thousand down and have me carry the twenty-thousand-dollar balance. Do you think I can trade this twenty-thousand-dollar note and first mortgage for San Diego apartments? Should I hold out for a cash sale? Or should I wait for the right trade?"

It would be easier to trade your note, secured by a first mortgage, than to make a direct trade of your house for apartments in another state. You can do still better with most apartment sellers if you sweeten your offer with more cash. As long as your place is now free of debt, your best bet would be to sell to your buyer with $5,000 down, arrange a new $15,000 mortgage which he would assume, then take back a second mortgage for $5,000. Your buyer still gets $20,000 financing. And you will have $20,000 cash plus a $5,000 second mortgage you can use in buying apartments.

Realtor Stanley Scotcher in Los Angeles tells of a deal along the lines suggested by the widow from Phoenix. He arranged a trade of a $23,000 first mortgage in Arizona for four Los Angeles flats valued at $58,000. The flats had a $30,000 first mortgage. Their seller took back a second mortgage of $5,000 to make up the difference.

## Is It Safe to Trade a $17,500 House for $250,000 Apartments?

Another phone call came from a St. Louis carpenter, who asked, "Is it safe to take over apartments worth a quarter million when all I'm trading in for the down payment is my seventeen-thousand-five-hundred-dollar house? I paid seven thousand for this house and fixed it up for about a thousand, so I'm only out eight thousand on it. Did most of the work myself. I have a loan commitment of ten thousand. The apartment seller is willing to take my house with this loan, which would give him ten thousand cash. Then the broker will take over the mortgaged house, plus five thousand cash as his full commission.

"I'm scared of this because it's bigger than I was looking for. I told a broker I wanted to trade for a fourplex, and he comes up with a lot bigger place. The apartment owners are an elderly couple who want to sell out and move to Long Beach, California. They own their place free and clear and will take back a long-term mortgage with low monthly payments. They're giving me an especially good financing deal because they've looked at my house and know how I'll fix up the apartments. Please tell me what I should do."

The carpenter added that he and his wife planned to manage the apartments themselves, saving the $150 monthly now paid for management. He had the property appraised by a licensed M.A.I., whose valuation came to $252,000. The gross income appeared sufficient to pay for expenses plus loan payments and leave an adequate in-pocket net.

The secret that will make this deal work out is the fact that the sellers will carry long-term financing all in one loan. This can keep your monthly payments low enough to give you a safe margin.

If two or three loans were necessary in order to obtain such heavy financing, the combined payments might be too high for safety. This could happen if a substantial short-term, high-payment second mortgage were piled on top of a conventional first mortgage.

Many kinds of opportunities arise where an investor can leapfrog a step or two in a pyramid to a million dollars. The possibility of trading a modest house for apartments worth a quarter of a million dollars, where the financing can be handled safely, looks like an opportunity to jump over several pyramiding steps in one move. Such a trade should appreciably speed your progress toward making a substantial fortune.

### Can I Trade My Home for a Condominium Apartment?

A San Diego, California, widowed schoolteacher, Mavis Yearnin, writes, "I want to trade my home for a $50,000 condominium apartment in Maui, Hawaii, where I plan to retire. My house is worth $45,000 and I only owe $11,000. I don't want to sell and pay taxes on my profit, or give my late husband's relatives a chance to make claims for the money. They might tie up a sale in the title company, but I don't think there would be any trouble if I could trade for an apartment home. Is this kind of trade possible?"

Absolutely! I know of many similar trades. If you can't arrange a direct exchange, make an offer to trade, subject to selling your property in a reasonably safe time, say in six months.

Incidentally, such a deal would be tax-free, regardless of whether you trade or sell your home and buy a condominium apartment home of equal or greater value within one year in two separate deals.

# 7

# How to Improve Your Property for Profit

# XV

## *What Property Improvements Should I Make?*

In the last few years it has become generally recognized that a considerable number of new millionaires are making their fortunes in the most profitable real-estate investment of all—the booming field of remodeling run-down homes and apartments. Remodeling projects continue to expand over 10 per cent a year, and reached $22 billion in 1973. I have been asked a wide range of questions about various aspects of improving property. This section will be concerned with physical improvements; Part 8 will cover improvements in operations.

### Does It Pay to Fix Up Apartments in Old and Conservative Boston?

This question was asked by Malcolm Duffield, manager of the Harvard Co-op book department, when I was autographing books in his store.

It pays to improve apartments and other properties wherever there are prospective tenants. The older the city, the more opportunity there is for making improvements. Most Boston property owners have heretofore let their buildings run down, leaving more room for improvement there than in many other parts of the country. However, some owners have profited by making their own improvements. Many are fast waking up to the fact that it is a short-sighted policy to bleed their properties, a course which can only lead in the long run to losses in value.

Imaginative buyers are taking over run-down properties, improving them and making profits. Alert civic leaders, like Martin Berman, president of the Rental Housing Association of the Greater Boston Real Estate Board, are influencing property owners to increase their income by making improvements. Berman states that members of his organization are making plans to spend about $20 million in rehabilitating and modernizing rental property. On the basis of similar programs elsewhere, it seems likely that these expenditures should increase values in Boston by a minimum of $40 million, producing additional net rentals of approximately $4 million.

### Does It Pay to Fix Up Single-Family Homes?

This question was asked by Elsie Clough of the Book Shop in Providence, Rhode Island. My wife and I stopped off there for an autographing party on the way to Boston from a Washington, D.C., lecture.

Yes. Spectacular profits can be made percentagewise in fixing up run-down homes. Of course, you need to own a lot of them to realize as high a total profit as can be earned from large multiple-unit apartments. There is usually a fixed maximum amount to be earned per dwelling unit.

Boston realtor Peter Turchon has been modernizing about five hundred run-down houses a year. He finds that he can make a profit selling a desirably modernized close-in older home for less than half the cost of new homes in the area. Run-down houses that have stood vacant for years sell or rent like hot cakes as soon as he renovates.

Turchon's spectacular success at specializing in single-family homes has inspired members of his family to similar activity. In a Boston suburb one of his sons has modernized forty-five large single-family homes with new baths, kitchens and exteriors. After remodeling, each building contains one to three extra apartments that rent readily.

Turchon's son-in-law has rehabilitated and sold 122 two-family duplexes. In another single project in a newer suburban area, forty-seven eight-year-old duplex ranch-style homes were spruced up for resale. On his mass rehabilitations Turchon makes a nominal over-all net profit approximating 3 per cent of the selling price. He buys in groups of twenty-five, fifty or more properties, so there is no specific cost or profit on each house.

### Is It O.K. to Speed Up Improvement Timetable?

Turchon has had sufficient experience to know that he can keep a large crew of workmen busy to the extent of completing about ten building renovations a week. Others just getting started make plans that seem to work out much faster on paper than the example described in my first book; then they wonder if there must be something wrong with their expedited planning.

For example, Benjamin Brown writes from San Francisco, "Two friends and I are setting up a corporation to follow your plan: to buy older places, paint and otherwise fix them up, and then sell. We intend to start with $3,000. The only difference in our plan and your example is that your formula calls for an average two-year turnover period, and ours will be twelve times as fast. We have carefully gone over the time it would take us to fix up a duplex. We know we can take care of everything necessary so we won't have to keep a place more than two months. If this develops as expected we'll jump into the program full time.

"We have double- and triple-checked over everything, but we are worried at so much shortening of your time plan. Please advise, is our speed-up plan feasible?"

Certainly your plan is feasible. The formula outlined in my book can be stepped up as much as you want, depending on available funds and the amount of time you plan to devote.

I know of many major moneymaking improvements that were made within your two-month time estimate. For example, twenty-year-old Alex Chavez of Albuquerque, New Mexico, bought a very run-down duplex for $5,000, paying $1,000 down. He writes, "My bride of six months and I did an awful lot of painting and cleaning up and we put in some new plumbing. We spent a total of $1,000, the remainder of our savings, to make these improvements. One apartment is now rented for $60 and we live in the other. The whole job was finished in two months' time, and the present appraised value is $10,200, which gives us a $4,200 profit."

The Chavezes kept their Civil Service jobs, handling this investment and improvement project in their spare time. I would certainly recommend that you do the same, retaining your present employment until you gain experience.

You might also want to review the tax implications of such rapid turnovers. If you make a business of continuing, short-term sales, you will have to pay ordinary income taxes instead of capital-gains rates. Undoubtedly you have figured on this possibility as a result of incorporating. Otherwise, it would pay to hold your property at least six months before selling, and to consider some up trading instead of outright sales.

Although you may have a property ready for sale in two months, you should allow ample time for selling and reinvesting. These steps might bring your turnover time closer to six months on the average. Once you get several projects going, your properties could move in a continuous process of buying, improving and selling. While you are getting started, though, you may need the profits from earlier deals to give you the down payments for further ventures.

### Is It Safe to Start in Improving Larger Properties?

Another speeder-upper is Edward Daniels of Connecticut. He writes, "Since I have a knack of understanding building and its construction, would you say it is reasonable to start with a property of $30,000 or so instead of the $8,750 example given in your book? I have $15,000 to invest if you think it safe to speed up your process.

Also, considering the size of buildings on the market in my area, in Norwalk and Stamford, I figure all the needed improvements could be completed inside of twelve months instead of the twenty-four you scheduled. Don't you think this speeding up would be safe?"

My formula should be considered as a guide to show the potentials on an average time-and-profit schedule that can readily be emulated or bettered. It starts out small and slow because the Enterprises were limited to an average savings of $2,500. With your larger savings it would be advantageous to buy as large a property as you can handle, as long as the basic suggestions in the book are followed.

It can certainly be safe to speed up the time on making improvements and turnover, so you can reinvest faster in larger properties.

### Does Paint Pay More Than Anything Else?

Sylvia Monroe writes from Long Island, New York, "I have already fixed up two houses since reading your book and have increased the values about $5,000. I am now purchasing a five-family apartment house for $22,000. The place is directly opposite a school, so I intend to rent only to teachers. As the apartments become vacant I'll paint and renovate—put in modern bathrooms and kitchens.

"I have a pretty good estimate of all repairs and improvements. They will cost approximately $4,000, and I plan to take care of them over a period of three years. At the end of that time I should be able to get $500 or more a month in rents. With that income and with the place nicely renovated, I should have no trouble selling for $35,000 to $40,000. I can hardly wait to get started on this new investment.

"One thing I have figured out I would like your answer on. Does paint pay more than any other single item of improvement?"

Both interiors and exteriors can be remarkably transformed by paint, which can often make the greatest increase in value per dollar of expenditure. Chapter II of this book tells how $400 worth of paint increased the value of a house by $4,000. Paint can change an eyesore to an eye-catcher. It can cover undesirable features and dramatize good ones. Gingerbread eaves, gables and dormers, for example, can often be rendered inconspicuous by painting them the same color as the roof. Windows and chimneys that are out of proportion can present a more pleasing appearance if the chimneys and window sash and trim are painted the same color as the exterior walls. Good features such as ample and well-placed windows and doors can be emphasized by the use of contrasting colors.

### Is Chicago Hopeless Because There Are No Exterior Paint Possibilities?

Robert Scholar writes, "Chicago, my home town, has lots of old income property. But, as near as I can determine, upwards of 95 per cent of the buildings are brick, not having the exterior paint improvement potential described in your book. Chicago is also decreasing in population, losing out to new brick single-family dwellings in the suburbs.

"How important is owning an exterior-paintable income property? What profitable improvements do you suggest instead? And how does the population loss to the suburbs affect the outlook for real-estate investment success in this area?"

Chicago offers unusual opportunities. I know of many investors who are doing well there, including Gloria Linari and her family and four couples who belong to a bridge club.

The Chicago area is growing rapidly. The percentage of decrease in the city population is slight and not at all alarming. The space abandoned by the lost population is needed for expansion of commercial and industrial activities. These factors are often overlooked when city population figures in a basically expanding area, such as yours, are analyzed. During several visits there I was amazed at all the magnificent new construction. Plenty of structures were going up in outlying areas, but new buildings were especially notable in the heart of the downtown area.

Although painting the exteriors can pay off handsomely, it is only one of many ways to increase values. With brick exteriors, you might consider installing trim or modernizing the entrance. Ask yourself, Will the front look more attractive with new or altered doors, windows, porch, steps or landscaping? Seedy-looking brick can be touched up. You can replace wooden steps with concrete or brick, replace wooden handrails with ornamental iron, and fill in or replace broken sidewalks with new cement. Sometimes you can modernize a front inexpensively by removing elaborate gingerbread, such as scrollwork, fretwork, bays and turrets. In many areas, however, such workmanship has grown antique enough to become greatly prized and should be preserved where feasible.

After improving the exterior, concentrate on painting and modernizing the interiors. Plaster in poor condition can be hidden by thin veneer paneling or other coverings. Excessively high ceilings can be lowered and improved by installing new ceilings of Celotex, fiberboard, acoustical tile or other decoration. Paint interior walls in colors that will make them look light and airy. Improve the floors by revarnishing, painting, or installing new linoleum.

Installations of modern electrical and plumbing fixtures make drastic changes at reasonable cost. Bathrooms can be modernized by putting in plastic, ceramic or other tile walls and floors, new towel racks, medicine cabinets, tubs and showers. Sometimes all you have to do to make a tenant happy is install a shower converter over a showerless tub. Old kitchens can take new cabinets or sinks; drainboards can be covered with formica, plastic varnish, tile or other surfacing.

## Should I Build Apartments on Top of a Funeral Home?

A Midwestern funeral director writes, "I own a very nice one-story funeral home, twelve years old and built of cement blocks. It is a little over 4,000 square feet and next door to a shopping center.

Do you think it would be a profitable idea to erect apartments on top of my building for the additional income? Since there would be no additional land cost, this looks like a natural to me. But I would like to have your objective view before I start building."

Before going far you should check any construction problems and costs with a reliable contractor. Would your present weight-bearing walls carry the additional floors without expensive structural changes and reinforcement? You should also ascertain the availability of adequate financing. Some lending institutions are rigidly allergic to making loans on hybrid structures that attempt to combine residential and commercial rentals.

A location that draws business prospects may meet with little favor as a place to live in. You should consider the location carefully from the standpoint of the average potential tenant. Since location is the number-one controlling factor, would this location draw tenants? I'm afraid that most people wouldn't want to live over a funeral parlor no matter how low the rent.

### Why Don't They Modernize Old Commercial Buildings?

Interior decorator Mildred Willis of New York City wrote, "I lived in a nice big Park Avenue apartment. They tore it down and a lot of other apartment and commercial buildings, too, to build new office buildings. Why don't they modernize instead of tearing them all down?"

In common with apartments, older commercial buildings are being modernized a lot more now than in the past. A 1973 national survey showed that total remodeling permits were about 15 per cent ahead of the previous year. Another survey showed that 75 per cent of all remodeling permits covered office buildings and other nonresidential structures, such as factories, hospitals and schools.

In New York City the Bankers Trust Company completed a

spectacular remodeling of its solid old eleven-story building in mid-Manhattan. The ceilings were so high that the firm was able to convert the building to eighteen stories by using modern low-ceiling heights. In Oakland, California, the old Central Bank Building was completely face-lifted and modernized.

Another outstanding example is the sixty-year-old Stewart Title Guaranty Building in Houston, Texas. A colorful façade of all-mineral panels makes it look brand-new. I have personally inspected these three modernizations, with many others. Their appearance and usability compare favorably with new buildings. Expenditures range from a small cost for face-lifting to between 50 and 75 per cent of new-construction expenses for complete remodeling and modernization.

There is a tax incentive to fixing up an old building as compared to tearing it down and building anew. All costs of modernization can be depreciated, and usually at a faster rate than new construction. With older structures built to last for centuries, demolition may be fairly expensive and this expense must usually be allocated to the cost of the land, which, of course, is not depreciable.

### Should I First Improve the Outside or the Inside?

This question was asked by Jane Hensley, following my lecture to the Evanston–North Shore Board of Realtors, in Chicago's northern suburbs. We were participating in a discussion with Educational Committee co-chairmen Lee Andruss, Jr., and Harold Metzgar.

I would start with the front, following the path that a prospective tenant would take. If the tenant is not attracted by your front yard and the front of the building, he'll never look inside. Next take a look at the entrance lobby and hallway, then the interior of the apartments. Thus, the front yard and building exterior might be first and the rear yard and building exterior last, unless it works out more conveniently to take care of the entire exterior at once.

## Does It Pay to Follow Personal Desires in Fixing Up Housing?

Columnist Beth Norman Harris interviewed me on her Los Angeles KFI radio show, *Meet a Celebrity*. Hollywood dress designer and author Edith Head was on this same show, along with several other authors. In honor of Miss Head, Mrs. Harris asked all participants to answer the question, "Do women dress to please men or to please women?" I was the last to be questioned. My answer was, "They dress to please women, and they undress to please men."

Afterward Mrs. Harris asked, "Do you feel that it pays for an owner like me to put in any improvements I would personally like to have in my own home?"

Like your first question, the answer depends on what your intentions are. For your personal use you should certainly feel free to follow your own inclinations. It would probably pay in terms of satisfaction, pride and enjoyment.

But personal desires should not be followed when you intend to rent or resell, unless the desired improvement increases the sale value by at least double its cost. A good example might be a dishwasher. It could pay very well in a luxury-type apartment. In a lower rent bracket it would not earn sufficient additional income to pay for its initial cost and maintenance.

## Will Tenants Move Rather Than Walk Seven Flights?

An anxious owner who was remodeling a seven-story apartment building telephoned me from Chicago. "I ordered a new automatic elevator to replace the present antique," he said. "This old one requires attendants on a twenty-four-hour basis, around the clock. The new one will be installed in about two months. It will give a lot faster service. The labor savings will be about twice as much as the monthly payments will cost me to buy this new elevator.

"My problem is this: The tenants know I'm going to raise the

rents after I'm all through renovating. They have put up with all
the dust and noise of installing air conditioning, which they now enjoy, without much griping. But several say this is the last straw.
They heard that the elevator would be out of service for three days,
and they're going to move before that. They said they were planning to move before they got a raise anyway.

"Of course the worst complainers are on the top floor. And the
elevator operators keep stirring things up in hopes I'll change my
mind and they can stay on the job. Have you had any experience
with this sort of thing? What should I do to keep too many tenants
from moving?"

I asked if the old elevator has been out of service recently for
repairs.

"Three times in the last year. Once it was out for a twenty-four-
hour stretch."

Your tenants will be more reconciled to inconvenience, even
though they expect rent raises, if they are kept well informed as
to your intentions. Deliver a written notice to all tenants as soon as
possible. Tell them that as part of your modernizing and for their
greater convenience you are installing a new, expensive automatic
elevator that will give fast twenty-four-hour service and will be less
apt to be out of service for repairs than the old one.

Even small concessions will be appreciated by your tenants if
you offer to make up for lack of service. Few tenants will move if
you advise everyone living above the second floor that they will be
given free rent for the three days there will be no elevator service.
This amount—10 per cent of monthly rents—should more than pay
in staving off vacancies, and you'll quickly recoup when you raise
the rents.

Some of the top-floor tenants may choose to use their rent concessions toward the cost of a hotel room. Others may schedule vacations or time off to take a trip. Most of the tenants will probably
walk the stairs. After all, President Truman walked farther than
that every day for the exercise. And President Kennedy advocated
fifty-mile hikes just to test endurance.

## Does It Pay to Put in New Furniture?

This question was asked by Edna Rymal Cox, president of the Southern California chapter of the National Home Fashions League, following my Los Angeles lecture to her group. Program chairwoman Marian Minogue, who worked as publicity director at Bullock's department store, explained that the organization was composed of professional women in the home furnishings industry.

Yes, in most cases new furniture can earn high returns. There was a time when this was not so profitable in many areas, because it was more of a general practice then to put in furniture. Today most new construction is rented unfurnished, so there's less competition for furnished rentals. A lot of older furniture has been outmoded by significant changes in styling, which emphasize simplicity for the most part. Tenants are likely to pay a premium for units that are furnished in attractive modern style.

## Does It Pay to Reupholster Stuffed Furniture?

Following my lecture to the California Apartment Association convention, this question was asked by Elfrida Swanson, president of the group's women's division. Vera Smith, secretary of the women's division of the National Apartment Association, joined in the discussion.

It often pays for personal use, where you desire special fabrics and want to retain fine old furniture for comfort or for sentimental reasons. It seldom pays for rental purposes. Laborious shopwork is so much more expensive than streamlined factory production. Trimlined new furniture on the market, designed for fairly rugged use, is quite inexpensive and costs a lot less than many owners realize. You can buy a new modern sofa set, for example, for less than you would pay to reupholster an old-fashioned set.

## Where Can I Buy at a Discount?

This question has come from many sources. Lee Hill asked it following my address to the Sacramento Women's Council of Realtors. In a letter from California's capital city, Elizabeth Browning states, "After reading your book, my husband, John, and I purchased a furnished sixteen-unit apartment house here in Sacramento. We certainly have found apartment ownership a real challenge which we enjoy exceedingly.

"We have a very competitive situation here, which demands that our units be in the best possible condition in order to keep them rented. So that we can stretch our improvement money as far as possible, we would like to know where we can buy at a discount. In your book you mention that wholesale suppliers advertise in the *Rental Owners Magazine*. I wonder whether this is a local publication or one available only in your area. Please advise.

"The Sacramento Apartment House Association, of which we are members, sends us a *Bulletin* in which a few local advertisers print their ads and mention that there is a discount to Apartment Association members. But this discount as a rule is not worth mentioning. We got a very nice discount on refrigerators by buying them direct from the company. However, this possibility is not mentioned anywhere in our *Bulletin*. Could you tell us where we can buy at similar discounts?"

The *Rental Owners Magazine* referred to in my book is a general name for the publications of local apartment and other owner associations, such as yours in Sacramento and mine in Oakland. Most of those I have seen carry advertising from manufacturers like Frigidaire, General Electric, Kelvinator, Westinghouse and Wedgwood. All of them give substantial discounts to bona-fide apartment association members. Perhaps your *Bulletin* committee has not contacted such companies recently regarding advertising. Or perhaps the companies did not feel your membership was large enough to warrant paid ads.

The National Apartment Association has recently started publishing a national *Rental Housing* magazine. Inquiries can be addressed to the new national headquarters in Washington, D.C. The publishers expect that all major national manufacturers who give discounts to apartment owners will place ads. The magazine is available for individual members of the association and to members of affiliated local groups such as yours.

Your local office is likely to have an exchange file of magazines put out by other associations. I have seen many such publications carrying advertisements of national and local companies, offering discounts to apartment association members. It is a common practice of many manufacturers to require that a membership card be shown before discounts are discussed.

## How Can I Join the Apartment Owners Association?

Contractor-builder D. R. Stuart of New Orleans lists "remodeling" on his letterhead. He writes, "I have read your book many times and enjoyed it, even though you are a little harsh on us contractors. I would appreciate your advice as to how I can become a member of the Apartment Owners Association."

You can join as an individual member of the national organization by writing National Apartment Association, 1825 K Street, N.W., Suite 604, Washington, D.C. 20006. The national office can also advise you of the name and address of their nearest affiliate in your area. I know there is a thriving local in New Orleans as I have lectured there.

Sometimes the locals are hard to find in the phone book because of the variety of names, for example, Rental Owners, Apartment Owners, Home and Apartment Owners, Apartment Association, etc. Many are listed under the name of the city, county, state, or area. For example, San Jose, California, is listed under Tri-County Apartment Association, covering Santa Clara, San Mateo and Santa Cruz counties. Who would ever think of looking under Tri-County? Many others are just as hard to find. So, when in doubt, write the national association!

# XVI

## How Can I Make Profitable Property Improvements?

San Francisco suburbanite Olive Robinson writes, "I bought my present home for $5,000, and it is now worth about $25,000. I owe $6,000 on the present loan and have a new loan commitment from a local savings-and-loan company, for $17,500. Part of the $20,-000 increase in value is, of course, due to inflation. But a great deal of the new valuation, 500 per cent of my original cost, is because of the improvements I have made. Much of it has been with my own hands, such as laying a three-quarter-inch oak floor, spackling, painting, laying linoleum, and plastic-tiling one bathroom.

"Redoing an old house to create atmosphere out of shabbiness is lots of fun to me. I should think it would be a lot more fun to do most of the planning and then hire the work. That's what I want to do in future stages, after avidly reading your engrossing book. But I want to stay in my present home in San Mateo, where I am all set up as an interior decorator, my only regular source of income.

"I plan to get the new loan, then use most of the money to buy apartments in San Francisco and arrange to fix them up. Is it safe to own both, to keep my home and buy apartments too? Should I get the biggest loan possible, or less, with lower payments? I am a widow of fifty-six with a son in college and would appreciate having your reassurance before going ahead. Although I know it is very inadequate, enclosed is check for $10 to help pay for your trouble in answering my letter. Is this a good time to start in San Francisco?

I mean right now, this month, considering international problems, continuing-recession predictions by some authorities, election uncertainties, present high interest rates?"

Thank you for your check, which I am returning, marked "Void." With your experience and acumen, and the amount of equity money available from refinancing, you should be able to keep your home, if you prefer, and borrow on it for further investment. As long as you are refinancing, get the highest possible long-term loan, to speed your progress. Keep a fair amount in reserve for contingencies and to tide you over until additional profits offset your higher payments. Your profitable house improvements should give you a decided advantage in continuing to fix up older rental property. Your $17,500 loan commitment proves that you have chosen wisely in making improvements. It also proves that your present evaluation of approximately $25,000 is sound.

San Francisco offers fine opportunities. I know of many recent successes there. This is a good time for you to start. As to a continuing recession, I think that present indications point in the opposite direction. Opportunities will keep rising in the Seventies and Eighties, along with expanding production.

At an educational seminar of the Evanston–North Shore Board of Realtors in Illinois, I shared the lecture platform with Dr. Arthur Upgren, professor of economics at St. Paul's Macalester College. It was refreshing to hear his realistic and knowledgeable views, bolstered with objective factual studies, rather than more theoretical approaches. We found that our predictions of future opportunities were almost identical.

### Are Many Women Getting into the Do-It-Yourself Act?

This question was asked by saleswoman Doris Burnham of the investment book section while I was autographing in Boston's Lauriat Bookstore.

Few women would attempt heavy-duty jobs like putting in new oak flooring, but they do handle many improvements. Equipment and techniques have been simplified to encourage more home improvements by the unskilled. It does not take any expert training to do painting with rollers or to use brush-on adhesive to install floor tile and plastic tiling for walls and drainboards. The growing number of women who take on such projects is helping significantly to swell the volume of do-it-yourself projects, with annual increases in the 10 per cent range. Manufacturers estimate that do-it-yourself work jumps over $2 billion annually, exceeding $30 billion in 1974.

With do-it-yourself projects costing less than half as much as contracted work, over twice as much improvement can be accomplished for the money spent. More technical problems, like extensive remodeling, plumbing and wiring, which usually require inspections, should best be handled by experienced contractors. But jobs like painting and gardening are easily handled by the neophyte. While more outdoor work is handled by contractors and by men, it is interesting to note that women do almost as much inside painting as men. A national study cited by David Kennedy, president of Kentile, Inc., indicates that 70 per cent of all interior painting was done by do-it-yourselfers, with the breakdown as follows:

| | | |
|---|---|---|
| Married and single men, working alone | 32% | |
| Married and single women, working alone | 25% | |
| Couples working together | 13% | |
| Total for men | 38.5% | |
| Total for women | 31.5% | |

### Is Do-It-Yourself Necessary?

This question was asked by former Doubleday editor Mary Lou Mueller, before she married a San Francisco banker, Leslie Dorking. Miss Mueller told me that my book made her so enthusiastic she wanted to invest in income property herself. But my do-it-yourself approach didn't appeal to her. Was my formula possible without the personal labor?

I guess too much work doesn't appeal to anybody! I revised the book, explaining that you don't have to do a lick of work, but can hire it all, and my formula still works out. Actually, doing the spadework gives you an extra push if you start with a small nest egg and are full of energy and young ideas, but it is not necessary. If you start with a larger nest egg, or move up the investment ladder, you are better off not to do the labor. It pays to hire others, as I do now, and spend your time shopping for good buys and supervising your property. Hired labor is tax-deductible, while your personal labor is not.

A lot of people fail to progress because they don't change their ways as they increase their holdings. They get a good start via the praiseworthy do-it-yourself route, then fail to pyramid nearly as far as they could, because they keep trying to do all the work. This is bound to slow them down, and often it discourages further advancement. It pays to analyze your operations periodically in order to make the most of your time and energy.

### Is a Renovation Program Possible in Virginia?

A Navy captain's wife writes from Norfolk, Virginia, "My husband and I are both devout church people. We are interested in developing a better world, spiritually and physically; at the same time we want a certain amount of comfort to go along with the security from a Navy pension that will soon be coming with my husband's retirement.

"Your program of fixing up rental properties appeals to us greatly. Goodness knows there are plenty of Navy personnel with low incomes who would like to have more decent housing at reasonable cost. We like the goals of improving property for the benefit of better living conditions for tenants and a better income for ourselves. We have about $20,000 to invest. We've found a couple of apartment houses here that we feel we could do well on. They are run-down and have low rents. We could fix them up and raise the rents a good deal. I just love decorating, and my husband's hobby is carpentry, and we're both anxious to get started.

"Our problem is that the two salesmen we talked to about this say that your program won't work in Norfolk, that the only way to make money in real estate is to ride inflation—and that is out of the picture here. Do you think there are possibilities in Norfolk, in Virginia, or should we go to Baltimore or Philadelphia or some other larger place?"

It's true, you can't depend on inflation's increasing values. Homeowners find, for the most part, that homes are most likely to sell at a profit when they make some improvements. Values increase when you do something to add usable space, like converting a garage to a bedroom or a rumpus room. When you upgrade the use of space on any kind of property, through modernizing, rehabilitating or building anew, you can earn a profit anywhere in the United States, certainly including Norfolk.

All the cities named have fine possibilities. But if you like Norfolk, why don't you follow your inclinations and stay? On a recent visit there I appraised some exceptional opportunities. You just happen to have talked to unimaginative salesmen. Among those who have told me of successful property improvements in your area is Geoffrey Myers. His firm, the Jamson Realty Company, specializes in "the purchase and renovation of real estate."

### Is It Too Late for a Waltham Couple of 60 and 67 to Start Remodeling?

A sexagenarian of Waltham, Massachusetts, writes, "I wish I could have had your book 25 years ago. I would have gone into property improvement and reinvestment a long time ago instead of only fixing up one home and playing it so safe with 4 to 6 per cent earnings from bank savings and insurance. I am going to need more income for retirement soon. Is it too late for a couple of sixty and sixty-seven, both in good health, to start building an income from property?

"We own free and clear a sixty-five-year-old two-story eight-room house in good condition. Good residential location near schools and bus line to Boston, only eight miles away. Waltham is a growing city again. Was in doldrums after some of our industries went South, where our skills are not needed and you can get cheaper labor. But now our skills are being appreciated and we are expanding as an electronics center.

"Bought house for $5,500 fifteen years ago. It is now appraised at $11,900. Has hot-air coal furnace, cedar shingles over clapboard, very well insulated walls. Have been thinking about putting $1,500 into a new gas heating plant, with extra aluminum storm windows and attic insulation recommended by gas company. No savings, by gas company estimates, but greater convenience, as gas would cost us about the same as present $300 per year for coal heat.

"If we fix up this place, small bathroom should also be tiled, at about $200, and kitchen modernized with new cabinets, linoleum, etc., at around $500. With these things done, at a cost of, say, $2,500, could I get the money back out of it if I sold? Am impressed by what you say about not sinking more into a property than can be gotten out of it.

"Waltham is full of old and often run-down apartments, tenements, and single homes, being a very old industrial city. Four-room apartments here rent for $85 to $90 unfurnished; stove but no refrigerator; some with, some without heat. Could invest about $3,000 to buy a two-apartment unit. Can save $600 to $700 per year additional, as in your example, for a few more years. But with inflationary prices, tighter money, higher interest rates, higher labor, wonder if the same advice your book gives would now prevail. Could I make better use of my modest resources even at my age by investing in such a two-apartment house that needs capital improvements?"

The accumulated nest egg you have in hand and your determination to better yourselves suggest that it certainly is not too late to start building up an income from property investment and improvement. Your free-and-clear home gives you a good backlog, along with other resources. Whether you sell or not, you can borrow enough on it for a good start on a worthwhile income-property program.

As you say, older Eastern cities like Waltham are full of old houses and apartments. Most of them have been allowed to run down. This situation naturally offers more opportunities for the investor who is farsighted enough to modernize. Whether you should spend the estimated $2,500 on your present home depends on the application of the yardstick detailed in my first book—would it increase the sale value $2 for each $1 spent on improvement? If not, your proposed changes are not a moneymaking investment. You would make them as a matter of personal enjoyment, if at all.

Some costs like land prices have risen since my first book was written, but this is only relative and does not limit opportunities. Automation and streamlined construction methods have actually cut costs in some instances, despite higher wage rates. It is best to buy as many units as your money will soundly handle. Consider the possibility of converting your two-story house to apartments. Before you decide on this step, however, get two or three bids from remodeling contractors and figure your potential income and resale value after conversion.

My Waltham correspondent wrote later, "After receiving your letter we went ahead with the mentioned improvements. Cost us $2,250 and increased the value about $6,000, as the new appraisal value is $18,000."

### Why Do You Give Contractors a Rough Time?

A Southern contractor phoned long distance seeking confirmation of the soundness of his refinancing arrangements. He planned to remodel a large run-down apartment house development. He expected to make about a quarter of a million on an initial investment of $40,000. After discussing his plans, already worked out, he said, "I had to ask somebody about this before going ahead. The profits look too good to be possible. I like everything in your book except for one thing, and that's got me riled. What have you against contractors? You give us a pretty rough time in your book."

D. R. Stuart of New Orleans made a similar complaint, mentioned in the previous chapter.

*Time* magazine wrote that half of my book is concerned with telling people what not to do. This includes warnings against a great number of situations and unreliable characters. Among them are some unscrupulous and bumbling contractors. However, I have warm regard for contractors in general and feel that the great majority of them are trustworthy and able. In fact, I advise investors to graduate from do-it-yourself as soon as feasible and to contract improvements in order to progress more rapidly.

It usually pays to deal with a contractor who specializes in remodeling, like my New Orleans correspondent. Some contractors avoid remodeling, chiefly because it takes more initiative and imagination than following a blueprint on new construction. A growing number realize that property improvement is a rapidly expanding business they should cater to.

Herbert Richheimer, for example, has remodeled four thousand houses on Long Island. He and another successful remodeling expert, Charles Abrams from White Plains, New York, have started a school that meets a real need. They have taught their "one-stop modernization" methods—whereby all work is handled by one general contractor—to builders from twenty-seven states.

### When Is a Building Worth Remodeling?

Richheimer states that any building is worth remodeling if it is structurally sound, unless it is in a totally run-down neighborhood.

### What's the Fastest Way to Waste Money Remodeling?

Richheimer's answers to this question: "Give the job to a fast-talking salesman, a suede-shoe artist for an out-of-town contractor. Pick one who may fly by night as soon as he is paid, leaving you with shoddy work, instead of a reliable firm in your own community. A member of your local contractors' organization has to back up his work with at least a year's guarantee."

## What Contractors and Contractors' Gimmicks Should I Guard Against?

This question comes nearly always, it seems, from housewives or widows. They have had or have heard about disappointing experiences with various contractors and their workmen. One New Jersey widow, for example, writes, "I have owned a duplex free and clear. I live in one unit, and the other has paid all my housing expenses. After reading your book I decided to convert my full attic into a third apartment.

"I answered an ad in the paper that said, 'Attics and basements changed to income-producing apartments for only $1,000.' The salesman who answered my phone call came right out to see me. He said, 'Sure we can put in your attic apartment for $1,000. That'll be $1,000 down, payable in cash. The total cost will be $2,000. But we'll make it easy on you and take your note for the extra $1,000.'

"He wanted me to sign a contract and pay the cash deposit right away. But I held off and checked his proposition and his firm with the Better Business Bureau. They said the police were after this outfit. They had a reputation of collecting a bunch of down payments, then skipping town.

"The Better Business man told me of another outfit that overcharges and the police can't do much about it. They collect a deposit, say $1,000, then charge, say, $5,000. It's always enough so they can keep all the deposit as their commission. Then they turn the balance of the contract over to a legitimate contractor, who naturally only does $4,000 worth of work.

"The Better Business Bureau recommended that I check with our local Contractors Association. They referred me to an expert remodeler who put in a nice 200-square-foot two-bedroom apartment for $4,000. He finished the job even better than he promised, and I am very happy with the results. I rented out the new apartment for $95 a month. I got a new mortgage for $12,000, which gives me $8,000 clear cash for more investing and improving of property. I'm very anxious to keep going. After just missing getting gypped, I now have a question: What are other contractor gimmicks to guard against?"

The Federal Housing Administration has compiled a booklet listing the names of unreliable contractors to guard against. Your first safeguard is to know your contractor's reliability. Besides the Better Business Bureau and the Contractors Association, there are other places to check regarding the reliability of good contractors and the unreliability of bad ones. Included are your local apartment or rental owners' association, real-estate board and home builders' association.

You can also ask the contractor for a bank reference and check there. Ask to see other work the contractor has completed, and ask the owners if they are satisfied. Is there any part of the work or the follow-up on guarantees of which they do not approve? Were there any problems on the crediting of payments, with liens or threats of liens from subcontractors or suppliers?

The safest bet, if you are in doubt, is to have the contract bonded. The additional cost is nominal and it might be wise in certain cases. If the contractor can't get a bond, you would be warned against hiring him. On the other hand, if he can readily furnish a bond, you probably don't need one.

### What Steps Should I Take Before Signing a Contract?

This question was asked by Everett Robinson of Wilderville, Oregon. He planned to improve the operation of his dairy farm by extensive additional construction, including a new creamery and a large barn.

Before signing a contract, you usually want bids from at least three reliable contractors. Specifications should be clearly spelled out, so that the contractors will be bidding on the same work. Each contractor is apt to give you additional ideas on how the job can best be handled, which will help you to check one against the other.

One may bid on the basis of two-by-three-inch studs, for example, while another plans to use two-by-fours or even two-by-sixes. Questions may arise on such details as:

> How close are the studs, for example, sixteen inches or twenty-four inches?
> How many coats of paint and what kind?
> How many layers on a tar-and-gravel roof?
> For how long is the over-all job guaranteed?
> For how long is specific work, like a new roof, guaranteed?

If the lowest bid is unusually below the others, it pays to double-check the completeness of the bid and the reliability of the contractor, but bear in mind the point that a reliable contractor may make a sound bid far below the others simply because they are busy and he has a slack period and wants to keep his crew working. Or he may do much of the labor himself.

Without telling the other contractors what the low bid is, I sometimes notify them that a certain contractor has underbid. Then I ask if they know anything about his work. They often volunteer such advice as, "He's a good man. I don't see how he beat our price." Praise from a competitor can be accepted as an accolade of reliability. They may say, on the other hand, "Sure he bid low. He always chisels. He thins his paint." They may point out other typical flaws of the job at hand, like "He skins his roofs." Criticism from competitors has to be taken with a grain of salt. But they often know of locations where the shortcomings have occurred—the most reliable exposure.

A point to be wary of: Sometimes a high bidder warns against practices which he or his labor forces do not approve, but which may produce just as good work. Some unions, for example, forbid efficient labor-saving devices like spray painting. Others insist that various materials, like flooring and wallboard, be laboriously installed in small segments even though it is manufactured in standard panels that may come as large as four by eight feet.

After costs have been determined by competitive bids, you will, of course, want to be assured of financing before signing a contract.

## What Should I Do After Work Starts?

This question was asked by Emma Sue Mann of Marianna, Arkansas, following my lecture in the book department of Goldsmith's department store, across the Mississippi in Memphis, Tennessee.

Even with the most reliable contractor, it pays to check on the work as it progresses. All contracts are subject to individual interpretations on various points that can usually be settled readily as work progresses, but which are costly to correct later. Whenever possible, obtain samples of the actual colors and materials to be used, to avoid misunderstandings. Color charts or manufacturer's samples can be checked, or you can specify duplication of other jobs completed by the contractor.

At certain stages of progress, the contract should call for payments to be made and they should not be speeded up. Disbursements should be arranged so that there is more work completed than you are paying for. Otherwise some contractors will leave you dangling interminably with an unfinished job while they concentrate on other work where they will receive some money. There are many advantages to getting a construction loan from a bank or some other lending institution, to cover new building or remodeling work. Most lenders will:

Verify the reliability of the contractor
Check the soundness of plans for construction and for repayment
Inspect the work as it progresses
Withhold payments until the work is satisfactorily completed
Insure that subcontractors and suppliers have been paid before
making final payment.

## What Should I Watch After the Job Is Finished?

This question was asked by Harry Andersen of Orinda, California. He and his wife, Janice, were completing a major construction job following his return from conducting a three-month group tour of Europe enjoyed by my wife and me.

The contractor may ask for full payment as soon as the job is completed. Never pay the full amount until required inspections have been made by lending and civic authorities, and until the statutory lien period has expired. On new construction and on any substantial remodeling work a specified amount, usually about one fifth of the total, should be held back until the lien period is over. After a "notice of completion" is recorded, subcontractors and suppliers are allowed a period, ranging from thirty to ninety days in various states, during which they can file a lien on your property if they are not paid.

Liens can be placed regardless of whether you have paid your general contractor in full, as long as he has not paid his bills. Besides the possibility of unsatisfactory work, this presents your greatest risk in hiring an unreliable contractor. He can skip out, leaving you with a lot of bills to pay, even though you have paid him the full amount you owe. The effect of a lien is similar to that of a mortgage for insuring payment: the holder can institute foreclosure proceedings if his claim is not settled.

A distinct advantage of dealing with a licensed contractor is that in order for him to keep his license most of his work must be guaranteed for at least one year. Other than that, certain equipment and certain installations, such as roofs, are guaranteed for a stipulated number of years by manufacturer and contractor. The time specifications are set forth in the contract.

### Why Doesn't the Government Fix Up Older Housing?

This question was explored by the Misses Tichenor and Peterson of Marshall Field's while I was autographing in their book department. They mentioned that many substantial older buildings were torn down in the Chicago area to make way for new public housing. It seemed that desirable housing could have been provided at much cheaper cost by fixing up the old structures.

Government housing bureaucracies throughout the country have previously succumbed to the destructive disease of bulldozeritis. However, Commissioner Bruce Savage of the Public Housing Administration in Washington states that he has found a cure. His department has recently started a new approach nationally and is now encouraging the rehabilitation of some older housing. As an experiment, a large and solid New York rooming house has been converted to modern two-, three- and four-bedroom apartments. The remodeling cost, about $10,000 per unit, is approximately half the cost of providing similar accommodations under new construction. A new project finished at the same time cost an average of $19,022 per unit. This government experience dramatically demonstrates the competitive position of improved older housing.

### What If the Tenants Can't Afford Increased Rents?

San Francisco auto dealer and County Supervisor Roger Boas asked this question as moderator of the KQED Educational TV discussion on property investment, in which, as mentioned earlier, I participated along with a Stanford professor of economics. Boas said, "You advocate improving property and then increasing rents. Even though the tenants may prefer the renovations, what if they can't afford the increased rent? Is it fair to deprive them of a place to live?"

If values increase beyond his budget, the tenant can get another dwelling in the price range he can afford.

It's like a woman trying on a fur coat she would like to keep. Suppose she can't afford it. She simply has to shop for something within her budget. The same economy applies, of course, to many things. To give another example, many a person would like to own a new car, but can't afford it. So he settles for a less expensive used car.

Those who can afford a new car expect to pay more for it. The same goes for a better used car, which you fix up and guarantee.

Most tenants expect to pay increased rent for better living conditions, which they crave. My general suggestions are based on creating better living quarters by improving property. Improving older properties provides desirable dwellings at less cost to tenants than comparable new construction.

## What Exterior Remodeling Pays the Biggest Profit?

This question was asked by Jack Dudfield, Santa Cruz County, California, a general contractor.

First steps, second porches, and third patios. These most profitable projects make up by far the highest portion of all exterior remodeling. Merely changing front steps and/or a front porch, for example, from worn-out wood to brick can increase value to ten times the cost and change an eyesore into an eye-catcher.

A 1972 survey by the Bureau of Building Marketing Research indicates that contract permits were issued for 1.5 million new patios added to existing structures.

## What Interior Remodeling Pays Off the Most?

"What major interior remodeling pays off the most?" asks interior decorator Barbara Straub of Long Beach, California, "and what specific changes?"

Modernizing kitchens and baths are the most profitable remodeling projects. The B.B.M.R. survey of contracted permits, mentioned above, found that over 3.3 million kitchens were remodeled and close to 3 million bathrooms. These are the key rooms a prospective resident inspects closely when planning either to buy or rent.

Kitchens are modernized dramatically by adding new cabinets, sinks and counters, new linoleum flooring, and new appliances, including exhaust fans, garbage disposers, and dishwashers.

Bathrooms can also be pleasingly transformed with new cabinets, a modern medicine cabinet over the basin with a large mirror and diffused lighting, and a storage cabinet under the basin which conceals unsightly plumbing. Also replace shower curtains with glass doors over the tub or shower stall, and cover the floor with bright linoleum or indoor-outdoor carpet.

# 8

# How to Increase
# Value by
# Improving Operations

# XVII

## How Can I Improve Operations?

I have been asked a wide variety of questions about ways to improve the handling of leases, receipts, raises and other details in the field of operations. While the physical improvement of property is commonly recognized as a means of increasing values, it is not unusual to make equally spectacular gains by improving operations.

### Can You Give One Real Moneymaking Case of Improving Operations?

This question was asked by Rex Barley, book editor of the Los Angeles *Mirror-News,* when he interviewed me on his KFI radio show *Books in the News.* Barley mentioned how unusual it seemed to him that there could be as many unimaginative property owners as my book indicated. Were my case histories somewhat exaggerated? Or did operating and physical conditions met by potential buyers actually offer opportunities for drastic improvements?

Once you take a close look at actual conditions you realize it is common to find opportunities for improvements. The case histories in which I mention names are quoted verbatim. Some improvements have been so phenomenal that I have toned them down in order to give an example that would be closer to average opportunities.

The outstanding commercial construction project in the free-enterprise system is Rockefeller Center in New York. And the most spectacular example of improving a single building's operations is Joseph Kennedy's handling of the twenty-story Merchandise Mart in Chicago. With ninety-three acres of income-producing space, the Mart is topped only by the Pentagon in size. Kennedy bought the world's largest commercial building in 1945 for approximately $13 million. He obtained a $12.5-million insurance company loan, which made his down payment only half a million, less than 4 per cent.

Marshall Field, the original owner, had depreciated the building to a book value of $21 million. He sold to Kennedy at a sacrifice because his firm, although strong in merchandising, was rather rigid as an income-property operator. Field was afraid of heavy vacancies that might come from the impending loss of government tenants, who occupied about a third of the building at low rents. To Field the government exodus presented a calamity. To an imaginative income-property investor like Kennedy it meant an opportunity. Under his aggressive management the Mart leased space to commercial tenants at considerably higher rents.

Four years after Kennedy's purchase the increase in value enabled him to get a new $17-million insurance-company loan. This gave him $4 million over his purchase price to use for making some property improvements and for further pyramiding. In ten years, chiefly because of a change in operations rather than physical change, the Mart produced $13 million in annual gross rentals, equaling the total purchase price. The new net gave it a value of $75 million, $62 million more than Kennedy paid. The new capital value rose to almost six times the original purchase price.

### Should I Raise Rents in Improvement Stages or All at Once?

A letter comes from Hilde Blodgett, of Massachusetts, who writes, "My husband, Harry, has a dry-cleaning route, and until we purchased your wonderful book all we could look forward to was the continuing problems of this service business. We started shopping soon after we both read your thrilling book. Four months afterward we bought our first piece of property, a fourplex in Salem.

"We bought the place for $15,000, with $3,000 down payment, and financing four times our personal investment. This compares with your example of only three times. Principal, interest and taxes cost us $116 per month. This place seems to follow your book to the letter: in a good neighborhood, near schools, transportation, beaches, shopping, etc., structurally sound, but needing renovation. Three of the tenants have lived here for sixteen years and the other one for three years. The rents were underpriced to begin with—$10, $10, $12 and $12 weekly—so we raised the tenants $2 each per week as soon as we took over.

"The outside needs a paint job, and the front steps need repairing. Just like you said, these items sure helped to pull the price down! Each of the apartments has five large rooms with front and back porches. The tenants furnish their own heat, sharing expenses, as there are two coal furnaces with each one heating two apartments.

"We informed the tenants that we intended making improvements, and we plan to install new kitchen sinks, new lighting fixtures, repair all switches and install a hot-water heater in the one apartment that lacks this facility. We figure all repairs and improvements will cost about $2,000, making our total investment $17,000. We don't want to overprice these apartments and cause vacancies, but we do want a maximum profit. We would appreciate your opinion as to a couple of questions: What rents should our tenants pay to make this a good investment for us? Also, as we plan to do this work in stages, should we keep raising the rents as we go along, or should we wait until all improvements are completed?"

It appears you have made a sound buy that should become a good moneymaker. Of course, rents vary in different areas, but yours seem as low as wartime rent-control levels. Your purchase price was fair on the basis of the old rents. After you make your improvements they should be closer to double the original rents. To allow for the $2,000 in improvements to pay off, you need only increase the sales value by $4,000. This can be accomplished by increasing the net income $400 per year, an amount you have already exceeded by raising the rents $416 a year. This action constitutes at least an improvement in operations.

Taking into account nearby-area rentals, with which I am familiar, and the cost of reproduction, your apartments should rent for a minimum of $75 and a maximum of $125 monthly after they are fixed up. You might find out what the rentals are in the neighborhood on modernized rentals, so that yours will be competitive. Rental values have nothing to do with your costs, but are pegged basically to the cost of reproduction for new buildings, less depreciation. That is why you can get a high return on judicious improvements, often far exceeding the examples I have given.

Normally, you will have maximum over-all income and minimum losses from vacancies if you increase the rents gradually as you make improvements. Eventually, as you reach the sound potential maximum, some of your present tenants are likely to move. If a unit becomes vacant, fix it up completely, if you can, in a minimum time. Then try to rent it immediately for what you think it will bring. You can always lower your sights, or consider additional improvements, if the apartment is not rented in a reasonable time. In your situation two weeks should be long enough to test the market. The increased rent you receive from a new tenant will give you a good verification of the market value of the other rentals.

### Are General Rent Increases Feasible, and When Should They Be Made?

This question was asked by San Francisco *Chronicle* reporter William Keller in connection with my appearance on KQED-TV. Many investors have asked me questions along the same lines.

The Blodgetts' experience in raising rents even before they made improvements suggests that the former owners could have increased their operating income by taking the same step. It is not at all uncommon to find that rents in desirable older properties are considerably lower than the going rates. They can be raised immediately or as soon as leases expire.

Generally, rents have increased along with tenants' income and operating costs such as taxes, utilities and repairs. In most cases where rents have stayed the same for some time, it usually turns out that the property is not maintained as well as it might be—but even in its present condition it should often pay a higher income.

An appropriate time to raise rents is, of course, after improvements are made, for then you have established a tangible increase in value. Other typical times are after announcements of increases in costs, which tenants expect to have offset by higher rents. Newspaper stories about higher real-estate taxes make good springboards. Another good time is in the early fall, when tenants settle down. A poor time to add to a tenant's expenses is when holidays approach and when Christmas costs are impending. If rent raises fall due along in November or December, it's a good idea to postpone action until after the first of the year.

On the general subject of raises, here is a quotation from Oscar Brinkman's *Washington Letter,* distributed to all members of the National Apartment Association:

In places where vacancies are not excessive, many apartment owners have found it feasible to increase rents moderately during the year. The early fall, before school starts and the heating season begins, has been found the best time to make upward rent adjustments, coupled with a simple explanation to tenants whose leases are about to expire that higher costs of operation . . . including taxes, fuel, repairs . . . make an increase necessary.

Increases of 3% to 5% are usually not regarded as excessive by tenants, many of whom have been able to increase their own incomes considerably more than that during the past few years. There is less complaint . . . and less termination of occupancies . . . when rent increases are put into effect *after* buildings, grounds, and apartments have been put into spic and span condition. There's such a large difference now between the rental rates of apartments in new, high-cost buildings and those in older structures that necessary upward adjustments of rentals in the latter cause no exodus of tenants.

## Should I Screen Present Tenants Before Buying?

Department of State employee Ralph Singleton asked this question following my lecture in Washington, D.C. "I can visualize finding an apartment building that checks out O.K. except that it might be filled with undesirable tenants. Would this be likely in a city with rapidly changing population, as in Washington? Should I protect myself by screening the tenants as to their suitability before I buy? Or should I wait and weed them out after buying?"

It would be a waste of time to try to screen apartment tenants before buying. The same thing applies to trying to push out undesirable tenants afterward by a clean-sweep process. It's best to accept them as desirable until they prove otherwise. I presume you are thinking of the cranks, Philadelphia lawyers, etc., who may be potential troublemakers. You can always evict them if they become undesirable. Of course, it is easy to evict them if they don't pay their rent. In most cases you would borrow unnecessary trouble by advance screening of tenants. Most of those living in the average building turn out to be perfectly suitable.

We are talking here about apartment tenants. If you happen to buy a commercial building, it pays to check credit ratings, ability to pay and legitimacy of the lease. In this type of operation, if the tenant moves or is unable to pay it may take several months or even years to find another tenant for the particular building and location.

With apartments, the main thing you want to check is whether the tenants are actually paying the rents quoted. You should review the entire rent roll with the manager and spot-check the rents in individual apartments as you inspect them. With some new construction, you should be especially wary of gimmicks the previous owner may have used—such as giving free rent to fill a building, then showing above-market rent schedules that are not in effect and will not hold up.

An example I spotted took place in a new sixty-unit garden-type apartment operation with a swimming pool. The tenants were promised two months' free rent on moving in, on condition that they sign a one-year lease. The lease provided that the first and last months were free, with the other months carrying a rental of $150. Thus the actual rental for twelve months was $1,500, an average of $125 per month instead of the $150 quoted. The difference of $25 monthly applied to sixty apartments, which made an overstatement of $18,000 in annual rental income. This represented a net-income figure, since it did not affect expenses. With apartment values generally figured at ten times the annual net, the sale value in this case was distorted upward by $180,000.

This misrepresented operation was easy to spot merely by reading the leases. It was verified by checking with some of the tenants when their apartments were inspected. A point to keep in mind: Before you buy, always read the leases, monthly contracts and inventories or other documents covering tenants' occupancy.

## Should I Check New Tenants Against a Rental Owners' Clearing House?

Sabina Connor writes from Pasadena, California, "A recent acquaintance tried to interest me in going into business with him on what he thinks will be a real moneymaker: to form a partnership to set up a central office for a landlords' clearing house for credit references, etc., on renters. Rental owners to pay $20 per year dues, which would give them the privilege of checking on tenant histories. Owners to be able to recover their $20 dues through firms who agree to give special discounts.

"The company to have a lobbyist in the capital to look out for landlord interests—especially in taxes. Property owners carry the burden of taxes for schools, etc.; renters do not pay for the schools, yet have more children in attendance, there being more renters than property owners. [sic]

"This all sounds as though it might be a good service, but it would require a monumental amount of work to organize. I am not

about to leap into fields I know nothing about, putting up money
that could easily be lost. Your book cautions on this score very
definitely—to stay in fields of proven merit and in which you know
at least something. Please answer my question with your comments:
Does this idea have merit?"

The ideas presented certainly have merit, as do many which may
perform a useful service, but they may have little likelihood of paying off. The odds against you, as I stated in my first book, are four
to one that you will fail when you go into any new business. This
compares on a ratio of sixteen hundred to one less favorably than
apartment investment, where the odds are four hundred to one in
your favor.

Many apartment associations already keep tenant histories, particularly a blacklist of poor payers and destructive and obstreperous renters who have been evicted. But some tenants change. A
tenant who is bad for one owner might turn out fine with another
under firmer collection and other operating policies. The chastening
effect of an eviction may make a tenant toe the line thereafter.
Some organizations continue maintaining their lists in conjunction
with a commercial credit firm, like the Retail Credit Association.
They can perform a useful guide if they are kept up to date by
apartment owners on an objective basis. Others have discontinued
the practice because owners have just not bothered to check before
renting. How can they tell whether a manager has blacklisted a nice
tenant for personal reasons? The majority of owners and managers
prefer to use their own judgment, backed up by credit and character
references.

Most of the services mentioned are performed by apartment associations, with minimum dues less than the $20 you quote. The
California Apartment Association lobbies in Sacramento and the
National Apartment Association in Washington. The support of
such lobbying is certainly vital in order to offset adverse taxation,
diehard rent control and other lobbies inimical to property ownership.

However, owner taxes are eventually passed on to tenants. They have to be, even in rent-control areas. Renters greatly exceed property owners only in New York City, where a two-thirds majority of the population are renters and their political strength has maintained rent control. Across the country, owners are in almost a two-thirds majority.

### Do Minority Races Always Cause Deteriorated Housing?

Arthur McInerney writes from New York City, "I am a sixty-seven-year-old native of Manhattan and wonder if it is safe to invest in my beloved city, or whether I should buy my first rental property across the Hudson in New Jersey. Does the change in population to Negro and Puerto Rican mean the eventual deterioration of rental property? Is it safe to rent to these minority races as tenants, or will they depreciate your values from the very first day?"

Minority races can be just as desirable tenants as anyone else if they are provided with desirable housing. Tenants of all races should be chosen on the basis of their ability to pay and to get along harmoniously with other tenants in the same building. In localities like Hawaii, harmony is achieved with unrestricted mixing of all races, a worldwide goal that should ultimately be achieved.

If an area is being taken over by a minority race, it pays to recognize the facts as they are and cater to this group. The biggest mistake is to allow properties to deteriorate because of such change. In all cases it pays to keep properties in good condition. Then you can continue to be selective in your choice of well-paying, well-behaved tenants. An owner who properly maintains his property can still choose desirable tenants, regardless of the race that may dominate the particular area.

Opportunities are available on a nationwide basis, and I'm sure you will find many good buys in New Jersey. However, the larger the city the greater are the number of opportunities for property investment. If you prefer New York, by all means shop for good buys there, where more rental units drop below the slum line every year than are built under redevelopment programs. In my opinion, this scandalous deterioration and need for complete rejuvenation is, to a large extent, due to the depressing effects of rent controls. Obviously, tenants with their important voting power are the chief proponents of rent control. Landlords in the past have helped to bring this condition on themselves by wide-scale bleeding of properties. Some have boasted about not spending a cent for repairs or improvements. They have been "penny wise and pound foolish." But owners of run-down buildings who overcome the psychological block of controls can make more money by fixing up their properties.

### How Can You Justify Overlapping Rent?

Most tenants have no further interest in an apartment once they vacate. Some are unhappy when an owner collects overlapping rents. An Alexandria, Virginia, correspondent writes, "On page 126 of your book is the statement, 'We arrange for the tenants' rent to start the next day, May 30, gaining two days' rent, since the vacating tenant paid to the first.' How can you justify collecting two days' rent from two people on the same property, even if it goes to pay your costs of rental advertisements, etc., or cleanup?"

A tenant who moves usually has no further rights in his apartment; those rights revert to the owner. Whether on a month-to-month rental or at the end of a lease, tenants don't always observe the usual requirement to give thirty days' notice before vacating. This breach may be difficult to enforce if the tenant moves out of town. A move on short notice sometimes causes an owner to lose rent before he finds another tenant. This may be offset at other times if the owner collects overlapping rents. Assume, for example, that the rent is paid to the end of the month and a sudden transfer or other reason requires a tenant to move on the fifteenth. If the owner rents again before the end of the month, say on the twentieth, he gains ten days of double, or overlapping, rents.

Often a tenant gives notice, then holds the property until the end of the month, in which case there can be no overlapping. Sometimes tenants move out with most of their belongings and hold the apartments, even though they have no further use for them, just to prevent the owner from taking over. They may keep their keys and leave a castoff suitcase with bits of discarded clothing. Even though such tenants are actually unable to occupy the apartment, because all their living accouterments are out, the owner can take over legally only if his leases so provide—as mine do.

In other cases, a tenant may actually stay on in the old apartment even though his new house or apartment is ready to be moved into. It pays for the owner to obtain a new tenant as soon as possible in order to avoid a rent loss at the end of the tenancy. If new tenants want to move in right away, you can offer the outgoing tenant a prorated refund for vacating immediately.

## What Is the Purpose of Rental Insurance, and Where Can I Get It?

Ross Hines writes from Phoenix, Arizona, "On page 179, in your example of insurance for the newly acquired Belvedere Apartments, you state, 'This is the amount we order, plus six months' rental insurance of $3,000.' Was this insurance to cover a possible vacancy so that mortgage payments could be met? Or what was the purpose of this insurance? Can I obtain it from any insurance broker in my area?"

Rental insurance covers losses from vacancies while you are repairing or rebuilding because of damage from fire or other casualties covered by your fire insurance policy. It costs very little proportionately, and is available as an additional item on your regular fire insurance policy for rental property. Depending on the type of fire coverage, the size of the property and how long it might take to rebuild, it sometimes works out best to have rents insured for a full year, sometimes for six months.

My insurance broker, Kenneth Bone, tells me that rental insurance is obtainable through any broker in all parts of the United States.

## I Took a Note Instead of Cash for Damages Deposit. Did I Do Wrong?

A San Diego widow writes, "I rented my nice two-bedroom apartment for $130 to a handsome young scientist with two children. I told him there would be a $100 deposit to cover any damages, which is my practice whenever I take children. It is returned on vacating if there are no damages, otherwise I deduct the amount covering the extent of any damages. I have always insisted on cash. But this young man said he was short because of moving expenses and all. He talked me into taking his promissory note instead, due in one year, when his lease is up.

"I have just realized that he could move out, leaving me holding the well-known bag with an unpaid note if damage has occurred. This young man is subject to transfer. Should I ask him to exchange his note for cash? Could they move out and leave me with a worthless note? Please give your advice and tell me, did I do wrong?"

A deposit has little practical value if it is not due until the end of the lease. Your tenant is under no obligation to redeem the note with cash until the due date or until it has been established that there are damages to collect, whichever occurs first. If he wants to remain as a tenant at the end of the year, you should demand redemption of the note with cash. However, what if your scientist works for an established company and leaves you with an unpaid note and damages? It is likely that all you will have to do to insure payment is advise him that the matter will be referred to his company. In California, if a tenant leaves an unpaid rent bill the owner can readily garnishee his wages by taking the case to a small-claims court.

You're right in realizing it's better to collect a cash deposit. Suppose, though, that you have a desirable tenant who cannot put up all of a fairly substantial deposit? You could accept part of it, say $25, and take a note or postdated check to cover the balance within a reasonably short time, say ninety days. Arrangements could be made for installment payments, with $25 down, for example, and $25 monthly added to the rent until the deposit is paid in full.

## Is It More Profitable to Rent by the Month or Lease by the Year?

This question was asked by Eileen Duke of Memphis, Tennessee, following my lecture at Goldsmith's department store.

It depends on local conditions and practices. Annual leases are more prevalent in the East, monthly rentals in the West. One arrangement may pan out about as well as the other. I strongly recommend a written rental contract, or lease, to clarify house rules and avoid tenant misunderstandings, regardless of the length of time covered. We are referring, of course, to apartment rentals. On commercial rentals it is a desirable country-wide practice to have longer-term leases, commonly running from five to twenty years.

## What Is the Fair Rental Value on a Commercial Lease?

Although my book is concerned primarily with dwelling rentals, a number of people have asked me questions about commercial rentals. C. I. Shaffer of Iron River, Michigan, writes, "I would like to get your opinion on a deal that I am working on. I own two lots, total frontage 60 feet and depth 120 feet, adjoining a chain store. They need more space and have offered me $60,000 for the lots and they want me to erect a store for them.

"The cost of construction plus the value of the lots would make a total investment of $160,000. I would have to borrow the $100,-000 construction costs. They will give me a twenty-year lease. In your opinion, what would be a fair rental on a deal of this type?"

On queries such as this I recommend checking with a local realtor who specializes in handling commercial property and is familiar with practices in your area.

While yardsticks on apartments are fairly uniform throughout the country, there are many more variables in commercial rentals. Determining factors are whether the owner or the tenant pays for certain expenses, such as taxes, insurance and repairs, and whether the rental is on a percentage basis or a flat rate. Percentage leases are being written more commonly on such property. They usually give you a flat minimum rental, covering a certain amount of the tenant's gross income plus a percentage of the merchant's gross receipts exceeding an agreed minimum.

There are all kinds of variations on such leases, depending to a great extent on local practices and on the usual arrangements of a chain store's home office. Percentages vary according to the type of business; a chain grocery store will not pay the same as a chain department store or a clothing store. Percentages of gross sales are tied primarily to varying ratios of expenses and net income. Because of fast turnover, a grocer takes a small markup on each item sold, while many retailers mark up their merchandise at double their costs.

## May We Buy or Copy Your Actual Lease?

As mentioned in Chapter X, requests by the thousands have come from people who want to buy or copy the leases I use and other forms that are mentioned in my first book. Henry Hix of Long Beach, California, writes, "After buying your book and reading it, I bought four more copies and gave them to my friends and one to my apartment manager. I told her that this was to be our bible in apartment house operations. In bringing my operations around to somewhere near your standards, I would like to use your lease form. May I ask you to please sell me 1,000 copies?"

Thomas Hollcraft of Portland, Oregon, asks, "What restrictions arise from copyright concerning the use of the lease contract and other clauses in your book? If these clauses are used verbatim for actual rental operations, would it be necessary to ask for explicit permissions, or would a blanket permission be granted?"

I do not have copies of the lease or other forms for sale, and my own are printed to order. You might be able to obtain similar leases from your local apartment owners' association. You are free to print or mimeograph any examples in my book, provided they are for your own use and not for sale.

## Do You Spend Most of Your Time Looking After Your Property Now?

This question was asked by students Maybelle Clevenger and Ran Stagner of the San Mateo, California, Simmons Institute, and by Madelon Le Fevre, an airline stewardess in Boston. Miss Le Fevre also states, "Your book was used as a reference in an extension course in real estate I took at Harvard. I went right out with $3,000 I had saved and bought run-down Boston tenements and fixed them up. A year and a half later I was told I would be transferred to San Francisco. I had increased the income so I was able to sell out for $17,000 profit, and am anxious to start afresh in a new city."

Looking after $5 million worth of property is still handled in my spare time. My local property managers take care of operating details. Most of my time is spent lecturing and writing.

## Should You keep Improving Operations?

When I entered the auditorium for a lecture to the National Apartment Association convention in Dallas, Texas, a diminutive white-haired lady stopped me and asked, "Just what is your speech about?"

"Basically on how to improve operations."

Then she exclaimed, "Oh, so you're a doctor! I have trouble with my floating kidney. You look like a kindly man. Could you examine me? Or are you a specialist?"

"Yes, I do have a specialty. It is curing sick, run-down properties."

Every property operation needs periodic examination and continuing improvement. Dramatic surgery may be required to turn a sick apartment house from a money loser to a healthy profit maker. Many improvement-minded owners keep making good profits by following my suggestions. Why do others, especially bleeders, lose money, thus lowering their property values and giving my disciples a better chance to make a good buy?

Because some apartment owners tend to neglect the essentials of property management, which may become lost in a forest of operating details. What is the fundamental purpose of improving operations?

*To Make a Greater Net Profit.*

This involves two basic goals which every property owner needs to recapitulate from time to time:

1. Maximum gross income.
2. Minimum expenses.

Some management decisions cover one or the other. Some affect both. For example, modernizing with new plumbing can increase rents and at the same time reduce repair bills.

# XVIII

## How Can I Improve Management?

My first book has a chapter on the subject of hiring apartment house managers, and another on how to supervise them. Relatively few questions have arisen regarding the hiring of managers, but I have received a number of queries about supervision. There was, too, one unexpected sidelight.

### How About Managers Who Copy Sample Letters?

The sample letters from prospective building managers that were published in my first book suggested the kinds of applications that are apt to lead to poor managers and to good ones. In the latter category, the desirable attributes include a wife's desire to stay home and be a good housekeeper; thus she can be on hand to show and rent vacant apartments and supervise or handle cleaning and other chores. A husband should indicate a willingness to do various handyman jobs, take care of minor repairs, etc.

A number of rental owners have told me of receiving letters from applicants who copied the best sample on pages 343–344 of my first book. I have received some verbatim ones myself, addressed to a newspaper box number. Other letters I have seen were minor rewrites of the original letter. Among those who have asked what I think of such application letters is Frances Styles, secretary of my Alameda County Apartment House Association in Oakland, California. "Should they be judged as insincere?" she asked. "Or should the statements, even though copied, be accepted at face value?"

Accept them at face value. The thousands of property owners who copy my suggestions are welcome to all the profits they can make; it is only good judgment to follow sound and proven investment methods. A similar attitude applies to manager applicants. Many have no idea what an owner is looking for, so it is a sound policy for them to copy letters that have worked. However, a verbatim copy is more open to suspicion, for a variation in wording is to be expected when the skills and goals of individual applicants are described. For the most part, though, letter writers can be given an opportunity to live up to the qualifications they list. In most cases their actual willingness and sincerity can readily be verified in a personal interview.

## Is It Necessary to Have a Resident Manager?

Hildred Zimmerman of Sausalito, California, writes of trading a home equity for a pair of flats in San Francisco. She continues: "While a stenographer for a public utilities company, I made a clear net profit on my flats of $230 each month and paid off the property free and clear. Then I traded up.

"I got $26,000 equity out of the flats and used this as down payment on a $55,000 four-unit brand-new luxury apartment house in San Rafael. I would like to manage it myself, but without moving there, as I have to live with my family in nearby Sausalito. Please answer this question: Is it necessary to have a resident manager with only four apartments? Or should I trade for larger property, say six, eight or ten apartments?"

California law requires a resident manager only in sixteen-unit buildings or larger. Such regulations differ in various communities. It usually pays to allow a nominal sum in order to have a responsible tenant on the premises. It is handier for you to have a resident manager who can show vacancies, keep up the yard, etc., even though you plan to closely supervise the property. Of course, if you live next door or nearby, this might not be necessary. It depends on how convenient the location is for you, and how much time you plan to devote to management.

### Is Rental Value of Manager's Apartment Tax-Free Income to Employee?

This question was asked by Bill Hayward, real-estate writer for the *Contra Costa Times,* Walnut Creek, California.

Yes, in most cases. An employee's living quarters are not taxable income if they are provided on the business premises, for the convenience of the employer, and the employer requires such residence. There would be no question on this score where government regulations require a resident manager. This tax advantage is, of course, an additional incentive in hiring apartment managers.

### How Should We Manage Distant Property?

Lois Roseboom writes from Missouri, "I inherited a house which is probably between seventy-five and a hundred years old. Structurally it is still very sturdy. It had been converted into four apartments, all with separate baths. Unfortunately, it was not in too good repair when we got it, one of those typical run-down places you write about. The house is situated in a small Pennsylvania town of 4,000 population on a large double lot three blocks from the main industry, Pittsburgh-Corning Glass.

"We have tried to manage the property by mail from Sedalia, and have appointed three different caretakers. None of them showed much interest. They even failed to collect rents and take care of needed repairs. Of course we did not have a chance to undertake the personal interviews you recommend. The place is getting in worse shape rather than better. We have had many vacancies, with taxes, insurance, repairs, etc., eating up most of our profit. We have had a 'For Sale by Owner' sign in front for two years, with our Missouri address. Had to replace it after last Halloween!

"Will sacrifice this fourplex for $12,500, but nobody who wanted to buy has had enough money to pay down. The building especially needs painting, and the yard cries for landscaping to replace the present weed patch. We own it free and clear of any loans. We are in moderate circumstances and don't want to put any money into the place. It has to pay its own way.

"In your opinion, what should be our move at this time? I'm hoping you can suggest a way for us to sell off this property so we can reinvest closer to our present home."

I strongly recommend turning supervision of your fourplex over to a nearby realtor. This is what I would do with property so far from home. A neighborhood realtor would be in a much better position to manage, rent and sell your property. His fees are nominal; he will be inclined to give your rentals and repairs more attention if he has the incentive of a future sales commission.

Therefore, tell the realtor what you have in mind: to fix up the property without spending any of your own money, fill it with paying tenants, then sell. Get rid of that "For Sale by Owner" sign. Two years without results should prove its lack of efficacy. It only cheapens your property, and in the end you might have to sell for less than if you had never put it up.

Ask the realtor to get bids to put the property in fair shape, then try to get a new mortgage, the largest that is possible. The financing should pay for all your needed rehabilitation and give you extra cash for further investment. The loan will also make the property easier to sell, for then a new buyer will need a smaller down payment. After the improvements and repairs are completed, you stand a much better chance of keeping all the apartments full, another factor which will help you sell at a better price.

If you don't know of a nearby realtor, ask the realty board in the community where your fourplex is located to recommend one. If there is no board of realtors in that city, there may be a county or an area board. For this kind of information, write to the Pennsylvania Realtors Association, 306 State Street Building, Harrisburg, Pennsylvania 17101. I have had personal contact with many of their members and am sure they would be happy to assist you.

(Information on realtors in other states can be obtained through the real-estate board nearest you, where you can get the addresses of distant boards and state associations. For the benefit of readers living in sparsely settled areas, addresses of nearest local boards and state associations are available from the National Association of Realtors, 155 East Superior Street, Chicago, Illinois 60611.)

### How Big a Deposit Should Be Charged to Hold an Apartment?

Apartment manager Jewell Terhune of Sacramento, California, was among those who asked this question.

Try to collect an entire month's rent to hold an apartment. The tenant may be unwilling or unable to pay this amount because he is short of funds. In that case a deposit should be collected, to be credited against the rent. The amount should be large enough to insure that the tenant will return to keep from losing it and that the owner will not lose rent. A deposit should be at least one and a half times, and preferably double, the rent for the holding period. For example, if an apartment rents for $150 monthly, an average of $5 a day, a charge of $10 should be made to cover each day the apartment is held.

Suppose a tenant looks at the apartment on a Friday and says he will move in on Sunday, when he will pay the balance of the rent. This would tie up the apartment for three days. The deposit, then, should be in the $30 range, with a minimum of $25. You should always collect a bonus exceeding the prorated rent. Once the deposit is paid you cannot rent to another tenant, even though a more desirable one may show up immediately afterward. Often there is lost time before you can start new rental efforts, such as advertising. In the foregoing case, if the tenant fails to appear on the Sunday you are forced to wait till Monday before attempting to rent to another tenant.

## When Should the Rent Start?

This question was asked by apartment manager Louise Cochran of Oakland, California.

The day the tenant ties up the apartment or when it is ready for occupancy, whichever occurs last. If the apartment is ready on the day the tenant pays a deposit, the rent should start that same day. This is because another tenant who wants to move in right away might appear immediately after a deposit is taken.

An apartment may not be ready until later, either after a tenant moves out or until certain repair work is to be done which will not permit new occupancy. In such cases the rent should start the day the apartment is vacant and ready for the new tenant to move in.

## Will a Transferring Manager Steal My Tenants?

This question was asked by Dorothy Kliks, president of the Oregon Apartment House Association, following my Portland lecture.

Not likely. Once in a while a manager threatens to take your tenants with her if she moves from your building and goes to work for another owner. In such an event, some sympathetic tenants say they will move, but most don't, especially if you hire an attractive and pleasing replacement.

## Should a Resigning Manager Stay as a Tenant?

This question was asked by Sam Lackman, following my lecture at Long Beach, California. Another who asked it was a Minneapolis utilities executive and apartment house owner, when I lectured before the Twin Cities Round-Table in St. Paul, Minnesota. He stated that his apartment manager had resigned after some years; she and her salesman husband had both reached sixty-five and had decided to retire on his company pension and their Social Security.

"Most of her friends are tenants in the building," he said. "She wants to stay near them by moving from the manager's apartment to another as a tenant. I kind of think that keeping my experienced manager in the building might be helpful in training the new one. But then I wonder. Do you think it might result in complications? Should I let her stay as a tenant?"

It would be very unusual if you and the new and retiring managers did not regret it afterward. An outgoing manager is usually co-operative in showing a replacement the ropes. But having a retiring manager stay in the same building can result in divided responsibility; tenants will continue going to the previous manager, whom they know better, with their problems or requests, such as a desire for redecoration or new furniture. The old manager then becomes a spokesman for the tenants, or at least a sympathetic listener. The best-intentioned ex-manager will bring up "the way I would have handled this," to show up the newcomer unfavorably and undermine her authority.

You will find that two triangles are created—one involving the two managers and the tenants, the other the two managers and the owner. On the surface, you may think it will work out, but it is likely to induce about as much harmony as letting a divorced spouse stay in the same house after the other spouse remarries.

I know of many discouraging experiences, and I have had some disappointing trials of my own. The owner may be motivated by sympathy for a sweet-tempered manager who has been a good employee. The arrangement often starts out smoothly, but in time the deposed manager turns out to be more of a hindrance than a help. She eventually leaves acrimoniously, whereas an immediate departure could have been harmonious.

## Is It Unusual to Double Your Equity by Improving Management?

Philip Gamble writes from Fort Lauderdale, Florida, "I followed your book very closely, using your checks and double-checks to evaluate the merits of apartments, and finally bought a twelve-unit property which had a good potential. Asking price was $99,-500. I purchased it for $83,000, with a $53,000 first mortgage. The seller took back a second mortgage for $15,000, and I paid $15,-000 down.

"Although the outward appearance was good, the furniture was quite old. The main drawback was that poor management had prevented the owner from making any money for two years. I put in some new furniture and found there was a big demand for it in this resort area. But the main thing I did was to put in a good manager. Have bonded her, and have set up your report and banking system. In fact, I keep your 'textbook' by the bed so I can easily check the answers to questions that arise.

"A very modest estimate would more than double my equity to $32,000 because of the increased income from improved operations. This is almost entirely due to a change in managers, as the new-furniture outlay has been nominal. Now I am ready to trade up for a property in the $200,000 price range. Is it unusual to double equity merely by improving management?"

This encouraging twofold experience is not unusual. Much more unusual is Joseph Kennedy's experience in increasing his equity more than a hundredfold when he turned a half-million down payment in the Merchandise Mart into a $62-million improvement in valuation.

### What If Tenant Contacts Owner Behind Manager's Back?

Nancy Bohn of Sacramento, California, asked this question, which is repeated occasionally by owners, tenants and apprehensive managers.

In such an event, the owner should be gracious but not overencouraging, and above all should make no separate agreements with the tenant without discussing the matter with the manager. Tenants seldom contact the owners if the owner clearly delegates authority to the manager. However, an exception may occur. A tenant may complain about the manager's attitude, her way of handling requests, her honesty or her personal habits.

Infrequently, a conscientious tenant takes the trouble to tell the owner about serious manager problems of which the owner has not yet become aware. One irate tenant revealed that the manager's husband was getting drunk on weekends and annoying some of the single women in the building, including herself. She said he was letting apartment repairs go unless the tenant was a pretty girl. In such cases he might waste several hours to fix a leaky faucet. These episodes usually occurred when his wife was attending Saturday night club meetings or Sunday church services.

The owner told me that he discussed these complaints with the manager. Of course, discharge would have been necessary if the situation was not corrected. But the manager convinced her husband that he should go to the club meetings with her and should start attending church regularly. Happily, a reformation resulted.

Investigation of most tenant complaints about a manager usually determines that the latter was simply carrying out the owner's policies. When she has to advise tenants of rent raises or changes in house rules, her task will be easier if she can blame someone else. I tell managers to say to tenants, for example, "The owner has asked me to raise your rent five dollars a month because of increased taxes." The manager is then viewed in a more favorable light by the tenant, with whom there is a day-to-day contact.

If the tenant contacts the owner about a matter in which the manager is carrying out orders, the tenant should be told that that is the situation. If there is further question, tell the tenant that the problem will be investigated and discussed with the manager, who is in complete charge. In most instances, the manager should then get in touch with the tenant. But sometimes the owner may want to renew the contact himself, usually with the manager present, in the interests of good public relations.

Of course, cases of dishonesty or misappropriation of funds should be referred to the fidelity company, the district attorney or the police for appropriate action. With any accusation, an employee should be considered in the right until proven wrong. Managers will be loyal to you if you are loyal to them. I believe in going overboard in standing up for them when they make honest mistakes. While managers should be encouraged to make decisions on their own, they should be advised that if they make a mistake it will be pointed out to them with suggestions for correction. They can expect an owner's backing if they err in judgment, but they should not make the same mistake twice.

When the manager handles details of operation on her own initiative, neither she nor the tenants should find it necessary to contact the owner. Matters needing the owner's attention can usually be discussed during periodic supervisory visits, which free the owner from handling day-to-day details.

### Did You and Your Wife Live in Your First Rentals? Is This Necessary?

Virginia Murphy writes from Belvidere Place, Montclair, New Jersey, "Your fascinating book held my interest more than most novels I have read. As a child I grew up in a section made up of Polish landlords and Irish tenants. My family was always included amongst the Irish renters. I determined some day to be a landlord myself, instead of a tenant, as my parents always have been.

"My husband, Harry, and I bought an older house in good condition for $15,000. We paid $2,000 down and secured a $13,000 first mortgage. It had been converted to include a three-room apartment. We rented it for $100 a month. After a little fixing up the house is now appraised at $19,000, and we have paid the mortgage down to $7,500. We would like to start pyramiding, but don't quite know what to shoot for. I mean, up to how big a property? Can you advise me how long you and your wife lived in your rental property? And is this necessary to get ahead?"

It is not necessary for you to live in your rentals to manage them, but doing so usually boosts you to faster and surer progress in the initial stages. My wife and I lived in ours and managed them up to and including our first thirty-unit building, comparable to the Cynthia Court in my first book.

You have an equity of $11,500 in your present property. This represents a sizable nest egg that should enable you to pyramid to something like the seven-unit Belvedere Apartments described in the book. The coincidence that you already live on Belvidere Place looks like a good omen!

## How Often Do You Make Periodic Supervisory Visits?

Another New Jersey coincidence involved Camden County realtor Marion Murphy (no relation to Virginia), who raised the above query following my lecture to a regional conference of residential appraisers in Pittsburgh, Pennsylvania.

"In July of 1961," she stated, "my son, Pat, and I bought for $4,200 a run-down house that was a sight to behold inside and out. The water pipes and radiators had frozen and broken, floors had buckled, ceiling plaster was badly damaged, and the house was filled with outdated furniture.

"My daughter, Rosemary, and I had made reservations for our first trip to South America, so I turned the house over to my son while I was gone. He hired workmen to install new baseboard heat, repair and sand floors, plaster and repaper walls, paint the interior and the exterior, remove all furnishings and other trash, install two flower boxes on the front porch, clear the grounds of weeds and trim the shrubbery. Pat said he followed the suggestions in your book very closely, with the goal, quoting you, to 'make a profit of at least one dollar for every dollar spent in repairs and remodeling.'

"The total cost of remodeling came to approximately $2,000. The house sold in short order for $8,750, giving us a profit of $2,550. Our office is in Audubon, in southern New Jersey. We handle sales and insurance mostly, plus appraisals. But we expect to branch out into more investment and property management. Tell me, how often do you make periodic supervisory visits with your managers?"

This question also comes up at most of my lectures to apartment owners. My periodic visits are made weekly when I am breaking in a new manager, or when there are special projects under way, like major remodeling or redecorating. Visits might be every day at times, in order to inspect various stages of construction or repairs. Supervisory contacts are regularly made on a semimonthly basis. This is adequate for keeping up to date as long as the manager is authorized to handle routine operating decisions.

Some owners pester their managers almost daily with minor details. By doing so they cause a great deal more harm than good and stir up heavier manager turnover. A manager should be encouraged to operate the building in the owner's absence as though it belonged to her. A greater feeling of importance goes along with taking more responsibility, and results in the performance of a better over-all job.

### Do You Have a Checklist for Expenses?

Among others, several checklist-prone pilots and stewardesses have asked this question, including General "Brick" Holstrom, who flew with Doolittle over Tokyo. He later retired from the Air Force to administer the Carmel Valley Manor Retirement Home, of which I am a director.

Although expenses vary considerably in different operations and communities, a checklist of minimum and maximum expectations can be helpful.

PROPERTY TAXES

May run between 12 per cent and 24 per cent of gross income, and between 1½ per cent and 3 per cent of market value. Community rates vary a great deal. So do local assessment ratios and practices, including allowances for depreciation. On the latter, some assessors are generous, some niggardly. Assessed values across the country vary from about 20 per cent to 100 per cent of market values, averaging 32.7 per cent, according to a 1972 study by the Census Bureau. The most common ratio is 25 per cent.

If taxes are higher than comparables in your area, explore the possibility of appealing for a lower assessment. Appeals may be made by individuals or by groups, such as apartment owners. Or you can hire an advocate, such as an attorney or accountant, who specializes in this field, usually on a percentage basis.

## INSURANCE

Check adequacy in relation to current values and coverages. Old policies on older values may be too low. Should cover comprehensive fire, liability, rental income, workman's compensation, and extended coverages such as windstorm loss, vandalism and malicious mischief. Optional coverages include burglary, robbery and fidelity losses.

Rates should run between $2.50 and $3 per $100 of coverage, and between 1¼ per cent and 1¾ per cent of gross income.

## UTILITIES

Includes lighting, heating, cooking, and garbage collection. In each category verify most advantageous schedule with utility company, as several schedules are often applicable. Arrange to pay bills bimonthly to save bookkeeping.

Will run between 4 per cent and 9 per cent of gross income, depending on local rates, whether tenants pay for utilities in their individual units, and other utility-consuming services all or part provided by owner, such as heated pools.

## MANAGEMENT

Varies according to duties of resident and over-all management, and whether the two are separate or combined. Usually will run about 5 per cent of gross income, over-all, ranging from minimum of 2 per cent plus free apartment for operations in the eighteen- to forty-unit range, to 4 per cent to 6 per cent for larger complexes.

## MAINTENANCE

Allow 5 per cent to 7 per cent of gross income.

GARDENER AND POOL SERVICE

Each about 1 per cent of gross income.

LEGAL AND ACCOUNTING

About 1 per cent of gross income.

VACANCIES

Should be held to 5 per cent maximum, with 2 per cent optimum. Often run to 10 per cent in older, poorly managed buildings and to 20 per cent in higher-priced new construction.

Note: Zero vacancies or 100 per cent occupancy sounds good, and may be fine for a short period. But if prevalent for several months usually means slack management, charging too low rents. The optimum of 2 per cent visualizes rents high enough to generate some vacancies, producing a higher annual income than lower rents with no vacancies.

SUMMARY

Efficient management should hold total expenses to a maximum of 35 per cent of gross income. May run to 50 per cent if owner provides utilities, furniture and furnishings, and amenities such as pools and janitor and social services.

# XIX

## *Do You Have a Checklist for Managers?*

In addition to requests for an appraisal checklist, correspondents have asked for a checklist they can use during their periodic supervisory visits with managers. Realtor Victor Zaro, specializing in property management, asked for such a list following my lecture and *Talk of the Town* radio appearance in Philadelphia.

### What Are the Routine Items to Look For?

He added, "Also, what are the routine items you look for that may not necessarily be discussed with your managers?"

The answer that follows incorporates my replies to many questions from realtors, appraisers and property owners concerning specific items in the field of manager supervision.

The items to look for are somewhat similar to those you look for when appraising a property for possible purchase. It is easy for an owner to follow the line of least resistance and put on a set of blinders when he visits his properties, overlooking items that should be fairly obvious. It takes hardly any additional time to make a habit of re-evaluation on each supervisory contact. If anything needs correction it can then be discussed with the apartment manager. Otherwise it might not be mentioned, unless a problem has been corrected since the last visit, or the yard or other parts of the building look unusually well kept. It is always good practice to praise the noticeable accomplishments, instead of commenting only when something needs correction. All details, including personal items like the manager's appearance, are considered for their effect on present and prospective tenants.

Other owners sometimes ask if they can accompany me on my supervisory visits with my managers. Two of my pastor friends, Clarence Reidenbach and Michel Vallon, have asked if they could join me to see what I check with my managers. The pastors are fellow philosophers who seek to broaden their knowledge in many fields, and I am sorry to disappoint them. But I tell them that most supervisory items are mentally checked, quite rapidly with experience. Actually, many details are absorbed rather than checked off. But I do note significant factors either satisfactory or out of line. Here are items to be alert for:

EXTERIOR

Are sidewalks, driveways and yard swept clean of papers and other debris?

Are lawns mowed, trimmed and green? Do they need cutting, weeding, reseeding, fertilizer, pesticides, water?

Is shrubbery trim? Is special attention needed, like pruning, thinning or replacement?

Is exterior paint, especially around the entrance, satisfactory? Should it be touched up?

If there is a pool, is it sparkling clear, free of dust, algae and debris?

Is the vacancy sign trim and legible, and can it readily be seen?

INTERIOR

Is the lobby or entrance hall satisfactory? Does it match present competitive conditions? Should floors, walls or ceilings be improved? Should the lobby furniture be repaired or changed? Should eye-catchers be added, like new furniture, planters, paintings, tapestries, vases, lamps or dividers?

Are the hallways clean and in good condition? Is a new paint job or a touch-up on walls and ceilings needed? Is the location of the manager's apartment clearly indicated on a sign in the lobby and another over her door?

## MANAGER'S APPEARANCE

Are the manager's doorway, entrance hall and reception room or living room—where she conducts business with tenants and owner—clean and in good condition?

Does the manager keep her clothing clean and neat?

Is her temper serene or is it vixenish, indicating a need for correction?

If the manager has children, are they well behaved?

If manager's husband is around, is he pleasant or boorish?

## MANAGER'S CONTACTS

Is the telephone answered satisfactorily—that is, does the manager give the name of the apartments and her own name, rather than start with just "Hello"?

If a response to a rental ad comes by way of the telephone, does the manager do a good selling job?

If a rental prospect calls personally, does the manager handle the visit properly? Does she encourage or discourage a prospect from becoming a tenant?

If a tenant stops in to pay rent, does the manager express thanks and give a proper receipt?

If a tenant asks for some service, such as more heat, or repairs, does the manager show a desire to please and otherwise indicate willing co-operation? Or is she abrupt, appearing to resent the tenant's interruption?

It should be mentioned that an owner's presence may sometimes cause a newer manager to make a poor showing because of over-anxiety to please. She may cut a tenant's visit shorter than appears desirable so that she can save the owner's time. The manager should be told to handle routine tenant contacts in her normal manner and that the owner will check over the books and other such details while waiting. If there is indication of a lengthy contact, such as making special arrangements in connection with a tenant's going on vacation, the manager should ask the tenant to excuse her. She should offer to contact the tenant after the owner leaves, or ask the tenant to return later.

### What Is Your Manager Checklist?

Besides realty owners, brokers and appraisers, apartment manager Margrit Bueckert and several airplane pilots have especially asked for this checklist, which goes into areas not covered in the previous section.

Before listing specific items, it is well to restate the over-all purpose of property investment: to earn the highest possible net income. To this end the owner should periodically review his means of increasing gross income and decreasing expenses in order to produce the highest net. With this objective, the basic controlling factors to keep in mind when checking various items with the manager are her primary responsibilities:

To keep the building full, with all units rented
To collect all rents when due.

These ends can be met only by exercising some selectivity—by screening tenants in terms of their ability to pay and whether they will fit harmoniously into the building and not cause other tenants to move out. Also, rent schedules should be realistic in order to keep tenants satisfied and avoid excessive turnover. The owner should usually discuss rent levels with the manager from time to time, then set them preferably just under the going market.

### Check on Vacancies

You cannot collect rents from nonexistent tenants, so the first thing I usually check with a manager is the vacancy situation. If the vacancy sign is out, I ask, "Which apartment is vacant?" If the sign is not out, I make it a practice to verify that it has not been neglected, or that there has not been a last-minute vacating notice, by saying, "I see you have a full house?"

## Audit the Collections

Once the status of vacancies has been determined, it saves time to immediately audit the rent collections. The problem of vacancies can be handled while you are going over the books, or afterward. But a number of questions that may arise can be settled automatically while checking income and expenses. The manager is expected to have the books in order so that the owner can audit them. Nothing is more exasperating on a day when you have a full schedule than to have a manager delay you by last-minute notations and calculations, or to have a manager say she has not had time to prepare the books.

Except for unusual emergencies, the owner should insist that the manager have the books ready for scheduled appointments. A manager's excuses about not keeping appointments with the owner and not having the bookkeeping up to date invite suspicion. There is a possibility that the manager cannot balance her books because she is using the owner's funds for her personal expenditures. If there are a couple of such occurrences in succession, it is well to insist on an immediate, comprehensive audit. The manager should always be able to account for all funds collected. They should be balanced by cash or checks on hand, receipted bank deposit slips, or receipts for authorized expenditures.

## Check Rent Receipts

Rent receipts should be listed by the manager in numerical order on a Banking Report, as shown in my first book, page 372. To avoid duplication, I am not reproducing any of the forms shown in the first book, even though I shall refer to them.

Rent receipts should be numbered and their numerical order should correspond with the chronological order. The only receipts the manager should use, even for deposits, are the numbered forms provided by the owner. The manager should give the original receipt to the tenant and keep duplicates to turn over to the owner.

The owner should verify the amounts on the receipts against the amounts entered on the report, placing a check mark opposite the money entry. For example:

No. 201 11/2 $125.00 √

As the receipts are checked, each should be scanned for accuracy and correct preparation as to the rental period covered, the amount of rent, etc. If any discrepancies are found between the receipted amount and the reported amount, they can immediately be straightened out with the manager.

Receipts should describe all rents, charges and deposits collected for the owner's account. If the manager keeps for herself the cleaning charges, which I advocate for most smaller operations, where the manager works part time, this item should be entered on the rent receipt but should not be charged to the owner's account. Key and damage deposits should be entered as income when received and as expenses when repaid. It's a poor practice to have the manager retain these deposits in a cigar box or some other such receptacle and make cash refunds from it. Needless accounting problems may result, as well as petty losses.

The manager should have the receipts totaled, and should prepare duplicate reports, one copy for herself and one for the owner.

## Check Authorized Expenditures

The manager should list all the authorized expenditures on her banking report, so that the owner can check the amounts against receipted bills. This covers items like nails, screws, tacks, washers and such necessities, for which the manager has paid cash as part of the general agreement that she may buy them as needed. It is a good idea where possible to have the manager indicate the apartment for which the expense item was used. Example:

11/3 Sears 2 Keys No. 206 $1.00

(Major items needed on a continuing basis, such as light bulbs by the case, or painting and plumbing repairs, should be billed directly to the owner.) The manager's expenses should be totaled and then deducted from the income.

## Check Bank Deposit and Cash on Hand

The balance should be covered by a receipted bank deposit or by cash on hand. It is expected that the manager will have made one or more bank deposits, balancing her books accordingly, just prior to the owner's audit. Any rents collected after the last bank deposit should be entered on a new banking report and balanced by cash and expense entries.

Deposited collections should always be audited. Regularly with a new manager and occasionally after she gains experience, it is a good idea to audit the recent collections that have not yet been deposited. Besides looking to see that the books balance, make sure that the manager has marked or rubber-stamped each undeposited check "For Deposit Only," so that it cannot be cashed. Make sure, too, that the amount of total receipts, either in one single bank deposit or in cash on hand, does not exceed the amount for which you are covered by fidelity, burglary and robbery insurance. For example, I have a blanket fidelity insurance bond covering $2,500 on each manager, and blanket burglary-and-robbery insurance covering up to $1,000 at each location.

After checking the rent receipts and the expense items, write below the entries the date and your signature or initials. I do not write "O.K." as the items are merely checked and not totaled. My wife runs them up on an adding machine in our office later, usually the next morning. Any arithmetical discrepancy can be straightened out with the manager on the next visit.

The manager prepares three copies. The original is for the bank, the receipted duplicate is for the owner, and the triplicate is retained by the manager. The numbered items on the above sample are:

1. The owner's name and address, imprinted by the bank
2. The imprinted name of the branch which maintains the owner's account

BANK DEPOSIT SLIP

(1)

JOSEPH ENTERPRISE
7070 PARADISE ROAD
SUBURBIA, COLUMBIA

2345    90-1268
        1211

(4) CYNTHIA COURT APTS.

(5) DATE  NOV. 19    19 74

Please list all items on the back of this ticket
or attach list and enter total deposit in this box→

| TOTAL DEPOSIT |
|---|
| $ 467.21 |

(6) FROM PARKSIDE BRANCH NO. 43

S. T. U.
Teller

(2) DEPOSITED IN

METROPOLE MAIN OFFICE  90-1268
CITIZENS NATIONAL BANK
METROPOLE, COLUMBIA

(3)  ⑈⑆⑆2⑆⑆⑈⑈⑆2⑆8⑈⑆009⑆ 2⑆45

3. The owner's automated account number
4. The manager's entry of the apartment house name or address
5. The date of deposit
6. The neighborhood branch bank's stamped and initialed receipt for the deposit. (Details of cash and checks are listed on the reverse side.)

## Check the Monthly Report

The monthly income report should be complete and ready to be turned over to the owner on his first supervisory visit after the end of the month. Collection entries will be the same as those entered on the bank deposit record. However, there is no need to keep bank deposits separated by months; the receipts at the end of one month can be mingled for deposit with those at the beginning of the next month. But the monthly report should show the receipts for the calendar month.

A completely filled out example is shown in my first book, page 368. The report should be scanned to see that the appropriate items are filled out properly and completely. Here are the entries to check:

TENANT'S NAME

Each apartment should be listed by number, showing the tenant's name. If there is no tenant, the reason should be given, such as "Vacant," or "Moved Nov. 15."

DATE WHEN RENT IS DUE AND DATE WHEN PAID

This entry serves as a red flag for delinquencies or rent paid in arrears.

NUMBER OF TENANTS

If there are additional tenants in an apartment and it is your practice to charge additional rent in such cases, has the stipulated extra rent been applied?

GARAGE

Has the extra charge for a garage, if any, been applied? Are all garages rented? If not, discuss steps that can be taken to rent them.

OTHER

Are key deposits, damages deposits, extra services, etc., included?

AMOUNT

Is the actual amount of the total receipts included? The manager should enter in this column only income that has been collected, not expected amounts. Are there any variations from the norm? For example, is only half a month's rent or less collected from an occupied apartment? Then there should be an explanation of why part or all of the rent is delinquent, and when it is expected to be paid.

MANAGER'S SIGNATURE

Has the manager signed the statement, certifying that her collections are accurate and complete?

There are many advantages to preparing a complete monthly report and keeping it on file. The manager can use it for a rent-roll record of amounts owed and due dates. The owner finds it a ready reference to consult in checking collections, delinquencies and vacancies. With such a report on file, the only bookkeeping entry normally required for income tax purposes would be the total monthly rents for an entire apartment house. This requires only twelve entries per year.

## Check Delinquencies

### Arrears Payments

If receipts or reports indicate that rents are being paid later than the due date, discuss with the manager methods of boosting tenants to a current basis.

### Nonpayments

If rents are unpaid, are there excusable reasons and earnest expectations of payment? Otherwise, has a written three-day notice been given to pay up or vacate?

Does it appear likely that the tenant may vacate without paying delinquent rents? Can valuables, like TV sets, be held to help insure payment? Does the manager know where the tenant is employed, or can she find out, so that collection steps can be facilitated?

## Check Leases

Has the manager prepared a written lease and inventory for each new tenant? Is each lease signed by the tenant and by the manager as the owner's agent?

### Triplicate Copies Are Advantageous

I have found it advantageous for supervisory and other purposes to have leases prepared in triplicate, with the third copy kept by the owner. The tenant should have the duplicate, and the manager should keep the original in her file.

### A Flag to Watch For

The flag to watch for here is the rent receipt for a new tenant, which covers special collections of key deposits and cleaning or other initial charges. Each such receipt when turned over to the owner should be accompanied by a triplicate copy of the lease. If this is not required as a routine matter, along with receipts for new rentals, managers may become slipshod and fail to execute leases as instructed. Requiring a triplicate copy enables the owner to verify the dates when a new tenant moves in and rent should start, and to make sure that the lease has been properly prepared and signed.

### Clear the Manager's Files

It is a good idea to have the manager turn over to the owner her copy of a lease when a tenant is vacating, to clear her files. The owner should keep copies of leases for a year or so after a tenant leaves, in case any legal or other questions arise. If a number of leases show up for the same apartment in one year, it indicates a need to explore possible shortcomings in the apartment that outgoing tenants may not have told the manager about. For example, is a neighbor tenant too noisy and in need of admonishment? Is a nearby furnace or air conditioner too noisy, needing repair, replacement, relocation, or more adequate noise abatement, perhaps a soundproof partition?

### A Case of Navy Night Owls and a Widow's Underdrawers

An example of what can happen occurred in an apartment house where the owner did not notice until the end of the year that there had been five changes of tenants in the same apartment. Not one mentioned the reason for vacating, and the manager failed to ask. The apartment was next door to the laundry room, and the owner wondered if the location had anything to do with all the moves. A phone call to the last outgoing tenant brought this statement: "I couldn't sleep a wink in that apartment, with the washroom going all night."

The manager stayed up late one night to check laundry room operations. After midnight two Navy nurses came home from their late-shift duties and brought soiled clothing, along with cold beer, to the laundry room. When the manager came in they were gossiping gaily above the noise of two washing machines. They were astonished to learn that their innocent late hours had caused annoyance to other tenants, and they said they would gladly do their washing during the day from then on; they had simply got into the habit of doing their laundering after their late shift.

The nurses mentioned another tenant, an elderly widow, who sometimes came into the laundry room when they were leaving. When she was questioned the next morning, the widow said, "I often wake up of a morning before daylight, and that's when I like to get up and do my laundry."

"Why?"

"Well, that's when there's no one else around. You see, I wear old-fashioned long cotton underdrawers. I wouldn't want to be putting them in the laundry when there's young folks around that might laugh at me."

The owner arranged to post a list of reasonable hours for use of the laundry room: from 8 A.M. to 8 P.M. weekdays, and from 10 A.M. to 8 P.M. Sundays and holidays. The room was locked at other hours, and none of the tenants complained. From then on, a new tenant stayed put in the adjoining apartment. As a bonus, the elderly widow told the manager that she had switched to more daring nylon undergarments rather than be made fun of. She found them more comfortable, after all, even though she thought they felt sinfully luxurious.

## Check Steps to Renting Vacancies

In most cases where a vacancy or a notice to vacate arises, the manager goes ahead and rerents the apartment. Thus, when the owner appears he may find that there has been a vacancy but it is already filled. The manager has already taken appropriate corrective action, reserving only the authorization of major expenditures for the owner's approval. But if the vacancy still exists, or if there is one coming up, what are the routine points for the owner to check? These should be the same details that the manager will have reviewed in her own mind before the owner arrives.

### Advertising

Has a vacancy sign been put on display?

Have waiting lists, co-operative rental centers or agencies been notified?

Has a for-rent ad been placed in the newspaper? Many papers have varying types of billing arrangements. The owner should set up an account that results in the biggest discounts.

Is the ad drawing good response?

If the response is poor, how should the wording be changed?

### Rent Level

Is the previous rent level satisfactory or is it time to increase?

Or is a decrease in order? It should be noted that sometimes a lowering of the rent may be necessary. However, this should be avoided, as rent levels generally are not decreasing but increasing, along with higher tenant incomes and higher operating costs. A lower rent may sometimes be quoted without actually reducing the base rent, for example, by omitting a garage or furniture customarily provided, or rents can be raised by charging the same rent for less service.

### Condition

Is the apartment in as good a condition as can be expected? Will it draw tenants on the basis of rent charged for the neighborhood, the number of rooms, etc.?

### Improvements

Are any improvement steps necessary in order to hold or increase rents? Is it better to make improvements than to lower rents? If lowered rents are forced because of deterioration, the condition may keep worsening, so why not fix the place up as soon as possible?

If an apartment has been shown to qualified prospective tenants as many as five times and still is not rented, you can take it for granted that something needs changing.

Should the apartment be painted, papered, recarpeted? Should it have new linoleum in kitchen or bath, or some other decoration or improvement?

Would it pay to put in new curtains and drapes? Plastic shades or Venetian blinds?

Would new heating or air conditioning pay?

Would it pay to put in new furniture, partial or complete, either for replacement or to change the status from an unfurnished rental? Sometimes when an apartment already has so-so older furniture, adding some inexpensive new items can transform it. Table or floor lamps, coffee tables, modern occasional chairs, breakfast sets can make a big difference. Maybe the furniture just needs to be rearranged, with a modern piece or two added—an end or corner table, a swag lamp or a painting.

If the apartment appears in good condition and the scheduled rent is judged as competitive, the next question to ask is, Should the manager improve her salesmanship?

## What Are the Follow-Up Auditing Steps You Take in Your Office?

This was one of the questions asked by Kathryn Convery, whose husband, John, is a C.P.A. and attorney in Walnut Creek, California.

Of course, a great deal of auditing has been done with the supervisory checking of the manager's books. In the office, as mentioned, rent receipts and expense items should be totaled to verify the manager's arithmetic.

It is a good idea to set aside for special attention the rent receipts on delinquent accounts. This makes it easy to keep an eye on them until the tenant either brings his payments up to a current basis or is evicted. Receipts of all tenants in arrears are kept in my current file for the individual building until the account is rectified. Then they are retained for one year in my regular closed file.

Each bank deposit should be entered in the appropriate banking record, with an identification to show where it originated. My properties are all identified by one or two initials—for instance "L" or "SL," signifying the apartments on L Street and the San Leandro apartments. When a bank statement arrives, deposits should immediately be verified. Although it is uncommon, managers preparing to abscond have been known to alter the figures on deposit slips. This way, any alterations or errors can quickly be detected.

Carry over to the bank statement your notation of the source of each deposit. While bankbooks may be discarded after a year or so, statements are normally retained for about five years, as more permanent records. Identification of the source of income listed on bank statements is helpful both for future checking and for income tax purposes. If you can readily identify the source of all funds, you invite fewer questions on tax audits, and you expedite smoother sailing.

## Do You Always Inspect Vacant Apartments?

Among several asking this question was resort hotel owner Tom Walsh of Washington, California, on the Yuba River.

This is a good rule to follow, and not only to verify whether the apartment is ready to rent or needs more cleaning or improvement. If you don't check vacancies on a regular basis a dishonest manager may rent the apartment without reporting any rent collections.

Especially watch for signs of changes since a prior inspection. In some areas a manager may rent an apartment to transients, especially over weekends. One apartment manager had a standing arrangement with a nearby motel to take overflow guests in her furnished vacancies. She pocketed this extracurricular income, giving the owner only the resulting wear and tear and higher than normal vacancy losses. She couldn't rent the apartments to bona-fide tenants when they were filled with transients, and she prolonged keeping some vacancies in order to purloin the undercover weekend rents.

Other big-hearted managers are liable to turn vacant accommodations over to visiting friends or relatives, a strict "no-no." Managers should be admonished that vacant apartments must always be held ready for legitimate prospective tenants.

# 9

# How to Finance Pyramiding

# XX

## *Is 100 Per Cent Financing Desirable, and How Can I Get It?*

The question in this chapter heading was asked by a realtor in the audience following my lecture at San Francisco Town Hall.

One hundred per cent financing is certainly wonderful if you can safely pay it back. After you have a sufficient reserve you should go ahead and get 100 per cent financing if you can. Usually you will find that your payments are so high it isn't sound when you are getting started with a small nest egg.

In practice sound financing will be closer to the 75 per cent which I cited in my first book as the average that can readily carry you to a million in twenty years. Incidentally, 75 per cent financing on other than F.H.A.-type loans was formerly available only from insurance companies, private lenders, and savings- and building-and-loan associations. Now even savings banks, as in New York State, find that 75 per cent financing on older apartments is a sound practice.

One hundred per cent financing means that you borrow all the purchase costs, putting in no money of your own. Many people who don't have cash in the bank arrange for 100 per cent financing by getting, say, a 75 per cent mortgage loan on a property and then borrowing the other 25 per cent elsewhere. Anyone with a steady job can get a salary loan from a credit union, a bank or a finance company, based on his income and obligations. Or he may borrow on his home, furniture, car or other security. Instead of selling the home, for example, or getting a complete new mortgage, he may be able to borrow what he needs by using the home as security. If one succeeds in borrowing all necessary purchase funds through such arrangements it can be considered 100 per cent financing.

Normally, 100 per cent financing means that you secure loans to cover the entire cost of the property. Many experienced investors do buy with 100 per cent financing or better. Just to prove how easily it can be done, when I was pyramiding from a half million to a million in the space of a couple of years, I bought a fairly large property without putting in a penny and wound up with extra cash in my pocket. I arranged a first mortgage loan through a bank, a second mortgage from the seller and a third mortgage for the realtor's commission. When the deal was completed the loans exceeded purchase costs, and the title company gave me a check for over $1,000—or something over 100 per cent financing.

### Is It Desirable to Borrow a Nest Egg from My Mother?

Fellow Bell Telephone Company worker Albon Ringer writes from Grand Rapids, Michigan, "One of the reasons compelling me to write this letter is the close parallel of our lives, although we are a few years apart. Both of us started as Bell System employees at the age of twenty-five. I work for the Michigan Bell Telephone Company. Have a lovely wife and three fine children. After reading your most informative book I am fascinated by the prospect of entering the real-estate field in my spare time as you did.

"There are a couple of questions I would like your opinion on. The first requires explanation. My oldest brother passed away, leaving my mother a modest estate. She has become interested in my serious desire to enter the apartment house investment field. She has advised me that I may use a portion of this estate to get started, with the stipulation that I repay her when I can. The interest rate is to be the same as she would have earned from savings. She trusts me implicitly. Being a religious man, as you are, I would never do anything to betray her faith. In your opinion, do you visualize this as an undesirable agreement? If so, how can it be made desirable?"

Borrowing a nest egg from relatives or friends is one way of getting started that would help you achieve 100 per cent financing. However, such a course can often turn good friends into enemies if you cannot repay at all or fail to keep your commitments without being hounded. There are bound to be disappointing results if you borrow for personal pleasure that you cannot afford. But borrowing from family or friends can work out if the loan is kept on a businesslike basis, with good expectations of repayment. This should apply as long as you use the money judiciously for investment. You could sign a promissory note, providing for regular repayments. You might pay only interest for a given period, say a year or two, after which time you should be in a better financial position. Then it would be wise to start at least token repayments on principal, preferably monthly and at least quarterly.

### Should I Have My Mother Cosign?

Joline Moore writes from Holly Hill, Florida, "I am in the process of varnishing (after removing the horrible paint) a sports fisherman boat. My mother and I own it and a sea skiff outright and hope to sell them for enough for a down payment on an apartment building.

"I expect to operate as an apartment owner alone. However, my mother's credit is better than mine. In case additional funds are needed for the down payment on the buy I locate, what do you think of having my mother cosign a personal note at the bank in order to get the money?"

Using another person's credit, through his cosignature, in order to borrow is almost the same as borrowing from him directly. If you don't repay, the cosigner becomes liable.

Your proposal might work out satisfactorily. The same factors apply as if you borrow directly from your mother. You might want to consider having your mother join you as a co-owner of the apartments you buy, sharing the benefits of any financing she helps to obtain. Or you might want to confine your first purchase to a down-payment range that you can realize without a personal, co-signed loan. In the absence of a significant stable income, a personal loan might best be held in reserve for use in emergencies or to help with improvement costs.

## Will a Bank Lend Me the Down Payment?

Another Bell System employee, Mark Timm of San Francisco, relates, "I have only a few hundred dollars in a savings account, but own about $12,000 worth of A. T. & T. stock. Bought it through an employee purchase plan during twenty-one years of service. I don't want to sell the stock and have never borrowed in my life. Have always rented. Now my wife and I want to buy and live in a Telegraph Hill fourplex. The price is $49,500, and the down payment is $10,000. Do you think a bank would lend the down payment? Or are they stopped by stock-exchange maximum financing rules?"

Stock exchange rules do not apply to borrowing on stock for a down payment to buy property. You may be asked to sign an affidavit that you are not borrowing in order to buy additional stock.

This is one example of eating your cake and keeping it. You can keep stock or other valuable property and still use it for a down payment. Just put it up as security and the bank will gladly lend you the money. So will your credit union or other lenders. With your steady employment record and income you could borrow a substantial amount even without this security. However, you will save money by paying a lower interest rate if you put up your stock as security.

Across San Francisco Bay in Oakland, Earl Byers, manager of the American Veterans Industries salvage stores, tells of borrowing $3,400 from his bank for the entire down payment on a $31,000 leased warehouse. Mortgage financing covered the balance of the purchase money. Byers put up exactly $92.86 of his own money in the transaction to complete the payment of closing or settlement costs.

## Why Do Banks Want Such Big Payments?

This question was asked by Henry Morgan when I was on his television show in New York. I mentioned that for the fastest progress one should borrow the most one can at each purchase or refinancing stage, and that the loan should be extended for as long a term as possible in order to keep monthly payments low. Morgan said, "I see your point. But why is there such a conflict with bank advice? Why do they want to keep your loans small and still have you make such big payments?"

I have had many discussions about the subject with bankers, including Bert Lynch and Chris Christiansen of Sacramento, Kendric Morrish and Fred Miles in Oakland, and Charles Neuman and Willis Bryant in San Francisco, and I have found that we think along similar lines on these points. But in general there is a lot of confusion about the fundamentals of financing because of different views on its many phases.

For example, the average banker's advice to the average borrower applying for a consumer loan is "Borrow the least you can get by with, not the most you can get. Pay the largest monthly installments you can handle." The smaller the loan and the faster it is repaid, the sounder it is for the bank to lend and the less interest cost there is to the borrower.

But my banker friends agree with me about investments: The more money you can borrow, and the less you have to pay back monthly, the more money you have for purchasing and improvements, and therefore the faster you can pyramid. To speed your pyramiding as much as possible you will want to arrange for the largest mortgage loans you can get, to run as long as possible. It is not sound, of course, to borrow more than you can repay. Always protect yourself by making sure you can meet loan payments out of income.

### Where Can I Get 75 Per Cent Financing?

Jay Dare writes from North Hollywood, California, "Your book is fine reading and has many helpful pointers that I am impatient to put to use. I'm one-third through and feel I have to ask you a question before waiting to finish it. Just where in the United States were you able to buy income property with such low down payments? Where can I get that 75 per cent financing? My wife and I have started looking for income property in the San Fernando Valley, Hollywood and various parts of Greater Los Angeles. We have found some fairly good buys in income property that needs improving. But we haven't found any that could be bought for less than one-third down, with maximum financing of 67 per cent."

This letter is typical of some I have received from readers who became impatient when partway through my book and asked questions that usually would have been answered by the time they reached the end. My experience with 75 per cent and better financing on personal purchases has all been in northern California, but similar financing is available anywhere in the United States. My files are filled with accounts from people who have done well all over the country, including Southern California.

It appears that what you are being quoted is, for the most part, the maximum available first mortgage from conventional financing, such as a bank or an insurance company grants. Because there is so much new construction in Southern California, conventional loans are tighter there than elsewhere. Therefore your banks would be inclined to lend a lower percentage than savings banks in the East, even if they had the benefit of the more liberal Eastern state laws. California laws now permit 80 per cent conventional bank financing, but few banks go this high. Where a first mortgage is insufficient to complete the financing, many deals are consummated with second, and some with third, mortgages. It is a spreading practice for the owner to take back a second mortgage as the chief means of subsidiary financing.

Keep in mind also that 75 per cent financing is a relative average to seek. Your figure of 67 per cent isn't far from it. The next purchase might work out with 80 per cent loans if the owner grants a liberal second mortgage. Or he might take back a big first mortgage, so handling all the financing.

Along with scores of contacts I have made with Southern California investors, I have talked with many leading realtors there. They have told of arranging major income-property deals with financing ranging from 75 to 100 per cent. Outstanding examples in different communities are related by Clive Graham in Long Beach, Don Roberts in Whittier, Art Leitch in San Diego and Marshall Jacobsen in West Los Angeles. The latter wrote after my lecture to the Santa Monica Apartment House Association, "Enclosed is the article I promised you after your speech last night. From my weekly column in the *Evening Outlook,* it concerns the importance of leverage in real-estate transactions. We have been advising our clients for many years to use what you call 'other people's money' in the purchase of investment property. Yet it has taken an event like your book to finally point out to the public the financial advantages of such a procedure."

### Can You Give an Example of 100 Per Cent Financing?

From Jay Dare's modest inquiry regarding 75 per cent financing, let's look at experiences in the 100 per cent range. Among others who have asked for an example of 100 per cent financing is Frank Blair of the *Today* TV show, in a New York radio network interview.

There are scads of them, including the case histories cited in my first book. Outstanding is Henry Ford, who pyramided into a billionaire enterprise on 100 per cent financing. He started without a cent of his own money and borrowed 100 per cent of the original capital that started his company.

Many fan letters have mentioned recent experiences. A number in my confidential, unquotable file, from builders, attorneys, accountants and title company officers, are in the 105 per cent range. A letter from a Miami, Florida, investor tells how he arranged loans that gave him $10,000 more than his total purchase and improvement costs on eighteen apartments.

The Statler hotels, before they were bought by Conrad Hilton to form the world's largest chain, were founded on virtually 100 per cent financing. Jealous competitors, as is often the case, called it gall, but Statler's bankers recognized his imagination and courage. They put up all the construction money on the strength of the thousands of advance reservations he had collected for the St. Louis World's Fair—all made before his hotel was even started.

A Texas developer paid $2,000 for a short option to tie up acreage valued at $1 million. This was his token start toward building a multimillion-dollar shopping center. The option provided that the seller would deed over the land when he received $250,000 in cash and the $750,000 balance in acceptable notes.

Next, the developer sold a one-sixth portion for $250,000 to each of five ranch- and oil-land investors. Each purchaser paid $50,000 down in cash and gave the developer a promissory note for $50,000 and the seller of the acreage a note for $150,000, secured by other properties. At this point the seller was paid off with the required $250,000 in cash and $750,000 in notes. The developer had turned his $2,000 into $250,000 in notes, which he owned without any strings attached. And he owned a one-sixth interest in the acreage, which was now free and clear.

Next, the developer secured long-term leases for the shopping center from national and regional retailers. These leases encouraged local operators to take over the remainder of the planned space. With the new leases in hand, the developer had obtained 105 per cent financing of the total construction costs, including architect's and engineering fees.

I know of other experienced investors, the John Burt Terhunes, Senior and Junior, who bought 129 desirable garden-type apartments in Sacramento, California, with 100 per cent-plus financing. They paid $1,525,000 and didn't put in a cent of their own money. After arranging long-term first, second and third loans, all of which they could safely handle, they received from the title company a closing check for $4,002.57 to consummate their deal!

### I'm Scared to Death of Borrowing. Am I Wrong to Be So Afraid?

Maudie Frustus writes from Minnesota, My husband is a postal clerk in a town near Rochester. We have seven children, three in college and four at home. We owe no one. My husband or one of the kids would come down with some sickness for sure if we owed. So every payday we keep putting a little by in the savings bank to draw interest. I don't believe in any form of borrowing. We never buy a thing unless we can pay cash on the barrelhead, that's our motto.

"We live on my husband's dad's farm and help with the milking and other chores. One of our kids slops the pigs, one feeds the chickens, and so on, that's the advantage of a big family on the farm. We also get all the milk, cheese, butter, eggs, bacon and ham we want or we could never even be able to pay expenses out of my husband's government pay, let alone save a penny.

"I'd like to see someone like us make more money by buying our own farm, or maybe rental property in Rochester, like some of our friends. We know we can never pay for such a dream unless we borrow a lot more than we put in, and that's one thing I'm scared of. Another thing, you borrowed with success in California. Some of my neighbors have done the same on a lesser scale here. But do you know of any successful heavy borrowing in this area? My husband isn't so sure I'm right to be as scared as I am, but he listens to me. Am I wrong to be so afraid? What would you advise us to do?

"P.S. Have not read your book, but read an article by Pat McCarty in the Minneapolis *Tribune* about you making a speech there

March 6, 'How to Make a Million in Real Estate.' Guess I better quit, but sure had to write you a fan letter to ask advice of someone who is a success. Please answer our problem. How can we get ahead and not have to borrow?"

Chances are you can't, to answer your last question first. A thorough reading of my first book, available at any Rochester bookstore or the public library, might help you understand. It is absolutely impossible to make a fortune today without borrowing.

It may reassure you to know that many people share your fear of the unknown. The fundamental investment truths of free enterprise are thus far unknown to you, but they are readily available if you take the time to read about them. For example, your statement "I don't believe in any form of borrowing" is a contradiction, because your savings are a form of borrowing on the part of the bank.

You are also confusing money investment with money consumption, two entirely different financial concepts. You are right to shun heavy borrowing for personal pleasures, but the money you borrow for investment should help not only to repay itself but also to make more money.

On one of my Minnesota lecture tours the master of ceremonies was Rochester realtor Leon Shapiro, president of the Minnesota Realtors Association. We had lots of time to compare notes as he drove through the "unseasonal" early-March snowdrifts. One day's trip took us south from Minneapolis to Mankato. After an intervening day's seminar in Minneapolis we drove north to Brainerd. Shapiro mentioned many outstanding examples of investment and heavy financing in your area. He and other Minnesota realtors told me of several deals that approached 100 per cent financing.

A carful of passengers made for stimulating discussions as Shapiro's snow tires slapped on the icy roads. The participants were Bernard Rice, executive vice president of the Minnesota Realtors Association, who had arranged the educational seminars; his secretary, Alice Benda; and my lecture associates, Fred Palmer of Worthington, Ohio, and William McKay of Van Nuys, California.

The discussion was frank, and many interesting details were brought out, but a great deal of the information was confidential, and can only be cited in general terms.

A case history that can be mentioned is a deal of Shapiro's that involved the purchase of a $25,000 rental property. The purchaser paid only $3,000 down, and a $22,000 first mortgage was obtained from a fairly conservative commercial bank. On its appraisal of the market value, the bank financed 88 per cent of the purchase price. Although the buyer put up just double the $1,500 realtor's commission, the seller cashed out, and no secondary financing was needed.

## Will the Sale Appraisal Value Decrease a Loan?

This question was asked by Alice Woodside, following my lecture in the book section of Capwell's department store in Hayward, California.

Some lending institutions make an appraisal, then adjust it if the selling price is lower. Others make loans on the basis of their appraisals, regardless of the selling price.

The Minnesota bank loan of $22,000 mentioned earlier was made on the basis of an appraisal that was considerably higher than the sale price, indicating that the purchaser made a good buy. When I participated in the Brainerd, Minnesota, seminar, two St. Paul realtors were fellow lecturers. They were John There, past president of the Minnesota Realtors Association, and Ray Jambor, cofounder of the Minnesota chapter of the International Traders Club. Jambor pointed out that maximum financing is easier to obtain on a trade when a lending institution appraises higher than the stated selling price and makes a practice of dropping to the lower figure. On a trade, the sale price may be omitted, with no reference whatever to values. Or the nominal selling price can be increased over the book value or the stipulated value to reflect the estimated paper profit of the trader.

Different lenders have different ground rules. Some stick to their appraisals, disregarding sales or trades. Some accept reasonable stipulated values on exchanges. Others insist on exchanging sales contracts rather than exchange contracts in order to set values. There are so many legitimate ways to prepare papers on exchanges that they can usually be arranged to suit any lender.

Realtor Joseph Costa of San Diego's Key Realty won the 1961 Richard Reno Exchange Trophy for the most oustanding California exchange of the year. In *California Real Estate Magazine* Costa reports how he juggled papers in order to obtain financing to consummate a four-way trade. On total valuations of $74,950, the following properties changed hands in a series of round-robin trades:

1. The owner of a $26,750 mortgaged duplex acquired three lots valued at $15,000.
2. The broker-owner of a $19,000 house wound up with the duplex.
3. A young couple who owned a $14,200 house wound up with the larger house.
4. The smaller house, subject to mortgage, and some cash went to the lot owner.

Completion of the exchanges was contigent on raising additional cash by refinancing the $19,000 house. Costa relates how he handled this requirement:

"By placing a new loan on the broker's house I knew I could generate about seven thousand cash. . . . While all the deeds and other papers were held in escrow the lender turned down the loan application because they did not consider an exchange of equity as a sufficient down payment.

" 'O.K.,' says I, and had the small-house owner sign a sales contract. Then I had the current large-house owner sign a sales contract. Consequently the escrow showed that they were each to pay one another thirty-three hundred dollars (this was the equity after adjustment). The lender was satisfied, and the escrow closed."

## How Do You Borrow Such Big Amounts?

Esther Prinz writes from Needham Heights, Massachusetts, "The formula described in your book seems little short of fantastic. My husband and I own a six-unit dwelling and could expect to realize $21,000 or better on it if we were to sell. I have prodded my husband into investigating other larger multiple-unit dwellings which we might buy if we sell the six-unit.

"The banks we have talked to seem so 'close' on giving mortgages in the neighborhood we ask for. How do you go about borrowing such big amounts? It is also not clear what the buyer in the first step of your pyramid uses as collateral for the '75 per cent financing.' Can you enlighten us?"

The collateral in my first pyramid step, as in succeeding steps, is the property purchased. The 75 per cent mortgage might be granted by a lending institution or by the seller, as happened with the purchase of the A Avenue house. If the first mortgage falls short of 75 per cent financing, the difference can usually be made up if the seller takes back a second mortgage.

It pays to shop around and not depend on one source of financing. Besides commercial banks you might want to check with savings banks, building-and-loan associations, insurance companies and mortgage brokers. In your shopping for larger properties it would be helpful for you to deal with a realtor, a broker who belongs to your local realty board. I am sure he can locate or arrange for more adequate financing.

## How Can I Get Ohio Sellers to Take Back a Second Mortgage?

Charles Nunley of Canton, Ohio, writes, "I am interested in following the advice in your book, which I thank you very much for writing. However, I have found in my preliminary shopping around in Canton that property sellers I have asked about it refuse to take back second mortgages to help with financing. One salesman I talked to said this is not a common thing in this part of Ohio. Have you ever looked at real-estate practices in Ohio? I would greatly appreciate a line of advice from you on this question: How can you get these Ohio sellers to take back a second mortgage?"

As pointed out in my first book, subsidiary financing by the seller or another party, perhaps a broker or a private lender, is commonly called a second mortgage in various parts of the country. This is especially true in the West and the Southwest, where secondary financing is a growing practice as a way of consummating sales. So-called second mortgages in the West are actually deeds of trust in many cases. In Ohio and the rest of the Midwest, secondary financing by the seller or other parties is commonly called a land contract. Some areas call this a contract of sale. Your salesman who has seldom arranged second mortgages has probably consummated a number of deals involving land contracts. The documents used and the legal status of the lender naturally differ on these various kinds of loans. But the ultimate result, whereby the buyer obtains subsidiary financing, is the same.

The practice of having a seller help with the financing is rapidly spreading eastward, as I have verified in discussions with investors and realtors in Boston. I have looked at properties and discussed local purchase and lending conditions in several Ohio cities—Cincinnati, Cleveland, Columbus, Dayton and Toledo—where I have lectured and made other appearances.

It profits little to ask questions about the possibilities of secondary financing unless you are ready to make an offer. It's best to shop until you find the buy you want, then make an offer that includes the desired financing. For example, your offer on a $20,000 purchase could state, "Subject to obtaining $15,000 mortgage or mortgages, with maximum payments of $120 monthly, including 8 per cent interest."

Some ads indicate, "Low down to qualified buyer," or "Owner will take back second to help finance." Similar wording might hint at generous financing, but most ads don't carry such messages. The purchase and financing deal you want can be obtained only after an offer is written up.

As mentioned, it is probable that your salesman has arranged for secondary financing under different terminology. He may lack the courage or imagination to work out such sales. You can be sure, though, that many subsidiary financing deals are actually being made right in his own neighborhood.

Any realty salesman will acknowledge that you need offers before you can make deals. Many a realtor has substantially increased his earnings after learning that if an offer is made subject to secondary financing it will often be accepted. (This same philosophy is spreading, to a great extent among the same alert realtors, to encourage offers subject to a trade-in of other property.)

## When Should I Stop Borrowing?

During a question-and-answer period following one of my talks in the Midwest, I was asked, "At what point in your career, if ever, would you feel that you should plan to be out of debt? In other words, when should I stop borrowing?"

You would probably never stop financing. But as an estate grows it pays to have some property clear as a safety measure. When you own a number of properties on which the loans are liquidating through regular payments from income, you are in a much freer position to finance emergencies or sudden opportunities if one or more properties is clear. It's better to arrange some heavier mortgages to help clear others, rather than having all loans partially paid down.

Heavy financing is necessary for pyramiding. The average investor finds that his pyramiding moves in surges of maximum financing, improvement and consolidation. Even a rapid pyramider should be financially extended only at the times when he borrows to the hilt in order to make maximum new purchases.

As pointed out in my first book, after improvement a property often merits a loan equal to or exceeding all out-of-pocket purchase and improvement costs, thus proving the soundness of the rental investor's position. When you have one or more substantial properties debt-free or almost clear, you can always raise funds readily by refinancing. Such a position enables you to obtain sizable commercial loans on short notice if desired, to tide you over while you wait for the processing of a favorable new mortgage.

## Is Real Estate Always at a Disadvantage Liquidity-Wise?

This question is oft repeated, and was emphasized by an Eastman Kodak supervisor after my 1974 lecture in Rochester, New York. The Kodak employee continued, "Real estate doesn't have the liquidity of my camera stocks. I've put most of my money into Eastman and Polaroid. Even though they have dropped a good deal on the market, I can sell in one day if I need to raise cash. Isn't real estate's lousy liquidity a basic disadvantage compared to stock?"

No. Not necessarily. If you sold your stock now to raise cash, you would take a terrific loss. The value of all stocks has dropped over 40 per cent in the last two years. A friend of mine who paid $60,000 for diversified "growth" stocks in the last few years has had their over-all market values slashed in half.

In the same two years real estate over-all has increased in value approximately 20 per cent. The realty investor who follows my program of improving property has an even greater gain. He can always raise quick cash by borrowing on his equities. Long-term financing can mean delays, but instant cash—the day you ask for it —can usually be obtained at any bank through a choice of two advantageous financing methods:

1. *A commercial loan* for up to six months, usually readily renewable for one year. This can tide you over until favorable long-term financing, sale, exchange, or other money-producing arrangements can be made.

2. *An improvement loan,* payable in three to ten years. Such a loan can be obtained to cover completed, current, and/or planned improvements, including modernizing, remodeling, painting, equipment, machinery, furniture and furnishings.

# XXI

## How Can I Determine My Net Worth and Establish My Credit?

Many people have asked me how they should go about determining their net worth and credit rating. A surprising number of people think they have no financial assets and are a long way from being able to invest, when an examination shows that they are actually fairly well off and already possess a sizable nest egg. The confusion arises because they do not understand the meaning of the term "net worth."

### Does Home Equity Constitute Savings?

One of my former bosses, retired telephone company executive Walter Reed of Oakland, asks, "Should I count the equity in my home as part of my savings? I have always considered this personal choice, to own a place to live in, as not particularly counting as a savings asset. I know I'm supposed to include my A. T. & T. stock and savings bonds as part of my savings. How about life insurance? Of course you would not count furniture and other personal belongings in the home, would you?"

Yes, you would. You include the value of your house, appliances, furnishings, car and jewelry. Anything that has a sale value counts as an asset in determining your net worth. You figure the present market value of stocks and bonds and the cash value of your life insurance. Sentimental value does not count when evaluating personal and real property. Neither do you discount to the price you would have to take at forced sale. Estimate the price you could get on the open market if you had a reasonable waiting time to sell.

After adding up all these assets, deduct what you owe. Include mortgages, installment loans and personal debts. The balance left is your net worth. Lending institutions usually have a standard form on which these items are filled out. A completed sample is in my first book, pages 395 and 398.

### Are You a Net or Gross Millionaire?

In speaking of whether a person is "worth" a thousand, a million or whatever the figure may be, the common financial measurement is on the basis of net worth. Some refer to the gross estate, as Billie Sol Estes did in boasting of his "fortune." According to court findings, which sent him to prison, his borrowing on nonexistent property made his liabilities exceed his assets, so he was actually worth less than nothing financially. Others who are more affluent may refer to their incomes as measures of their worth. Internal Revenue Service statistics for 1972 showed 1,011 Americans with adjusted gross incomes of a million or more, where there were only 306 in 1960. But net worth is the accepted measurement.

Reverend Clarence Reidenbach of Oakland asked, "Are you a net or gross millionaire? A member of my congregation, treasurer Bert Philips, asked me if I thought only your total assets came to a million. I said, 'No, I'm sure Bill means his net, that his total assets less his debts come to over a million.' Which one is right? If I'm right, how can I prove it?"

You're right. My total assets are close to five million, and I owe almost one and a half million. My financial statement is on file with Dun and Bradstreet, several banks and other financial institutions.

## Should I Tell My Banker the Truth?

A taxicab driver writes from New Orleans, "My brother and I borrowed $1,000 from the bank on a one-year personal loan. This was our down payment to buy a run-down $7,000 duplex in the black section here. We fixed it up ourselves, mostly paint and new roof and steps and front porch. We have nice new tenants who are paying $150 a month in rents now, double what the previous owner got. We want to keep our credit good so we can buy more houses to fix up.

"Our problem is that we have spent on improvements the $1,000 we expected to save to pay off the loan. We can only pay a couple of hundred on the loan, which is due next month. Should we tell the bank the truth? Or give them a cock-and-bull story, like hadda pay that much for grandmother's funeral or something like that? Airmail stamped envelope enclosed, so please rush reply. We are grateful for what your advice has made for us so far. We will be especially thankful for your quick answer to our problem."

Tell your banker the truth. It pays to be frank with creditors. It helps establish your honesty, besides helping you to sleep well at night. Even if you had been improvident it would still be best to be frank. In your case, you have used the money for a worthwhile purpose, when you could easily have borrowed the extra cash through an improvement loan if you had tried.

As long as the present situation keeps you from paying off the loan, I would go to your banker at once. Don't wait till the last minute. It will be easier to renew the loan before it falls due, and it helps that you can pay at least something to reduce it. Perhaps your banker will refinance the duplex sufficiently for you to pay off all your loans now—your mortgage and down payment. Why don't you ask him? This would enable you to set aside your projected personal-loan payments as savings toward the down payment on another purchase.

### Should I Start with a House and Borrow Only 75 Per Cent?

A postoffice clerk writes from Bakersfield, California, "I have $11,500 saved and am interested in buying an eight-unit apartment house. It is listed for sale at $59,500 and can be bought for $52,500. There is a $47,500 first mortgage from a savings and loan.

"Are eight units too big for my first buy? And should I look for a house instead, like the example in your book, to establish my experience and mortgage credit? Also, is it safe to take over such a high mortgage that would be over 90 per cent financing? Should I restrict myself to 75 per cent financing?"

The bigger buy your finances will let you handle, the better. My first book starts out with a one-family house in the $10,000 range only because Joe Enterprise has to work with a $2,500 nest egg. My book offers average potentials readily matched and often surpassed, as with the financing you mention.

For faster progress borrow as much as you can on each long-term loan as long as income is sufficient to pay expenses and mortgage payments.

### Should We Refinance or Sell Our Home?

Michele Le Franco writes from New Orleans, "My husband and I are both high school teachers in our early forties, and we have a boy and girl in high school. We have $6,000 in savings, which doesn't seem much after fifteen years of teaching. We own a home that is worth about $27,500. The original $20,000 mortgage is paid down to $8,000. We want to buy a small apartment house to start, maybe four to eight units. We are uncertain what steps to take and would appreciate your answering our questions.

"Would it be best to refinance our house to gain additional funds for investment? Or should we sell or trade it, even though it means moving to smaller living space? How much of our savings should we hold in reserve?"

You have already accumulated above-average savings toward your investment nest egg. Your cash savings alone approach the national median, not counting your house equity. Especially while you are both working and can continue saving, you can borrow fairly substantial amounts from your credit union, bank or other lending institution. All they will require is your signatures. This gives you a good credit backlog, and you would not have to hold as much in reserve as some investors do. You could therefore commit all your cash savings to an investment opportunity, with your credit in reserve.

As long as you want to progress through investment, it would pay to get a new loan, the highest possible. You should be able to borrow at least as much as the original loan and possibly more. The $12,000 or so in additional funds would equal twice as much as your present cash savings, giving you about $18,000 for a cash down payment to get you off to a flying start in investment.

## Do I Have to Borrow Through a Broker's Loan Officer?

A Boeing aircraft machinist writes from Seattle, Washington, "Salesmen have told me, 'We have our own loan officer and we can swing loans that you couldn't get through a regular loan source.' Can they really get better loans, or is this just a sales pitch? Do they and other loan brokers cost you more? Are you obligated to go through the loan officer in the real-estate broker's office?"

You don't have to go through the broker's loan officer. However, many leading realtors are exclusive agents for certain loan sources, such as specific insurance companies. In other cases the broker's presentation of your loan may obtain better results than you could on your own, to a bank or building-and-loan association, for example. The lender may stretch his yardsticks a bit in order to encourage the broker to present more loan business.

Loan brokers may charge from ½ of 1 per cent to 10 per cent for their services. One or 2 per cent is more common for conventional first mortgages, and 5 to 10 per cent for second mortgages arranged through private parties. When a real-estate broker helps negotiate a loan, or a building contractor performs this service for an owner, they are often repaid ½ to 1 per cent, for example, by savings-and-loan associations.

### How High an Interest Rate Should I Pay in This Day of Tight Money?

This question was asked by instructor John Brill after my San Francisco Town Hall lecture.

Naturally, you should pay the lowest rate you can get. Mortgage interest averages about 8 per cent across the country. It tends to be somewhat higher in the West, around 8½ per cent, and as high as 9½ per cent on less favorable financing. It runs a bit lower in the East, from 7½ to 8 per cent.

Interest rates, like all other costs, are a relative factor. If rates go up, the rise is reflected in the cost of new construction. Such increased reproduction costs have to be passed on to tenants, the ultimate consumers in the case of rental property.

### Is There a Maximum Interest Rate That Can Be Charged on Mortgages?

This question was asked by Grace Barker, manager of the book department at Adam, Meldrum and Anderson's, in Buffalo, New York, when I was there autographing books. A similar question was asked concerning California loans by Laura Reid of San Leandro, following my lecture at Capwell's department store in Oakland.

The maximum interest rate on mortgages that can be charged in various states runs between 6 and 10 per cent. Both principal and interest are sometimes voided if a lender makes a loan at interest that exceeds the legal rate. Maximums that are considerably below

market levels freeze out available mortgage funds, so the nationwide trend by state legislatures is to increase legal interest rates.

State laws vary. For example, the maximum rate in California is
10 per cent, an amount that is often charged on second mortgages
when a lender puts up the money. The laws of some states void only
the interest in case of overcharging.

In most cases where there are maximum-interest laws it is legal
to charge a discount or bonus in making a loan. This affects the
cost of the loan, but has generally been defined as money that does
not constitute interest. In a typical example, a lender made a $2,500
second mortgage at 10 per cent and collected a 10 per cent discount. The note required a repayment of $2,500, but the borrower
received only $2,250.

This kind of financing is more common with builders of individual homes in areas where money is tighter. One builder arranged a
$10,000 loan at 8 per cent, but he had to pay a 10 per cent dis-
count, so he received only $9,000. The builder had to include this
extra $1,000 in his cost of construction, which he eventually passed
on to the home buyer.


### Should I Pay Off All Bills at Once or a Little at a Time?

Marguerite Porter writes from Los Angeles, "Saw the piece
about you in *Esquire*. I purchased a home in 1949 and my two children and I have lived here until this time. Have added a new roof,
painting exterior and interior and complete new bath with new hot-
water heater. Have a boy starting college and a girl finishing high
school.

"Having this house equity has been a Godsend. Four months ago
I had to have major surgery, just when some personal loans had
built up. I borrowed $6,500 on this property to pay off the loans
and surgical expenses and give me a cash reserve until I got on my
feet. I still have $1,900 left in the savings bank, but I am still home
recuperating. My pay has gone on, but it has dropped to 50 per
cent of my regular salary. Am returning to work from sick leave in
three weeks.

| | |
|---|---:|
| "I still owe on car and two other loans | $2,500 |
| Arrears on life insurance | 300 |
| Miscellaneous debts | 200 |
| Total | $3,000 |

"After reading your improvement program and realizing how I have already benefited by fixing up this house, I would like to buy rental units to make a profit as you have done. Along with saving up the down payment, I know I have to maintain good credit. Your advice would be greatly appreciated on the following: Should I use up my savings to reduce the car loan and pay off all other bills? Or should I wait and pay off a little at a time out of monthly earnings? Which would be best to insure my credit?"

It would normally be best to pay off your small miscellaneous debts and your arrears obligations, such as your life insurance. Leave the larger loans, like the one on your car, to be repaid from income. This arrangement will leave you a reserve for emergencies and will give you a start toward your investment nest egg. After you get all your debts paid off you can plan to build up enough to buy your first income property.

## Should I Sell My Second Mortgage for a 40 Per Cent Discount?

Lydia Parsons writes from San Jose, California, "My husband, Harry, and I bought a copy of the tenth printing after having twice borrowed your book from the public library. Did you know you coined a new word in the English language? Clayton Realtors here headed an advertisement with HERE'S A NICKERSON FOR YOU. Congratulations!

"Already you have helped us a great deal in our knowledge of what to do and what not to do in improving property. We have a small income, and our main asset is the ability to make improvements ourselves. We hope to do that, then sell for a profit or obtain extra income from rents. Do you still like duplex property for a small investor?

"We renovated and redecorated our present home according to your plan and could easily sell at a substantial profit, but we like living here. We own a second mortgage of $3,300 that we could sell. The proceeds would go to pay some bills, and the balance be used for a down payment on another property. The mortgage brokers we talked to will buy it for a discount of 40 per cent off, which seems like a heavy sacrifice. But we are obligated to sell it or our home, or else wait for some time before we can get moving on your program. What would you advise?

"P.S. Don't you think San Jose seems to be booming dangerously? Rentals average $90 to $150 a month, but even slum property seems high in price. Would you be willing to suggest a firm or person who could assist us in buying the 'run-down property' we are anxious to locate?"

Instead of selling your second mortgage at a discount, try to use it as the down payment on a home or duplex that you can fix up. Many owners will take such security at full value for the down payment, even those who might be reluctant to trade for smaller property.

Now that you have improved your home, you could probably refinance it with a new first mortgage that will be sufficient to let you pay off bills and take care of improvement costs on the property you buy. Otherwise, you can always arrange separate F.H.A or other financing to pay for improvements. Even though it is more costly, it might be advisable in order to expedite your progress, as long as you can meet the payments from income.

It would not be fair to my realtor friends in San Jose to suggest any one of them. By answering suitable ads, such as the one you quoted, you are likely to line up realtors who will co-operate with your property-hunting desires.

Booming San Jose is presently overbuilt on higher-priced rentals in some areas. However, there are good opportunities for the kind of operation I recommend. Also, for one who has experience it is possible to do quite well with competitive new construction. With your ability to improve property, you should certainly make good progress. Duplexes, and also single-family homes, can work out fine, especially for the small investor.

## Do I Have to Pay Off a Defaulted First Loan to Save a Second?

This question was asked by one of Tro Harper's saleswomen in his San Francisco bookstore, where I was autographing books. She said, "My husband and I have a chance to sell our home to give us money for income-property investment. A buyer has offered to meet our full asking price of $20,000. The present loan is $9,000 and we have a commitment for a new $15,000 first mortgage. The buyer offers $2,500 cash down and also wants us to take back a $2,500 second deed of trust. We just put our property on the market. Now we think we can get a better deal, maybe all cash, if we wait. We hesitate to accept because we understand we have to pay off the entire first deed of trust or lose our second deed in case the buyer doesn't keep up his payments on the first. Is this true? What would you advise?"

Accept the offer. You and your realtor established this as a fair price, and very likely you will not do as well if you wait. Very often your best offer comes right after a place is freshly put on the market. In a similar Oakland case, a reluctant seller turned down a $25,000 offer that involved a $3,000 second mortgage. The offers on his house kept dropping until, a year later, he sold for $21,000 cash. In your case, the $2,500 loan you take back could be practically all profit compared with later cash offers.

Until the depression years, in the case of a foreclosure action resulting from a default of payments on a first deed of trust, the holder of a second deed could have his investment wiped out unless he could raise the entire amount of the first deed. Since that time, the laws of various states have altered this practice. California statutes now provide a three-month reinstatement period after a notice of default has been filed. If the owner doesn't make up the payments by the end of that period, the holder of a second loan can step in and reinstate the first loan by bringing the payments up to date. In such a case, or if the second deed itself is in default, the second lender may foreclose and take possession of the property under similar proceedings.

### Can a Minor Get Credit?

A student writes from Seattle, "I am seventeen, just married, and have read and reread your 'investment Bible.' It has inspired my wife and me to start saving that nest egg so we can follow your text as a guide to financial independence. We are both students and both working evenings in a restaurant, I as a short-order cook and my wife as a waitress. We are impatient to start shopping in earnest for our first piece of income property. Have a couple of questions to ask.

"Although it is legal for a married minor to make a contract, how do banks and other lending institutions regard loans to minors? Is there any possibility of receiving adequate financing?

"What is your opinion of the Seattle area for making a go of your program? I've looked at listings in the paper and have found two in our planned $10,000-to-$15,000 starting range that would warrant further investigation if we just had the down payment to start negotiations."

Saving a nest egg is by far the hardest task on the road to a fortune. If you and your wife keep that in mind it will help you to achieve your goal. Seattle should be a very good investment area.

It is generally legal and binding for a minor to contract for necessities, such as lodging, food and clothing. A lender can foreclose on a minor just as he can with anyone of legal age if the mortgage payments are not made.

Lending institutions have varying rules regarding loans to minors, whether they are married or single. Lately, with the increased number of applications from ex-G.I.s under twenty-one, from students and from young married couples, there has been considerable relaxing of the rules. In some cases a cosignature by an older person may be necessary to secure extensive financing. For the most part the determining factor is not age but personal financial stability. Along with the value of the property to be mortgaged, your loan will be gauged by your ability to repay, the dependability of your income, and your payment habits with previous credit.

### Can a Foreigner Get Credit?

Erich Bueckert writes from East Germany, "I have a chance to go to West Germany and then to America, where my cousin has a job for me as a skilled machinist. I want to save money and buy property and fix it up. I will become a citizen as soon as I can, but hope not to wait so long to own property. One thing worries me. Can a foreigner like me get credit to buy property?"

Yes.

### Can a Black Janitress Get Credit?

Glenna Truman writes from a small town in Texas, "I bought your book at Foley's in Houston after I read in the paper you were giving a lecture there. I am a widow thirty-seven years old, with a son who is a senior in high school. Have a steady job doing janitor work in the Bijou Department Store. Have worked there twelve years. Don't make much, but it's steady, which is important to me. Have saved $1,600. We live in a small house and pay only $35 a month rent. I can buy it for $3,000. Want to fix it up like you say in the book. It would cost about $500, with my son and me doing the work. Then it would look better than places renting for $60 a month, so I would rent it out for that.

"Then I would take the money and buy another small house and just keep at it, if I can only get started. The only thing is, the owner wants all cash though he owes nothing on the home now. I want to borrow a $2,000 mortgage or more, so $1,000 of my money will pay him off, and I'll have the rest for fixing up. My son says the bank won't loan me the money to buy this place because I'm black, and especially because I'm a black woman. He doesn't want me to go down there and ask because he says it would make him a laughingstock at school with his mother a black woman getting uppity ideas. He has asked his counselor (black), and the teacher says anybody knows a black person can't get credit the way a white person can.

"I have always given and will keep on giving a tenth of everything I earn to the Baptist Church, where I am a Deaconess.

"Please give me your kind advice so I can show your letter to my son, and I will also take it down and show it to the bank if you say it is all right."

Credit in most of the United States and the world is not based on race or sex. Your ability to obtain a loan does not depend on whether you are black any more than it does on whether you are a woman. It does depend on these three chief factors:

*Your Security:* what you own now or plan to buy that will insure your loan

*Your Income:* what you earn now and what you plan to earn from your purchase

*Your Integrity:* how punctually you have repaid previous loans, if any; how steadily you have kept employment; how regularly you have made savings deposits; and how faithfully you have kept tithing and other community commitments.

These are all guides to help a lender determine your ability to repay his loan. With the improvement program you have in mind, a lender should feel that your house gives ample security. Holding a steady job for twelve years makes a strong credit recommendation, and so does faithful church participation. If you haven't had previous loan experience, the fact that you have maintained a regular savings program proves your good payment habits.

I would recommend talking over your plans with the manager of the local bank where you have your savings account. He is already familiar with your ability to save. Feel perfectly free to show my letter to your banker, besides your son and his teacher-counselor. The latter is partly right, to the extent that blacks in many parts of the country are among those earning below-average incomes who have not established a good credit history. The shortcomings of a low income and a poor payment record affect anyone's credit, regardless of race.

Also, it is all too true that unreasoning prejudice has previously denied credit and other benefits of free enterprise to minority races. I know of former cases where leading insurance companies refused mortgages to qualified blacks. Some also refused to employ blacks. Both discriminations are now, of course, illegal. The same companies are now making loans regardless of race, just as they are now giving employment regardless of race.

Any individual should receive credit who proves himself by holding down a steady job, paying his bills and accumulating savings. I'm sure that in most of the country you would obtain the credit you ask for on the basis of your proven ability to repay.

### Is Bankruptcy a Good Way to Get Ahead?

This somewhat twisted question was asked by a chef, following my lecture in Atlanta, Georgia. He continued, "My uncle who learned me how to cook has gone through three restaurant bankruptcies. Once was in his own name and twice he was a corporation. 'Nothing to doing it over and over,' he says. 'Easy as shooting fish in a barrel.' He borrows money up to the hilt by offering high interest. Then he stashes cash in banks across the line in Alabama. Keeps doing this until he goes busted. Leaves his suppliers and money loaners holding the bag.

"I'm studying the idea of copying him. Aim to start my own restaurant and borrow all I can. I'd buy a big apartment house with the cash I stash away. Do you think this is a good idea to get ahead?"

Absolutely not! You can't go far in real-estate investments without good credit, and bankruptcy certainly will hurt if not ruin your credit. Besides, your uncle stands a good chance of going to prison for fraudulently concealing assets. He's bound to be exposed sooner or later.

You will go much further, besides sleeping better of nights out of jail, by guarding your credit and faithfully paying your bills. You should start your realty investment right away with a small nest egg, rather than waiting for a big buy with bigger but illegal funds.

# XXII

## *Where Is the Best Place to Borrow Money?*

Wherever I have lectured, people have asked this question. It was raised recently by a member of the audience following my lecture at San Francisco Town Hall.

It pays to shop carefully for money and the best possible financing, just as it pays to shop for property. Some people get into the habit of always borrowing from one source. There isn't any one best source for all circumstances. In December, for example, a certain bank or insurance company might be out of mortgage money, and in January the same lender might have a whole year's quota on hand.

Nationally, the major source for long-term income-property loans has long been insurance companies. However, building- and savings-and-loan institutions, along with savings banks, are now taking over greater proportions of mortgage financing. Banks used to grant no longer than ten-year loans on non-F.H.A. mortgages. Now many go to twenty and even twenty-five years on favorable terms. In California it's a regular practice for banks to provide twenty-five-year loans at 9 per cent interest, with 75 per cent financing.

## Home Borrowing

According to a 1972 Department of Commerce study, savings-and-loan associations financed 48.6 per cent of all mortgages for one- to four-family non-farm homes. These institutions, which are especially strong in the West, play a less active role in financing commercial and farm loans.

Commercial banks financed 16 per cent of home loans and an important portion of commercial and farm loans. Other sources of home-financing loans were as follows:

| | |
|---|---|
| Mutual savings banks | 12% |
| Government agencies | 9% |
| Life insurance companies | 6% |
| *Individuals and others | 8% |

> \* This category includes labor, trust and pension funds, mortgage companies, endowed institutions and credit unions.

## Installment Borrowing

The major sources of installment borrowing for improvement loans are commercial banks, credit unions and personal-loan companies. As a rule commercial banks and credit unions charge considerably less than other installment lenders. Although credit unions often charge less interest on secured loans than on unsecured loans, their rates are usually fixed in relationship to the size of the loan. Thus, while they usually charge less than banks on smaller loans, banks have more flexibility and often set a smaller interest charge on larger installment loans.

## What Financing Is Best to Pay for Improvements?

This was one of the questions asked by book department manager Margaret Sawders when I was autographing at Horne's in Pittsburgh.

The most easily obtainable financing available for improvements is the so-called home-improvement loan, which also covers other dwelling units, such as apartments. The maximum for both single-family homes and multifamily buildings is controlled by the owner's equity, with a repayment period extending up to ten years. Some banks set limits of $10,000 or so. Others will lend up to 80 per cent of the owner's equity, without limit.

The interest depends on the size of the loan. The regular interest rates in 1974 averaged about 11 per cent, but the range of various loans, based on amount and duration, can be as low as 10 and as much as 12.5 per cent annually on the unpaid balance.

According to the Housing and Home Finance Agency's *Bulletin 2 of the Urban Renewal Service,* property bought and rehabilitated in urban-renewal areas is eligible for F.H.A. financing under Section 220. The owner of a building with fewer than twelve units can obtain a mortgage as large as 90 per cent of the modernized value.

Improvement loans are seldom recorded as liens against property; therefore they are not secured like a mortgage or deed of trust. A solution that would encourage more improvements would be long-term mortgage financing comparable to F.H.A. new-construction loans. Most of the actual financing to cover larger sums approaching $10,000 and over is handled by long-term mortgages.

I know of a number of recent bank loans of more than $10,000, however, for apartment house modernization, remodeling and furnishing; usually they ran from five to seven years. Some commercial banks could not legally make second mortgages, but they recorded extensive improvement loans as liens, using the property as security in the same way it is used to guarantee a second mortgage. In these cases the borrowers were able to meet the comparatively high monthly installments out of income. They wound up with the most favorable financing after the improvements had been made and the rents increased.

For the average investor, refinancing to pay for improvement loans usually works out best in the long run if this practice is followed:

1. Get a short-term loan to pay bills.
2. Make the improvements.
3. Raise the income and therefore the market value.
4. Arrange the highest possible long-term mortgage.

The last step often provides added cash for further investment; additionally, the money can be used for paying off the old mortgage, short-term loans and improvement bills.

## Why Didn't You Get an Improvement Loan to Speed Turnover?

T. A. Wilkinson, Jr., writes from Aiken, South Carolina, "I am moving to Charlotte, North Carolina, and plan to start investing there in the same manner as outlined in your book. In my new job I will be associated with the largest real-estate broker in the city, which I feel will be a tremendous asset.

"There is one question that sticks in my mind which I would appreciate having answered, and that is, Why is it on your A Avenue house you waited to make improvements out of income, and spread them over a long period of time? Why didn't you get a 'home improvement loan,' so you could pay for the work much sooner, enabling you to turn over at a much earlier date? This was the pattern followed after A, and I just wonder why it was not done for A."

The improvement work at A Avenue, the Enterprises' first property, was spread over a fairly lengthy period chiefly to illustrate an example on the conservative side. The time period could readily have been shortened, since there was no additional financing beyond the purchase-money mortgage. This example was also useful because it showed how the improvement work could be broken into segments.

Accelerated progress in the initial stages of pyramiding would certainly be possible through an improvement loan or other financing that would let you do all the necessary work as soon as possible. Such borrowing is recommended as long as you can finance the payments plus the expenses out of income.

## Why Not Quit My Job to Speed Progress?

Although Wilkinson has feasible speed-up plans, not all ideas to move faster are necessarily sound. A telephone company installer writes from Boston, Massachusetts, "I have a little over $3,000 saved up in the local credit union. I have found a number of real hot sleepers in row houses that fit your plan to a T. They have been milked by sharpie owners who let them run down. With such short-sighted policies their rent collections keep going down. They have lots of vacancies. A perfect setup for your plan to buy cheap, fix up, raise rents, and sell at a good profit.

"Anyway, I am a born do-it-yourselfer, like to get in and pour on the labor as long as I can see a good benefit. I have been with the phone company seven years, making fair pay. Bought a nice suburban three-bedroom home, a hundred-year-old Cape Cod which I fixed up myself. I can see where I could move a lot faster if I quit my job and spent full time fixing up properties. Don't you think that is a good idea to help move ahead faster? Why didn't you quit sooner instead of working seventeen years for Ma Bell? What do you advise?"

You are likely to be better off in the long run if you handle real-estate investment for a few years on a spare-time basis, as I did. Keep saving out of those steady Bell System wages and see how well you do. After you get up the ladder and have had a little more experience you will be better able to measure your probable rate of progress and decide when you can safely quit your present job and devote more time to property investment. You may find then that you will be ready to take the step in two or three more years or that it will take you five or ten, depending on your progress and your investment income.

Looking back, I realize that I would have quit my Bell System job several years sooner if I had visualized my investments' potential return. They produced more income than my salary for some time before I resigned. It was a case of getting into the habit of commuting to a salaried job. But I'm glad I didn't jump the gun and quit too soon after starting to invest.

I believe you will progress further and faster if you hold on to your job for a few more years. Investment success is governed by the maximum use of credit. Your credit in the initial stages, with fairly modest savings, will be limited without a stable income. In addition, you can pyramid faster with steady wages to back you up, because you can more safely put all your available funds to work. You will be in a better position to borrow additional amounts through personal loans to take care of emergencies. Without this certain wage backlog that gives you a definite credit reserve, you would need to hold a larger cash reserve for emergencies.

## Why Isn't Easy Financing Uniform Throughout the United States?

Oil worker Leon Escamillo writes from El Paso, Texas, "Most of the loan companies here charge 8.6 per cent interest on real-estate loans. I asked at a couple about their general policies and they said they will lend only 50 per cent of their appraisal value on older houses and apartments. I have found some good buys here for $10,000 or so, but they are hard to finance, so haven't tried to buy any yet. I need a little more guidance to get started.

"When I lived in Newark, New Jersey, working for the oil company at Bayonne, the banks seemed to have plenty of money. It was easy to get a 75 per cent loan at 6 per cent interest on an old duplex house I bought and fixed up. Why isn't financing uniform in all the states? What would you advise me to do down here in Texas to get 75 per cent financing?"

There are many ways to finance; examples covering them will be found in my first book. It doesn't do much good to attempt dry runs, nor does it settle anything to talk to real-estate brokers and lenders about generalities. You should first find a suitable place that you can handle, then make an offer subject to your getting the financing you require. Very often the seller will finance a heavy first loan or will take back a substantial secondary loan. Or an alert realtor will help work out financing by shopping around at various sources.

Interest rates have increased all over the country. I'm sure you'd find them higher now in New Jersey, but supply and demand vary in different areas.

Savings are heaviest in Eastern states, while the demand for mortgage money is greatest in the West and the Southwest; but, except in the case of national insurance companies, there are difficulties that prevent the spread of Eastern savings across the country to cover Western financing. Eastern savings institutions, such as the one in New Jersey which gave you a desirable duplex loan, are bound by many statutory restrictions. This situation was emphasized by Robert Tharpe, president of the Mortgage Bankers Association of America, when we both lectured to the convention of the National Association of Realtors in Dallas, Texas.

"Obsolete and inhibitive statutes," he said, "prevent a free flow of investment funds across state lines, impairing more uniform financing. There are many states which impose 'doing business' penalties on out-of-state business, and which have blocked these states from savings bank and pension fund investment. There are states where antiquated restrictions on the ratios to value at which their institutions may lend either keep the conventional mortgage from becoming the independent, competitive force it should be or else lead to unsound appraisal practices as a means of circumvention to grant higher loans. We have lived too long with these forces of legal obsolescence. It is long past time to rouse ourselves and do something about them. I propose that the National Association of Realtors and the Mortgage Bankers Association of America join together for a vigorous assault on these obsolete and antiquated laws."

### Should I Borrow on Life Insurance in Order to Invest?

A Portland, Oregon, preacher writes, "Your book has convinced me of the sound uses of your program, but my wife hates to borrow or let loose of our savings. We have $2,000 in the savings bank.

Another $3,000 will be realized from selling a piece of land we have had in the family since 1897. A small profit that doesn't amount to much if you count the time. With our $5,000 I hope to build our estate enough to keep us in at least comfort when I retire in another fifteen years.

"We have a question or two, mainly from my wife. How much would one require now in this Pacific Coast economy to get started? You say $2,500 plus $50 monthly savings from personal income. Could you run this plan without a chunk out of your salary each month? On a minister's pay I have a tough time caring for my brood, with no leeway for savings. Could the plan be carried out with our money as above and without borrowing any of the down payment at all from any agency?

"Should I borrow against two life insurance policies I have and leave some of my savings in the bank? I have excellent credit with the Ben Franklin Savings and Loan Association in Portland. Is this a good place for real-estate borrowing?"

In your circumstances I would not borrow on the life insurance in order to purchase property. You have plenty of cash. Save the policies for an emergency reserve. It seems that most wives have a cautious tendency to preserve the status quo. However, many women—wives as well as spinsters and widows—are successfully venturing into realty investment.

Plowing in more savings speeds up progress, but it is not necessary. My advocacy of continued savings has a second purpose: to discourage investors from getting thoughts of millionaire living with the first small-property ownership. The savings-and-loan association is a good place for heavy purchase-money borrowing. If you need more money for improvements, an improvement-type loan is easy to get at the bank.

I know of many recent purchases on the Pacific Coast of single homes and duplexes with down payments ranging from $1,000 to $2,500. A $2,500 start is reasonable for run-down but basically sound property that readily responds to improvement. Portland is a good place for property investment. You should be able to buy a suitable property there for not over $3,000 or $4,000 down, leaving you a fair cash reserve for improvements and unforeseen eventualities.

## How Can I Save Months of Doglegging for Loans?

Dr. Marvin Rodney of Loudonville, New York, writes, "Are there experienced people in the New York 'megalopolis' area (Boston–New York–Philadelphia–Baltimore–Washington) you might recommend to a 'little investor' regarding the purchase of real estate, using the annuity type of approach through a syndicate or trust?

Also, by what obvious, available means can one select the best available lenders in a strange area, and yet save the months that can be lost doglegging it to every one of the larger institutions?"

If you don't already have a good mortgage contact, such as a bank or savings-and-loan company, mortgage brokers will gladly review the lending possibilities in a given area. Their fees range from 1 to 5 per cent, depending on the size of the loan, area practices and other factors. In some areas lenders pay part of the fee when they have a surfeit of funds. The borrower's cost is usually taken from loan proceeds and should never be paid in advance. Mortgage brokers are mentioned in the section on financing in my first book and are listed in the telephone book under "Real Estate Loans," "Loans" or similar classifications. They have available mortgage funds from labor union and company pension funds, from trusts and from private lenders. Also, many large institutional lenders, such as insurance companies, operate through mortgage brokers rather than maintain their own staffs to grant and process loans. Mortgage brokers may also have information on real-estate syndicates or investment trusts in your area. Some of them maintain contacts in this field and operate as real-estate brokers themselves. You might also check with your banker and with the local real-estate board for the names of realtors who specialize in this field.

Recent laws have encouraged the formation of real-estate investment trusts. These enable small investors to share in the ownership of desirable larger properties. Such trusts are buying up apartments and homes, and they are constructing or buying hotels and motels, office buildings, leased retail stores, and factories.

### Should I Deposit All My $100,000 at 6 Per Cent in Savings-and-Loan Companies?

Dallas oilman Marion Stickle phoned long distance to say, "I've read your book three times and outlined it. I've been giving all my attention to developing my oil interests. I'm going to divide my time from now on, fifty per cent to the oil business and fifty per cent to following your plan of buying and fixing up apartments. I'm transferring forty thousand dollars now from my Dallas accounts to a California community, and I'll have about a hundred thousand available in a short time. I want to use it to help establish some financing contacts. I understand you can get the biggest mortgages from savings-and-loan associations, so I plan to spread the money around among them in various twenty-thousand-dollar deposits, all insured. They will average six per cent or better while my money is sitting there and I'm shopping around. What do you think of this idea? Have you any suggestions?"

The general idea has merit, but I would establish at least one contact with a commercial bank as soon as possible. Make a savings deposit there even though the interest is lower, and also set up a commercial account. Ask to see the bank manager, so that you will not be a stranger if you should later apply for a loan. Commercial banks look with more favor on a loan applicant who is also a depositor. In fact, some refuse financing to nondepositors. The bank manager who welcomes you with a big smile when you open a sizable new account should remain friendly when you come back to ask for a loan. Your reception may not be nearly so warm if your first contact is for the purpose of making a loan. Commercial banks are more interested in apartment mortgages than they used to be, and they tend to grant more favorable terms than formerly. They are branching out in order to put increased savings deposits to use. Combined, they also have major investment control of about $25 billion in trusteed corporate pension funds.

A bank contact is indispensable as a speedy source of ready cash. With such a credit reserve, you can finance to the hilt on major purchases, for example, committing about all your cash on hand. To give another example, you don't have to build up substantial deposits in order to pay taxes, when you know you can usually get the money from the bank the same day you ask for it. Also, commercial banks provide an extra reserve for payment of improvement loans when other credit is not readily available to you. The commercial bank where you have maintained deposits and established your credit will tend to grant more liberal financing of improvements, including major repairs and new furnishings and equipment.

### Can I Finance Real Estate Through an S.B.I.C.?

A Chicago-area shopping-center developer writes of having difficulty obtaining the necessary financing for a new project. He adds, "I have heard in a roundabout way that you can get good real-estate financing through a small-business investment company. Do you know if this is feasible? Where can I get more information about S.B.I.C.s in this area?"

Yes, S.B.I.C.s can make real-estate loans on riskier ventures than might be feasible for a more conventional lender. Their financing costs are naturally higher, to offset the greater risks they take. They often demand a heavy share in ownership and profits. They can lend up to $500,000 on a single venture without special government authorization.

I know of a Florida marina development that was about to collapse because the owners needed an additional $300,000 to complete their project. Their plans included a shopping center, waterfront apartments and boat parking slips. An S.B.I.C. offered to advance the $300,000 in exchange for 50 per cent ownership. There are many ways in which unusual financing can be worked out by one of the 338 S.B.I.C.s in operation in 1975. For names and addresses of S.B.I.C.s write to Small Business Administration, Investment Division, Washington, D.C. 20416.

### Should I Borrow to Modernize a Dairy Farm?

A letter from a Wisconsin couple states, "We are dairy farmers in Clark County. Read in the Minneapolis *Sunday Tribune* about your advocacy of improving property through financing. The future doesn't look any too good for us unless we modernize to meet competition. With labor going up faster than income, we need to put in milking machinery and other mechanized equipment to replace hired hands.

"Our problem is this, now that our land mortgage is almost paid off: We have always thought we should stay out of any more debt. But it would take a full lifetime to lay aside enough money to pay for needed changes. The longer we wait the higher the costs, and the more we keep going backward. The neighbors that operate like us are no better off, so it isn't just us. We all belong to the same dairy co-op. In our area the ones who are driving new Lincolns and Cadillacs are those who have already borrowed to modernize. I don't know how they all managed their financing. I know one got the money for some of his new equipment through our co-op credit union.

"We don't care about the big cars, but we thought maybe we could better ourselves. We would like to look into this, but don't want the neighbors to know until we have our plans all worked out and put into operation. The article about your advising others to get ahead gave us encouragement. Please consider our problem. How would your borrowing and modernizing experience with apartments apply to a Wisconsin dairy farm?"

You can easily finance your farm modernization, especially since your land is almost paid for. Your affluent, mechanized neighbors have already shown you the way. Many fan letters from your state and neighboring states like Minnesota and Iowa tell of people who have switched from profitless to profitable farming by borrowing in order to mechanize.

Talk to two or three equipment dealers and get their ideas, then verify them with your county farm agent, dairy co-operative or other adviser. Ask for suggestions from neighbors who have already modernized. Most likely they'll be proud to show what they have done, and to tell you what to do and not to do, based on their experience. After deciding what equipment you need, figure your expected modernization costs. Add about 10 or 20 per cent extra to cover contingencies.

Next, figure the total gross income you would expect to make after modernization. Deduct the anticipated expenses you will have after your labor-saving devices are installed. (They should be lower than your present expense.) The balance gives you your new net. Present these figures to your local banker and ask for a new, long-term mortgage to pay off your present loan and the modernization costs. You should end up with a greater spendable income than at present. This is the easiest way to handle modernization. If you already had a substantial mortgage, you might have to consider financing through a shorter-term equipment loan. This could be worked out through your equipment dealer, through your bank, or through the credit union operated by your dairy co-op.

### How Can I Acquire Proper Financing?

Fred Millar, another dairy farmer, writes from central Michigan, "My net worth is $79,720, composed of a 226-acre improved dairy farm with a market value of $30,000 free and clear, a dairy processing plant, the Geneva Cheese Company, of equal value, plus cash, stocks and other assets. I would like to acquire an apartment building or other income property to increase my estate.

"With the above net worth, what size property do you suggest I look for to start? How can I best acquire proper financing with these assets? How much money, in your opinion, could I borrow? I live about 100 miles from Detroit, and only a few miles from Flint, Saginaw, Bay City and Pontiac. This looks to me like an area of splendid opportunities. Do you agree?"

Your area, as you say, is one of splendid opportunities. As I've said elsewhere, your best bet to raise cash for further investment is to get the biggest possible loans on your present real-estate holdings. You might then consider buying the largest income property you can handle, or you might trade one of your properties, if this is your inclination, after putting a mortgage on it.

After raising money from mortgages, you can still borrow from the bank on your business operations, as long as you remain in the dairy processing field, where you have proved yourself. The amounts available to you would be determined by your net earnings and net worth, and by the credit situation in your particular lending institution at the time of your loan application.

## When Should I Keep and When Should I Pay Off an Old Loan?

This question was asked while I was autographing at Paul Elder's bookstore in San Francisco. An apartment buyer was trying to decide whether to assume an existing mortgage or to arrange a new one.

Decide on the basis of whether you gain more by saving on interest or by acquiring the most funds. At times it pays to keep an old loan. For example, assume that you are buying property for $20,-000 on which there is a $12,000 insurance company loan at 6 per cent interest. You desire financing of $15,000 and can get a new first mortgage in that amount at 8 per cent interest. In such a case you might plan to keep the present loan and try to get other financing for the $3,000 difference. The seller might take back a second mortgage for this amount at 8 per cent. Even if you paid a higher premium rate, like 9 per cent, for a second mortgage, you would still be better off. The foregoing is predicated on the present loan's running for a fairly long term so that the payments on both loans would not be excessive.

On the other hand, if the property you want has a loan on it with a higher rate of interest than you can get by refinancing, pay off the old loan. In a recent Richmond, California, fourplex purchase there was an existing fifteen-year mortgage at 9 per cent, held by a savings-and-loan association. The existing loan was originally $12,500 and was paid down to $12,000. The buyer was able to get a new twenty-year $15,000 loan at 8 per cent from a commercial bank. Monthly payments on the new loan were slightly less: $126.80 on the existing $12,000 mortgage, and $125.47 on the new $15,-000 loan. Even if you cannot get additional funds, you would still want to reject the old loan and take a new one because of the lower rate of interest.

### Would It Pay to Refinance My Own Present Loans?

This question was asked by another of Paul Elder's customers, who had overheard the previous discussion.

The general considerations involving a purchase-money mortgage would also apply in most instances to the question of refinancing your present loans. Astute individual and corporate borrowers continually review their loan programs in the light of up-to-date financing costs. For example, in the easier money markets of the early 1960s the Bell Telephone companies refinanced a billion or so in bonds. New funds costing an average of 4½ per cent paid off bonds floated in the 5½ per cent range in the tighter money markets of the late '50s.

### Should We Make a Commercial or a Mortgage Loan to Invest?

Sidney Einstein writes from Brooklyn, New York, "My brother and I own and operate a New York City taxicab company with a market value of $20,000. Outstanding against it is a commercial loan, paid down to $2,000.

"Secondly, my brother owns his own duplex house, value $15,-000, with a mortgage paid down to $3,500. He lives in half and rents the other part out.

"Third, my father owns a building with twenty-three apartments and five stores. The market value is $50,000, with outstanding first and second mortgages totaling $26,000. We wish to pool our resources and trade up the latter. We would like to think we are going about the financing correctly, and would appreciate your advice.

"Should we borrow the maximum of $8,000 on our taxicab company from a commercial bank? Should my brother renew his duplex mortgage for the maximum amount? Or would it be a sufficient down payment to trade up the apartment building, taking over the increased mortgage payments on a bigger property?"

First try to up-trade the equity in the apartment building, holding other credit and funds in reserve. If you can develop a more favorable deal by offering additional funds, long-term financing with low payments is the best means of raising the money. A new mortgage on the duplex looks like your best source for obtaining cash. On any refinancing, as you have indicated, arrange the maximum loan obtainable in order to make the biggest investment.

I would leave the commercial loan till last, as that would normally involve a shorter term and higher payments. This potential credit gives you a good reserve. You could use it to pay for accelerated improvements on either the present or the newly purchased properties.

## What Is the Difference Between "Acceleration" and "Escalation"?

This question was asked by former missionary Jo Nichols of Phoenix after my lecture to an Arizona Apartment Association convention. Questioners often ask about each of these terms, and sometimes both, indicating a measure of confusion between the two entirely different meanings.

### Acceleration

This term has been optionally included in mortgages for many years by lenders to give them added protection. Borrowers should protest its inclusion and where possible avoid it. With this provision, the due date on a note may be "accelerated" to due immediately, on demand. This happens with certain stipulated occurrences, customarily if payments are not made on time, and optionally if the property is sold.

### Escalation

This is a newer term, inserted in fine print by some lenders, particularly savings-and-loan associations. It provides that the interest on a mortgage may be "escalated," or increased, whenever certain lender's interest costs increase. For example, the escalation may be tied to an increased rate of interest paid by the lender on savings accounts or to the Federal Home Loan Bank or both.

The California Apartment Association and other property owner groups have protested this practice as unfair unless it works both ways, with mortgage interest going down when the lender's interest costs decrease. The up-and-down proviso is called a "variable" interest rate. It has been used in Sweden and other European countries for some time, and is gaining sanction by the Federal Housing Administration and the Federal Home Loan Bank, particularly if available at the option of the borrower.

## What Is "Participation"?

This question was asked by retired newspaper publisher Pat Campbell of La Selva Beach, California.

Here is another term coming into reluctant borrower usage, enforced by some lenders, notoriously insurance companies, in the tight money markets of the 1970s. With this questionable practice, the borrower is simply told, "We will lend you the money only if we participate as a partner."

Typical was a deal offered me on a proposed thirty-year $500,-000 apartment house loan at 9 per cent interest. The insurance company lending the money expected to receive regular payments on the loan, *plus 10 per cent of the gross income,* becoming a 10 per cent participating partner without paying any operating or purchase-money costs. Certainly I have refused all such offers, and I know of many other like-minded investors who would not accept proffered "participation" loans.

But many contractor-builders have been caught on a limb financially. They frantically sought long-term mortgages to bail out short-term construction loans, while their bank accounts flattened from making payments on nonproductive land purchases. In order to stay in business, they have been forced to accept arm-twisting "participation" loans, with some lenders demanding as high as a 50 per cent partnership.

Several property owner groups denounce the practice of forced "participation" as unconscionable, demanding that it be outlawed. A 1974 statement of policy by the National Apartment Association calls on the federal government to "Prohibit the practice of mortgage lenders coercing borrowers to agree to an *equity participation* as a condition for making the permanent loan on a multi-family project."

## How Can I Overcome Tight Financing with a Wrap-Around Loan?

Questions similar to this are often asked in a tight money market, including "How can I avoid high interest with a *wrap-around* loan?" and "How can I save points and other refinancing costs with an *overlapping* loan?"

Knowledgeable realty investors and home buyers are now using to a great extent a relatively new instrument called by the above terms. The same procedure is also called an *overriding* or *all-inclusive* loan, mortgage, or deed of trust.

In a typical purchase a twenty-four-unit apartment house sold for $250,000. The buyer traded in a duplex valued at $40,000 and paid $10,000 in cash, making a total down payment of $50,000. There was an existing $150,000 bank loan, payable $1,030 monthly, including 6 per cent interest. In easier money markets the buyer might attempt to obtain a larger loan. Or the seller might transfer the loan to the buyer and take back a second mortgage or deed of trust for the $50,000 balance. However, at the time of purchase, new loans in the area carried 8½ per cent interest. The bank quoted the same 8½ per cent interest plus one point, $1,500, for transferring the existing loan to the buyer.

To overcome these costs the buyer gave the seller a wrap-around loan in the form of an overriding deed of trust for $200,000, payable $1,500 monthly, including 7½ per cent interest. The buyer paid the $1,500 monthly to the seller, and the seller continued to pay $1,030 monthly to the bank.

### Advantages to Buyer

The buyer, of course, saved one per cent interest over-all, compared to the 8½ per cent required on a new or transferred loan. If a wrap-around loan had not been made, he would also have paid 9 per cent interest on a $50,000 second mortgage. In contrast to another alternative, a contract of sale, the buyer has greater protection by having the property deeded to him in conjunction with signing the overriding deed of trust. Also, the latter provided that payment in full could be made without penalty, giving the buyer the option of refinancing at lower interest whenever available.

### Advantages to Seller

The seller made a 1½ per cent continuing profit on the difference between the 6 per cent paid the bank and the 7½ per cent interest paid by the buyer. This actually netted about one per cent, as he would have collected 9 per cent on a $50,000 second mortgage if he had not taken back the wrap-around loan. Also, in case of default, in most states an overriding deed of trust, the same as a regular deed of trust, can be foreclosed in about four months. This

contrasts with a probable year's delay in getting a court judgment
to enforce a defaulted contract of sale.

### Advantages to Lender

Many banks or other institutional lenders may not legally advance funds on a second mortgage or contract of sale, but may be
able to finance an overriding deed of trust. In a typical wrap-
around refinancing, there was a bank loan of $175,000 at 6½ per
cent interest on a forty-unit apartment house valued at $300,000.
The owner wanted to borrow $60,000 to pay for major moderniza-
tion. The bank holding the loan offered to advance the $60,000 by
making a new loan of $235,000 at 9 per cent interest, thus paying
off the existing loan.

A rival bank offered a wrap-around loan of $235,000 at 8 per
cent, taking over the payments on the $175,000 loan rather than
paying it off. The second bank, of course, made a gross profit of
1½ per cent interest on the existing loan, while the borrower saved
one per cent overall. The first bank did not object to the overriding
arrangement as long as loan, tax and insurance payments were kept
current.

# 10

# How to Save

# on

# Income Taxes

# XXIII

## *Have You Ever Been Audited?*

Several fellow apartment owners have asked, "Have your income taxes ever been audited?" Realtor George Burchill asked this question in San Jose, following my lecture to a joint meeting of the Lions Club and the Realty Board.

When I answered yes he asked, "Could you divulge any information that might be of help to other investors?"

I do not profess to be a tax consultant, but when questions arise in this field I am glad to share the information gained from my experience and study. In several instances I have obtained technical advice direct from informed representatives of the Internal Revenue Service. Their letters in my files customarily state that I may use the information they contain, but that permission cannot be granted to quote directly.

### Audited Three Times

Since my first book came out I've been audited three times, once by the state of California and twice by United States Internal Revenue Service agents.

One revenue agent told me that his boss had read the story about me in *Time* magazine and remarked, "This fellow Nickerson must be honest or he wouldn't have revealed his operations in so much detail in his book. But how could he have made a million and paid so little in income taxes? Check his operations with a fine-tooth comb from the time he first started investing."

All my transactions were audited in depth, including all purchases, sales and trades since I first started. Of course, normally the statute of limitations applies to returns after three years—six years if the gross income is understated more than 25 per cent—but the agent's supervisor ordered a lifetime audit on the basis that he was pursuing the possibility of fraud. There is no time limit where fraud can be proved.

This auditor's identification card was reassuring to me, as it read "Revenue Agent," not "Special Agent." He would still make a meticulous audit in search of possible errors, but if a special agent had been assigned it would have indicated that there actually were serious expectations of proving fraud. I got the impression that the Internal Revenue Service people were motivated as much by curiosity as by anything else in probing my virtually tax-free road to a million.

### How Long Should I Keep Books and Papers?

Documents pertaining to financing and transferring property should be kept indefinitely. A taxpayer should protect himself by keeping other vital records and books for at least six years, or until an audit is completed; then they may be destroyed. All the agent has to find is, say, a $10,000 bank deposit that is not declared as income, or a deducted expenditure of several thousand that cannot readily be proved, and he can in effect accuse you of fraud unless you produce acceptable explanatory evidence. The burden of proof is on you to identify the source of any undeclared funds credited to your account. You are presumed guilty unless you can prove your innocence, a reversal of the usual application of justice.

Typical of the items questioned on my returns was an apartment house purchase involving a $15,000 cash down payment. This sum had never been declared as income. Where had the money come from? A satisfactory answer to such a question would be difficult to prove if substantiating documents were not retained.

Fortunately I had saved my books on all income and expenses

from the very beginning, and I had kept every scrap of paper concerned with financing, refinancing, purchasing, selling and trading. Thus I was able to prove conclusively the legitimate source of all funds. My escrow statements and loan papers showed that the questioned $15,000 had come from refinancing another property after it was improved and the income had increased. Funds obtained through financing are, of course, not taxable income.

After the revenue agent got through he said, "Your operations are certainly O.K. It helps that you kept all the evidence. I've audited a lot of books, but this is the first time I realized clearly how you can make a fortune in real estate without paying much in the way of income taxes. I'm going to buy your book myself!"

### Is There Little Escape for Authors?

The second U.S. audit of my records was initiated in connection with the approximately $150,000 I earned in royalties from the initial sale of over 340,000 hardcover copies of my first book about real estate. Among those who have asked the foregoing question was San Francisco columnist Herb Caen, author of *Baghdad by the Bay*.

Heavy ordinary income taxes slash into the successful writer's windfall royalties from a best seller. The capital-gains escape hatch has been shut down since Dwight Eisenhower's *Crusade in Europe* pushed him into the ranks of millionaires. A patent holder is still able to pay capital-gains rates and could spread back over a five-year period his income from protracted work; but the holder of a book copyright has to pay ordinary income taxes and was limited to a three-year spreadback, provided he actually spent two years on the book. This limit applied even though he may have spent a much longer period of unremunerated time on the book—as did Katherine Anne Porter in writing *Ship of Fools,* a work that took twenty years.

At the same time that the Internal Revenue Service was applying these confiscatory tax measures against authors, some Administration and Congressional spokesmen advocated the granting of subsidies to encourage more writers and artists. It seemed more logical to encourage them by a more reasonable tax application spread over lifetime earnings. Despite the vaunted power of the pen, writers as a group have appeared rather supine in accepting cavalier tax treatment.

### Is There Tax Relief for Windfall Income?

Happily, both administrative and legislative leaders became concerned about the problem of windfall income. President Kennedy in his 1963 tax message to Congress advocated the averaging of tax treatment for highly fluctuating incomes such as those of best-selling authors. Fairer taxation was also sponsored by leading legislators, including Vice President Humphrey while a Senator, and Mayor John Lindsay of New York while a Congressman. So a majority of national legislators from both parties approved the Income Averaging Method of computing taxes on windfall income.

In effect at the time of revision of this book in 1975, this method is optional for royalty and most other income. Essentially, it allows you to compute your taxes on an unusually high amount of income at lower tax rates, based on your average income for the previous five years. Income Averaging is reported on Schedule G, and details of allowable income, computation, etc., are covered in special I.R.S. Publication 506, revised October, 1973, and available from the Internal Revenue Service without charge.

But enough of digressing into the field of writing. In the rest of this chapter I'll answer questions regarding tax audits as they pertain to realty and general areas, based on a number of studies and reports and my three exhaustive personal audits.

### What Are My Chances of Being Audited?

Commissioner Donald C. Alexander reported to Secretary of the Treasury Shultz for the fiscal year 1973 that one out of fifty-seven federal income tax returns was examined, mostly through I.R.S. office audits. This compares with the one out of fifty-five returns audited the previous year. The volume of field audits conducted on the taxpayers' premises was only 20 per cent of all returns audited, but these audits were considerably more exhaustive.

All returns are routinely checked for mathematical errors. One report showed that where errors occurred they averaged $84 when against and $70 when in favor of the government.

Various selection methods will increase the number of audits. Complex business and investment returns stand a greater chance of being audited, and that chance increases with the size of the income. In fiscal 1972 one in eight businesses with incomes of $30,-000 and over was audited, and one in eight nonbusiness taxpayers with incomes of $50,000 and over. Nearly all returns in the higher figures are given at least a cursory office examination for unusual entries or items that depart from averages. Automation helps select returns that carry out-of-line ratios. Generally, all returns showing incomes of $30,000 or more will get a thorough going over. One out of fourteen corporations was completely field audited. This figure probably approaches a close estimate of the audit chances of a property investor.

## What Are Average Deductions?

Among others asking this question was Cuma Schofield of North Fork, California.

If your deductions are out of line with the average, your return is likely to be audited, in which case you will be asked for documentary proof. On page 376 are average itemized deductions for various incomes, along with the average tax for all returns filed with itemized deductions, based on I.R.S. preliminary statistics for 1972 released March, 1974.

## Should I Dread a Tax Audit?

This question was asked by a Los Angeles apartment owner following my May Company lecture under the sponsorship of book

| ADJUSTED GROSS INCOME | MEDI-CAL & DENTAL | TAXES PAID | CONTRI-BUTIONS | INTEREST | OTHER | TOTAL DEDUC-TIONS | INCOME TAX |
|---|---|---|---|---|---|---|---|
| Under $5,000 | $637 | $ 535 | $ 234 | $ 417 | $ 158 | $ 1,981 | $ 75 |
| 5,000– 10,000 | 457 | 716 | 284 | 639 | 249 | 2,345 | 509 |
| 10,000– 15,000 | 333 | 1,030 | 344 | 931 | 332 | 2,970 | 1,150 |
| 15,000– 20,000 | 294 | 1,404 | 424 | 1,097 | 357 | 3,576 | 2,026 |
| 20,000– 25,000 | 291 | 1,778 | 544 | 1,208 | 376 | 4,197 | 3,069 |
| 25,000– 30,000 | 336 | 2,184 | 692 | 1,360 | 428 | 5,000 | 4,236 |
| 30,000– 50,000 | 393 | 2,983 | 1,031 | 1,686 | 636 | 6,729 | 6,961 |
| 50,000– 100,000 | 462 | 5,145 | 2,092 | 2,855 | 1,226 | 11,780 | 17,562 |
| 100,000– 200,000 | 630 | 10,066 | 6,023 | 5,880 | 3,004 | 25,603 | 44,987 |
| 200,000– 500,000 | 900 | 22,538 | 20,704 | 13,744 | 7,804 | 65,690 | 114,308 |
| 500,000– 1,000,000 | 705 | 54,437 | 71,419 | 31,614 | 19,931 | 178,106 | 304,195 |
| 1,000,000 or more | 142 | 153,603 | 385,809 | 68,596 | 60,146 | 668,296 | 991,990 |

buyer Al Busch. The property owner hesitated while I autographed a book for him, then said, "I took some deductions I think are O.K. but am not sure of. For instance, some of my depreciation may be a little more liberal than it ought to be. Don't you think I should dread a tax audit? Doesn't everyone?"

There's no reason to dread an audit as long as you keep adequate records and your returns are as honest and complete as you can make them. You are entitled to take all the deductions and special applications allowed. In being unsure about some things you're in the same boat as most taxpayers. It is only natural to wonder whether an audit will cost you more taxes. The chances are it will, but no sizable amount is likely to be involved in a problem such as the one you speak of.

Although an audit may be somewhat time-consuming and inconvenient, it may also, especially if it comes very early in your career, be advantageous—in that it gives you an evaluation of the soundness of your accounting procedures. If adjustments are to be made, the earlier this is done the easier it will be and the less it will cost.

Depreciation deductions on most buildings, for example, are usually open to question, since they are subject to so many variables and are dependent on individual judgment. There are guidelines to follow, and you can normally figure what will probably be acceptable. Still, it is impossible to be certain whether or not your return will be challenged until it is actually audited.

Once an audit is made you can feel fairly assured that the affected tax returns will suffer no further jeopardy. I.R.S. administrative rules provide that audited returns may not be re-examined except for unusual cause and on approval of the district director.

### What Should I Do When the Tax Man Cometh?

I have been asked many questions as to how far the taxpayer should co-operate in answering a revenue agent's request for information and evidence.

It helps to establish your honesty of purpose if you wholeheartedly answer all questions and produce any documents, accounting books, receipts, etc., that the agent asks to see. If the return in question involves fairly routine items or a moderate income, you may be asked to bring certain papers to the Internal Revenue Service's local headquarters for an office audit. In such a case you will be told which papers are wanted, and it pays to take them along.

In more complex audits, such as mine, in which it would require a number of trips to produce all the papers the agent may ask for as his audit progresses, he will arrange for an appointment at the office where your books are kept. A field visit saves a great deal of the taxpayer's time, and the agent's also, as most papers can be readily produced on the spot as the audit develops.

### Should an Accountant or an Attorney Participate?

Seymour Turk, a publishing company executive, asked, "Don't you think an accountant or an attorney should always participate in a tax audit?"

Whoever is in charge of keeping the books should participate in the audit from the beginning. If a tax accountant or attorney is regularly consulted in investment operations, he should always be advised of the audit and his participation left to his judgment.

For the average audit the agent will first establish certain facts and then state his tentative findings. The taxpayer should call in an attorney or accountant at least to advise him—preferably, to help deal with the revenue agent before the settling of any controversial findings that indicate a greater tax liability. Usually it is better to have the lawyer or accountant participate from the beginning. An adviser's fee is, of course, tax-deductible. Almost invariably it is less than the amount of taxes he can save.

### How Does the Agent Check Income?

The agent looks for signs of unreported income. For example, does the taxpayer's standard of living seem higher than his reported income would warrant? The agent checks all the bank statements of the taxpayer and his family for the years under audit—usually the last year filed, which is the year before the audit, plus the two preceding years. Every deposit is open to question and should be identified. Therefore, as stated earlier, it pays to label each deposit when you check your monthly bank statement.

The agent presumes that all deposits represent taxable income unless the taxpayer can prove otherwise. Thus any nonincome deposits should be so labeled (examples: "Sale of A Avenue house," "Refinancing Cynthia Court Apts."), and supporting evidence should be readily available. For a real-estate investor, each income-producing property may be audited; the agent may check rent receipts, statements, names of tenants and other evidence to verify that all income is reported.

Some owners keep a bulky pile of rent receipts over a period of years. To avoid this I have each apartment house manager sign a monthly statement certifying the amount of rent collected from each tenant. This practice has proven acceptable on all my audits. One point to mention is that whenever an amount other than the full rent is reported for an apartment, there should be an adequate explanation. Examples: "Vacant," "Moved Nov. 1," "Delinquent rent to be paid Dec. 5."

### How Does the Agent Check Exemptions?

This question was asked by a steel company executive's wife, Rosemary Nickel of Hillsborough, California.

After checking income, the agent verifies exemptions. He is especially interested in unusual claims, such as for a dependent other than one's wife or children. He wants to know the ages of children and whether they have an independent income of $750 or more. If appropriate, he may ask if they are students or if they have married during the year.

One agent told me that a father may sometimes claim a daughter as a dependent if she marries toward the end of the year, figuring he has supported her for over half a year. However, the father cannot claim her as a dependent if she files a joint return with her husband for that year, even though she may have married on the last day of December. If her new husband does not claim her as an exemption, and the father can prove that he has provided over half of her support, then he may take the deduction.

### How Does the Agent Audit Itemized Deductions?

This question was asked by Sacramento, California, pizza parlor owner Laton Willis.

The agent will probably ask for receipts or other evidence if the tax return shows itemized deductions in any sizable amount, especially if they exceed the I.R.S. guidelines for the reported income. For example, in connection with contributions, I was asked for a statement signed by a church financial officer as proof of an above-average donation. The agent may also explore whether property gifts were valued correctly, and whether the recipient of a contribution actually qualifies as a tax-deductible charity.

### How Does the Agent Check Interest?

Receipts will be asked for, especially if the interest payments are above average. In my case, the I.R.S. office audit had already flagged my returns as showing disproportionately high interest deductions. This is only to be expected for a large property owner who goes in for heavy financing to pay for purchases and improvements. I showed a passbook, a bank statement or a paid-off note to back up every interest item I had claimed.

### How Does the Agent Check Taxes?

Another heavy deduction flagged by the I.R.S. office audit was property taxes. The agent was especially inquisitive about my tax deductions for 1960, the year when most of my book royalties were earned; I paid two years' taxes on most of my properties in this one taxable year. It is perfectly legitimate for a cash-basis taxpayer to prepay or postpone his income and expenses in order to gain the best tax advantage. Naturally, the revenue auditor verified the receipted dates stamped by each property tax collector, for he is instructed to take nothing for granted.

Property taxes, business license fees and state income taxes are easy to prove from paid bills. Other taxes, such as state and local sales taxes, may present more difficulties. In most cases they are estimated. A revenue office supervisor in California advises me of his rough yardstick: that one-third of the adjusted gross income will be subject to sales taxes. If this income is $12,000, then $4,000 will be acceptable as the amount spent on items subject to sales tax. To short-cut his computation he simply takes 2 per cent of the adjusted gross income in a 6 per cent sales tax area. An amount that substantially exceeds his resulting computation would be subject to question and flagged for further audit.

The California example is cited to show how the I.R.S. sometimes uses rules of thumb. Sales tax ratios vary in different states because of myriad exemptions. One state exempts food from sales taxes, another drugs, and so on. The Internal Revenue Service continually studies average deductions on various items. Now Optional State Sales Tax Tables have been compiled and included in *Instructions for Form 1040,* showing average sales taxes in most states in relation to income. Here are examples of 1973 guideline figures for a family of three or four in California: $118 for adjusted gross income of $7,000 to $8,000; $150 for $10,000 to $11,000; $199 for $15,000 to $16,000; and $234 for $19,000 to $20,000.

### How Is Expense Account Information Checked?

This question was asked by John Ferris, real-estate writer for the Oakland *Tribune.* Property owners have asked the same question.

Travel, entertaining and other expenses incurred for business or investment purposes, including the management of income properties, can be perfectly legitimate under tightened expense account rules. Even so, the agent is especially interested in expense account information. He will check the adequacy of bookkeeping entries to show the amounts claimed and legitimate reasons for their allowance as business expenses. He may verify the amount, time, place and purpose of each expense. He may explore whether nondeductible items have been hidden under advertising, promotion or sales expenses. He may ask for receipts or ticket stubs for air, train or other commercial transportation. He will especially ask to see diary or calendar entries for meals, lodging, entertainment, or other business and travel expenses.

The tax auditor will delve into automobile expenses, and he is not receptive to estimates. He wants mileage records on business auto travel. For depreciation purposes he wants sales and trade-in statements covering car purchases. He may ask for receipts covering expenditures for repairs, tires and accessories. Auto and other travel expenses can usually be covered acceptably by filling out Treasury Form No. 2106 and retaining applicable receipted bills. This "Statement of Employee Business Expenses" makes a useful form for the self-employed, including artists and investors.

### How Are Medical Expenses and Other Deductions Checked?

This question was asked by Dr. Wilson Matlock of Fresno, California, following my lecture to the Fresno Rotary Club.

All deductions will be balanced against allowable averages. Proof will surely be demanded if they appear excessive. Some substantiation may be required even if they are below average, but in all cases receipted bills are adequate proof.

### What Is Looked for Under Depreciation?

This question was asked by John Haviland, treasurer of the National Apartment Association, following my lecture in his home town of Portland, Oregon.

The agent is apt to review your depreciation schedules in detail from four major standpoints, as outlined below.

## OWNERSHIP

Are the depreciated assets actually owned by the taxpayer? Tax bills and other evidence may be requested. Sometimes a taxpayer claims depreciation and other expenses on property in which he owns an interest that does not entitle him to individual tax deductions. An example is ownership of stock in a corporation which owns property. In most cases the corporation takes the deductions and they are not allowable for the stock owner.

## ALLOCATION OF COST

Is the proper amount taken into account in reporting the cost of nondepreciable land, of long-term depreciable buildings, and of short-term depreciable items such as furniture, fixtures, machinery and equipment? The average taxpayer wants to allocate his costs as heavily as possible to the faster-depreciating accounts and as little as possible to nondepreciable accounts. The revenue agent looks for ways to reverse this accounting process.

In the absence of other qualified evidence, such as a bona-fide appraiser's statement, the agent will probably ask to see bills that show tax and assessed valuations which were in effect at the time of the property acquisition. Then he will review the tax assessor's ratios of land and buildings and other property. If the taxpayer's allocations are close to that ratio, or if they are not as heavy as that ratio in the area of depreciable items, the agent usually accepts the depreciable amounts shown on the return. Otherwise he will no doubt propose arbitrary adjustments.

On property taken in trade the agent may check to see whether the depreciation has been properly accounted for. Has it incorrectly been based on the market value of the new property? Or has it correctly been based on adding the depreciated cost of the traded property to any prorated additional costs of acquisition?

## LIFE OF DEPRECIABLE ASSET

Has too short a life been applied? This question is paramount in the agent's mind as he considers ways of increasing your tax liability. He examines all applicable factors, such as the various kinds of depreciable assets, the type of construction of buildings, the age of the property, the life of short-term assets. There is likely to be a considerable amount of questioning and discussion in this area before the agent arrives at his conclusions. He will rely a great deal on *Tax Information on Depreciation,* Publication 534, prepared by the Internal Revenue Service, which in many instances tends toward longer-than-realistic lives in the space-age world of faster obsolescence. Any deviation from I.R.S. guidelines in favor of the taxpayer will probably require documentary substantiation.

## AMOUNTS OF DEPRECIATION TAKEN

Do the amounts jibe with the foregoing findings on cost allocation and stated life? Is the same method consistently used for particular assets? If not, is there good reason for changing? Are accelerated-depreciation amounts justifiable? The agent will pay particular attention to the allowability of items such as:

*Investment Credit of 7 Per Cent.* Is the depreciable asset used in a business operation that makes it eligible for 7 per cent investment credit? For example, this credit, under specific qualifications, normally applies to business operations, like hotels and motels, but not to rental income properties, like apartment houses.

*First-Year Depreciation of 20 Per Cent.* Is this applied to eligible personal property, like furniture, with a remaining useful life of six years or more?

*Declining-Balance Method.* At a beginning rate that may double straight-line depreciation, did the original use of the asset commence with the taxpayer?

*Time Limit.* Were the accelerated-deduction provisions, such as the foregoing, made within the allowable time limit?

The time limit coincides with the deadline for filing a return. Taxpayers on a calendar-year basis, for example, have a deadline of April 15 in the following calendar year. Suppose the taxpayer passes up allowable accounting choices in his favor, such as first-year depreciation and the declining-balance method? They can be claimed on a revised return filed before the deadline, but they cannot usually be retrieved on an amended return filed after the deadline, or on subsequent returns filed for following years.

## What Does the Agent Look For Under Repairs?

The agent looks for items that run significantly larger than the average for other returns and the pattern of the taxpayer's previous returns. He may spot-check various bills to see if they back up bookkeeping entries. If he finds any that are questionable he will ask to see more. If a bill seems unusually large he will want to verify its accuracy. If the amount appears correct, then he will consider whether it is applied to repairs in error. Should it be listed as a capital investment instead? A large roof-repair entry, for example, might develop into a charge for a new roof and therefore is not a legitimate annual expense. It should be entered as a capital expenditure and depreciated over the appropriate number of years.

## What About Other Expenses?

Similar yardsticks may be applied to expenses other than repairs. The agent may want to see tax bills, interest accounts, utility bills and salary verifications. He may ask to see Social Security reports and employee salary statements in order to verify the salaries paid.

One area where property owners are apt to be questioned concerns the value of quarters provided for managers and other employees and carried as an expense for the owner. This represents a cost to the owner in loss of rent income. But it is not allowed as a deductible expense unless it is also shown as income, as is done by some owners to jibe with Social Security returns, where a reasonable market value for such quarters must be reported as employee income.

## How Does the Agent Check Casualty Losses?

This question was asked by warehouse operator Wallis York of Sacramento.

An agent will probably explore these questions in considering casualty claims:

1. Does a casualty loss qualify as tax-deductible?
2. Has the damaged property already been fully depreciated?
3. Is part or all of the claimed loss covered by insurance?

## What of Capital Gains?

The agent will probably look into property transfers for their tax application. Are trades properly executed as nontaxable, either up trades or across-the-board trades with no boot, or bonus, taken? What were the mortgages on the properties traded?

If property has been sold, should a capital gain apply? Has it been held over six months? Did the owner take back a mortgage and defer capital gains over the life of the loan? The agent will check the loan and sale arrangements to make sure that not more than 30 per cent of the principal has been received in the tax year of the sale.

Taxpayers may get tripped up here by counting only the down payment, neglecting to include the portion allocated to principal from installment payments. If this sum pushes principal payments over 30 per cent, the entire capital gain falls due for the year of sale.

## Does the Agent Have a Quota?

This question was asked by Liane Puckett on her radio show, *San Ramon Valley Report,* on Station KWUN, Concord, California.

Technically no. Agents used to operate under quota systems and were expected to return to the office with a predetermined minimum amount of added revenue. Former commissioner Mortimer Caplin ordered that field audits be conducted on a "quality" basis, more detailed than heretofore, and at the same time that quotas be dropped. Quotas may be out, as confirmed by Commissioner Alexander in 1974. But revenue agents and their superiors, right up to the top, feel a pressure to collect considerably more than their salaries and expenses incurred in making field and other audits.

When Caplin asked Congress for greater appropriations in order to hire more agents, he estimated that approval of his request would mean a revenue gain of $.3 billion from a 30 per cent step-up in audits. Thus the new agents, like the old, were expected to more than pay their way. By 1973 audits produced over $5 billion.

The job of the Internal Revenue Service is to collect taxes. On borderline cases the revenue agent naturally draws conclusions in the government's favor, just as an accountant interprets the regulations in favor of his client. What are the results? Caplin himself has stated that taxpayers in general are honest and thorough. Regardless of this appraisal, four out of five audits result in nicks here and there that mean added revenue for the government.

### How Long, O Lord, Will the Audit Take?

This question was asked by a widow whose husband had left her with a business operation plus income properties, all valued at over a million. She had fired her husband's competent C.P.A., who had handled all the books and tax returns. In his stead she had hired a favorite nephew, just out of high school, with no experience, little training, and an inclination to spend more time fishing than keeping books. A revenue agent had already spent two weeks going over the shambles the young man had made of her books. He gave no estimate of how much longer his audit would take.

The revenue agent may complete his field audit in one day, or he may take several days or weeks. He may spend a day or so getting preliminary information, return later for another day or two to complete his probing, then return one or two more times to discuss his findings and iron out any disputed points that are matters of interpretation. It depends on the complexity of your returns, the completeness and the organization of your books, and the ready availability of supporting evidence, such as documents and receipted bills.

It also depends on the agent's familiarity with your particular type of operation. In this regard, the Internal Revenue Service is stepping up the quality of its training program, so that better-educated specialists will be able to audit complex returns. The keenest brains in Treasury have concentrated on effective training procedures for all agents, old and new, and uniform application should result for audited taxpayers. More discrepancies will be ferreted out where they exist. On the other hand, time will be saved and there will be smoother sailing for a taxpayer whose books are in order.

Both classroom and on-the-job training will help to sharpen the quality of audits. Field training and supervision means that two agents instead of just one may visit you. One will be a supervisor or instructor.

### Will I Suffer Any More "Quality" Audits?

One businessman told me of his experience in 1962 when an agent came calling. The agent advised the taxpayer to prepare for a lengthy visit, as he was under instructions to make a new kind of "quality" audit. Commissioner Caplin had given orders to the I.R.S. to delve into minute details whenever a field audit was made. The businessman's return showed heavy entertainment expenses, which he agreed to adjust. Then every business expense item was gone over in interminable detail. The agent scrutinized a multitude of minor receipted bills instead of accepting nominal bookkeeping entries, even though he agreed they were not out of line.

"It looked like he was pushing me around so I would lean over backward on legitimate deductions on future returns," the taxpayer told me. "It took six days to finish this audit. It only took a day and a half on one I had three years ago. Do you think I will have to suffer any more of these so-called quality audits?"

No. The I.R.S. thought that such prolonged "fishing expeditions" would result in more revenue per man-day. Some comparatively fruitless "quality" audits have taken up taxpayers' and agents' time for weeks, when essential points could have been covered in a day. This smother type of auditing reached its peak in 1962, when the I.R.S. found that the amount of increased revenue per agent-hour actually dropped. With more agents in the field, the garnering of additional tax assessments was considerably lower than in 1961.

So, effective in 1963 and thereafter, instructions have gone out to stop all the detailed checking into inconsequential items. Agents are to pass over nominal bookkeeping entries that are not out of line. They are to concentrate on major entries that appear questionable or that depart from the norm—items that will produce the most additional revenue. This means a fairer shake for all taxpayers. Expect an increased possibility of being audited, with a decreased probability of prolonged probing that points toward harassment.

### What If I Disagree with the Agent?

After completing his examination, the revenue agent will advise you of his findings. They may be made on his own responsibility or after consultation with his supervisor, depending on the complexity of the return and the agent's experience. He will review any areas where he feels there should be greater tax liability and on each point at issue will ask if you agree. There will probably be some cases where the agent can point out an obvious error; if minor adjustments are involved, many taxpayers agree to them on the spot.

In a great many cases there is room for argument, because the suggested tax is subject to personal judgment and interpretation. In some cases the taxpayer can throw additional light on his position and persuade the agent to retreat. And it may happen that having a tax return audited will suggest areas to the taxpayer where he could reduce his taxes.

In any case it is not wise for a taxpayer or his representative to agree immediately to any sizable adjustment. He should ask what the preliminary findings mean in the way of higher taxes. Then he should request an extension of time before settling so that he can review the whole matter, look for supporting evidence in his favor, such as tax court rulings, and consult a tax attorney or an accountant versed in the field at issue.

While it is true that agents are in pursuit of all the taxes they can collect, and tend to be hard-nosed about judging borderline cases in the government's favor, they want to be essentially fair and are co-operative in giving the taxpayer ample time to seek advice and supporting evidence. Of course, on open and shut cases there will be no compromises. Still, agents are instructed to settle borderline disagreements without time-consuming court action if this is reasonably possible.

### Can Compromises Be Worked Out?

Where there are several moot points, some compromises may be worked out. The taxpayer may agree to one concession in exchange for having the agent concede another. In one example related to me by a tax attorney the taxpayer depreciated two older apartment buildings over a twenty-five-year life. He used the same life span to capitalize extensive remodeling and additions on one, costing about as much as each building. A 4 per cent depreciation charge resulted. The agent proposed to recapitalize all three accounts over a life of thirty-three and a third years at 3 per cent. It was finally agreed that one building would go to a 3 per cent depreciation, the extensively remodeled one would remain at 4 per cent, and the remodeling work would be accelerated to a twenty-year life at 5 per cent.

Thus the agent was able to go back to his supervisor and show that he had followed his instructions to stretch out the useful life of the taxpayer's buildings, while the taxpayer wound up with the same total depreciation for the three accounts. Incidentally, the taxpayer came out ahead on future returns. Shortly thereafter, he disposed of the building which he had agreed to adjust to only 3 per cent depreciation.

If you and the agent agree on the amount of tax deficiency or refund, he will present a waiver, Form 870, for your signature, showing the proposed increase or decrease in your tax liability. Signing the waiver speeds up refunds or stops 6 per cent interest on deficiencies thirty days thereafter, even though payment may be made later. What else does the waiver waive? It releases restrictions against the I.R.S. on tax assessment and collection. Another form, No. 872, is available if you do not agree to the proposed adjustment, but are willing to extend the agent's time for examining your return. If you refuse, the agent would have to slap on an arbitrary assessment in order to circumvent the statute of limitations.

### How Can I Appeal the Agent's Findings?

If you and the agent fail to come to an agreement, you can appeal directly to the U.S. Tax Court, Court of Claims, or District Court. Usually you can save time and money if you first request an informal conference with a Revenue Service District Conferee. Formerly this conference step was handled by the agent's primed supervisor, who was naturally inclined to fight for the agent's contentions rather than mediate them. Time and expense can often be saved by an informal meeting with a full-time conferee. Although he too is motivated by the basic I.R.S. responsibility to collect as much tax as possible, he can be expected to appraise the merits of both sides before arriving at his conclusions. Don't think that you can't lose in an attempt to better yourself. In some cases a conferee has overruled an agent's proposed compromises, and the taxpayer has wound up in a worse position. It is a good idea to weigh the implications carefully before passing up a comparatively favorable compromise with the agent.

If an agreement is reached at the informal conference, you will be asked to sign the previously mentioned waiver Form 870. If no agreement is reached, the revenue agent submits his report to the district director, together with the conclusions of the conferee. You will receive a copy of this report, along with a "thirty-day letter." If you decide to continue your protest against a proposed tax increase, you have thirty days in which to do one of two things:

1. File a formal appeal under oath to transfer the case to the I.R.S. Appellate Division, where a government attorney, rather than an accountant, presides over conferences. About 70 per cent of presented disputes are settled there. In arriving at settlements, the government attorney and the taxpayer's attorney weigh their probable chances in tax or other courts.
2. Write for or simply wait for a ninety-day statutory notice of deficiency.

After receipt of the ninety-day notice, you have ninety days in which to act. You may appeal directly to the U.S. Tax Court. Eighty per cent of its cases are settled before a final court decision. You can also appeal to the tax court if you are dissatisfied with the formal findings of the I.R.S. Appellate Division.

Starting in 1974, simplified "small claims" tax court procedures are available for claims up to $1,500.

Instead of appealing to the tax court, you may pay the additional tax, and then you have two years to file a claim for refund, using Form 843. If the claim is disallowed, or no action is taken within six months, you may file suit for refund in the U.S. District Court or in the U.S. Court of Claims in Washington, D.C.

If you take no action within the ninety days cited, the district director will automatically assess the tax. After paying it you can follow the steps described above to obtain a refund.

### What Are My Chances in Court?

The odds are more in your favor in the lower courts, but weighted against you in the higher ones. In small claims tax court settlements for 1973, the I.R.S. reports that taxpayers succeeded in winning 530 claims completely and 1,149 partially, while only 316 were totally lost.

Taxpayers won 96 district court cases in 1973 and lost 178. In the U.S. Court of Claims taxpayers won ten decisions, lost thirty. On appeals to circuit courts taxpayers won only sixty-one cases as against two hundred losses to Internal Revenue. The Supreme Court awarded only one win to a taxpayer, versus eight losses.

An experienced tax practitioner advises me, "You may have a good chance in tax court if you have a borderline case that might fit income tax laws, even though contrary to I.R.S. regulations. If your position appears contrary to income tax laws, but they seem unjust, better pass up tax court, where you're almost sure to lose, and go direct to district court, where you still might win."

### Will Tax Deficiency Penalize Next Year's Estimate?

At my San Francisco Merchandise Mart lecture a furniture dealer asked, "Suppose I file a tax estimate for this year, based on the taxable income shown on last year's return. Normally there would be no penalty for deficiency even if this year's income greatly exceeds last year's. I've already made more this year than last, and there's still three good months to go. I've just come up with a tax deficiency for last year on a field audit. It shows greater taxable income than I figured, mainly because I loused up the handling of installment sales. That's behind me now. What I want to know is this: Will I be penalized because this year's estimate is now under last year's income?"

No. The tax court has ruled that you can't be penalized on this year's estimate, regardless of a reassessment of your last year's income. You are safe as long as you estimate exactly on the basis of last year's filed return. Unless you expect a great reduction, it is a good safety measure to estimate this year's income on the basis of the previous year's return.

### Does the Agent Want to See Every Penny of My Expenses?

No. You can save bookkeeping by rounding to the nearest dollar. For example, show $10.01 to $10.49 as $10, and $10.50 to $10.99 as $11. You and the government should break even moneywise, and it will save time for both.

# XXIV

## *How Can I Save Taxes on Operating Income?*

The largest number of questions regarding operating income are concerned with depreciation, the chief factor in saving taxes. The inexact science of calculating depreciation will be the chief exploration in this chapter.

### Can I Make Money and Have a Legitimate Tax Loss?

A typical question comes from a physicist at the University of California Radiation Laboratory. He states, "I bought a twenty-four-unit apartment building with 80 per cent financing in San Francisco. It's about thirty years old. It pays for itself from the income and gives me a nice profit besides. But look what happened when my C.P.A. got through figuring out my income taxes. He deducted enough depreciation to give me about a $2,000 tax loss that offset part of my Lab salary. Here I am, putting money in the bank that comes out of my building. Can it be legitimate to show a tax loss?"

Yes. A number of large real-estate syndicates pay no income taxes whatever. Their highly qualified tax accountants completely offset income by their handling of depreciation and leasehold amortization, in addition to interest deductions on financing. Many property owners, large and small, come close to balancing their income with depreciation. They are often able to show a tax loss when depreciation is coupled with the interest deductions that accompany heavy financing.

By the use of shorter useful lives, accelerated straight-line depreciation can apply to older buildings as compared to newer ones, and also to remodeling of older structures. However, greatly stepped up depreciation can help offset initial costs of brand-new construction, furnishings and equipment. As explained later in this chapter, first-year deductions can be used where applicable, and straight-line charges can be doubled by using the declining-balance method. A classic example on a larger scale is quoted from the 1958 annual report of the Sheraton Corporation:

The new Philadelphia Sheraton, completed in March, 1957, has achieved the success originally anticipated. The profit from operations before fixed charges aggregated $1,860,000 for the first year's operation. . . . Due to the 200 per cent depreciation deduction allowable under the 1954 Revenue Act which makes this new project most attractive, not only were there no income taxes to pay but in fact a small deficit in "reported earnings" provided additional cash benefits when applied against the earnings of other Sheraton hotels having a less favorable tax basis. Payment of income taxes for the Philadelphia hotel must, however, eventually be expected, since depreciation figured on a "declining balance" basis means only postponing the early tax payments. The advantage lies principally in the opportunity for rapid debt reduction which is made possible during the first few years of high depreciation reserves.

It might be mentioned that Sheraton's 1958 policy of "rapid debt reduction" contributed to its falling behind in its seesaw battle for world supremacy with Hilton. The latter lived up to his name by continuing his financing to the hilt.

Sheraton's over-all depreciation in its fiscal year 1958, mentioned above, totaled $14,163,623, stepped up from $11,919,759 in 1957.

## How Did the Enterprises Avoid Income Taxes?

Dr. C. E. Rector writes from Spooner, Wisconsin, "Page 513 of your first book carries the statement, 'Net operating income before loan payments: $10,603.' Now, if the commercial building I own netted that amount, by the time I paid federal and state taxes I would only be able to keep about 55 per cent. In your book the total amount was carried through as available for reinvestment. This was also true of each transaction, beginning with the house on A Avenue. Question: How did the Enterprises get out of paying taxes on the net operating income of the apartments?"

The Enterprise operations as described in my first book should be virtually free from income taxes. In the statement you mention, and in other summaries as well, interest on loan payments is tax-deductible. Also, many improvement costs, such as painting, can usually be allocated to repairs as an annual deduction. The balance of net in-pocket income can be offset by depreciation on furniture and building. One advantage of providing furniture is fast depreciation.

## Why Aren't All Property Operations as Tax-Free as Apartments?

In a subsequent long-distance call, Dr. Rector discussed his commercial-property operations, which subjected him to a 40 per cent income tax. He then asked the above question.

Commercial and industrial properties with relatively high land values and longer-lived buildings do not offer depreciation deductions comparable with apartment properties. Heavy land costs are, of course, not depreciable.

With all property you have to make plans that take advantage of the best tax applications. Tax benefits don't just fall into your lap. Tax expert J. K. Lasser tells of one operation where "an income [after taxes] of $506,234 was turned into $984,734 by a different tax technique."

Faster depreciation methods have generally been in effect since 1954. However, a 1960 Internal Revenue Service study showed that only 17 per cent of real-estate owners took advantage of permissible stepped-up deductions. In some cases the taxpayers were not aware of the advantageous tax changes and continued to apply old-time standards. On the other hand, I know of a number of moneymaking apartment investors who did not take all their allowable deductions because they were already breaking about even on their taxes. Instead of showing a tax loss, which might not be recoverable, they failed to take special allowances and they stretched out depreciation over a longer period than is generally applied.

### Is the Government Likely to Shorten Longer-Than-Average Lives?

No. Government agents are not prone to shorten depreciable lives to force a tax loss, and they will probably leave your schedules alone if the depreciable life appears longer than guideline averages. The only change they usually contemplate in depreciation lives is lengthening them if this will result in greater taxes. Depreciation deductions saved for future use by stretching out useful lives are not apt to be challenged if they reflect actual retirement and replacement practices.

### Can I Postpone Depreciation That I Don't Need Now?

This question was asked by an investor who took a tax loss on stock sales. He didn't need the approximately $3,000 in depreciation that was allowable on his real estate. He asked, "Can I postpone this depreciation until next year, then double up with $6,000?"

No. Depreciation not taken in a given year cannot be recovered later. You can save in the range of 10 to 30 per cent of a possible depreciation loss for this year by changing your useful-life schedule. You could change from twenty-five or thirty years to forty or fifty, for example, if this fits your investment operations. But this change would lower your depreciation for next year also, rather than increase it. Useful lives can be lengthened or shortened for good reason. Changing back to a shorter life the following year would certainly be open to question. Later on, however, if circumstances warrant, you might acceptably revert from, say, forty years to thirty.

## Are Audited Depreciation Schedules Binding?

This brings up the question of changing depreciation schedules after they have been established by an audit. One investor built some new furnished apartments in Arlington, Virginia. Allowable accelerated depreciation could have given him a tax loss, if he had so desired. He didn't have sufficient offsetting income, as did the Sheraton in Philadelphia, so he adopted depreciation schedules well below the maximum allowable, and they were all approved in a tax audit the following year. The next year he found that his repair and replacement expenses were growing, and he needed a bigger depreciation reserve than anticipated. Certain furnishings, such as drapes and carpets, had been put into a ten-year depreciation account; in some apartments they had worn out in less than three years.

The owner said, "I want to put some of these fast wearers into a separate depreciation account and speed up the deductions on them. But I have heard that once the Internal Revenue approves my schedules, neither they nor I can touch them. Is this true?"

No. The Special Technical Services Division of I.R.S. informs me it does not consider that audited depreciation for one or more years has a binding effect on depreciation rates or amounts for subsequent years. The taxpayer may make changes if he has good cause, and the I.R.S. may advocate changes subsequent to an audit.

However, revenue agents seem to have a policy of leaning over backward to respect each other's findings. In order to avoid unwarranted reconsideration of depreciation rates, certain administrative rules have been established. An agent making a subsequent audit may not re-examine depreciation schedules approved in a previous audit unless he is able to give sufficient grounds to get such a go-ahead from his district director.

### Will the I.R.S. Agree to Binding Depreciation Schedules?

Yes. If you wish a binding agreement on a particular property, you may apply to your district director, stating your estimated useful life, method and rate of depreciation and salvage treatment. After I.R.S. investigation or correction, Form 2271 is prepared and signed in quadruplicate, and it is binding on both parties. It can be modified only by joint agreement, or if facts or circumstances arise which were not apparent when the agreement was made. It can readily be modified if a change in tax law or I.R.S. regulations, such as the new *Tax Information on Depreciation,* applies.

### Can a Homeowner Take Depreciation on Rental?

A professor at the University of California, Berkeley, plans to rent his furnished home for three months while he tours Europe with his family. He asks if he can claim depreciation along with other prorated expenses.

Yes. To help balance the income you receive you are entitled to take one-fourth of a year's depreciation on your home and furnishings.

### Can a Co-op Owner Take Depreciation on Rental?

A Waikiki, Hawaii, schoolteacher asks, "Can I take depreciation on my co-operative apartment when I rent it out on my year's sabbatical leave?"

Yes. I.R.S. rules entitle a tenant stockholder to take depreciation for periods when he rents out his property or uses it for other business or investment purposes. Like homeowners, he is also entitled to deductions for real-estate taxes and mortgage interest.

### Can a Summer-Home Owner Take an Entire Year's Depreciation on a Full-Season Rental?

This question is asked by a correspondent who plans to rent his mountain summer home for the full three-month season, the only time it is accessible for use.

Yes, if it is not usable except during the rental period. If you use it for part of the season, then only the portion allocated to the rental period is deductible.

### Can I Take Depreciation the Year I Sell for a Profit?

The Revenue Service has been backed by the tax court in a challenged ruling that if there is any profit no depreciation is allowed to the extent of that profit. Generally, where property is sold for a profit, depreciation is not allowed for the year of the sale. This is another advantage of trading, as depreciation applies to both properties on a prorata basis in the year of an exchange.

On a sale greater than book value, tax planners can try to arrange transfers toward the beginning of the year. A sale or contract in the fall can forfeit depreciation for the entire year. Delaying the signing of a sales agreement until January can give you full depreciation for the previous year.

### How Can I Benefit from Depreciation When I'm Down to Zero?

This have-your-cake-and-eat-it question was asked by a New York department store operator who owned both a business and property.

Other store owners have managed to benefit from depreciation after their properties have become fully depreciated. They sell to a real-estate syndicate, taking back a long-term lease. The sale is on the installment basis, so profits at capital-gains rates are spread out over the years of the loan. The tenant still benefits, because the syndicate takes depreciation based on the sale price, usually in amounts large enough to fully offset income; this tax break is reflected in lower rental for the tenant. Another tax advantage is that the cost of the land is now charged off in rent, whereas it was, of course, originally nondepreciable.

Similar moves have been made by store owners who have not taken full depreciation, but who have owned their property for some years and find it greatly increased in value. The comparatively low depreciation is based on the original low cost, but the lease-back tenant and the new syndicate buyer can both benefit from greatly increased depreciation which is based on a sale price pegged at present market value.

### How Should I Allocate Apartment House Depreciation Accounts?

This question was asked, among others, by Mobile banker Gordon Wright following my lecture at the University of Alabama, Tuscaloosa, which was jointly sponsored by the university and the state realtors' association.

The taxpayer should usually try to allocate his accounts so that they will yield the greatest depreciation and still be realistic enough to win I.R.S. approval in case of an audit. After buying a furnished apartment, for example, it takes some figuring at tax time to properly allocate accounts. You want to make fast-depreciation accounts—covering such items as furniture, machinery and equipment, which are not an integral part of the building—as large as possible. Of the remaining cost you want to allocate the largest possible part to land improvements and then as much as possible of the balance to the slower-depreciating building account, leaving the smallest allowance to nondepreciable land.

Some accountants use rule-of-thumb ratios, allocating a certain percentage to land, land improvements, building, furniture, fixtures and machinery. Such ratios are sometimes accepted on audit, often not. They may save time and effort as useful guides, but there are too many variables to allow them to reflect accurate values on an individual property.

Buyers may arrange for a sales agreement to assign certain values to the various components of a property purchase. Such co-operation usually matters little to the seller as long as he makes the sale; he will probably agree to any breakdown the buyer asks. Therefore the I.R.S. takes a dim view of such agreements.

Some owners arrange for an independent evaluation by a qualified appraiser. This may be a wise precaution if the apparent values differ materially from the property tax valuations. An examining agent may accept or reject such an appraisal, no matter how expert it is, if the I.R.S., as mentioned in the previous chapter, gives great weight to tax appraisers' breakdowns of valuation in locations where assessments are considered fairly up to date and sound. Total valuations may differ considerably from market values because different adjustments are used in various areas. For example, one state may fix taxable values at 25 per cent of the market, another at 50 per cent. But the percentage allocations to different accounts are apt to be fairly accurate.

Appreciable variations between an owner's estimates and the property tax allocations usually turn out to be bookkeeping differences, not actual ones. Many items, such as carpets, wall beds and room air conditioners, may be appraised for property tax purposes as part of the building. For purposes of income tax depreciation they can be separated and charged off at a much faster rate than the building. If your allocations differ widely from those of the property tax authorities, it pays to check with the property appraiser's office and get a statement from him on his system. That way you will be forearmed in case your allocations are challenged on audit. One point to watch is the value of land improvements, such as sidewalks, driveways and landscaping. The tax assessor may value these items as part of the land, whereas the new *Tax Infor-*

*mation on Depreciation* shows an approved useful life of twenty years.

### Is It O.K. to Split Accounts?

Accounts may be split to get bigger deductions on faster-depreciating items. Accounts may also be consolidated in order to simplify bookkeeping. Oscar Brinkman, consulting editor for the National Apartment Association, cited the following in his informative *Washington Letter:*

A successful operator of many apartment buildings has used this "life schedule" for depreciation deductions from gross rental income of a building constructed some years ago:

| PROPERTY | LIFE (Years) |
|---|---|
| Heating equipment | 10 |
| Elevators | 15 |
| Roof and guttering | 10 |
| Linoleum, corridors | 8 |
| Kitchen cabinets | 5 |
| Refrigerators | 5 |
| Gas ranges | 4 |
| Medicine cabinets | 2 |
| Linoleum, kitchen | 4 |
| Casement windows | 10 |
| Venetian blinds | 4 |
| Building equipment | 4 |
| Building shell | 25 |

There are other items, of course, that can be fully depreciated over *short periods,* such as curtains, drapes, rugs, etc.

### How Should I Determine Useful Life?

This question was asked by apartment owner Limuel Willis of Menlo Park, California.

You can gain the greatest allowable depreciation by estimating the shortest acceptable useful life. A $100,000 apartment building with a fifty-year useful life depreciates at 2 per cent, or $2,000 a year. A twenty-five-year estimated useful life on the same building results in a doubled 4 per cent allowance of $4,000.

The early I.R.S. bible, *Bulletin F,* was considered by most accountants to be on the unrealistic side. It was replaced in 1962 by *Depreciation Guidelines.* At this writing in 1975, the latest I.R.S. bible is the 1974 edition of Publication 534, *Tax Information on Depreciation,* which lists recommended "Asset Guideline Classes and Periods." Although this is intended to be only a guide, examining agents are inclined to follow it rather closely. It pays, therefore, to have good substantiating reasons when you depart from I.R.S. *Asset Guideline Periods,* which shows a useful life of forty years for an average new apartment building. The 1974 *Asset Guidelines* in some respects is less informative than the practically obsolete *Bulletin F.* The 1974 I.R.S. publication shows no guides for different classes of building construction.

*Bulletin F* had different suggested useful lives based on "good," "average" and "cheap" construction and made suggestions in relation to these variations. Classifications were not defined by the I.R.S. but were subject to readily definable construction terms. Class A steel buildings were certainly "good." Reinforced concrete or brick are usually considered "average," but they may be classed as "good." Wood-frame or frame-and-stucco may be perfectly desirable for a given area, but they are classed as "cheap." These are all comparative terms, used for purposes of appraisal and also in determining the degree of combustibility for fire insurance premium rates.

Where other than average new construction is to be depreciated, the taxpayer and the I.R.S. may still rely to some extent on suggested variables as in *Bulletin F* as a guide to adjustment of useful lives and rates.

Cheaper wood-frame construction, for example, takes a faster suggested depreciation of 3 per cent under *Bulletin F* as a composite rate on new construction. Assuming they are new, both "good" steel-frame and "average" concrete or brick construction take a composite rate of 2½ per cent. A suggested life of fifty years, or 2 per cent depreciation, is given for the latter categories if equipment—such as heating and plumbing—and fixtures are handled in an account separate from the building account.

The taxpayer may apply faster depreciation schedules than shown under *Asset Guideline Periods* if his replacement and modernization practices are realistically reflected. A wide differentiation can be applied to newly acquired older buildings. Under the new *Asset Guideline* rules, an owner who bleeds his building is penalized on audit, while an owner who modernizes and rehabilitates can depreciate at an accelerated rate. But there are wide differences of interpretation on the same operation.

Take a twenty-year-old apartment house of average quality, under average operations; when new it was depreciable at forty years. I have heard I.R.S. people maintain—nonsensically, I thought—that a new owner should go back to a forty-year depreciation schedule, figuring only 2½ per cent a year on his cost. On the other hand, I know of some owners who have arbitrarily deducted the twenty years of past life, leaving only twenty. Both approaches are certainly subject to challenge.

Suppose the building is already over forty years old. Could the Internal Revenue Service prove a remaining useful life of forty years? Would an owner be justified in taking all his depreciation in one year? Obviously not. You have to take into account the improvements made since a building's erection, and also its present state of repair. A depreciation faster than 2½ per cent should certainly be acceptable. A thirty-year remaining useful life would almost surely stand audit. Probably twenty-five years would be an acceptable adjustment. All would depend on the many applicable factors which bring about deterioration and obsolescence.

## Which Depreciation Method Should I Choose?

This question was asked by realtor Gladys Jacks of Rio del Mar, California.

The choice of method depends on your over-all tax liability. A speculator builder who has a high operating income will want to take the highest allowable depreciation. So would a part-time investor with a sizable salary or professional income.

A long-term investor may have enough depreciation at nominal straight-line rates to offset most or all of his in-pocket income. Any accelerated method that results in a tax loss usually means lost depreciation that could be saved by leveling methods. The 1960 I.R.S. study previously mentioned showed that 83 per cent of property investors used straight-line depreciation. It is certain that more than 17 per cent would have chosen accelerated methods if they had been aware of them. Listed below are the applications of various methods to usual apartment operations.

### Does New Investment Credit Apply to Apartments?

No. This special deduction from income taxes was approved by Congress in 1962. A maximum investment credit of 7 per cent, with specified limitations, can be applied directly against income taxes. Primarily it covers tangible personal property bought for business operations. Transient-type lodging, such as hotels and motels, qualifies if more than half the living quarters are used by transient tenants. Apartment houses do not qualify under normal operations, as they do not cater to transients and, basically are considered investments rather than business properties.

### What Is Additional First-Year Depreciation?

On tangible new or used personal property, such as apartment furniture and equipment, which has a useful life of at least six years, you can deduct 20 per cent of the cost in the year you make the purchase. This choice does not apply to buildings or their components, such as wiring, plumbing and central heating and air conditioning. It must be made by the filing deadline, which would be April 15 following a calendar tax year, and cannot be claimed on an amended return afterward.

The maximum allowance in one tax year is $2,000 on a separate return and $4,000 on a joint return. What if a couple filing a joint return expect to spend much more than $20,000 on eligible personal property in one year and wish to take the fullest advantage of the 20 per cent first-year allowance? Deliveries or payments expected toward the end of the year might be postponed until the following year.

One couple ordered close to $40,000 worth of allowable furniture for two new apartment houses, all installed in one calendar tax year. Because they operated on a cash basis, they paid about half in one year and arranged to pay the balance on January 10 the following year, thus taking almost a $4,000 deduction each year. A pitfall to watch here is giving a note to cover delayed payments. If an installment loan had been arranged, with notes signed in the first year, then the applicable property would be considered as purchased in one year.

Additional first-year depreciation does not apply to property taken in exchange, except for any allocated boot or bonus paid. The I.R.S. gives as an example the trading in of an old truck where $500 was allowed toward the purchase of a new one costing $2,-000. The boot paid, which is the $1,500 difference, qualifies for additional first-year depreciation.

Where the first-year allowance is claimed, any other depreciation would apply to the remaining cost. The allowance is not subject to prorating for just part of a year. The full 20 per cent can be claimed even though the property is paid for on the last day of the tax year. A taxpayer contemplating a five-year useful life on some items, such as rugs, might well stretch the life to six years in order to claim the first-year allowance. Many taxpayers put all personal property into one account. A ten-year composite useful life is commonly applied to new furniture and equipment.

## When Can I Use the Declining-Balance Method?

The biggest depreciation that can be taken in the initial years is by the declining-balance method, whereby twice the straight-line rate can be deducted in the first year. This method can be applied to both buildings and tangible personal property, without figuring salvage value. Each year the declining-balance rate applies to the remaining undepreciated basis.

The maximum of twice the straight-line rate can be taken only on housing property acquired new after December 31, 1953, that has a useful life of three or more years. A builder of a new apartment house can use the maximum rate. So can a buyer if he purchases the property before it is rented. Once the property is rented, a subsequent buyer cannot apply the maximum rate, even though he bought it only a month or so after erection.

### Can I Apply the 200 Per Cent Rate to Remodeling?

Yes, even though a straight-line or 150 per cent declining-balance rate might apply to older apartments, you can take the maximum 200 per cent declining-balance rate on capitalized housing improvements, such as remodeling, renovation or rehabilitation.

### Can I Pick My Own Declining Percentage?

Any rate, such as 125 per cent of the straight-line rate, that does not exceed the maximum allowable can be used in the declining-balance method. Most accountants apply the maximum. On property not subject to the qualifications previously defined, a maximum rate of 150 per cent of the straight-line rate can be applied. This includes new or used housing property acquired before January 1, 1954, nonhousing property bought anytime, and used housing property acquired in 1954 or thereafter.

### How Can I Use the Sum-of-the-Years-Digits Method?

Limitations are the same as on the 200 per cent declining-balance rate. In addition, salvage value must first be deducted before figuring sum-of-the-years-digits depreciation. A different fraction applies to each year on a reducing basis. Thus a $2,500 auto with a five-year estimated life, used by a realty investor in his operations, might have a salvage value of $500. The balance of $2,000 could be depreciated as follows: five fifteenths for the first year, and in succeeding years four fifteenths, three fifteenths, two fifteenths and one fifteenth.

## Can I Change My Accounting Method?

Yes and no. The method can be changed, with limitations, according to I.R.S. publication 538; it depends on the situation. After the amount of depreciation with the declining-balance method drops below the level which could be taken with the straight-line method, many taxpayers change to straight-line. A change from straight-line to declining-balance or sum-of-the-years-digits for other than residential rental property requires I.R.S. approval, but this switch is not apt to be accepted except in unusual circumstances.

## What Depreciation Choice Have I When My Home Is Converted to Income Property?

According to the I.R.S. publication *Your Federal Income Tax,* 1974 edition, if you bought your home in 1954 or thereafter and were the first user, and then converted it to business or rental use before July 25, 1969, you may use the sum-of-the-years-digits or the declining-balance method at twice the straight-line rates. If your home was bought before 1954 you can only use straight-line. If converted after July 24, 1969, your only choice other than straight-line is the declining-balance method at a maximum rate of 125 per cent of straight-line, provided the property has a useful life of twenty years or more.

## Is the Amount Always the Same with the Straight-Line Method?

Where the straight-line method is used, any salvage value must be deducted first, as with the sum-of-the-years-digits method, and the same rate must be applied in each succeeding year. The amount deducted would remain, except for a change in the estimated life and for a fractional application to the first and final years. The life may be reduced or lengthened because of a change in operating experience or an I.R.S. audit.

## Must There Always Be a Salvage Value?

No. If personal property has a useful life of three years or more, salvage value of 10 per cent of cost or less may be disregarded. And 10 per cent may be deducted if the salvage value exceeds that amount. In practice, autos and other equipment used in realty operations may carry a useful life of between three and five years, with a salvage value in the 20 per cent range.

Such items as apartment refrigerators usually have a nominal salvage value, as indicated on the I.R.S. table on page 411. Discarded furniture, such as sofa sets and carpets, may be worthless, depending on how long they are used before you dispose of them or replace them. It often costs more than the junk value to haul off such items.

Once buildings usually carried a salvage value. Demolition contractors used to pay owners for the privilege of tearing down a building, in order to sell the scrap. Rising costs of labor and equipment and obsolescence of old materials have reversed this procedure. Demolition costs now exceed the recovery from junk sales, so you have to pay to have a building torn down. Obviously, this leaves no net salvage value. Yet some revenue agents may still insist that you consider net salvage value when computing your allowable depreciation. But most tax authorities, including J. K. Lasser and the Research Institute of America, recommend that you no longer take building salvage into account.

## How Do Methods Compare?

Although omitted in later editions, the 1971 I.R.S. booklet *Your Federal Income Tax* shows a table comparing various methods that apply to an apartment owner. The example stipulates new refrigerators costing $2,625. This would pay for about twenty standard refrigerators at apartment house rates. The example gives an estimated life of ten years and a purchase date of January 2, so a full year's depreciation can be taken in the year of purchase. The I.R.S. estimates the nominal salvage value of all the refrigerators at $100, less than 10 per cent of cost and, therefore, not taken into account as salvage. In the first year an additional depreciation of 20 per cent, or $525, is taken. The example for apartment refrigerators gives a realistic life of ten years, which many accountants use.

In the following I.R.S. table, which gives a detailed comparison of the three methods, I have italicized the figures for the years in which depreciation under the second and third methods dropped below straight-line. With an item similar to the one in the table, taxpayers would routinely change from declining-balance to straight-line depreciation in the fifth year.

DEPRECIATION OF NEW REFRIGERATORS COSTING $2,625.00

| YEAR | ANNUAL DEPRECIATION | | Sum-of-the-Years-Digits |
| --- | --- | --- | --- |
| | Straight-Line (10%) | Declining-Balance (20%) | |
| First-year additional depreciation | $ 525.00 | $ 525.00 | $ 525.00 |
| First-year ordinary depreciation | 210.00 | 420.00 | 381.82 |
| TOTAL DEPRECIATION, FIRST YEAR | $ 735.00 | $ 945.00 | $ 906.82 |
| Second-year depreciation | 210.00 | 336.00 | 343.64 |
| Third-year depreciation | 210.00 | 268.80 | 305.45 |
| Fourth-year depreciation | 210.00 | 215.04 | 267.27 |
| Fifth-year depreciation | 210.00 | *172.03* | 229.09 |
| Sixth-year depreciation | 210.00 | 137.63 | *190.91* |
| Seventh-year depreciation | 210.00 | 110.00 | 152.73 |
| Eighth-year depreciation | 210.00 | 88.08 | 114.55 |
| Ninth-year depreciation | 210.00 | 70.46 | 76.36 |
| Tenth-year depreciation | 210.00 | 56.37 | 38.18 |
| TOTAL | $2,625.00 | $2,399.51 | $2,625.00 |
| Salvage value or unrecovered cost | None | $ 225.49 | None |

## Can "Juggling" of Income and Expenses Be Legitimate?

Yes, a taxpayer on a cash basis may juggle cash flow to gain the best tax advantage. This does not refer, of course, to "juggling the books," in the sense of falsifying records. It applies to spreading out, accelerating or deferring income or expenses in a way that will result in the least taxes.

Some revenue agents take the position that such accounting moves are not permissible if they are done solely for the purpose of saving on taxes. Contentions along these lines have been carried by the I.R.S. into the courts. Court decisions, as in the Kay Kimbell, Howard Veit and James Oates tax court cases, have held, in effect, that such declarations concerning the general practice are pure nonsense. Tax law recognizes the averaging of bonanza income by authors, inventors and others, for example, purely for tax savings. The cited tax court decisions and I.R.S. Revenue Ruling 60-31 authorize methods of deferring income in order to save taxes. There are limitations on some methods, but it is considered only good business to conduct your operations in such a way as to gain the best tax treatment. Every recognized tax authority, including Lasser and Kiplinger, agrees with this philosophy.

## How Can I Juggle Capitalized Expenditures?

A legitimate example mentioned previously was the case of a couple on a cash basis paying for approximately $40,000 worth of apartment equipment over two tax years in order to apply 20 per cent first-year depreciation to the entire amount. The equipment was all purchased and installed in one tax year. Even though half was paid in the following year, the entire amount was eligible for first-year depreciation. When payment is made by January 15, a full year's regular depreciation would usually apply. One month would normally be deducted if payment is made on January 16, leaving eleven twelfths of a full year's depreciation.

In a reverse example of juggling payments, a taxpayer who expects to take big furniture and equipment deliveries next year could step up partial payment this year. Even if delivery is arranged for next spring, a down payment could be credited to this year for tax purposes if it is made by December 31.

### How Can I Juggle Capital Gains?

On sales of capital assets at a profit, consider the advantage of deferment of delivery, consummation or payment until the following tax year or years. Profits on personal-property sales usually apply to the year in which payment is received. On real estate, the date of transfer of the deed, or possession, usually applies, unless the principal payments do not exceed 30 per cent in the tax year of sale. Then capital-gains profits can be spread over the life of the mortgage taken back by the seller.

### How Can I Juggle Operating Income?

Monthly apartment rentals do not offer much opportunity for juggling operating income. Leases consummated toward the end of a calendar tax year could provide an agreement for cash security deposits to be paid in January. If it is desirable to defer taxable income, notes should not be taken. Ordinarily they are ruled as constituting payment in the year the note is delivered. But a contract or an agreement could postpone receipt of taxable payment.

Other income from sales and services can often be deferred by holding off the billing and by making special contract arrangements.

### How Can I Juggle Expenses?

In a tax year in which you expect heavy net income you can step up your allowable expenses and other deductions. An example was my payment of two years' worth of property taxes in the year I received heavy book royalties. January loan payments can be made in December to step up interest deductions. You can prepay interest for a full year in advance.

End-of-the-month utility bills and other expense items that are normally held to the following January 10, for example, can be paid at the end of December. Heavy repairs, such as painting halls and exteriors, that are planned for the following year might be stepped up to the current year. Or you might sign a contract with a reliable contractor to do the work next year, giving him a heavy down payment, say 50 per cent, this year.

All deductions should be looked over to see if they offer possibilities of juggling. For example, two years' contributions can be handled for tax credit in one year. After making the current year's contributions, an annual pledge, as to a church, can be made to cover the next calendar year; then it can be paid by December 31, enabling you to receive two years' income tax credit.

There is no question of the fact that such items are allowable for annual deductions. Questions arise chiefly when juggled payments cover assets with more than one year's life. But if the expense item is expected to be used up within the next calendar year, you can still take it as this year's deductions provided it is paid by December 31.

J. K. Lasser mentions a poultry farmer who saved $70,000 in taxes in a high-income year by ordering a six months' feed supply for the following year.

### How Can I Offset Increasing Property Taxes?

An income-property owner must pass his increased taxes on to tenants, explaining why the raises are given. Long-term leases should provide that the tenant will pay any increase in property taxes and also insurance.

### How Will Proposed New Income Taxes Affect Operating Income?

Among others, several educators have asked this question. Included are Professor Boris Nelson of the University of Toledo in Ohio and school administrators Roger and Irene Schulte of Hayward, California.

Preliminary discussions, pending legislation, and actual revisions point to better rather than poorer tax breaks for future changes affecting depreciation on real-estate improvements. Tax bureau reformers want to make a lot of changes toward what they consider more equitable over-all practices. As one example, they plan to apply capitalization treatment to oil- and gas-drilling costs, which are now charged off as expenses. They also plan to apply depreciation treatment not to exceed capital costs in place of present depletion allowances. Whether these changes go through or not, the tendency will be toward bringing some of the more favorable tax treatment of such risky forms of investment more in line with regular real-estate practices.

In order to encourage real-estate investment, including remodeling and new construction, revised and pending tax laws point toward approval of faster depreciation write-offs on new construction. Operating, in-pocket income, which you put in the bank, will still be offset to a great extent by depreciation. The initial costs of buildings and furniture can be charged off in annual installments. Land costs cannot be depreciated, of course, and this is a drawback to the owner of commercial properties. Their land values are proportionately high compared with building values. With apartment houses, where land values are usually considerably less, a much higher proportion of total costs can be charged off as depreciation.

Naturally, older buildings can be depreciated faster than new ones, which is another advantage of buying and improving older properties. A further consideration in favor of providing furniture is that it takes a much faster depreciation than the building.

Although all interest and tax payments are now deductible from income, there is considerable pressure to reduce allowable non-business deductions of this nature. However, interest and tax costs for business and investment purposes, such as buying income property, would still be fully deductible. One effect of the proposed changes, if they go through, will be to increase the net cost of home ownership for those who now deduct all property taxes and interest on their home mortgages. This would make rental units more competitive economically, but the discouragement of home ownership might also lead to more public housing. I think that interest and tax costs will continue to be fully deductible when the legislative and administrative skirmishing is over. A number of Congressmen, in both public and private statements, have confirmed this judgment. After all, homeowners constitute almost a two-thirds majority of the nation's voters!

Some investment-property buyers, such as professional people with high personal incomes, like to arrange unusually heavy mortgages. Thus, while they have heavy earnings, more income can be offset by interest. When they get ready for retirement their loans can often be paid off, leaving them with a substantial spendable income.

# XXV

## How Can I Save Taxes on Pyramiding Profits?

According to a 1974 Treasury study, about seven million taxpayers benefited from preferential capital-gains treatment in 1972. This chapter will deal with questions that have arisen concerning various ways of saving taxes on profitable sales, and how to avoid paying taxes entirely by making tax-free exchanges.

### Can You Explain a Simple Tax-Free Exchange?

This question was asked by a woman realtor while I was autographing at Fowler Brothers Bookstore in Los Angeles. She added, "I suppose a simple tax-free exchange would have to be small, like trading two houses?"

Basically, a simple exchange means that only two properties are involved. They can be large or small. If you trade one piece of property for another without giving or taking boot, or bonus, you have an even, tax-free exchange. A simple example might involve trading a commercial building for a duplex, with neither party giving boot. If you pay a boot, then you are trading up, which is also a tax-free exchange to the up-trader. The boot may be in cash, or it may be some other valuable consideration; for example, you might assume a larger mortgage.

A multimillion-dollar exchange that was comparatively simple mechanically involved Sheraton's trading the Astor Hotel on Times

Square for the Ambassador, now called the Sheraton East, on Park Avenue. According to the Sheraton Corporation's report for 1958, the Astor was valued at $11,950,000 and the Ambassador at $10,-750,000, so Sheraton received a boot of $1,200,000. Only the boot was subject to capital-gains tax, with the exchange tax-free up to the valuation of the Ambassador.

### Should I Sell, Trade or Lease?

Mrs. Forrest Hills writes from Southern California, "My husband and I own a two-story studio building in the heart of Hollywood, in a popular apartment house neighborhood. It is worth in the vicinity of $25,000. The property has been rented in the past and used by us for teaching and little-theater activities. We are both professional musicians. My husband is over sixty-five and draws a small Social Security benefit. I am fifty-three, so it will be nine years before I can receive my Social Security payment, which will be about $100 per month under existing law. We have no heirs or dependents.

"I work in an office and turn most of my earnings back into the property. Several brokers and builders have offered purchase arrangements along these lines: a substantial down payment, a second mortgage, and a twelve-year loan at 8 per cent interest, with payments at $200 a month. I have been contemplating selling and letting them build a new apartment house. I prefer not to involve myself with new construction, and do not wish to make an outright sale because of taxes.

"If I take back a second trust deed, is there any way to protect myself in the event of foreclosure if the new owner doesn't keep up his payments on the first loan? Surely there is some way to protect this valuable asset. My husband and I would be most appreciative of your kindness in answering my all-important question and suggesting any alternatives you think we should consider."

Despite your reluctance, it appears that with your desirable site you could build new with 100 per cent financing of the construction costs. You can make very good profits with competitive rents in an economically sound building in a good location.

### Should I Consider Trading?

If you want to avoid any uncertainties arising from new construction, your greatest opportunity would probably come from trading your commercial building for as large an apartment house as you can safely handle, one with a proven existing income. No income taxes would apply on your profit from trading for a property of greater value, as long as the purpose of both is to produce income. With the apartment house you could acquire, most of your in-pocket income should be offset by depreciation.

### Should I Consider Leasing?

You might consider giving a fairly long-term lease, say ten years, to a tenant who would improve the property to increase its value. Depending on a variety of arrangements and circumstances, if the sale value is $25,000 the lease value is likely to be in the neighborhood of $250 monthly. You could include a proviso that the tenant will pay all taxes, or at least those above present rates, to make sure that additional taxes will not cut into your income. You could give the tenant greater incentive for improving the property by agreeing to an option for him to buy at the end of the ten years on specified terms.

### Should I Consider an Installment Sale?

You could stipulate a 25 per cent down payment, for example, which would enable you to defer income taxes. If you receive 30 per cent or less on the principal in the year of sale, the capital gains can be spread over the life of the mortgage. Approximately a third of a million taxpayers take advantage of this method of deferring capital gains every year, according to an Internal Revenue Service study.

One way to spread out even the down-payment income would be to split it in half, for example, and collect it over the first two years. You could take 15 per cent in the year of sale, say in the fall when possession is given, then collect another 15 per cent down the following tax year, in January or later if you operate on a calendar-year basis. The balance of 70 per cent could be paid as you desire, commonly over a ten- to twenty-year period.

The second major payment could be made when construction starts if the buyer is going to erect a new building or remodel extensively. These percentages can be manipulated any way you choose to spread out your installments and applicable taxes, as long as the maximum on principal is 30 per cent during the tax year of the sale.

### Does the Second Mortgage Holder Have to Pay Off the First?

If the buyer plans to build new, his construction loan would have to be a first mortgage, or a deed of trust. Then either you would have to be paid off, thus stepping up your capital-gains tax, or you could agree to subordinate your loan to the new first mortgage. Subordination would make your loan a second mortgage. However, you would not have to pay off the first loan in order to protect your interest in case the owner fails to keep up payments. This question keeps cropping up on various related transactions because that commonly used to be the law. Now all you have to do is keep up the payments yourself. When making a loan on income property you can include the proviso that in case of default you can take over collection of the rents in order to offset loan payments and expenses.

### Can I Report an Installment Sale on an Amended Return?

A Miami businessman tells of selling income property with 25 per cent down, taking back a fifteen-year mortgage, and reporting a capital gain of $18,000. "A year later I read your book and learned of the installment method of reporting profits. I'm still within the period allowed for amending returns. Can I get a refund by sending in an amended choice of the installment method?"

No. The installment sale must be reported by the deadline for filing a tax return for the year of sale. A 1974 sale by a taxpayer who files his taxes on a calendar-year basis, for example, must be reported by April 15, 1975. If the return is filed early it can be revised up to April 15. A revision or an amendment to report an installment sale would be invalid if it were filed on April 16 or thereafter.

The year of the sale is the controlling factor, not the year in which a first payment is made. The two usually coincide, but not always. Thus an installment sale recorded in December 1974 on which the first payment is made in January 1975 would still have a filing deadline of April 15, 1975.

### How Do Mortgages Affect Tax-Free Exchanges?

This question came up after my lecture to the Women's City Club of St. Paul, Minnesota, arranged by Lillian Case of the St. Paul Book and Stationery Company.

Let's say you trade a free-and-clear house for a duplex, giving a $10,000 mortgage on the latter, or perhaps assuming an existing loan. The mortgage would constitute a bonus, called a boot, just as if you had paid $10,000 additional cash. The party paying the boot has a tax-free exchange. The party receiving it has a tax-free exchange except for the boot, which is subject to a capital-gains tax.

If both properties have mortgages, the difference between them would constitute boot. Suppose the house has a $5,000 loan and the duplex a $15,000 loan, and the properties are traded with these loans being assumed. Then a boot of $10,000 is paid by the duplex buyer and is received by the house buyer.

## How Does Depreciation Affect a Tax-Free Exchange?

This question was asked by apartment owner Wycliffe Sweet of Oakland, California.

As long as you receive no boot, depreciation has no bearing on whether your exchange is tax-free or not. However, depreciation has to be taken into account in figuring your new depreciation basis. If you paid $12,500 for purchase and improvement of a rental house and depreciated it $2,500, then the depreciated book cost of $10,000 would be your basis. To this you add the boot paid in order to establish book costs from which to figure new depreciation. Here's an example:

### HOUSE DEPRECIATION ACCOUNT
*(Bought and traded unfurnished)*

| | | |
|---|---|---|
| Original cost of house | $11,500 | |
| Deduct land value | —2,500 | |
| Cost of depreciable building | $ 9,000 | |
| Add capital improvements | +1,000 | |
| Total cost of building plus improvement | $10,000 | |
| Deduct depreciation taken | —2,500 | |
| Remaining depreciable cost | $ 7,500 | |
| Land cost carried forward | +2,500 | |
| Depreciated cost of building plus land | $10,000 | $10,000 |

### DUPLEX DEPRECIATION ACCOUNT
*(Acquired furnished)*

| | | |
|---|---|---|
| Mortgage assumed on duplex | $15,000 | |
| Deduct loan given up on house | —5,000 | |
| Difference, representing boot paid | $10,000 | 10,000 |
| BOOK COST OF PROPERTY ACQUIRED | | $20,000 |

If the house included furniture, either originally purchased or acquired later, its cost and depreciation would also be figured into the house account. In newly set up depreciated accounts, the land will carry no depreciation, but the furniture may be depreciated on the basis of a ten-year life and the building on the basis of a thirty-year life. Allocation of the $20,000 book cost might be figured proportionately according to tax bills as follows:

|  |  | DEPRECIATION | |
|  |  | Life Years | Percentage |
|---|---|---|---|
| Land value at 20% proportion | $ 4,000 | None | None |
| Furniture value at 10% proportion | 2,000 | 10 | 10% |
| Building value at 70% proportion | 14,000 | 30 | 3⅓% |

In an exchange of this sort, market value has no effect on the new depreciation account or on tax liability. Suppose the market value of the duplex is $25,000 and its acquisition thereby represents a turnover profit of $5,000 to the house seller. His depreciation would be the same as previously figured, and his exchange would still be tax-free.

### How Does Depreciation Affect a Sale?

In the above house accounting the basis on which to figure a capital-gains tax would be $10,000, taking the original costs plus those of improvements, less the depreciation. Therefore, sale at $15,000 would represent capital gain of $5,000 on which to figure tax liability.

### What Is the Maximum Capital-Gains Tax?

This question was asked by executive secretary Sam Marks after my lecture to the Menlo-Atherton Board of Realtors in California.

The maximum capital-gains tax on an investor's assets held over six months is 25 per cent, if net long-term capital gains do not exceed $50,000 per year. In many cases a turnover profit is paid for at less than 25 per cent, as a long-term capital gain is taken into account as ordinary income in the amount of 50 per cent of the gain. The $5,000 house profit shown above would be listed on the capital-gains portion of the tax statement, then halved to $2,500 as the basis on which to pay regular taxes.

This assumes there are no compensating losses. If the house seller had also sold stock, for example, at a loss of $5,000, then the loss and the gain would offset each other, and no tax would apply.

### Can I Make a Tax-Free Exchange of a Vacant Lot for a Duplex?

This question was raised after my lecture to the Christian Writers Conference at Berkeley, California, moderated by Dr. Ralph Johnson of the Baptist Divinity School.

Yes, if the lot is held for investment purposes.

### Can I Make a Tax-Free Exchange of a Home for Income Property?

Executive secretary Ruth Nichols asked this question following my lecture to the San Mateo–Burlingame Board of Realtors in California.

Yes, if you first convert the home to income-producing purposes. If you rent the home and then trade it up or even, you can have a tax-free exchange. Otherwise you would have a capital-gains tax to pay on your profit, the difference between your trade-in value and the cost of your home, including improvements.

### Must a Home Be Rented for Six Months to Be Considered Income Property?

This question was asked by Santa Cruz realtor Polly Dudfield at my Emporium lecture in Palo Alto, California. She added, "Accountants have informed me that the Internal Revenue Service is apt to challenge a conversion to income property unless a home is rented for at least six months. What is your opinion?"

Revenue agents can dream up some stiff interpretations, like this, even though no regulations back them. There have been cases of approved conversions from home to income property where no rental occurred. The owners advertised or listed their properties with realtors as available for rent, then traded before they actually rented. In most cases the owners made improvements after deciding to rent. They kept records of rent-inducing expenditures and advertising.

Cases of converting without ever renting are somewhat unusual and difficult to prove. Your position should be fairly sound if you actually rent to a tenant, even if it is only a month, before trading. You should keep duplicate rent receipts and other information concerning the tenant, so that he can be contacted for corroboration.

### Can I Take a Tax Loss on the Sale of My Home?

This question was asked by Shirley Forrest when her airline-executive husband, James, was transferred to Washington, D.C., requiring them to move from Danville, California, to Silver Springs, Maryland. The sudden transfer raised the possibility of a loss. The Forrests wanted to explore various tax ramifications before making a final decision on disposal of their home.

No tax loss is available unless you first convert to income property. If you rent out the home and then sell, you can be eligible for a tax loss. Any loss is figured on the basis of cost or market value, whichever is less, at the time of conversion to rental property. If the market value is less than cost, it usually pays to make improvements to increase the market value before renting. This should increase the rental value and the resale value, decreasing a loss or turning it into a profit.

Sometimes a potential loss can be changed to a gain merely by renting and keeping the property in good repair. Depreciation, repairs, maintenance and upkeep costs can be charged against income, and you can take more time to wait for a better price. Accelerated depreciation can be taken if this is your first rental, and the property was bought new after 1953.

## How Can Company Reimbursement of Loss on a Home Be Tax-Free?

Some companies have compensated their employees in cash for any losses on a home sale because of a transfer. One employee stated that his company was willing to reimburse him, but the Internal Revenue Service had previously ruled in a similar case that the cash reimbursement constituted income to the employee; furthermore, such income could not be offset by showing a tax loss on the home sale. The employee asked, "How can this be handled so I don't have to pay taxes on reimbursement of my loss?"

No income applies to an employee if the employer buys the home at cost. The employer may then dispose of the property as he chooses. If he resells at a loss, his company then has a deductible loss.

## How Can I Make a Three-Way Trade and Avoid a Capital-Gains Tax?

An auto salesman, phoning long distance from Oklahoma City, said, "I own a vacant corner lot that I paid $22,000 for several years ago. An oil company wants this as a service station site, and they've offered me $40,000. I've already picked out a $200,000 apartment house that I want to buy. My broker offered an exchange, so the apartment owner could sell to the oil company. That way I'd save taxes on my $18,000 profit. But the apartment owner says, 'Sell your property and get your money for a down payment first. That's the only way I'll talk business.' How can I work out a three-way trade so I won't have to pay a capital-gains tax?"

Get a signed offer from the service station company to buy the property at the stipulated price. Then have your broker write up an exchange offer for the apartment house, subject to his being able to sell the service station lot for $40,000. The title company will arrange for you to deed your lot to the apartment owner and vice versa. Then the apartment owner can deed the lot to the oil company. For a tax-free three-way exchange, these steps cannot be short-cutted by your deeding the lot directly to the oil company.*

### How Can I Make a Five-Way Tax-Free Exchange?

A Baltimore realtor was working on an exchange of a fourplex for a thirty-unit apartment house. The owner of the latter wanted to cash out and agreed to accept the exchange only if the realtor guaranteed the sale of the fourplex. The realtor found a duplex owner who wanted to trade for the fourplex. Then he found a rental-home owner who wanted the duplex, and a buyer for the home. He had written up purchase offers in every case, planning to bypass the mechanics of trading. Then the up traders became worried over tax liabilities and balked at signing deeds until their tax-free positions were clarified.

Although five parties are involved, this is a fairly simple step-down process which is easy to work out. The apartment house and fourplex owners should exchange deeds. The apartment seller then exchanges the fourplex deed for the duplex deed, then the duplex deed for the single-family-home deed. Finally he deeds the home to the cash buyer. All the up trades are tax-free; the down traders are taxable only on the boot they receive.

### What Is the Maximum Number of Parties to a Multiple Tax-Free Exchange?

This question was asked by Chicago *Daily News* columnist Tony Weitzel on his *Town Crier* radio show.

---

* I was informed later that the deal I suggested had been consummated without hitches.

Once you pass the point of making simple trades, there is no limit to the number of parties who may participate in a multiple exchange. Any even or up trades would be tax-free. The down trades would be partly taxable, as previously explained.

Realtor Jim Reid of Alamo, California, a member of the Traders Club who specializes in exchanges, tells of consummating a multiple exchange involving eight parties and eleven pieces of property in eight parcels in five different states. Reid states that some of the traders had not even seen the properties acquired. He mentions that sight-unseen acquirement is not unusual on an exchange, although it is rarer on an outright purchase. Part of his commission on the eight-way exchange included the equity in a Phoenix, Arizona, house which he had never seen. He had arranged for its appraisal by a Phoenix realtor, however, and was turning it over to the latter to sell. Thus the house would be acquired and sold unseen.

Reid added, "I arranged another exchange of a vacant commercial lot in Sacramento for rugged mountain property in Idaho. It was ideal for hunting, but little else. You couldn't even get to it in winter. This trade was completed with neither party seeing the property he took over."

### Can I Make a Tax-Free Exchange of a Farm for Apartments?

A hospital fund-raising executive writes from Pittsburgh, Pennsylvania, "I wish I had read your book twenty-five years ago, I made a little money following the depression, buying low, fixing up as you advocate and then selling. But I stopped too soon. I would have kept going had I known about the pyramiding potentials from financing and tax allowances as you explain them.

"I would like to ask a couple of questions. My situation is that I am fifty-seven years old. Have a good salaried job. Own a 341-acre farm near here. Usually get out there only on weekends. My wife and I are getting tired of the winter weather we have and are thinking of relocating in Florida, California, or some other Southern state when my time for retirement comes.

"This farm that I have involves trade-ins of smaller farms. My equity should be about $100,000 after the sales commission and the $8,000 mortgage are paid. Do you think a straight trade or a three-way trade for apartments could be worked out? Are there brokers who specialize in this sort of tax-free exchange?

"I have been told that if a farmer sells a farm and then reinvests his equity in another farm within a year he doesn't pay capital-gains tax. Is this true? And what if he doesn't invest in another farm but puts his money in an apartment house? Can this also be done tax-free?"

Generally speaking, any even or up trade of investment property is tax-free, as in trading a farm for an apartment house. They do not have to be the same kind of property. However, an actual exchange must take place, either direct or multiple, as in a three-way trade. The profit on a sale is generally taxable at capital-gains rates even though the funds are used immediately for repurchase of a similar investment property.

An exception is a so-called "involuntary conversion" for public use. If a farm, apartments or other investment property should be condemned, for example, to make way for a throughway, you can reinvest the proceeds of the sale and avoid the capital-gains tax. You must buy similar investment property by the end of two years following the year you receive a profit from selling, if the involuntary conversion occurred after December 30, 1969. If the conversion date preceded December 31, 1969, the replacement period ends one year after the close of the first tax year in which you receive any profit.

### Can the Tax on Home Profit Be Deferred by a New Purchase?

A similar exception applies to the profit on a home sale, whether it is voluntary or a forced sale from condemnation. No capital-gains tax applies if the proceeds are used to buy another home within one year after the sale of the old residence.

## Is a Combination of Home and Investment Separable for Tax Purposes?

If you do not live on the farm, it would all be construed as income property. If you reside there, the residence portion of its value on sale could be reinvested in a residence on another farm or elsewhere without tax liability. But the income-producing portion of the farm would be subject to the tax application on any other investment property. A capital-gains tax can be avoided only by an exchange or an involuntary conversion.

## Where Can I Find Traders Club Specialists?

For specialists dealing in tax-free property exchanges all over the country, contact your nearest board of realtors and ask for recommended members of their Traders Club, Exchange Club or Exchange Committee. If such information is not available locally, write direct to the Commercial Investment Division, National Institute of Real Estate Brokers, 155 East Superior Street, Chicago, Illinois 60611.

When I lectured at the realtors' national convention in Dallas, president William Monsees of the Fort Lauderdale, Florida, Traders Club spoke to the National Institute of Farm and Land Brokers. He stated, "A growing amount of trades involves the tax-free exchange of farms with large capital gains for apartments and other city income property."

## Is the Tax on an Exchange Actually Free or Only Deferred?

Arthur Skeadas writes from St. Louis, Missouri, "I understand from your book that profits realized from up trades of income property are not taxable. However, a real-estate dealer and teacher said that they are taxable, and that the tax liability may only be deferred. I'd greatly appreciate your clarification."

Richard Taft writes along similar lines from Washington, D.C.,

"On page 454 of your book you state, 'No capital-gains tax applies when you trade up, giving your property plus a boot for the property you acquire.' According to a Washington attorney, 'Any sale or exchange of property is a legal basis for a capital-gains tax.' Would you please resolve this apparent contradiction by telling me: (1) the source of your statement; (2) if this statement is still true in 1974; and (3) if you have found this statement to be true in your own dealings. Thank you for your help in this matter."

The answer to Taft's questions 2 and 3 is yes. These questions about taxing trades indicate the importance of establishing points at issue. Sometimes two apparently contradictory statements may each be valid when the subject matter can involve many provisos. An even or up trade of income property is tax-free unless an ultimate sale is made. Then the capital-gains tax that applies would be considered as deferred from the date of the first exchange.

At the time an investor trades a piece of property up or across the board for another, there is no income tax whatever due on the transaction. You can keep trading on this basis indefinitely. Still no income tax applies to turnover profits as long as you do not sell outright or take boot on a traded property. Trades are considered by the Treasury Department as continuations of the same initial investment, and the holding period for tax purposes is governed accordingly. Thus the proper date of acquisition that you should show for property taken in trade is your original purchase date.

Once you sell—and this is what the Washington and St. Louis advisers have in mind—you would be taxable for all capital gains, beginning with the first property traded in. For example, assume you trade a duplex for a higher-valued fourplex, and no tax applies. If you later sell the fourplex, a capital-gains tax would be based on the trade-in basis, which is the depreciated cost of the duplex. In the house and duplex accounts mentioned at the beginning of this chapter, a sale of the duplex at $25,000 would result in a capital-gains tax on a $5,000 profit.

If you trade the duplex for an eight-unit building, still no tax applies, and so on without limit, but always bear in mind that you are not taking boot on a trade. If you sell the higher-valued eight-unit building, then you would be subject to a capital-gains tax on the profits from both trades. Beginning with your original cost on the house, you would have to take into account all the costs of acquisition, financing, improvement and sales, less depreciation. These accounts are carried forward as you progress. With the acquisition of the aforementioned duplex, accounting would start afresh, on the basis of depreciated costs of $20,000.

My sources for tax information include those cited in my first book: *Your Income Tax,* by J. K. Lasser, published by Simon and Schuster; *Your Federal Income Tax* and *Tax Guide for Small Business,* published by the Internal Revenue Service.

### How Can I Make a Tax-Free Sale of a Poultry Ranch to Buy a Farm?

Telephone executive Earl Mackintosh phoned long distance from Hayward, California, and said, "I want to buy a four-hundred acre northern California farm for a hundred and forty thousand dollars. The owner wants sixty thousand or so down and will take back a mortgage for the balance. A subdivider wants to buy my eight-acre poultry ranch for sixty-four thousand. This represents a terrific profit on which I would have to pay a capital-gains tax. How can I work out this deal and not have to pay any tax?"

Arrange an exchange agreement between you and the other landowner. Deed the poultry acreage to him in exchange for his farm equity. Then he can sell to the subdivider, and your transfer of properties would be tax-free to you.

The farm owner would wind up paying the same capital-gains taxes if he sold in the same year to the subdivider. He could probably spread out his tax liability, however. He could consummate the trade for your poultry ranch in one tax year, in which only the profit on his boot would apply. Then he could complete the poultry-ranch sale the following tax year.

### Should I Refinance Before Trading or Selling?

Ethel Moughon writes from San Bernardino, California, "My husband and I are planning to trade our motel for apartments in northern California. The monthly payments on our motel are too high for a new party to come in and make out. Too many separate loans! We have a question involving the income tax angle. We would like to refinance by borrowing more than enough on a new loan to pay off all the present loans and give us lower monthly payments plus ready cash. If we sell or trade, would we have to pay a tax on this extra amount of cash we get over present loans? And would you advise that we go ahead and refinance or wait and let the next owner secure his own loan?"

With excessive monthly payments on present multiple loans, it would usually be advantageous for you to refinance in order to obtain a new long-term loan with reduced payments, as long as the refinancing does not appear too costly. The lower payments would give you greater in-pocket income, and any resulting cash would put you in a better position to reinvest in other property.

However, if refinancing is quite costly, requiring high loan fees and bonuses, for example, and you are able to manage with the present situation, it would probably be better to wait and let your buyer arrange for new loans. His acquisition could be written up subject to obtaining the proposed financing, if desired.

The cash you obtain by refinancing will not be taxable, of course, when you get the additional funds. Many investors have made fortunes by refinancing, instead of disposing of, desirable properties in order to keep pyramiding. If you sell, the total sale price, including equity and loans, controls the amount you receive and account for when you are figuring capital-gains profits. The fact that you obtain a bigger loan should have no effect on the taxable gain applying to your sale, unless your loan exceeds your book costs, and you report an installment sale.

### How Would Loans Affect an Installment Sale?

The effect of loans must be computed carefully in a sale reported by the installment method. Any assumed loan amount above book costs counts as cash to the seller, included in the 30 per cent maximum receivable on principal in the year of sale. It also increases the percentage of profit for each year reported.

### How Would Loans Affect Tax-Free Trades?

You would not be liable for additional taxes in trading as long as you traded up or across the board, counting any mortgages, personal or commercial notes or other loans. This means you would trade equities with the same loans, or the loan you assumed would be greater than the one you gave up unless offset by equivalent cash or other consideration to make up the difference.

For example, if both traded properties have $100,000 mortgages you have an even trade. If your mortgage is $100,000 and you acquire a property with a mortgage of $150,000, you are trading up. If your mortgage is $100,000 and the other is $75,000 you will be taking a boot of $25,000, unless you make up this difference by giving cash, a note, a second mortgage on the acquired property, or other valuable consideration.

### When You Sell for a Profit and Then Buy New Apartments, Is It Necessary to Live in the Property You Acquire to Get the Capital-Gains-Tax Benefit?

This question was asked after my Memphis lecture in the book section of Fred Goldsmith's department store. The inquirer was a middle-aged housewife whose hobby was interior decorating. From applying her hobby to the property of others, she branched successfully into buying and improving her own apartments.

I have been speaking of income property. This could be either a house or apartments that you rent out. You don't have to live in income property in order to save on income taxes. On a cash sale as an investor, you would be entitled to the capital-gains benefit as long as you held the property for at least six months. Or you can trade for a property of equal or greater value and pay no tax at all.

You are probably thinking of the tax treatment if you sell your home, in which case entirely different tax rules apply. You can sell your home, of course, and buy a new one within a year without paying any capital-gains tax. Both the old and the new homes must be your principal residence, the place where you live. To make the over-all transaction entirely tax-free, the cost of the new place must equal or exceed the adjusted sales price of the old. There would be a proportionate tax on the difference if the new home cost less.

### Do I Have to Put All the Cash Proceeds into a New Home to Avoid the Tax?

No. You don't have to put any of the cash from a home sale into your new home, even if you arrange 100 per cent financing. The total cost must be equal or more, but you can finance it as heavily as you wish and use the cash for other purposes.

Joseph Sanchez writes of paying $9,500 for an older Los Angeles home, spending about $1,000 to fix it up, then selling for $17,500. He obtained all cash above his mortgage. Then he bought an $18,000 home in the San Fernando Valley with 100 per cent financing. Next he used his cash funds, including his tax-free $7,000 profit, as the down payment to buy a Hollywood fourplex that needed fixing up.

### When Does the Six-Month Holding Period Start?

A San Antonio, Texas, investor writes, "I am putting up a new apartment building. What acquisition date should I use for income tax purposes: the date of my lot purchase, the date that construction starts, or when it is completed? I want to know when my long-term holding period applies for resale."

Your lot-acquisition date, for the purpose of establishing your holding period, is the day after you take possession or the day after the deed is transferred or recorded. The established practice on a newly constructed building is to start the holding period the day after construction is completed or the day after the building is accepted by the owner from the contractor.

The foregoing I.R.S. rules sometimes result in a long-term gain on a lot, and a short-term gain at ordinary income rates on the sale of a building on the same lot. For long-term capital-gains treatment on your entire property, hold off the apartment sale until at least six months after completion of the building.

### Does It Sometimes Pay to Sell Rather Than Trade?

This question was asked by Judge Sherrill Halbert at my Ambassador Club dinner lecture in Sacramento. The judge, who served as club president and master of ceremonies, added, "I am referring to a professional such as a doctor or lawyer, with heavy taxable income he would like to offset as much as possible with depreciation. Wouldn't it pay to sell at capital-gains rates rather than trade, in order to have more depreciation to deduct at 100 per cent against ordinary income?"

Yes, sometimes. A professional investor, say a doctor or lawyer who envisions high personal income for many years, might come out ahead by paying the lower capital-gains rates that would apply when he sells, and then by buying larger property, rather than trading. His allowable depreciation would step up considerably, based on his new costs, instead of being lowered by the depreciated costs of his traded-in property. When the occasion calls for it, selling instead of trading is advocated by astute accountants.

The tax advantage of selling rather than trading would hold if he has taken only straight-line depreciation, but would be offset by any accelerated depreciation exceeding straight-line. The average investor is better off to postpone any taxes as long as possible. Circumstances may change. Maybe a person's net personal income will drop, even if he is a professional man. He may put in less time, take an assistant or have other reasons for a lower net. Or maybe he'll buy, a large enough new or old furnished apartment house to give all the offsetting depreciation he needs. In that event, he might find that he had paid a capital-gains tax for little or no advantage.

### How Will Proposed New Tax Laws Affect Pyramiding to a Million Dollars?

Pentagon colonel Homer Huskey asked this question after my lecture in Washington, D.C.

Probably less in real estate than in any other form of investment. No change is expected in the basic concept of capital-gains treatment for profits from real-estate turnover by long-term investors. The maximum capital-gains tax will probably remain at 25 per cent, but the present holding period of six months may be extended to a year. This more realistic period is intended to further distinguish between speculators and investors in terms of the taxes they pay. It should have little effect on anyone who follows my formula for making a million in twenty years. The sample million-dollar pyramid set forth in my first book contemplates an average turnover time of two years.

Even though all such expenses must be passed on to tenants, it is generally recognized that the apartment house owner pays more than his share of real-estate taxes. But turnover profits and operating income should stay comparatively free from income taxes. No other country charges capital-gains taxes comparable to ours on property sales. Because of growing foreign competition for investment funds, there is a concern not to enact more punitive laws affecting real-estate investments.

A general rule that is not expected to change is that trading smaller properties for larger ones will be considered as a tax-free

continuation of the same investment. Another tax factor not expected to change materially is the one that permits capital gains to
be spread over the life of a mortgage, if the seller takes back a
mortgage of 70 per cent or more. This rule encourages sellers to
take back big loans and enables buyers to invest with smaller down
payments, increasing the field of prospective purchasers.

After you have larger, more desirable properties which you have
built up to good income producers, you may prefer not to sell or
trade. Many people keep pyramiding in such cases by borrowing on
their retained properties and using the funds for further investment.
A friend spent $100,000 for purchase-plus-improvement costs of
an apartment house, then borrowed $150,000 on it. His loan had to
be repaid, of course; but the $50,000 obtained for investment cash
would not cost a cent in taxes under any foreseeable law.

There is considerable pressure to remove capital-gains treatment
from such items as profits on stock options and royalties on timber
and coal, and to reclassify them as subject to ordinary income taxes.
Such plans naturally are of concern to property owners, who wonder if they will be similarly affected. But it appears that general tax
planning tends toward removing real-estate treatment from many
non-real-estate investments, and leaving most of the favorable features of real-estate taxation pretty much as at present.

I believe the future will hold continuing incentives and expanding opportunities for the growing ranks of enterprising investors
who seek to share the American Dream by pyramiding in real estate.

# Index

## A

Abrams, Charles, 258
Acceleration, 363-64
Accountant, participation in tax audit, 378
Accounting method, change of, 409
Adams, Wayne, 212
Advance fee, payment of, 231-32
Age limit for entering business, 21-22
Age of a property, 181-82
Agreement
   to buy, cancellation of, 161-62
   to sell, cancellation of, 162-63
Albany, New York, 42
Alexander, Donald C., 374, 386
Aliens, broker's licenses for, 152
American Bar Association, 153
American Research Council, 209
Amory, Cleveland, 188
Andrews, Dana, 16

Apartment owners association, *see* National Apartment Association
Apartments
   above funeral home, 243-44
   buying and selling, 43, 47-51, 66-67, 150-52, 186
   co-operative and condominium, 107-8
   deposit charged for holding, 289
   depreciation accounts, allocation of, 401-3
   investment credit, new, applied to, 406
   note traded for, 232-33
   tax-free operations, 396-97
   trading fishing boat for, 223
   trading for commercial property, 213-15
   vacant, owner's inspection of, 314
Appraisal
   checklist, 175-79